A STONE'S THROW

A
STONE'S
THROW

Travels from Africa in Six Decades

Genesta Hamilton

Hutchinson

London Melbourne Auckland Johannesburg

This edition first published in 1986 by Hutchinson Ltd.,
an imprint of Century Hutchinson Ltd.,
Brookmount House, 62–65 Chandos Place, London WC2N 4NW

Century Hutchinson Publishing Group (Australia) Pty Ltd.,
PO Box 496, 16–22 Church Street, Hawthorn, Melbourne, Victoria 3122

Century Hutchinson Group (NZ) Ltd.,
PO Box 40–086, 32–34 View Road, Glenfield, Auckland 10

Century Hutchinson Group (SA) Pty Ltd.,
PO Box 337, Bergvlei 2012, South Africa

Photoset by Rowland Phototypesetting Ltd.,
Bury St Edmunds, Suffolk
Printed and bound in Great Britain by
Redwood Burn Limited, Trowbridge, Wiltshire

ISBN 0 09 165910 8

To Robin and Liza

A stone's throw out on either hand
From that well-ordered road we tread
And all the world is wild and strange

RUDYARD KIPLING

INTRODUCTION

This book is made up of extracts from my Diaries, begun before the First World War in a very different world.

I remember so many things. First of all, when I was very young, and crawling, I found a tower of bricks my brother had built, and knocked it down – odious child, I was. We sailed off round the world, Father, Mother, a valet, a maid, my brother and me, with two nannies. In New Zealand I was very disappointed to find the hotel page-boy in uniform instead of feathers. *En route* England we passed a volcano in full eruption. Father held me on the rails and told me never to forget this wondrous sight. I never have!

My grandfather had lived at Anstie Grange, a fairly large house in Surrey with a stunning view to the South Downs. While he lived, my father 'broke the entail' with the consent of the three generations involved, so that we eventually left Kitlands (also in Surrey and my first love among country homes) and came to live at Anstie.

I remember parties at Anstie, before the Kaiser's war, the house full of Father's shooting friends and Mother's foreign ones (called by the family Sarah's Foreign Legion), the long processions every night into dinner, two by two, Father and the Principal Lady first, Mother and the Principal Gentleman last; all arm in arm – the men in white ties, the women in glorious, gaudy evening dresses, and wonderful jewels. I hid behind the long velvet curtains in the hall to see them go by, all sparkling and beautiful.

I remember the servants' balls, in the big houses, one ball to each house, Mother leading off with the butler: a band, supper, me dancing with the head gardener, and so on down the ranks. We, the Family, retired after the first three dances, and the servants kept it up till dawn.

I remember the pack of animals we took for walks – my two dogs, a couple of hound puppies, two goats and a sheep – all obedient and intelligent, and keeping well out of the way of the very scarce traffic (horses and carriages, and one car in a month, was all we saw). Mother and I went round Coldharbour village in the pony sleigh each Christmas with presents – tobacco, tea, and red flannel for petticoats. Village children were so polite; the boys touched their caps, the girls curtsied to us. They had such pretty manners. All the boys later went off to the Kaiser's war, and many were killed.

I made friends with the gypsies who used to camp on Leith Hill, and visited them during my rides. This was strictly forbidden and Stapley, the coachman, tried to stop me, but in vain. There was exquisite beauty around my home, from a sea of bluebells in the woods to autumn's flaming colours, and the bare winter branches, decorated with frost and snow. With the mass of servants we had, Anstie was like a village: gardeners, stablemen, chauffeurs in cottages and sixteen servants living in the house.

Father was very clever, with a brain descended through his grandmother from Lord Napier and Ettrick, who invented logarithms. Father became rich. Income tax at the time was about 6d in the £. He was fun, and endlessly helping others. Once he told me he worried because however much he gave away, it never hurt him personally. He was very modest too, and absolutely worshipped mother who was very beautiful, with dark blue eyes, auburn hair, and the Gambiers' faultless features.

Mother loved entertaining. Lots of handsome men and lovely ladies came to her parties and dinner parties. At our house in London the footmen wore livery, the table was laden with flowers, and the dining-room floor was so unsteady it had to be reinforced from the kitchen below. There had been a ghost, which was exorcized, and there was one room in the house into which I could not enter. There were endless stairs and little heating. As it was the way one lived then, no one minded. In the Kaiser's war the few bombs that fell made the poor old house jump, and it began to crack and crumble. We finally sold it, and moved to a beautiful house in Park Lane, with drawing-room panels imported from France.

We had no cars until about 1910. The first one took us quite slowly to Scotland and back, with a certain amount of punctures *en route*.

So the years passed quietly for us, until suddenly I was grown-up – skirts longer, hair up. I was fifteen and the Kaiser's war was upon us.

Genesta Hamilton, July 1986

1914

On 3 August, at midnight, Great Britain declared war on Germany. I was fifteen years old. Mother and I went to London. The first sight I had of the war was a convoy of ambulances crossing Albert Bridge.

At Anstie we are living very simply with only three servants. It is perfectly comfortable and much more peaceful. But of course the house is not so well kept as before. There are troops everywhere; they commandeer vehicles and have taken over orphanages, Christ's Hospital and horses. In London they camp in Hyde Park. On the Continent there have only been skirmishes so far, but a battle is expected soon. There are a million men on each side and the battle front stretches over 250 miles. It will be the biggest battle in our history. People say that the war may last any length of time, from three weeks to three years.

I heard a story which points to the fall of the Germans. Before he came to the throne, the present Kaiser Wilhelm's grandfather, Wilhelm I, asked a fortune-teller when he would be king, and she told him the exact date. Then he asked when his kingdom would be made an empire, and she said 1870. Then he asked when it would fall, and she said 1914.

The Allies are Great Britain, France, Belgium, Russia, Serbia and possibly Italy and Japan. Our enemies are Austria, Germany, Romania and Turkey. The Indian princes sent troops and money at once. The Canadians help us splendidly and have sent thousands of men and horses.

My brother Griggs has joined his regiment, the Surrey Yeomanry, and at present is in England, but longing, as they all do, to go to the front. My cousin Fred Heath has joined up, and cousin Martin Heath is already at the front. Uncle Fred has been given command of Coast Defence in Scotland. Uncle Gerard has been told not to go back to South Africa, as he may be needed here. They are both generals in the Royal Engineers. Uncle Herbert is needed at Portsmouth and so cannot go to the war; he is an admiral. Both he and Uncle Gerard have been knighted.

1

18 AUGUST

Bertrand de Comminges, whose home is in northern France near the German border, is staying with us because of the threat of war. He is a dreadful bother and does nothing but tease; still, he is only thirteen so I suppose he must be forgiven. He sleeps here and goes away during the day. The Germans have taken Liège.

This morning we went to the Grenadier Guards camp outside the Palace and then to Horseguards Parade, where there is a recruiting office. We heard cheering and just caught sight of Winston Churchill. We also saw (at least Mother thought it was) Lord Kitchener in uniform. Several companies of troops have been marching under our windows. The recruits swarm in, but there are still many loafers who would be better in the army.

This afternoon we went on top of a bus, which was fun. We ran up to the City and there met Hal Gore Browne, back from Burma, who has joined the army. He said his brother Eric has volunteered for the front and is now a captain in the Post Office Rifles. Their sister Dot and her nurses have taken possession of Guildford Hospital because all the nurses there have gone overseas.

19 AUGUST

The French have taken another town in Alsace, Saarburg. Mother stopped there once for lunch but did not like the look of it, so went on. That was in the spring of this year.

Eric Gore Browne dropped in today. He looked so thin, poor chap – I don't believe he has enough to eat. Still, 'à la guerre comme à la guerre'. He took us to see his quarters. The men were sleeping on the floor and I couldn't tell the difference between them and their kit. They have a great deal to carry on their backs, besides a heavy rifle. Their rifle magazines hold five bullets and are loaded in the usual way, but Eric says the guns kick hard on firing.

Our family is doing well. Out of eight cousins, seven are serving: Raymond and Fred, Cuthbert and Martin, Griggs, Stewart and Billy. I am surprised Leo doesn't go. [I heard later that he was medically unfit.]

The great battle has started. The Germans are trying to crash through the Belgian defences, but the Belgians are stubbornly holding on.

22 AUGUST

Major Goulburn from Betchworth came to lunch. He said he has been doing all he can to save the hunt, and thinks he has succeeded. We are going to hunt a little as soon as the harvest is cut, on whatever horses we have got left. After lunch we went to see Griggs in his camp. He was looking very fit. He sleeps in all sorts of places – in barns, in mangers, and sometimes in the car. He is going to have a mock alarm and asked us to go and see it. I hope we will.

3 SEPTEMBER

The Germans are now in France. There has been fighting in Compiègne, where Bertrand's home is. The British captured ten German guns there. The list of British casualties is out: my cousin Muni Sneyd's cousin, Lord Hawarden, is believed dead and another friend of hers also. Two of Mother's friends are on the list, one wounded and the other missing.

On Monday, 31 August there was a recruiting meeting at Holmwood, arranged by Father. The speakers were first St Loe Strachey, High Sheriff of Surrey; he was very good. Then Sir James Goodrich, and finally Canon Palmes, who was excellent. He said at one moment: 'What is patriotism?' and an old man at the back, pretty drunk, began, 'Whoy, that ain't no good, that ain't.' Cowham, our butler, tapped him on the shoulder and told him to be quiet. Dr Robinson pushed through to him, but when the man began again he was ungently hustled out.

6 SEPTEMBER

This morning we started for Herne Bay; Griggs's camp is in a lovely place for fine weather, but very exposed if it rains. The whole Surrey Yeomanry is there; the horses packed together in lines, with the officers' quarters behind them. We found Griggs in his tent.

7 SEPTEMBER

Started for the camp early and saw the regiment galloping over the hills. It was a fine sight. Stayed in camp all day and talked to the horses and the men, several of whom, being Surrey people, knew us.

8 SEPTEMBER

Today we went to Canterbury. The cathedral is wonderful. There is a French chapel in it which was used for the Huguenot refugees. Mother's ancestors, the Gambiers, worshipped there.

Mother and I went to the camp to say goodbye to Griggs. While we were there an airship was sighted; she finally came right over us. The horses did not like it at all, and were very frightened. We were stopped five times by police on the way home; they were on German spy duty.

10 DECEMBER

On 7 December we went with Harry Crofton, my blind cousin, to Aldershot. The place is swarming with troops, of which a good half are Kitchener's army men. We went to the aviation ground. A few months ago there was nothing but a few aeroplane sheds and one airship shed. Now there are several of the latter, while the rest of the ground is covered with planes.

Then we went on to the German prisoners' camp. It has a fairly low line of ordinary barbed wire, behind which is the guard, to whom we distributed cigarettes. It is bitterly cold, they say, and they long for a change. Further on there is a quite low wire entanglement and still further a very high electrified wire, behind which are the Germans. They came out later to load a motor lorry and I really must say they are a nice-looking lot, quite different from what I had expected; they are tall and strong, with fair hair and blue eyes.

We went on to Waverley Hospital, where my cousins Marjorie Heath and Janet Broadwood were working. The wounded are so patient. One boy in Marjorie's ward is only seventeen years old. He got into the army by saying he was eighteen, and his birthday is on 8 February; he has had two operations already and has to have a third. Another man, Driver Bradley, to whom Harry said: 'Well, how are you today, old man?' answered: 'Oh, the pain's still there!' As a matter of fact he was very bad, but he did not complain.

Another looked very white and thin. Mother said, 'Are you ill or wounded?'

'Oh, I'm both, madam,' he answered, and he did look bad. Yet he was quite cheerful.

We had to leave the hospital but I could have stayed there for ever, and now I hope Mother will let me work in one somewhere.

19 DECEMBER

Mother took me to a Belgian hospital for the wounded this afternoon. One of the men was very badly wounded, and several had bronchitis. One had a shrapnel wound all down his body, from head to feet; but he was cheerful, joking and keeping the other men laughing. In another ward there was a woman, the wife of one of the men; she had escaped from Brussels, leaving her little daughter there with her sister. She had had an adventurous journey: when she reached the boundary between Holland and Belgium someone threw a narrow plank over a tiny canal and she ran over.

She said that the Germans in Brussels usually took no notice of you, but if they asked you the time and you told them in French instead of German they were furious and broke your watch.

4

24 DECEMBER

We spent Xmas with Griggs. As we passed Gravesend I heard guns. I think it must have been an air raid, for a Zeppelin came over Sheerness and dropped a bomb. Our guns fired at it. I afterwards met a boy who was there at the time, and he said nobody took any notice at all.

When we arrived we unloaded at a tiny cottage belonging to a charming old lady, and had tea with Griggs. He was quite alone in the farmhouse with Kite, a groom from Anstie, and Birch, his servant. So Mother decided to ask Miss Knowles (the 'Lady of the Cottage') if we might take the beds she had got ready for us, and the furniture, over to the farmhouse.

25 DECEMBER

A lovely day for Christmas. After church and church parade we went to the oasthouse where the men were billeted, to have lunch with the gun section. Griggs sat at the head of the table, Mother on his right and Father next to her, while I sat on his left. Father had Sergeant Latham beside him; Corporal Steel sat next to me. We drank the King's health and afterwards the cooks' and the waiters', then the waiters' and the cooks'. There were speeches, and Mother gave away presents.

1915

20 FEBRUARY

At Anstie the Civil Service of London Rifles, Prince of Wales's own, come and drill in the grounds and shoot at the rifle range.

In London the men drill in the Park, and the other day they were all charging. In fact they charged my cousin Muni Sneyd and me, who were walking up a path. But as they were rather far apart we walked on between two men and escaped capture.

We were going to have troops billeted on us at Anstie, but for the second time it has been stopped.

28 APRIL

Uncle Herbert [*Admiral Sir Herbert Heath, just now C-in-C Portsmouth, and future Second Sea Lord*] has asked us to Portsmouth to see the launch of a new battleship. We drove from Anstie and arrived in the late afternoon. After tea, Uncle Herbert took us all over the dockyard. We saw the old docks, where wooden ships were built long ago, and we looked at this new super dreadnought. She is the same size as the *Queen Elizabeth*, who has been doing such good work in the Dardanelles. They had tied a sham bottle onto the stern and first Mother, then I, 'broke' it. She will be christened the *Royal Sovereign*. She is not a sister ship of the 'Lizzie', not nearly so expensive or so fast, but built on rather elaborate lines – I mean for the men, each of whom has a 'den' to himself.

29 APRIL

Uncle Herbert, Aunt Bessie, Father, Mother, my cousins Madeline, Posey and I started off in two cars to see the launching. The yard was full of the men who have built the ship, and there was a guard of honour of sailors. Behind the ship a small platform had been erected, on which we all stood.

When Lady Dalmeny arrived, she inspected the guard of honour. She was very plainly dressed in dark blue, with a big fur and a small hat. The religious ceremony came first. It was short and imposing. Then the constructor ordered the men to take away the blocks which held the ship. The order came, 'Clear away!' and the men scrambled off and swarmed ashore. Lady Dalmeny took the hammer, while the constructor took the chisel and held it on the cords which fastened the ship. Five strokes, the cords were severed, and the *Royal Sovereign* was free! As she broke the bottle, Lady Dalmeny said, 'Good luck to the *Royal Sovereign*.' The ship kept quite still for a second, then came a little grating noise; she quivered from bow to stern and glided down the dock. A loud cheer came from the men and a second one as she slid gracefully into the water. The launch was over. She dropped anchor in the harbour and a tug came and pulled her into a floating dock.

There was a garden party at Admiralty House before lunch, after which Uncle Herbert took us all out in his barge. We went to see *Royal Sovereign* in her floating dock where she will be worked at for nine more months, having her engines, guns and armour fitted.

We saw the two forts in the harbour; the soldiers waved at us but of course we took no notice, being in the admiral's barge. We were shown the fortifications: iron posts, which submarines cannot get through, driven into the bottom of the harbour. Coming home I steered and the old sailor, Mills, was so nice.

20 JUNE

Today we went to the hospital at Heathyfield; on the way we had tea with Dot. While she and Mother were talking, I went round the ward and talked to a man named O'Brien, who has been all through it and finally lost a leg. He said that at Neuve Chapelle the German losses were tremendous, and at one place they found eighty English and two hundred Germans, all dead. It just shows how we can fight – eighty killing two hundred!

He told me many interesting things. He said they saw a crucifix standing in front of a wall; shells had riddled the wall, but the crucifix was not touched. Then again, a shell exploded near another crucifix and blew it into the air, and when the figure came to earth again it was not broken.

Some people have seen strange visions of men in armour on the battlefield; once at Neuve Chapelle and once at Mons. Whenever we are in real trouble, the Germans suddenly stop firing, saying that they cannot fire at what is between the armies. I asked O'Brien if he had seen them, and he said no. But he said extraordinary fancies came to one on the battlefield such as one had never thought of before. Dot said that they had had two 'vision men', but they were gone.

The men make many things as part of their therapy: mats, belts, babies' bonnets, trays etc. There are two Canadians there. One has only one arm, and he works his things on a sort of frame. They have also got a man the top of whose head was blown off, who draws very well. He only started drawing since coming to the hospital.

5 SEPTEMBER

We heard today that Griggs had married Alesta Alexandra McAuslane on 28 August at Westbrook. This was a fearful shock to us; apparently he was billeted on the family and they got him to marry this person. Father and Mother were thunderstruck and horrified. In the army you must ask your colonel's permission to marry, but Griggs had not done so.

22 SEPTEMBER

We started in the car *en route* for Mrs Hervey's at Northiam. When we reached Rye we went to the old fortress, dating from 1135, which was used first as a stronghold and then as a prison. The cells are small and very dark but the ones above are better; they have at least got windows.

23 SEPTEMBER

This morning we heard gunfire.

Friends told us that, while they were watching some Canadians marching towards the harbour on the way to the front, one of them broke ranks and held out his hand, saying 'Wish me good luck.' So all along the lines they were shaking hands with these men and wishing them good luck. One Canadian suddenly said, 'Will nobody kiss me before I go?' A girl held up her hand and said she would, but the man kissed two others. The girl, however, was not to be defrauded of her kiss and held up her hand again, so he kissed her too.

27 SEPTEMBER

We got a wire from Father saying that poor Raymond [*Uncle Arthur's son*] had been killed in this last fighting. He is the second of my Heath cousins to be killed – Martin was killed on 18 May this year.

13 OCTOBER

Back in London we had an air raid, which shook our two-hundred-year-old house. You could hear plaster falling inside the walls. We saw the Zeppelin illuminated by our shrapnel, which was bursting around it.

We went down Oxford Street and stopped to speak to a policeman, who said that he had seen the Zeppelin go west a short way, then do a big dive and, turning round, go away eastward.

We took a bus and went to the City, passing a fire just outside the Lyceum Theatre. We went on to St Paul's. There was nothing to be seen there so, while we were waiting for another bus, an army friend called Gerry crossed to speak to some special constables who were on duty. When he came back he said: 'They've dropped three bombs: one just outside the Lyceum, one in the Strand and one in Piccadilly. Several people killed.'

Of course, I knew there must be casualties but Gerry's words brought it home to me and I began to realize the nearness of the war.

At the fire there was a fairly big crowd but no one was allowed near it. So we moved on a bit, but were stopped by policemen looking for a spy. When we had passed, we saw a bright light in one of the top windows of the Hotel Cecil. The crowd outside the hotel grew larger every minute. Gerry went to see what was happening. When he came back he told us there was trouble inside the hotel, where angry Canadian officers were fighting foreign waiters. He heard someone say they were sending for the Guards, so he thought we had better go home in case there was a riot. I should have loved to stay to the end, but I had to go with my parents.

1916

4 FEBRUARY

On 7 October 1915 a possible governess for me had come to lunch with us. [*I was seventeen and wanted a job, not a governess.*] She called herself Eva de

Bournonville, and said that she came from an old French family. Her grandfather, or great-grandfather, had emigrated to Copenhagen, where she was born, but her father had gone to Sweden and she became a naturalized Swede at the age of eight. I liked her. Attractive, short and slight, she had a very pale face, straight nose, rather thin, pale lips and big, dark eyes. She was neatly dressed and talked seven or eight languages, including German. She had been working in a Swedish embassy and had come to England to try to get a censorship job at the War Office.

During lunch this lady spoke a little German to Mother, who knows it well. The lady spoke it very fluently. The talk turned to spies. Suddenly Mother turned to her and said, in her disconcerting, straightforward way, 'How do we know you are not a spy?'

Tossing her head, the lady opened her bag and produced a card signed by the Danish Minister in England, saying that she was all right. We looked at the card. Then she went away. It was obvious that she no longer wanted to give me lessons.

Two months later a plain clothes policeman visited us. Mother called me. The officer asked me what I knew of the de Bournonville; I told him all I could remember. He told us she really *was* a spy and was now in prison in Holloway. Some time later, a friend came to see us who had been at the woman's trial. She said there had been thirty-seven witnesses against her. She was condemned to death, but appealed and her case went to the Home Secretary. She received penal servitude for life, which no doubt means that she will be released after the war. We thought this sentence far too light for a proven spy. She was the only woman spy who had been working on her own. It was she who had directed the last Zeppelin raid on London. Our Intelligence knew she was trying to come to England long before she arrived. Apparently she came to us because one of my uncles was a general at the War Office, another a general commanding at Portsmouth and a third Second Sea Lord.

6 JUNE

Father came home tonight with the news that Lord Kitchener of Khartoum has been drowned. Next day the papers said he and his staff (including our friends Sir H. F. Donaldson and Colonel FitzGerald) were on their way to Russia in HMS *Hampshire* when she struck a mine and sank in ten minutes. As there was a very heavy sea running, the two torpedo boat destroyers which accompanied her had been detached and sent back to harbour. Consequently when the ship sank there was no one near to rescue the men. It is a terrible blow.

Mother bought shirts for the troops overseas, and so her name became known in the trade. One day a salesman appeared, trying to sell her mackintoshes – he said they were the best quality and that Lord Kitchener and his staff had bought some for their journey to Russia. So though none of us, and not even Lady Donaldson, had known about this trip, it was not a well-kept secret and enemy spies may well have known. We believe the *Hampshire* was torpedoed, not mined, as the press said. It is strange that the *Hampshire*'s escort was sent back to harbour just because of rough seas. Were the messages faked? Certainly the enemy knew Kitchener's plans and movements.

24 JULY

Last February, before Gerald went to the front, he had six days' leave which he spent with us. He brought to the house a man in the Gordon Highlanders – Captain Brian Brooke, son of old Captain Brooke, 'Father of the Gordons'. Brian is a magnificent man – tall and broad, with red hair and brown eyes and thoroughly Scottish (except, of course, no accent). Last May, when they came on leave, we saw him again. I called him Sir Galahad. Mother called him Brian Boru. [*Her history was muddled; Brian Boru was Irish, not Scottish.*]

On 1 July the Great Push started. On the 3rd we had a wire to say that Gerald had been seriously wounded in the leg, and Mother went over to Rouen to see him. Some time later we heard that Sir Galahad was also badly wounded and that he was at the Empire Hospital, St Vincent's Square. By this time Gerald was at Netley Hospital, recovering slowly, and Mother was back in England.

We went to see Brian. He was badly wounded in the neck and his left arm was paralysed. I saw him three times. Then, tonight, we went on to the hospital from Victoria Station, having come from Anstie.

25 JULY

Sir Galahad died last night under chloroform, as a result of the operation. He was operated on at 7 p.m. and died at 9 p.m. He was twenty-seven years old. Brian had a curious aversion to flowers. Our rooms in the Portman Square house were full of them, and Brian always sat with his back to them if he could. The last time we saw him my arms were full of roses from Anstie. When the porter said he was coming past the glass doors, I asked Mother where I could put the flowers as he hated them so much. She said, 'Don't be silly, hold them.' He saw me still holding them, and looked away. Perhaps he had 'the sight' and a foreboding that flowers meant death for him. Almost the last thing he saw was me holding those flowers. I could not get this memory out of my mind.

2 SEPTEMBER

We started for Folkestone this afternoon, Mother and I and our maid Elizabeth. We journeyed up with a Frenchman who had been in the trenches and was then sent over by his government to see about munitions. He said the war must last at least one more year – I believe it will finish in February 1918.

11 SEPTEMBER

This afternoon we saw the Somme films; they are very terrible. The worst part is the actual advance; you see the men in the trenches, then the officer jumps onto the parapet and waves his arm – the signal for 'Advance'. The men spring up and leave the trench, but two are killed at once and slip back. Two or three more are caught in the wire, and another is entangled and left behind. He is shot. It is terribly vivid and gives one some slight idea of what this war is like. Brian was wounded in this advance. He fell, but got up and went on, then was hit again; this wound was mortal.

Also you see dead Huns being buried; and some nerve-shattered prisoners being brought in were quite pathetic. They were almost mad, and kept holding their arms up, signifying '*Kamerad*'. It was pitiful to see the half-puzzled, half-terrified expressions on their faces. I hate them as much as anyone does, but you can't help feeling sorry for them.

29 OCTOBER

I joined the pantry staff at Anstie, which has been turned into a first-line hospital for fifty officer patients. There is a modern operating theatre and everything is up to date. There are fifty staff, including doctors, nurses and orderlies; my cousin Dot (Doreen) Gore Browne is the commandant. Father pays all the expenses, which are vast.

Last night they telephoned from Anstie to say that there would be a convoy in and that I was to come down from London today. I arrived in time for lunch and went to the pantry afterwards to work. Everyone was tired, because the convoy had arrived about 1 a.m. and they had been sitting up until two in the morning, and then came on duty again at 7 a.m. My fellow workers are Mrs Kenny, Miss Martin, Evelyn Elgee, Poppy Hind and Olive Monk. We are divided into two lots; Mrs Kenny and Miss Martin are the two 'bosses'. We work like this: all six go down at 7 a.m. and work until 3 p.m., when three go off and the others carry on until 6 p.m. Then the three who have been off come and take their places and go on working until it is all finished and they retire to bed. Next day it is our turn to go off at 3 p.m. and come on again at six, until all the washing up is done, about 9 or 10. So we have a good eleven hours' work a day, and more if a convoy is coming in at night.

26 DECEMBER

We had a signal that a convoy is coming tonight. Doreen Gore Browne, tall, statuesque and beautiful, in a red uniform with a very long white veil on her dark hair, stood in the doorway holding up a lantern; a perfect vision of safety and comfort to the tired, strained and suffering men as they arrived. We have had two more convoys.

Of course, we in the pantry don't meet the patients much, but I know one or two. There is Macky – Mr Mackness, a lung man. He was terribly ill, and they had to operate on him twice; he is better now, though he has relapses. Then there were Cheery Charles, Precious Percy and Carrots. The cheery one is Lieutenant Fitz-Randolph, Canadian, very amusing. Percy – Captain Abbott – another jolly soul who loves the ladies, is popular. Carrots is Mr Matheson – red hair, of course – a very nice Australian boy.

It is thrilling to see a convoy come in. They usually arrive late at night. All the HAs [*higher authorities*] assemble on the front steps to meet them. First come the walking cases, in the hospital cars; then four or six Red Cross ambulances, each carrying four patients. RAMC men appear, to unload the stretchers. There are also our own three orderlies, Battersby, Chapell and Duxbury. No matter how cold or wet it is, they move about without hats to show that they belong to the house. When the ambulances arrive they help to draw out the stretchers and put each one on the ground for a minute or so, standing back to let the patient breathe fresh air. Then two men pick it up and take it into the house – out of the pantry's ken.

Now for our Christmas festivities, which took place on Boxing Day. There was to be a dance; we were all free from 2 p.m. until the time we went to bed. We joined the patients in the hall and sang songs, then had tea with them. Then stockings filled with presents appeared, each marked with the name of the person it was for – one for each of the staff and patients. We played games – hunt the slipper, musical chairs, etc. Then we ladies retired to robe ourselves for dinner – mufti was allowed so we wore our prettiest evening clothes. We proceeded into the dining room two by two, as in the old days. Mr Broadhead took me in – he is a 'leg man' and such a nice boy. Dinner was delicious. I danced the first two with Mr Leslie, Black Watch. Then I danced with Mr Healey, the Australian whom I call Anzac. He dances beautifully. I had six dances with him and one with Captain Roper. Then we knocked off. But first we trooped into the dining room and had some drinks and sang 'Auld Lang Syne'. Never have I enjoyed myself more than I did that night.

1917

1 JANUARY

Thanks to that enterprising person Anzac, tonight there was another small and heavenly dance, in uniform, and after dinner. When it was time to stop we went into the dining room, and the sight of big glass jugs and glasses on the sideboard evoked shouts of joy, which turned to howls of sorrow on the discovery that the jugs contained nothing but water!

8 JANUARY

There are many funny moments. I took a tray up to a new patient and he said, 'Awful place for a hospital, this is.'

I couldn't think what to say, but eventually replied, 'It *is* rather far from the station.' Later I heard that he had asked someone who I was, and was appalled to hear that I was the owner's daughter!

Last night Anzac gave me some snapshots he had taken of Gallipoli, France and the hospital – very good ones. He told me of a friend of his, the best he had ever had, without exception. They used to share everything, and were great friends. The other man had just received a pot of jam, and before opening it he said, 'I think I'll go and see if that dugout is all right.' While he was there a shell exploded and a piece hit him, cutting his jugular vein. He was carried up the steps, and he just had the strength to say to his friend, 'I leave you that pot of jam, Healey!' before he died.

Today, I left Anstie for a month's leave in London. Such a send-off I had! The pantrymaids came to the front door and some of the patients too. Then Sister Mary appeared and took me into the hall, to say goodbye to the men there. Then I had to go to the office. Then I bolted back to the hospital car and was embraced by the pantry staff. Someone said, 'Don't leave them out of it!' and when I looked at the bow window in the hall I saw a lot of men in their white dressing gowns, bedroom slippers etc., waving walking sticks and laughing. At last we got away and they all cheered. I had already been round the wards saying goodbye, and had quite a long chat with Macky.

18 JANUARY – LONDON

A few days ago Mother told me that she had arranged with Dryden Sneyd, my cousin, to give a little dance, which took place tonight. Dryden is a field gunner; he had been in France for ages, was awarded the MC and is now home on a month's leave. The dance was a great success. Billy Heath, my cousin, came and, though wounded in the foot, danced all the time. Muni Sneyd brought a party of twenty, among whom were several Australians.

19 JANUARY

Today has been quite eventful. First we went to the Carlton and had tea with Captain Phillips. He was a doctor and had joined the Australian Army Medical Corps. He was very interesting about Australia and said that he found the manners and customs of England so strange and hard to remember! We asked him to come back with us to supper, and we put some records on the Vocalion and danced. Uncle Mike Gambier and Aunt Irene turned up and stayed a short time.

When Mother went to the door to let them out there was a muffled roar. She thought it was the Zepps again. This was about 7 p.m. However, there was nothing to be seen, so we forgot about it until half an hour later when Alice, the parlourmaid, appeared with a telephone message; there had been an explosion somewhere in north London, and our little kitchenmaid, who was out for the evening, had fainted in the tram from shock and a policeman was bringing her home in a taxi.

Captain Phillips being a doctor, we turned to him for instructions. When the taxi arrived she was put to bed with hot water bottles and brandy. For some time she was half-conscious, and kept talking about flames and Zeppelins. Then she went to sleep and woke up later quite all right, but very shaken. We are afraid this explosion was at Woolwich Arsenal – a disaster for the munitions.

12 FEBRUARY

I went to Anstie with Father tonight. I am overjoyed to be back here. Start work tomorrow.

16 FEBRUARY

This was an eventful day. To begin with I heard in the village that my cousin, Captain Fred Heath, younger brother of Raymond who was killed in 1915, had been seriously wounded in the neck. This was the first I had heard of it – the village grapevine knows everything.

This evening we were told that a convoy of thirty was coming in at midnight. Great excitement among the upstairs people, as there were only twenty-five free beds, but someone raised some others and everything was beautifully arranged. It was 2.30 when the convoy arrived – thirteen walking cases and seventeen stretchers. The last man was tremendously bandaged and looked – what we could see of him – very ill. We sent up drinks and waited until 3.45, when I was sent to bed because I had been up early. And the last case, the very last to be taken in, was Fred Heath himself! I felt he was coming somehow, but for all that it was a great surprise.

17 FEBRUARY

Commandant took me up to see Fred this morning. He looks very ill and is in great pain. His right side is half paralysed and he cannot speak. It is extraordinary that he should be here – he had not asked to come, nor even mentioned the place. How strange the way things work out.

I only had three hours' sleep last night. Am fagged out.

27 APRIL

Much excitement when we heard that a plane had crashed out Snake's Hill way; doctor went out and brought back the pilot, who proved to be the famous ace Captain A. de B. Brandon, DSO, MC, who has brought down two Zeppelins. He was badly hurt, leg fractured, but is getting along well now and walking on crutches.

Anzac has gone and Fred has also left. He is now at the Empire Hospital, St Vincent's Square – the place where Brian Brooke died. He is going on well, but needs special treatment. Great joke – Mother is always at daggers drawn with Fred's parents at their house, Kitlands, and they were not allowed at Anstie. But she could not forbid them visiting their son at Anstie, and they came through the wood every day to see him.

Kitlands is another family home, said to date from Saxon times. It is a rambling old house, enlarged from time to time and set in a wonderful garden. Here there are walls of rhododendrons, glades of roses and azaleas and some exotic and quite famous trees, brought back from distant lands by my grandfather, the sailor Leopold Heath, and given to his brother Douglas who was a dedicated gardener.

17 MAY

I had my leave two days ago, and now we are in the West Country for a while, starting with Plymouth. Fred has come back to Anstie and is to stay there until he is fit. He has made a very good recovery, speaks and walks (still on crutches) quite well.

18 MAY

Captain and Mrs Brooke are here too. Their boy, Pat, is ill in his ship with typhoid, and she spends all her time with him. Pat is making slow progress. He is the youngest of the boys of the Fairley branch of the family.

We went for a walk towards Devonport where we saw the Russian man o' war *Askold* (five funnels, hence her nickname of 'Packet of Wood-bines'). She is here refitting as she has run out of ammunition, and we have none to fit her guns.

23 MAY

Newton Abbot is a quaint little place. Went to the market this morning. We were interested in the Dartmoor ponies – small, very strongly made, with an Arab look about them.

25 MAY

Had a ride this afternoon with Father. I had a strong little dun cob. We went up over the moors, but I am disappointed in Devon scenery. Moors, indeed, on the top of the hill, but cultivation up all the slopes – very dull. I rode down a narrow, twisting track; my sure-footed Dartmoor pony never made a mistake. When we returned to the top, Father was angry with me for the first time in my life, as his big horse could not follow the narrow track, and he was worried.

26 MAY

Pat Brooke has died, ten months and one day after Brian. He is the third son the Brookes have lost in this war, and they have also lost their son-in-law. One of the sons and the son-in-law were both VCs. The last remaining boy is in India and married. The poor parents are devastated with grief – all their splendid sons gone, except one. It makes one's heart ache and there is nothing one can do to help.

16 JUNE

Back to Anstie.

1 AUGUST

Today the hospital closes for three weeks' cleaning – badly needed, in spite of our efforts! We have been getting rid of patients by degrees; most have gone to the Cambridge Hospital. Today the last six went.

17 AUGUST

Came to London a short time ago; Father and I went on to Portsmouth to stay for a weekend with Uncle Fred [*Lieutenant-General Heath-Caldwell*], who is the GOC there, and Aunt Connie. There was a small dinner party for the Commander-in-Chief, Admiral Sir Stanley Colville.

18 AUGUST

In the morning we went round the harbour in the Admiral's barge, escorted by the charming coxswain. Then on foot round the dockyard and saw torpedoed ships, one of which, the *Ettrick*, had her bows completely blown off. She was escorting a transport and had managed to intercept a torpedo fired from a German submarine, thus saving the other ship.

Dinner at Admiralty House, where Princess Victoria (once) of Schleswig Holstein is staying. She is charming and most amusing. Her side beat us at billiards.

19 AUGUST

Went to church at the regimental chapel – a delightful service, nearly all singing. Lunch on board *Superb*, Uncle Herbert's flagship, which is in dry dock undergoing repairs. Captain D'Ath took us round her. She is a wonderful great ship, a dreadnought.

On our way home we saw tanks in the distance and found our way there. Princess Victoria and Lady Adelaide Colville were there; they had both been in one, and Uncle Fred said I might go. One squeezes through a tiny door into a dark and oily interior. It was very bumpy and very hot, yet we were going over smooth ground and the top was open. I would not have missed it for anything. [*These were the first tanks to go overseas – the first ever built.*]

3 OCTOBER

To Aberdeen for a few days, then on to the Brookes at Fairley. The house is full of mementoes of their dead sons, and hanging up in the hall is Brian's old rifle with a record on it of the beasts he shot.

The spae-wife told my fortune and was good about the past. For the future – *nous verrons*. While I was there we went to the regimental sports and to a garden party given by the Gey Gordons. (*Gey*, I am told, is Gaelic for 'terrible', and the clan had earned itself this name centuries ago. People who don't know any better call them the 'Gay' Gordons.)

Joined Father and Mother and went on to Aboyne. While we were there I was lent a fat piebald pony belonging to the hotel. I went with Father to his shooting moor, Lumphanan, and explored the hills around. On top of one is a disused quarry, and a big pond with a low wall round it. It gave me quite a shock when I first came on it, it was so still and deep; and, as a storm was coming up, there was a weird, dark look about everything. It fascinated me.

30 OCTOBER

London. There was a raid tonight. I was asleep when I found myself being hauled out of bed. The Take Cover whistles were going down every street, also hooters which the army uses on its cars – they are more noisy and certainly more penetrating than any whistle. We trooped downstairs in every degree of undress.

The guns started in the East End. Every now and then Mother would go to the door and open it half an inch. The guns grew louder and louder as the Boche came nearer. Once or twice we heard the hum of the Zeppelin, but couldn't see it. Shrapnel from our guns tinkled down outside. This lasted for about two hours. Then it suddenly stopped.

6 NOVEMBER

Today I came to the Hill Hospital, Farnham, to work in the wards. The commandant is my cousin, Dot Gore Browne, who also runs Anstie. This place is for other ranks.

30 NOVEMBER

There is a camp not far from here, at Frensham, where some Serbians are stationed. This morning they marched along the high road, singing most beautifully: a weird, eastern-sounding chant which they sang in parts. They looked rough and untidy, but they are grand fighters. I wish I could hear them singing again; it was fascinating and haunting.

12 DECEMBER

Today I was present at my first operation. It was not very serious – a hand. I got through it safely!

These boys' pluck is simply incredible. Everyone talks of it and everyone knows it, but you don't realize it until you are with them yourself. One boy was having his arm massaged by my blind cousin, Harry Crofton. I am not sure what was wrong with it, but it had been in a sling for ages and this was the first time it had been massaged. I was behind him and could not see his face, but his head was twisted sideways and down onto the table with the agony of it, and he gasped, but never let out a word or groan.

25 DECEMBER

High festivities today and lots of work preparing things. They had a truly Xmas pudding for lunch: full of threepenny bits and silver emblems. They all had fires in their wards, too, which was a great joy, and we spent the afternoon hanging small presents on the Christmas tree. Then came tea, with crackers and cakes to their hearts' content; we put paper head-dresses on top of our caps, and looked festive. After tea we took the presents off the tree again and handed them out. The boys drew for them in a box of numbered tickets, and then we hunted frantically round for the things indicated on the tickets, feeling their waiting eyes upon us, and deafened by the absolutely indescribable noises of the musical things they got. I believe this will be the last war year; next year will bring us victory and peace.

1918

14 JANUARY

Some time ago Dot and I settled to go away to Southsea for a fortnight, and today I was to pick her up. But this morning I woke up to find five inches of snow on the ground and everyone in varying tempers. The boys sent me off amid snowballs and cheers and I started out feeling that a holiday had really begun. Then the car hesitated, skidded on its hind legs, swerved, stopped and backed cleverly into a ditch. The hill was very steep, it is true – still, we were only about ten yards off the top, so it was all the more annoying. I left the chauffeur to his own devices and started to walk. The mud and ruts in the road were frozen hard and covered with snow, so walking was a cold, hard, slippery job; but I enjoyed the whole thing. Reached Rowledge House at last; Dot and I sat over the fire, having missed the first train, and waited for the taxi to take us on to the next one. A fatigue party of patients pushed the car up the hill, and it arrived in time to get us to the station, where we waited three-quarters of an hour for the train.

Reached London an hour late, found every comfort ready for us at Portman Square, and sank into a paradise of clothes.

15 JANUARY

We both lazed most of the morning. Mother had a glorious store of lovely things for us. Had a long journey, and failed to get tea despite the efforts of a nice soldier. At Portsmouth we drove in an old shandradan of a cab to our hotel. It is on the seafront and our room, large and pretty, is quite delightful.

17 JANUARY

With some difficulty we arose in time to get to Government House for lunch with Uncle Fred and Aunt Connie. The attractions of our room are so numerous and varied, that dressing takes a comfortable couple of hours. From our beds we can watch the ships of war going out and coming in: torpedo boats, destroyers, dredgers, submarines, armed trawlers and some queer little fellows that beside the others look like toy boats, which go about in strings of five or six at a time.

Next day Uncle Fred came to tea in our room and told us about each ship as she passed, and about the three forts – Horsesands, Nomans and Spitabout. The boom stretches from here to the Isle of Wight with just one gap, guarded by two ships.

Presently the searchlights came on, and their effect on the water was indescribably lovely. The shaft of light lies on the sea in a streak and the waves gleam a vivid silver – not the soft white it is in the moonlight, but dancing, dazzling, bright silver, leaping and running along like a fiery sword. Then the searchlights went up and up until they were pointing straight into the sky. Suddenly they went out, and then there was nothing to be seen except the few points of light in the ships.

20 JANUARY

Today we went all over the dockyard which was very muddy. One of the submarines we saw was covered in rust – she had been submerged for a long time. And there were a lot of tiny chaser tanks, called Whippets, which have done good work. They can do ten miles per hour, and of course it is hopeless for an enemy to think he can run away from them, or have any effect on them with a rifle. There was also a brand-new US ambulance train and a wonderful new ship that contained a piece of the old *Revenge* which fought the Spanish fleet, and was named after her. The dockyard is just like a little world – a very important little world – by itself.

21 JANUARY

Today we waited from 6 a.m. until 12 noon for the guns at the castle to go off. Many unusual (to us) things happened. We saw the target towed out and soldiers come from the castle. We saw several submarines and the seven faithful 'fleas', tiny boats jumping about in the wash of bigger ships; we saw the men round the guns, the soldiers returned to the fort and still nothing happened. So we thought no more about it – which, of course, was the quickest way of starting them. We leaped! The guns were very big and everything rocked each time they fired their 15 rounds. Outside, we saw several shattered windows.

26 JANUARY

We went this morning to the wharf, where the first boat to come in was *D25*. She dogs our footsteps – wherever we go, there she is. She was moored outside the Isle of Wight yesterday, where we went and she is always the first ship we see. Her wash foamed up against the sea wall and splashed us, as though in greeting.

27 JANUARY

Garrison church, after which we went to the Bastion. Aunt Con and I were armed with a note from my uncle. We were let in and two officers showed us over – everything is painted in camouflage. While we were there, a formation of five aeroplanes came over us, very low and fast. They came straight for us and buzzed like angry wasps. The four front ones passed over us but the fifth was some way behind. She was flying quite low and suddenly turned right over, twice, without stopping, not head over heals but wing over wing. The plane shut off her engines and dived still lower, almost onto the sea, then shot up again. It was lovely to watch.

16 MARCH

Came back to the Hill, where I am now a VAD nurse. My cousin Dick Crofton appeared, very brown and fit, but thin. He is in the Royal Horse Artillery, with the Chestnut Troop – the 'Golden Beauties', they are called.

He and I went to Anstie, where six of us staff go every Wednesday for Red Cross nursing lectures. After the lecture Dick and I went for a ride. Oh, the desolation of the woods! The Duke's Warren has gone, so has half the Redlands, and the birch plantation along the sandy bit is completely swept away [*the timber was used in the trenches*].

19 MARCH

More thrills. A lad in the hut has developed a rash. Hut isolated. Commandant comes. I am ordered to London. I protest – no good.

20 MARCH

Today went to the Grafton Galleries to see the war photographs, which are extremely upsetting because they were taken on the battlefields. Such sad scenes – we hate wars, but they are forced upon us by our jealous neighbours. One German general once said, after seeing London, 'A fine city. I would like to sack it.' Barbarian.

The German offensive has started. It is going to be more terrible than anything before.

23 MARCH

We have retreated a good bit. Captain Martin, a friend of Mother's, came in. He is cheering about the fighting. Dick turned up to say *au revoir*. His leave is not up yet, but he is going back at once.

24 MARCH

We are still retreating – back to the Somme; all those lives lost taking this territory in the first place – for nothing. Uncle Herbert, who is now Second Sea Lord, came after tea. He was quite cheerful, despite the news.

25 MARCH

The fighting is terrible – endless slaughter on both sides, but mostly theirs. Uncle Fred, who has left Portsmouth so that a man from the front can take his place and have a rest, is now in charge of the Royal Air Corps, his new amalgamation of the Royal Naval Air Service and the Royal Flying Corps. He began this mammoth task with only one ADC. Later he was given several more men, but got no recognition. He said to me rather sadly, when his two brothers were knighted, 'They've forgotten all about me!'

15 MAY

Mother and I are in Southsea. So much has happened since I last wrote. I developed a septic arm from a small area of chapped skin I had on my hand, and which I had touched with a dressing. I had to have an operation, then we went to Anstie for me to convalesce. They had a tennis tournament there, which made them very happy. The garden is exquisite this spring, and I never saw so many wild flowers as there are this year. Mother and I went to see the Pageant of Freedom. It was very beautiful: the colours of all our Allies were waved on the stage, and Clara Butt was magnificent as Great Britain.

I am still not allowed to work and this idleness frets me.

16 MAY

Yesterday to tea with Mrs Nelson-Ward who has the most enchanting little old house – a gem, and so beautifully done up. The family are descended from Nelson's daughter, Horatia, whose mother was the beautiful Emma Hamilton. Mrs Nelson-Ward has a harp which once belonged to Emma Hamilton; she plays and sings charmingly.

Today we had lunch with Admiral Nelson-Ward at the old George Inn, where Nelson slept his last night ashore. Mother and Dolly went to Haslar Naval Hospital, which has not enough nurses to help the sailors. I spent a happy afternoon with the harp. [*Much later, Mother sent me the harp in Kenya where it was damaged by the sun. I gave it to a British museum.*]

18 MAY

Isle of Wight. Father and I went out in a boat this morning; there is a half-mile limit all round. Round the corner is a wreck, the *War Knight*; she was sunk on only her second voyage.

21 MAY

We went to watch the divers at work on *War Knight*, and then to Carisbrooke after lunch. A splendid old place, a good deal of it is in ruin. We saw the famous donkey which treads the wheel for the old well. They say that the single war economy for the Isle of Wight is to have one donkey instead of two!

24 MAY

I have heard more about *War Knight*. The fishermen say that she was run into by an oil tanker, and she herself was carrying several barrels of oil. Both ships caught fire, and *War Knight* flamed like a sheet of lightning right up the mast; the crew could not escape.

25 MAY

Pat Brooke died a year ago today.

26 MAY

On the water in the morning and again, having nothing better to do, in the afternoon. It is delicious in the evening, warm and still; everything smells sweet and the moon on the sea is exquisite. And then you see *War Knight* and think of the war, and the men we've lost.

We 'did' Carisbrooke thoroughly and I had a look at the museum, which contains a lot of Stewart relics. Princess Elizabeth, daughter of King Charles I, died here, and not even *her* room was respected by the utterly contemptible trippers who write their insignificant names all over these sacred walls! The place ought to be shut until people can behave better and I doubt that will ever be, for democracy is not improving the nation's manners.

28 MAY

Captain Martin had to go and inspect an Electric Light School. He is so alarming with his one leg – hops down steps on it, and is very agile. We went to the aerodrome from where he was to start, and when the 'bus' arrived, the pilot got out and came to us – such a child, full of technical slang! We shall miss Captain Martin – he is fun.

Dick is now in France, doing very well: captain and MC, still with the Chestnut Troop. My cousin Billy Heath is with him. He has been awarded the DSO, but of course won't say why.

10 JULY

We saw the Zouaves march past. They were imposing, very brown and war-scarred, splendid-looking troops, not quite youthful. The crowd forgot to be British and cheered madly.

12 JULY

We heard the Zouave band play at a requiem service in Westminster Cathedral today. It was very impressive. Crowds of candles and clouds of incense. A huge catafalque below the altar, draped with black and gold brocade, and covered with the French flag, six tall candles around it. The Zouaves stood motionless the whole service through, with their *p'tit officier* facing them. There was much singing and finally their band played the 'Sambre et Meuse', a lovely, strange and haunting air. We pursued them when the service was over, caught up with them and cheered vociferously.

9 AUGUST

We are going to Scotland. Our train left Kings X and we said farewell to Bessie, who, after twelve years of faithful service, is leaving us to drive an ambulance. We shall miss her sunny hair and apple cheeks. Dulcie Hore and I shared a compartment, and Griggs joined us at Grantham and slept on the floor of Father's and Mother's carriage. It was a beautiful journey, grey and soft. I could hardly bear to go to sleep, it was so lovely to look at.

10 AUGUST

We arrived at Aberdeen and after breakfast Griggs and I went for a walk and reached Market Square. The women wear plaids over their heads. We came on to the Huntly Arms at Aboyne where we have got a sitting room and five bedrooms. Retriever Rex and spaniel Raven are with us. Raven is highly strung and very shy, but she has recovered from the journey and is now quite light-hearted.

11 AUGUST

Uncle Herbert arrived breezily in a smart naval car. Some of the ladies here find him attractive, which is not surprising.

14 AUGUST

There are six of us here and the men go off each day to shoot and fish. The game is getting the best of it – luckily we do not depend for our daily food on the contents of the game bag! Dulcie and I go for walks and today, on the way up Birsemohr Hill, we found Birsemohr Loch, a gem of a place with tall reeds growing at one end and a small island in the middle; then it stretches right away to the slope of the hill where fir trees and heather, growing up to the edge, are reflected in it.

17 AUGUST

Started out on my tubby piebald pony to Lumphanan, with the car following. Left the shooters, wandered up the hill, sat down comfortably with my back to a stone and, obeying Cameron's [*the keeper's*] instructions, admired the view. It was admirable, too. All these lovely hills, rising one behind the other for miles, and Lochnagar's three peaks lifting above them with clouds hanging halfway down it and the sun on its crest. Sun and shade alternating on the nearer hills.

30 AUGUST

One day we drove to Tarland to find the Coulsh, which was once the home of a Pictish chief. Since this is Scotland it is hard to find – no direction boards, no entrance fee, no uniformed guardian, no crowd of curious and irreverent trippers, no electric light, just a farm and a small boy with a shock of red hair and a candle. The entrance is a small hole in the grass, built up with stones and just large enough to get into, bent double. Of course it is pitch-black inside and that is where the boy and the candle come in. There is a fairly long, low passage which suddenly gets tall enough to stand upright in, and at the end is a dome about eight feet high. I wondered how this chief lived, how he died, how many wives he had and how many people he killed.

I stayed the night at Corsee and that evening we went to the town hall to watch the dancing. All the lassies flocked in at the beginning, when there were thirty-six girls and two men, but more males gradually arrived. They danced Scottish dances, and it really was striking to see how all these girls and men in ordinary blouses and skirts, jackets and trousers, with never a kilt among them (except the soldiers), nor a plaid, could dance every native dance so stylishly. They had eightsomes and foursomes, Schottisches and something called the Circassian Circle, and they danced them all perfectly.

8 SEPTEMBER

Matthew, the pony boy, told me a very sad story, news of which reached Aboyne two days ago. A shepherd on Cloch-na-ben Hill came upon a wrecked aeroplane with the body of the aviator pinned beneath it, dead. They say he came from Montrose, where, according to Matthew, thirteen spies have been caught. Petrol tanks in planes have been pierced, so while they are flying the fuel is leaking away.

12 SEPTEMBER

The news from Russia today is terrible. The Tsar has been murdered in a cellar, with the poor little Tsarevich. And now they say that the Tsarina and her four daughters were murdered with him. Of course no news comes direct, but this is as authentic as any news from Russia can be nowadays. It is horrible to think of those lovely girls killed in that way; they were so young and so beautiful. They and their mother were nursing in the war. Petrograd is said to be in flames in many places, and massacres are going on in the streets. A few days ago the Bolsheviks murdered Captain Cromie, the British Naval Attaché there as he stood on the steps of our Embassy. The mob is mad for blood, Russia is in chaos.

24 SEPTEMBER

A very high wind, but I wandered down to the river Dee for the last time. While I was there I saw some cows walking along the opposite bank, threading their way through the trees, imperturbably (cows do everything that way) followed by an elkhound and a pretty girl with her hair down her back and her arms bare, wearing a blue frock. The dog sat on a rock and watched the river for a while, every now and then looking over his shoulder to see if the girl was all right. She tried to shoo away some stray cows which had joined her lot; he instantly dashed to help her and fiercely barked them away. It was a very pretty sight – the beautiful cows, the little brown farm girl, the protective dog and the grey Dee. The river was very grey and very swift as there had been a lot of rain. I am sorry to leave this place – it has been such a good leave here. It's Anstie pantry when I get back.

26 SEPTEMBER

Got back rather weary. Monsieur Aahl, the Norwegian Secretary, came to dinner. He is politely seeing the last of Litvinoff, the Bolshevik – I suppose there is no other word for it – 'Ambassador' here, who is being sent back to his own country (the best place for him) in return for British subjects detained in Russia. Litvinoff is apparently quite young and seems rather harmless. But I don't like or trust any Russians, except the unhappy, exiled 'gentry'.

30 SEPTEMBER

So here I am, back in the pantry and very happy to be here. It now consists of Mrs Kenny, Miss Dames, me, Miss Calvert and Miss Plat. It's a case of being in at the death of the war!

3 OCTOBER

Bad luck haunts me. The doc says hospital air doesn't suit me and that I am to leave tomorrow by the 9.45 train!

I've just been here long enough to hear of the deaths of two of our old patients – such charming boys. One is Mr Cobden. He was discharged from the army, joined the Flying Corps and was killed in France on 21 June.

The other is Mr Smith, an Australian who was wounded in the leg – he nearly died of a haemorrhage one night. I remember he said to me one teatime when I was taking up the tray: 'I know you love your horses, Miss Heath.'

I said, 'I do – but how did you guess?'

'Oh, I saw you with one of them in the yard the other day and you were "loving" him!'

I thought it the nicest thing. He and I were quite good friends. And now he's dead.

8 NOVEMBER

The news is thrilling. Last night there were wild peace rumours, and we danced about and felt quite hysterical, and this evening I rang up Captain Martin and asked him. He could – or would – tell me nothing definite, but it's in the air. It will be through in another couple of days, and then . . .! Well, I hope we shall take it decently and not maffick about it. But it is utterly impossible to be calm after four years of this nightmare, the Victory! Next time I write in this book, I expect it will be IT.

9 NOVEMBER

Not yet, but very, very nearly. Foch met the German delegates, and they were so dumbfounded at his terms that they sent back a courier to Berlin to ask 'What can we do?' This evening Pat from the War Office rang me up to say that the Kaiser has abdicated.

I said, 'May I spread it?'

He said, 'Yes, go on,' and I fairly ran. I told it in the hall, in the kitchen, in the sister's room, in the office – Glory! And thank God.

11 NOVEMBER

It has come. Pat rang me up about 10.30, and said, 'Five o'clock this morning!'

'The armistice?'

'Signed and delivered.'

So at last, after four years, it is ended, finished. It is very hard to realize – it has been such a part of one's life. I can hardly remember pre-war days; it sounds ridiculous, seeing that I am nineteen now, but I have simply grown up into it.

The telephone has been ringing all day. London has gone mad, of course – all the bells are ringing and guns are firing. There are crowds everywhere, and throngs outside Buckingham Palace. I am going up tomorrow. The men are coming home before long.

12 NOVEMBER

What a day! Dot and I came to London by the early train, and Father met us at the station.

We hurried out again as soon as we had reached home, and went to the Mall to see the royal procession from Buckingham Palace to St Paul's for a service of thanks and remembrance. A thick crowd had gathered; everyone carried flags and looked absolutely happy. There was a thin cordon of police – we met Sir Montague Ommanney with Lady Ommanney, and he said: 'I know no other capital in the world where the King and Queen can go out with only eight mounted police for guard, and only police to line the streets!' He got it absolutely right in saying that the loyalty here is unique and, I'm sure, lasting. The procession was as simple as it could be. First came four mounted police, then a few equerries, next the royal carriage with the King, the Queen and Princess Mary. The cheering was glorious; above the heads of the crowd were flags and flags, waving madly. The King and Queen looked utterly happy, but Princess Mary was restrained – I expect she was near tears. I heard she went wild with joy when the news came through, and behaved, so Pat said, like a small schoolgirl. It is wonderful when you realize that so many kings are losing their thrones – Germany, Austria–Hungary, Bulgaria and Russia have gone – yet our King is *ours*, firmer than ever on the throne, and beloved.

Trafalgar Square was wonderful! A seething mass of people, and flags – flags everywhere. Everyone cheering and shouting, drums, bugles and every sort of noisy instrument. People crammed up the steps of the monument, some on the lions' backs, an improvised jazz band, soldiers and girls dancing in rows, linked arm-in-arm. Big trolley buses went by, packed with men and women in khaki, cheering and waving their flags. We bought several for the house. There has never been a war like this before, and the ending of it is wonderful.

The Armistice terms have been astonishingly stiff, and apart from that Germany is in a terrible state – the people are starving, there is no food at all. President Wilson proposes to send them some. Yet on the hill the other day I met Emerson the moss-gatherer, whose boy had been a prisoner there and escaped after seven attempts. While he was in Germany they tortured him; one of the things they did was to brand his legs with burning coke – he will carry the scars always.

'I could tell you other things, Miss,' said Emerson, 'but I won't, it wouldn't be right.'

I wonder where the widows are. I have not seen any since I have been up. Now must be the most terrible time of all for them.

13 NOVEMBER

After lunch, to *Chu Chin Chow* for the fifth time. It was packed, and we could only get three seats in a box. They brought in a new scene – the Allies, draped in the flags of their countries. First Belgium, then France, both were cheered terrifically, then America – storms of cheers (really America doesn't deserve so much as the others – they didn't come in for a long time), next Italy, and finally, having given us time to get our breath, Lily Brayton as Britannia. The house nearly came down! They played 'Rule Britannia', then we stood up and sang 'God Save the King', then 'Land of Hope and Glory' – which is just what England is now.

On the way home we stopped to see the exhibition of mechanical models. There are models of some of the torpedoed hospital ships, a lovely one of Italian scenery, a collection of war trophies, and a submarine that sinks – incidentally it sends up a lot of bubbles, which no submarine would think of doing – as well as an airship poised above a battlefield and an astounding German dugout, lined with concrete, and dug down several yards below the surface – all nice and dry, ready for our men when the chase began!

After dinner Father, Mother and I went down Oxford Street and Regent Street to Piccadilly Circus. The same mad crowds, processions every minute, always the countless flags, drums, bugles, dinner gongs. Girls draped in big Union Jacks, two passed us with one French flag round both of them, flags worn as caps. Soldiers with flags hanging out of every pocket, the weirdest dances, bands of cheerful sub-lieutenants, flocks of small street Arabs, and lorries crammed with people, with the luckiest one sitting on the bonnet. Once we got into a ring of dancing, shouting Tommies – it was marvellous!

Father, with due regard for his watch and his womenkind, put his weight against them, and they gave way happily, like so much elastic.

The British crowd is usually so good-natured, but later on that night they tore the placards off captured German guns and made a bonfire in Piccadilly of them – that was not so bad, but the fools threw handfuls of live cartridges on them! And in Trafalgar Square they burnt one of the guns, piled the wooden benches on it, and hurt the firemen, which is horrible. But on the whole they are behaving well, and it is only late at night that they run wild – probably on drink.

14 NOVEMBER

Spent the morning teaching Cuthbert to dance – he is not too bad. Mother and I lunched at Lyon's, which is terribly respectable! Then we went on to the Regent Palace Hotel (which was one of last night's sufferers – they smashed an *iron* door) in search of my brother Griggs and his wife. After dinner we retired with them to a quiet place to talk, which was a bore as the grill room was very gay, with people dancing on the tables like Carmen and throwing bottles about like Englishmen!

15 NOVEMBER

London seems to be quietening down a little – they must be getting rather tired. Came to Anstie in the car, piled high with fireworks outside and wool and bandages inside. Not much room for us! A dance here this evening, and there was *one* man! Miss Gordon from the kitchen made me a good partner.

16 NOVEMBER

Hounds met here at 11 a.m.; the hospital trooped out and stood in admiring rows. I rode Templar, the best hunter I have had. It was grand – the first time I have been out since the war, except once, cubbing. Cuthbert arrived for tea, and soon after we had the fireworks. They were lovely, and the whole village came down to see them.

17 NOVEMBER

I went to church at Coldharbour. It was quite a nice service until the parson, Mr Denman, urged us to *pray for the Kaiser*! I was frozen stiff with horror and fury – how *dare* he say such a thing! One doesn't pray for Satan!

4 DECEMBER

Poor Dot has got flu very badly; she is so weak and tired, which makes it worse. Her mother is with her, and I hope she will be better soon.

6 DECEMBER

Dot has got pneumonia on the left lung, quite badly. Sister Dunbabin came over from the Hill to nurse her.

10 DECEMBER

Dot has safely passed the crisis, and is on the mend.

12 DECEMBER

Came to London in a hurry because Mrs Philpott seems to have got flu. I was joined by Mr Wallace (once of here) at Epsom. I saw him tearing down the platform and put a hand out of the window, so he got in and was very amusing and interesting. Also he carried my bag, which was a great blessing.

16 DECEMBER

Blind Harry Crofton arrived last night. He and Father departed for France this morning; escorted by detectives, with the navy to see them safely on board at Folkestone, and the army to take them off the other side and carry them around. I think we may reasonably expect them safely home in three days' time.

17 DECEMBER

Mother and I went to Anstie for the day to say goodbye to everyone – the hospital is really coming to an end. I don't remember ever having seen the view as lovely as it was today – a wonderful purple-blue right out to the Downs, and the sunset a burning red-gold.

19 DECEMBER

Heart trouble of last summer breaking out again. Small heart attacks, and I must stay in bed. So I missed seeing an ex-German U-boat, lunch at the Carlton and welcome to Haig, tea with Mrs St Aubyn, and a dance at the Hoptons.

20 DECEMBER

Dulcie Hore and I came to Anstie in the car, and I went straight to bed. I am in Mary's room on the top floor. There are now only six patients left, and about twenty staff all told. What will it be like when they are all gone?

23 DECEMBER

Mother came down. I am much better and got up today. I played the most scientific bridge tonight – the strong, silent sort, where you count cards, and do sums and refrain from talking about frocks or hunting, and pull your partner's play to pieces after each game.

25 DECEMBER

Communion service at 6 a.m., which meant getting up at five. I was able to go out first for a few minutes – it was exquisite. The clearest, deepest blue sky, enormous stars glittering like diamonds. A red splash low down in the east, prelude to the sunrise, and, almost straight overhead a silver-white moon. It was a perfect Christmas dawning.

After the service it was bath and bed again – wisely. Dressed for the second time, and worked all the morning decorating the hall and dining room for lunch, for which we were ten at one long table down the middle of the room. Two geese, Father and the doc at opposite ends of the table carving. Father made an excellent little speech, and we drank His Majesty's health and one another's, and then went into the hall and everyone hunted for presents.

At teatime I cut the cake – a marvellous three-decker with real icing sugar (a true luxury in these post-war days) on it – with Cock o' the North, my *skean-dhu*, which was slow work. Many games after and carol singing.

26 DECEMBER

We all went to the Boxing Day meet at the White Horse in Dorking. A very fine frosty morning, but the ground was hard. It was a pretty meet, and a big field for these times. I nearly wept at not being allowed to ride.

On the way back we stopped at the telephone office. Mother went in to compliment and thank the people there – they really have been splendid, working long hours and always helpful and polite. It was just the day for a long motor drive – but petrol was lacking. Hounds had a rather poor morning and a good afternoon, I heard. And for us, in the evening, bridge. Again.

This is the hospital's last day.

27 DECEMBER

Today Anstie Grange Hospital closed. It was too sad. The ambulances left at 2.30, and we tied their pet plum pudding mascot on the back with a piece of holly stuck in it. We said goodbye to them all and waved them out of sight to the last corner of the drive. It is horribly empty and big now. There is no one and not a sound anywhere; just half-filled ashtrays and a few books lying about.

After two years and a quarter of a hundred noisy, cheerful people everywhere, to me it is as if some big thing has died, and left the place empty and silent.

[*During the years that Anstie was a hospital the Union Jack flew on the roof every day and was taken down at night. Many years later Mother sent the flag to me in Kenya and we flew it on special occasions. I finally brought it to England and gave it to Coldharbour church, where it hangs above the war memorial to the men who died in Hitler's War – those from Coldharbour and from my family.*]

1919

29 JANUARY

We went, a family party, to the United Services Ball at the Albert Hall, nearly three thousand people in fancy dress or uniform and very beautiful. Father was in pink, Mother as a Kurd, Aunt Irene *poudré*, and my dress was eastern and really lovely. The floor was superb, the band rather more used to the operas than to our music – but good enough all the same. Coloured searchlights played all the time, this wonderful kaleidoscopic crowd moving and shifting and blending.

6 FEBRUARY

Things have been quite exciting lately. The whole of the labour class seems to have gone on strike – miners, railwaymen, tubemen, electricians, waiters, cooks and . . . *page boys*! In a hotel now you will get no meals and no hot water, so you either break the ice before getting in or go dirty. The electricians say that they are going to cut off the lights and leave London in total darkness. The government is being surprisingly firm; they sent troops to Glasgow to bring sense to the Clyde shipbuilders and they have called for volunteers for the power stations; also they have made it an offence to interfere with the water or gas supply.

The electricians said they would turn out the lights at six tonight: it is now seven, and all serene. The Peace Conference has been rather put in the shade, but, as I suppose we have passed the crisis here, we may be hearing something more about it.

15 FEBRUARY

Motored to Anstie for the day in the new Vauxhall. The car is good for touring, runs very smoothly and can do 80 miles an hour. The air was like velvet, the view all blue and everything smelt of spring, fresh and delicious. It was a perfect day. When we got there we found the roads covered with frozen snow which is just beginning to melt, hovering between slipperiness and slush.

Anstie has been rather chaotic – eight of the radiators burst. Mrs Philpott has just avoided drowning and has been tearing about with baths and pails and mops, pulling up the carpets and cursing the frost. I wandered round, was greeted exuberantly by all the dogs and blessed by one of the woodsmen, Curly, who is a dear. Came back to London through the loveliest sunset, which flooded everything with a pinky gold light.

22 FEBRUARY

Dick arrived early this morning and we went to the meet at Bookham. Found almost at once and at first had quite a good run, but the going was bad. This evening Mr Griffin (an American naval officer) arrived and after dinner Miss Piggott came up from Bearehurst, and we four danced to the jerky melody of the pianola.

7 MARCH

My friend Mr Griffin collected me, and we went to the movies. Mr Griffin is going to Russia next week to chase Bolsheviks through the ice [*The British had sent a force to Archangel during the Civil War*].

11 MARCH

Mr Capehart and Mr Griffin – Bob – came to dinner. Then on to the Mitfords' dance with them.

18 MARCH

Here begins a thrilling tale. We took on a chauffeur called Bates with a touching history, for our sympathetic ears, of four years as a prisoner of war. Today he vanished entirely, leaving his extremely anxious wife on our hands. There's no sign of him anywhere.

19 MARCH

Still no sign of Bates, and we passed the day hunting for him. I went to the City and had a talk with Mr Nichols in Father's palatial office.

A Pole, Count Ostrorog (whom I met at the Torrs' last week) came to dinner, and we all went on to the Carews' dance. He dances well.

20 MARCH

Our elusive Bates has been traced to Brixton. His wife has gone there.

21 MARCH

A particularly lurid day. Bates came to the house and I dismissed him (Mother is in France). He made a scene. He was drunk. However we all emerged alive, but then Griggs had to go down with him and the butler to Dorking to look at the cars there.

28 APRIL

The snow is about ten inches deep on the flat and there are five- to six-foot drifts in places. I know because I sat in one, and the spaniel came and sat on my chest – she is a heavy dog – by way of helping me.

5 MAY

I am twenty today. I don't know that I quite like being so old, but we'll see how things go on later. We came to London, and are staying at the Wigmore Hotel. Tonight we all went to the Slavo Dance at Prince's.

18 MAY

Bob Griffin, whom I imagined to be battling with icebergs and Bolsheviks, suddenly rang up and said when could he come round and see 'you-all'. We sampled the river at Richmond and found it very crowded, but otherwise delicious. He came back with us to dinner.

20 MAY

On the river again, this time to Kew, and Bob came. It was rather hot. Bob and I fought, the first time since I have known him, and over politics too. It was a novel experience. However, he goes north again tonight, so we parted friends. His ships are at Inverness, and he really will sail straight for Russia now. I fancy they won't be gone very long.

4 JUNE

A great day! We went to the Derby and took Captain Lake and Mr Capehart. There were thousands of people, among them bookies, gypsies, three-card-trick men, coaches, motors and buses, and a crush in the grandstand you couldn't move in. We won a little on Paper Money and lost it all on Wendy. Next time we go I should like to ride there from Anstie; it is the best way to see it. As it was, we stood on the roof of the car and bore the rain patiently until Mr Capehart went off and fetched an umbrella for me. He borrowed it from an old lady superintending the coconut shies, and when she saw him she cried, 'Ow, the ducky little sailorboy! Bring it back dearie won't you?' Of course he did.

5 JUNE

Hurlingham this evening with Mr Lake, the sailor brother of the captain's. He is very nice and had spent the morning with three of his brothers, all receiving decorations. One got the MC, two got the DSO, and he got the DSO and DSC – a very distinguished set of brothers.

10 JUNE

Started off for Cambridge, with Mr Lake to see I got there safely. I was going to stay with Lady Wood – but I'd no notion *where*. There wasn't a sign of Sir John anywhere, so we went about asking people which his college was. Ran him to earth at last, and found the rest of the party, so poor Mr Lake was able to escape.

11 JUNE

Watched the tennis tournament after lunch. Cambridge was beaten. Tonight we went to the Duds Ball, where we stayed till 5.30. I met a boy named Drummond-Hay, nicknamed Truffles. The band got merrier and merrier – one musician was carried out, and another crowned himself with a wreath of flowers and danced a *pas seul* on the platform.

12 JUNE

Went on the river after lunch and slept peacefully in the boat. John struggled with the tea and sat with his feet in the water, muddying it. He also poled us home most efficiently. We only crashed six boats, and made ourselves very popular. He held on his way regardless.

Tonight we went to the Naval Ball at the Guildhall. There were twice as many people as there was room for, so we stood round waiting for chairs for supper. John had brought a bottle of champagne, so we didn't faint.

When it was over, at 5.30., we had our photographs taken in the marketplace, looking perfectly awful in the morning sun.

13 JUNE

Truffles came round after lunch and took me over the colleges. He did it very well, telling me the history of each one. We walked and walked. I remember the river from King's Bridge, and the Cloister at Queens', which is lovely; very old, quiet and dim and away from everywhere. You can imagine the ghosts of generations of students passing up and down, not minding the silly little human beings who come round to look at their old haunts, and go away wondering at them.

After dinner we went on the river, Lady Wood and John in one canoe, Truffles and I in another. We lashed them together with our handkerchiefs. John sang to us and we drifted along that lovely stream seeing the lights fade out, and the sunset die down, till the stars appeared one at a time and the pale moon watched us. It was dark when we got in, and beautiful.

I leave tomorrow; it has been heavenly.

17 JUNE

To Ascot. It was a broiling hot day and a wonderful sight; crowds of ladies in lovely frocks. The royal party arrived about ten o'clock and drove up the course escorted by mounted gentlemen of the Household. The King, Queen, Princess Mary and the Prince of Wales were in the first carriage, drawn by four perfect horses.

19 JUNE

Ascot again, just as hot and just as beautiful. This time we saw the royal carriages leaving, they drove off between lines of ladies and gentlemen, all curtseying and bowing, and the Queen smiling and looking so happy.

28 JUNE

Peace has been signed today. It is the fifth anniversary of the murders at Sarajevo which started the war. The documents were signed at three o'clock, and suddenly all the guns round us started firing twenty-one rounds each, all round the ridge, one taking it up after another – almost, I suppose, for the last time. There was a lot of happy noise everywhere later in the evening, fireworks and rockets.

How wonderful to think it is peace at last. I wish I was in Paris now.

6 JULY

This is the day of universal thanksgiving all through England. Dulcie and I got up early and went to Westminster Abbey where we waited, shivering, for the doors to open. There was a wonderful service, the music beautiful – there is nothing like music . . . I hope Heaven realizes how incredibly, overwhelmingly thankful and grateful we are.

10 JULY

Jim Wood, my pilot friend, appeared today for two minutes. He departs tomorrow morning for Finland, in an oilship. He wanted to take me up in his plane, but it didn't come off.

Tonight we went to the opera – *Romeo and Juliet.* Melba sang exquisitely and the duet was heavenly. And oh, the people! – the dresses and jewels were lovely, and some of the ladies were too!

16 JULY

We had been bidden to the garden party at Buckingham Palace. An enormous stretch of lawn and five thousand people, all in elegant clothes, with the great stone Palace in the background. The King and Queen went their separate ways, receiving people and speaking to them, passing down a lane of guests while Mamas presented nervous débutantes, and it all looked perfectly beautiful with the sun pouring down. We wandered about meeting friends and seeing all sorts of interesting people – a lot of royalties, diplomats, generals and one or two actors.

After tea Admiral Nelson-Ward presented Mother and me to the King. It was very informal and easy; he shook hands with us, said a few words to Mother, and then moved on. Dot was also there and she stayed the night with us.

18 JULY

The Peace Procession takes place tomorrow; in front of Queen Victoria's monument a stand has been erected where the King and the royal party will take the salute. Round the front of the stand are seats draped in red cloth and backed by the white and gold pylons and the flags.

19 JULY

Forth we went in the early dawn, Father, Mother, Dulcie, Griggs, Aleste and I, through the Park to Woolland's, [*Knightsbridge*], where we have got seats for the Victory Procession.

The Park was full of sailors and Wrens, pretty neat girls in that most

38

becoming uniform for which Uncle Herbert is responsible. [*He told me that he and Dame Catherine Furse, commanding the Wrens, had been ordered to inspect the new uniforms for these girls. He insisted on shorter skirts and smarter hats, to the Dame's disapproval – but he got his way.*] There were groups of decorated naval officers, glittering with gold, swords, shoulder knots and medal ribbons. Father came to a halt here, looking for Uncle Herbert, so we went on.

At Woolland's we had excellent seats on the ground floor, raised, and looking onto the street. The only drawback was the pane of glass in front, which made coolness impossible and cheering useless!

At 10 a.m. the processions left Albert Gate, sweeping round the corner and past us to march down Sloane Street. The men marched alphabetically by country. The Americans headed the column, with General Pershing leading them, splendid on a very fine horse. The men were most impressive. They marched eight abreast, all in khaki, rifles shouldered and bayonets fixed, glinting as they caught the sun, swinging round the corner.

The Belgians came next – little men in long brown coats and brown shrapnel helmets, with a cheerful little bugle band. They were terrifically cheered! There were not many of them, but they were hardy and tried. The very first into the war, here were the survivors; they have had terrible losses.

After them came Chinese generals with their staff, all mounted and very smart. Each country's troops carried their own banners. The Americans made a perfect group, a sudden wave of colour, a forest of flags. The Belgians carried theirs sloped over the shoulder, I thought it less impressive.

Following them the Czechoslovaks – then the great fighter, Maréchal Foch! How the crowd cheered! He rode carrying his baton in his right hand, looking very unselfconscious and superb. He took no notice of us at all. His general followed him, then a band, and then his soldiers – Chasseurs, infantry, colonials, Zouaves in their picturesque clothes, Tirailleurs, some fine-looking sailors and cavalry.

The Greeks came next, then Italians, Japanese and Poles.

The Portuguese followed but I think the crowd was getting its breath for the next outburst, which came with the Romanians. They have suffered too, and their men look splendid. Then the Serbians – tall, well-built men. They were cheered and cheered again.

There was a pause after the last of the foreigners. Then our own men appeared. First the navy, Sir David Beatty leading, marching ahead alone, followed by an officer carrying his flag. Then came his admirals and staff, dozens of them including Uncle Herbert, who looked for us, smiling as ever, but did not see us. Men of HMS *Queen Elizabeth* were next, then the battle squadrons, each with their flags. And the Naval Reserve men, among whom were the minesweeper crews; nobody had done better work than them.

There were merchant captains too, who supplied England with food all through the war in spite of their heavy losses. There were naval nurses and naval chaplains, all decorated. Dame Catherine Furse led the WRNS; they marched most beautifully and looked perfectly charming in their smart new uniforms. Sea Scouts brought up the rear. The crowds cheered madly.

A band. Another pause. And then the army! Staff officers leading followed by leading officers and men of the 19th Expeditionary Force. They were the very first to go to France, and here were the survivors, having fought right through to march in the Victory Procession.

The massed standards of the Household Cavalry, cavalry and infantry regiments came. Then the artillery, wildly cheered by the crowd (the cheering led by an officer aloft upon a lamp-post, who took off his cap and waved his stick and yelled). Behind them, riding a very beautiful chestnut, came Uncle Gerard at the head of his engineers. He saw us and saluted. I stood up and waved frantically to him. The sappers were marching behind carts containing some of the mysteries of their trade: field telephones, pontoon boats and tool wagons. Then came the infantry – about two lines of each regiment, marching, most of them, twelve abreast.

Four tanks were very thrilling, lumbering along with an officer running backwards in front of them, directing them. Then the Jersey detachment. Then some splendid Australians, New Zealanders and South Africans, each with a detachment of nurses. Then the VADs, 'Very Adorable Darlings', marching as well as anyone and looking perfect. They got tremendous cheers.

A band. A pause. The Royal Air Force. Hundreds of them, and among the officers leading was Colonel Samson, an ace, and a wonderful man. The WRAF brought up the rear, and ended the procession, the most wonderful and historic procession that has ever taken place in England. I am thankful to have seen it.

After dinner out again to see the fireworks in Hyde Park. They were exquisite. Fountains of gold, great gold flowers opening towards you, cascades of colour, showers of ruby and emerald stars, the crowd gasping at it.

Beacons are lit all over England tonight, on the highest hills. The sky over Hampstead was bright yellow, flickering with reflections. The people! Thousands and thousands of them all over the roads, mostly quite sober, a few not. Some were dancing that funny arm-in-arm dance Trafalgar Square specialized in on Armistice night, singing, ringing joy-bells, and all covered in flags. Some girls had tied the Union Jack handkerchief-wise on their heads, and had sewn them onto the blouses.

It has been a wonderful day, but it's somehow hard to realize it means peace. People are supremely happy, but they're not swept off their feet with relief and thankfulness as they were on Armistice night. *Then* it was the soul of the country you saw, *now* it's just the spirit of gaiety. One of the most glorious sights today was our regimental colours – so many of them in tatters. They are the soul of the army.

21 JULY

Today we drove to Southend, where Admiral Fremantle has asked us to lunch in his ship, HMS *Revenge*. After lunch I went all over the ship. An attractive boy with a mop of yellow hair and a cigarette stuck behind one ear showed us over his own special turret. He told us all about it and said the entire turret, with its two great guns, weighs 2000 tons. The average time of firing from one shot to another is twenty-one seconds, but this particular ship gets through it in eighteen seconds. He took us into the place where they get the ranges from. The amazing thing is that, though the shock outside the turret would blow you six feet high when the gun is fired, inside there isn't a sound!

11 AUGUST

Said goodbye to everyone and packed ourselves into the train for Edinburgh. Ran into Dick Usher in the lounge; he is stationed here with the Scots Greys. [*Many years later Dick came to live in Kenya with his wife. After a few years they parted and he married again. Three days after the wedding they left in Dick's plane for their honeymoon. The weather was bad, with low cloud. He flew into a mountain and she was killed; he shot himself.*]

16 AUGUST

I drove the car from Aboyne to Lumphanan to join the shooters, tucked it into a farmyard and walked up Quarry Hill to the pool. Fascinating place. The slabs of rock are pinky grey, and the water is a still purple and very deep. On the top of a hill with the moors all round it, it is a gem of a pool. I have loved it for three years.

26 SEPTEMBER

The railway strike starts tonight at midnight.

28 SEPTEMBER

All the main lines have stopped working and the government is commandeering all the petrol, so goodness knows when we shall get south! In London there are no trams, tubes, taxis or buses, and lorries are hard at work bringing food into the city. This strike paralyses everything. Trade unions are involved and the government has its hands full, but they are sure to

41

come to a settlement soon. Meanwhile a few trains are being run by volunteers.

30 SEPTEMBER

Every day I have been out with Tom [*Farquhar, Lady Farquhar's eldest son*] all over the country, being looked at by his friends and endless relations!

3 OCTOBER

Today Tom and I went by train to Cambus O'May, biked to a farm where we left the machines, and walked on to the Burn O' the Vat. It is a lovely place, a deep, rocky cleft running up with this small burn in the middle of it. In one place there is a waterfall across some rocks which make what is called Rob Roy's Cave, where he hid a while from his enemies.

Two nights ago the Northern Lights were showing. They looked like running streamers of white, streaky clouds, moving up and down the sky; they streamed and flashed and faded and lit up in patterns – the sky was alight with them. They were all white, not coloured. The curious thing is that they came from the south-west! They are more strange than beautiful, but I am glad to have seen them.

4 OCTOBER

This is our last day here, as somehow Hann the chauffeur has got the petrol to take us south by car.

7 OCTOBER

The strike is over. The first train was run last night – we heard the cheering. We are still going by car and started for Carlisle this morning. The Border country is grand and curious, with steep, bare hills, very narrow valleys and sheep everywhere.

8 OCTOBER

En route Chester, we came through Windermere. Magnificent, wild, windy and as grand as Scotland.

Chester is a beautiful old town. But motoring isn't all joy – the roads are cut to pieces and full of holes, through which we bump in an anguished silence.

9 OCTOBER

This morning I went over the cathedral alone. It is built of rose-red stone, and the light inside is a very soft pink. The organ was playing gently, I wandered about. There are many In Memoriams to men who have fallen in this war, and there is also a banner presented by the hospitals of Cheshire. After the cathedral I walked along the walls, then looked at the shops, some of which have quaint old carvings on the woodwork. A great many have been rebuilt, but in good taste.

10 OCTOBER

Left for Cheltenham. Drove through Shropshire, which seems to have stuck in the eighteenth century. Everyone is very slow and very polite, and the carthorses are magnificent, but the scenery is flat, dull and cultivated.

11 OCTOBER

Tom and I are engaged.

Left early for London. Home at last! I started reading the engagement letters. It took me two hours without stopping or pausing, from five till seven. After dinner, at it again!

16 OCTOBER

Every day is composed of letter-writing and shopping. Life is grand being engaged – the best thing I have yet tried. Today I went to the Hill Hospital lunch party – it was fun. Everybody ragged me and I hope they'll all turn up at the wedding. It's going to be on Wednesday, 10 December, at St Margaret's, Westminster.

1 NOVEMBER

Anstie. This is a great day. To tea came about a hundred of the villagers. Tea was in the dining room, dozens of tables, and scores of babies turning up in all sorts of odd places. After tea we went into the hall and had a couple of hours of a really good conjurer. Just before the end, Hoddie, our carpenter, ex-navy, made a charming speech and presented me with a wedding present from all the Anstie and village people – a lovely cruet set in silver. I was so pleased and scared I didn't know what to say; it was wonderful of them. They left after that. Bless them all. I don't suppose I shall see them again before the day.

30 NOVEMBER

Over to Mick's for tea. He looked Tom all over and sympathized with him. A chilly run home. This is the last time I shall be here as *me*. Everyone looks rather worried. I'm beginning to feel that way, too!

10 DECEMBER

Got up after breakfast, and Madame Dion, the dressmaker, arrived to dress me. The wedding dress is georgette, hand-embroidered all over with a girdle of pearls, some of Mother's Limerick lace for the train (from the shoulders) and a huge tulle veil. The bouquet is a sheaf of madonna lilies. Went downstairs and left the house with Father for St Margaret's. Hann driving, with Kite our groom on the box.

Mr Locke and Mr Nelson-Ward married us. It must have been quite pretty, and I only wish I could have seen more of it. Teddy Blake, a friend of Tom's, was best man. Tom sounded as if he was on parade when he answered, and I don't suppose I sounded at all! At last we reached the vestry and I was signed away to Tom. Then, back home, shook hands with everyone I could see and dashed upstairs to the photographers. Then to the drawing room, and an endless procession of people appeared, and I am *Mrs Farquhar*! Down to the cake and champagne, which I drank out of the tiny glass Madame Irgens gave me ten years ago for today! I drank everyone's health and got quite tipsy. My beloved Sally [*French governess*] was there, and Everett, Truffles and hundreds of others. At last I went up to change for going away, and came down to be pelted with flowers. We dashed into the car, and left for Victoria Station and Paris. Dear Mick was on the platform, cheerful and sarcastic, also Nanny and the cook.

So farewell to Genesta Heath!

21 DECEMBER – PARIS

Tom and I went after dinner to see Pavlova dance. It was exquisitely beautiful and she herself is like a rather tall fairy, with a lovely figure. I bribed someone else's taxi to chuck the someone else and take us home for twenty francs.

22 DECEMBER

We saw Richelieu's Palais Royal and the King's Palace, those immense gardens and courts and great sweeping staircases; and then of course we saw the Arc de Triomphe, through which an airman flew for a rag and was punished for it by the government!

23 DECEMBER

Our last day here! Mostly shopping, and then left in wagon-lits for the Riviera, for St Raphael.

24 DECEMBER

Woke up to the brightest, loveliest sunshine, everything sunny and happy and lazy.

25 DECEMBER

Christmas Day. We took a charabanc over the mountains to Cannes, and rammed a French military car on the way. All the people got out, the two drivers shouted at each other, everyone shouted at everyone else, till at last the French officer made them push the car a bit, got them apart, and we went serenely off.

For the next half hour our chauffeur talked loudly about his hardships and said at last, *'Ce sont des militaires, on ne peut rien dire. Je ne dis rien, moi!'*

Cannes seemed quite nice, a big town full of English people. We had come over the Esterel Mountains, which are steep and rugged, but not pretty.

31 DECEMBER

New Year's Eve. Went to the casino after dinner and got our supper table. The room was crammed with people and very noisy, with a small dancing space in the middle and three bands. They rang twelve strokes on a gong, then came 'Auld Lang Syne', the 'Marseillaise', 'God Save the King' and the 'Brabançonne', while everyone sang and shouted and drank each other's healths. Then we had supper, and then danced and ragged and threw paper reels at each other. At last I was so tired I couldn't do anything more.

What a year this has been for me!

1920

7 JANUARY

We got a boat this afternoon after a lot of hard talking and crossed to the islands. She is a good little boat, a racing boat, all sail. We saw the wreck of an Italian ship which was carrying timber when she was driven ashore on rocks.

12 JANUARY

In a charabanc to the Gorges du Loup. It is amazing country, immense hills, bare and high with these wonderful roads winding up, all in perfect condition. The Saut du Loup is where the stream springs out from the rock so that one can walk behind it. We reached a village called Gourdon, about a thousand feet up on the top of a rock with a view over the sea to the Corsican mountains.

4 FEBRUARY

We went to Monaco and over the palace which is very beautiful, though quite small. This place is a gem of a town; small, immensely rich and perfectly kept.

8 FEBRUARY

On donkeys to St Agnès, an old Saracen town in the mountains, hidden away behind a cleft in the rock. We climbed on foot to the old castle, perched on the topmost crag, and on the way I got into a panic for no reason at all and hung where I was until helped by Tom. It is a wonderful old town, at least a thousand years old, with low-roofed houses where the donkeys lived underground. I suppose the houses were built so low because these coast villages were constantly raided by Saracen slavers, and the villagers hoped they would not see the houses.

28 FEBRUARY

Boarded the *Maréchal Bugeaud* for Algiers.

29 FEBRUARY

This is a terrible boat – she rolled even in harbour, and the sea is now quite rough. There is a party of Foreign Legion recruits on board. They must be miserable – this is the first of their many tough times to come.

1 MARCH

Landed at last, and went to the St George Hotel on the hill. The Arabs are interesting to me, though Tom saw more than enough of them in the war.

This hotel is beautiful. The garden is full of flowers, beds of stocks and freesias, with purple and scarlet bougainvillaea and wistaria climbing all over the house. It used to be an old Turkish palace – the Turks owned the country before the French took it. Strange that people who had created such beauty could then live in such abject discomfort and filth. The hotel has been modernized up to a point, and is full of old carvings and quaint window sills. Outside is a wide, shady marble terrace.

2 MARCH

Went to the town and were promptly picked up outside the mosque by an Arab soldier who took us inside. We took off our shoes and wandered around. It did not seem very impressive; it is dark and quiet with several rough, round pillars, and hung with coloured rugs and cloths. Near the door there is a large basin for the Arabs' ablutions – feet, hands and face – before and after praying. It sounds as if they ought to be a clean race, but oh, the flies!

Then the soldier took us through the Arab quarter. We wandered about trying not to tread on the beggars and not to *look*, even, at some of them. Finally reached a place where he said there were dancing girls. We went up some rickety stairs, round a gallery over the courtyard and into a small room with a huge brass bed enclosed with curtains. There was a lamp burning on the floor; the whole place looked dark and nasty. Our guide said that four girls would dance for forty francs, or one for twenty; so we said no thank you, quite politely, and left. We ended up in the French cathedral, another converted mosque, which would have been gorgeous except for two noisy children's school groups, both going round it at the same time.

24 MARCH

Left today for Biskra in a sleeper.

25 MARCH

Changed our train for a perfect horror at El Guerra and bumped on through miles of dreary country, poorly cultivated since the soil is hard and stony. There were herds of goats and sheep with little Arab boys guarding them; and a Bedouin camp with squat, dark tents. The women wear bright, full, coloured dresses. Stopped at Batna for lunch and again at El Kantara, which is called the Gate of the Desert. Here there is a wide, palm-bordered river with immense red rocks, the 'gates', towering up on each side of the line. They are terrific. Beyond the 'gates' is the same stony desert. El Kantara is an oasis, where it snows in winter. At last we reached Biskra and ended up at the Sahara Hotel, which has nothing wrong with it except the baths.

26 MARCH

This is a lovely place, with clear, dry air. Our room looks onto the gardens where several old Arabs sit spitting and talking in their explosive language all day long. There is a nice guide boy here, Bel Kassim. He took us over the market this morning and through the bazaar – a marvellous sight. Biskra is one of the marketing centres of the Sahara. Everywhere there are hundreds of Arabs, squatting on the ground, wandering about, playing games under the arches of the buildings, sitting in their shops, all dressed in white burnouses. They are all of the same type, tall men, averaging over six feet, with pale brown skins, well-cut features and magnificent black eyes. Camels, donkeys, sheep, goats, jostling and braying at each other. Some of the men are negroes from the south – big men, very black, with squat noses and beady eyes. We wandered about the whole morning, fascinated.

After lunch we walked to the Garden of Allah and roamed around it. It is a big place with sandy, well-kept paths and immense trees, many palms and hundreds of others making a dark green, scented shade. There are very few flowers – Kassim picked me some. After leaving the garden we went to call on the Agah who was working in his bureau. We were taken into a large room hung with rugs, saddles, veils, ornaments, bridles, photographs, swords and a large painting of the Agah.

27 MARCH

Went off on camels at eight this morning for the sand dunes. It is the first time I've been within biting distance of one, and I used to hate them. They look so absurd. Tom's camel roared the whole time, weaving his ridiculous neck about and loathing us all. He frequently lay down, then got up and wandered off on his own. At last we got under way and suddenly I loved it; so swinging and easy. My old beast seemed resigned to everything, and never made a fuss. Kassim rode a tiny donkey, his toes touching the ground on each side. We went to the dunes and then turned through a real plague of sand flies. At the oasis we had lunch and slept in the shade. We saw an Arab fertilizing dates by hand, a most delicate operation. Started home when it was cooler, and got in very stiff and very happy.

Tonight we went to a café to see the Ouled Nails dancing. They seem to be a tribe of dancing women; they are all fat and danced the *danse du ventre*, jerking their tummies up and down, round and round. Two of them danced the *danse des mains* which was prettier than the other dances but not so interesting. The music is unmelodious: a big drum, a little drum, a violin with two strings (three if it's lucky), a banjo and a pipe that drowns everything else. Once a horrid sight came in – a Sudanese negro dressed in a kilt of jackal skins covered with mirrors, and a high head-dress. He carried a tom-tom and had a face like a monkey. He jumped about, sang, beat the tom-tom and fluttered his tongue at people for money. When given any he jumped at it and licked it up.

28 MARCH

Kassim had a carriage waiting for us, so we drove through Vieux Biskra. One book I have read says it is wrong to call it that, as there was once a warrior named Ould-Biskra; the town was called after him and 'old' may be a corruption of 'ould'. It was very quaint and pretty with mud walls each side of the town, palm trees leaning over the tops of them, children dressed in mixtures of bright colours, and unveiled women with enormous silver ear-rings that touched their shoulders. These are negro women – one very rarely sees true Arab women out of doors. Water runs down the sides of most of the tracks and often you see an Arab washing bits of himself in the streams. And yet they are covered with fleas who live in their clothes. We took home at least a couple every time we went out.

29 MARCH

At seven this morning we started off for Sidi Okba on horses – of sorts. There was a really good, well-fed, well-bred chestnut belonging to a friend of Kassim's – he stuck his fine little nose in the air and tried to run away with me when I wanted to canter. Then a starved and overworked black with subdued manners and a head like a mule; and a pathetic white creature, all ribs and bones. These two came from a stable and I'd like to kick the owner out, then rest and feed those poor horses.

Some of the desert we crossed is firm, baked sand, good for galloping; but further on there are small hummocks with green stuff growing out of them. The horizon line is always that mysterious, wonderful purple, promising everything – but which no one ever reaches. Tom wandered about bird-hunting and it took five hours to do the fourteen kilometres to the village. We passed herds of grazing camels, guarded by cheerful brown men with pleasant faces and white teeth; long carbines were slung over their shoulders. The camels looked at us as only camels can look, snaky neck slightly twisted, head half sideways and very stiff, supercilious, half-shut eyes. There were Bedouin camps with low, black tents, fires burning, animals tethered or hobbled, and big dogs barking and rushing at us. At Sidi Okba we had lunch in a pretty garden, while Kassim played his flute and a splendid-looking Arab sat on a bench, turning the other end into a drum. I bought some ear-rings, a knife and one or two ornaments, hideous and quaint.

We went over the mosque where Sidi Okba is buried. He was the Prophet's barber and came here from Arabia with a strong army, preaching Mohammedanism – 'believe or die'. He was extremely brave and fought many battles. He was killed fighting the defenders of Timgad and was buried in this mosque. Outside his tomb are heavy glass ornaments, cloths, coloured paper and pictures of Mecca. At the side of the mosque, facing

Mecca, hangs a large crystal ball. Outside the mosque is a court with pillars, dazzling white in the sun. There is a fine Roman door made of carved wood with great wooden bars down it, all carved.

We went up the minaret and the Arab guardian told me some interesting things about the history of the place. He said the Romans were the first rulers of all this land, and that he didn't know where the first Arabs came from. The Roman door was brought from a temple in a village halfway between Biskra and Touggourt, a negro village for freed slaves 200 kilometres south of Biskra.

We went through the village (catching some of Sidi Okba's special brand of fleas) and at last said goodbye to everyone, mounted and rode home. The camel-herders had caught a jerboa which I bought. It had soft grey fur, huge black eyes, tiny forelegs and long hind ones, and travelled in big hops; they live in the sand all day and come out at night. I carried him in front of me and he put his nose inside my coat. I let him be because I thought the sunlight might be worrying him, and just held the string his leg was tied to. The little beast scrambled right up my coat and came scratching out at my neck. Halfway home I let him go; he would probably only have died. He bit me hard and scratched with those claws of his, but we got him untied at last and he hopped away.

After that we galloped, because there was a sandstorm coming up. It looked wonderful; a purple distance, a flaming red sky and a driving mass of low clouds that seemed like evil genii let loose, crowding up to whirl the sand. The mountains were covered with a wicked red haze, moving behind Biskra and then seeming to turn and come back on it. We got in to the hotel and shut the windows. The real storm missed Biskra, but a lot of sand penetrated the rooms.

31 MARCH

Tonight we went to an Arab café to see the sword dance. Two men had swords – heavy, curved scimitars – and one knelt on the floor. The one who was standing whirled the sword round his head, round his neck, caught it in the other hand, played with it, whirling it all the time so quickly you could not see the blade. He slashed forty or fifty times at the man on the floor, who parried, then the first one whirled his sword again, quick as lightning. The 'music' came from a big war drum pounding away and a shrieking pipe. It was a splendid show.

The other dancing was the same as usual; but one of the girls, a very lovely Ouled Nail, danced up and made eyes at Kassim. He looked virtuously at the floor. Then she asked him for a cigarette and got it. At last she leaned forward and said something to him, at which he shook his head and she went away. I said, 'What a lovely girl', and he said that she had offered '*Si*

cela fera plaisir à monsieur et madame, de danser toute nue'! I think he would
have blushed if he had been fair enough.

1 APRIL

At last we had to leave Biskra – it has been so interesting here – and came
to Batna where we got a car and motored out to Timgad. The country is a
green plain, bordered with mountains. It was lit by a gorgeous sunset,
crimson behind the hills, with the sky above like a clear green opal and the
plain below the purest gold. An old camel looked fine for the first time in
his life, standing on a hilltop, black against the sky. We passed Lambese,
where there are many ruins practically untouched, and reached Timgad
after a forty kilometre drive. The hotel here is absolutely bare, nothing but
necessities, but it is quite adequate, food passable and the people are
charming.

2 APRIL

Spent a fascinating day among the ruins. All this country was part of the
Roman Empire. Lambese was a garrison town; Timgad was built for a
marketing centre, to make friends, and trade with, the native Berbers who
lived in the hills and objected to being ruled by anyone. Timgad, called by
them Thamugadi, was founded by the III Legion of colonial troops, under
the Emperor Trajan in about AD 100. The tribes were always raiding, and
the Romans didn't like the early Christians who lived there, either. At last,
at the end of the seventh century, a Roman general arrived one day to find
the town in flames, pillaged and sacked, with the Berbers camped outside
the walls. After that it simply fell to pieces, earthquakes shook it down and
the rains covered it with earth from the hills, so that no one in Europe knew
it existed. The first man to find it was a Scotsman named Bruce (Bruce was
a famous traveller; I believe it was he who discovered Petra. No French
book mentions him – they want people to think *they* were the first to find
Timgad, in 1745.) I dare say he was one of Prince Charlie's exiles. He
mentioned the town in his memoirs, but couldn't say anything about it as
only the Arc de Trajan and a part of the capitol was showing above ground.
Then in 1880 a French group arrived and started excavating. In these forty
years they have done wonders.

The town used to cover about sixty acres. There are two good roads
crossing it, Cardo Maximus (from north to south) and Decumanus Maximus
(east to west). Beneath these roads are drains which still work, with movable
stones at each end so that they could be washed out. They are deep enough
for a tall man to stand in, upright. The Arc de Trajan, which stands over
the road to Lambese, is magnificent and very strong. There is everything
that every Roman town has – forum, theatre, capitol, even a library. So far

the excavators have found thirteen public baths – besides baths in each of the big houses. There are marketplaces and some charming little temples, also Christian churches and monasteries, and a beautiful baptismal font, in perfect mosaic, some way outside the town. They have found fine statues, and one or two exquisite bronzes. It is fascinating to wander about among the ruins and think about those Romans here, two thousand years ago, and their courage as they fought off the Arabs. These usually left the Christians alone, but once they took five priests, carried them away to Lambese, and from there to the mountains where they were left for wild animals to kill.

During all the years that the Romans were there, Berber Arabs never ceased harassing them. Today we saw the Byzantine fort, where, I suppose, the last stand was made. It is a big strong place, and the walls are full of human bones. Little Arab boys chased us with Roman coins to buy, and we picked up one or two which we hoped were not fakes. When the Romans controlled this arid country they brought water many miles in a large aqueduct for the people, the cattle and the crops. No one brings water now; the aqueduct is ruined. Biskra has a few wells which suffice the handful of people living here.

4 APRIL

Easter Day. Out just once more in the morning to say goodbye to Timgad, then we had to leave for Batna. Stopped at Lambese on the way and saw the museum there, with a splendid mosaic. Lambese was much bigger than Timgad, with ninety thousand inhabitants. It has hardly been excavated at all – one has only to buy some land and dig, to find almost anything. Nobody bothers about it! At Batna we had tea at the Hotel des Etrangers, which is run by a nice Englishman who was very interesting about the country and the Arabs. He has travelled a lot out here, and even made friends with the wild and fierce Tuaregs, who live a long way south of Ouragla. They gave him a fine throwing spear.

Left for Constantine and got in very weary and dirty. Staying at the Cirta; it is the best hotel here, but not expensive.

5 APRIL

This town is centuries old, built on the side of a deep gorge. The Romans had a strong garrison here. We went down the gorge, along a tiny track, and looked up at tremendous cliffs towering above us. They are completely disfigured by drainpipes, largely decaying, down the rocky sides, and trippers' names which are scratched everywhere on the rocks. There are hundreds of birds: vultures, ravens, pigeons and storks, who stand silent and motionless on every roof. We crawled along while Tom stopped perpetually to look at these boring things through his glasses – all in the boiling sun. I was profoundly thankful to get home at last. The gorge would be marvellous if it wasn't for mankind.

Looking out onto the big square in front of the hotel we see herds of pack-donkeys passing, almost hidden under enormous burdens – sacks of meal or loads of wood – plodding along on their tiny feet with their big ears drooping. Carts pass with six or eight or even eleven horses in them – miserable, starved Arab beasts, all bones and sores; four of them do not equal the strength of one European horse.

Today we heard a monotonous chanting and saw about a hundred Arabs singing a funeral song and carrying two bodies to the mosque. They were not in coffins, but covered with green clothes embroidered in scarlet.

The Arab women wear black from head to foot, with a white veil. There is a big Jewish quarter; the women are very good-looking, with white skins and large dark eyes. They wear gay colours: green and red, yellow and blue turbans, big gold and mother-of-pearl ear-rings, anklets, bracelets and necklaces. They put pretty little pointed caps on one side of their heads, and on top of the whole thing Paisley shawls! Heaven knows where they came from.

6 APRIL

This afternoon we went out with Colonel and Mrs Sparrow, friends of Tom's, an Arab climber and two other Arabs on an egging expedition. We went to the gorge, down a steep hill under the most appalling drain, a truly French drain, round a corner and came suddenly out on an astonishing sight. On our left was the gorge with a splendid cascade of water about sixty feet high, roaring down the crevice. A few yards on was another one, sparkling and crashing into a pool, beyond which it spread away to the river, wide and quiet, full of rocks and stones, with lovely country each side of it. Above the cascade stood several hundred feet of sheer cliff.

Tom wanted some eggs. One of the nests was across the gorge; we sat and watched the three Arabs cross the water and climb a tall cliff opposite. One climber is a perfect monkey. Give him a tail and he would go anywhere! As it was he made good with a rope. He went to the point, made fast the rope, tied himself up and swarmed down the rock, hanging on with toes and fingers, a drop of hundreds of feet below him sheer down to the river. After that display he went after two other nests in just the same way, creeping about on the face of the rock like a snake. He was slung down a crevice and tucked himself up and sang while another man fetched him a stick. He let down his turban to pull the nest up, hanging on by one hand. He said he has been climbing these rocks all his life, hunting pigeons – '*moi pas peur des rochers, moi enfant des rochers!*'

7 APRIL

We saw the old Governor's Palace, where the Arab chief of the town once lived. It is a beautiful place with many courtyards leading one out of the other. Each one has a balcony running round a square, covered with red and purple bougainvillaea, wistaria, arum lilies and orange trees. It would be quite perfect if it wasn't full of podgy little men in European clothes scuttling about. We also saw the mosque of Salah Bey, the best we have seen here but not very fine; none of these mosques are. Tom says the Syrian mosques and the Egyptian ones are magnificent. These all look like failures!

1922

[After two years in England we decided to visit East Africa.]

27 OCTOBER

On board SS *Neuralia, en route* for a safari in British East Africa. Our party consists of Tom and me, John Rawle, Mello van Reichersberg Versluys, his invaluable valet Joseph, and Blixen [*husband of the writer Karen Blixen (Isak Dinesen)*], who is our white hunter and whom we pick up in Nairobi. This is a funny little ship, only nine thousand tons, but she doesn't roll much. The crew are nearly all Lascars, with silent feet and grave faces. There are dances every night – 'everything except sleep,' the chief steward said. Mello and I danced this evening to a gramophone, but the ship was rolling, and sometimes it felt as if you were climbing a mountain, and sometimes as if you were being thrown down a precipice.

29 OCTOBER

We are in Biscay, and the sea is like a range of grey mountains, breaking into snow at the top. We have been receiving SOS messages from some ship in distress, but apparently two other ships have already reached the spot she was supposed to be at, and found nothing. There's a big sea running.

This morning our tea tray, which was sitting on a camp stool, bowed gracefully to Tom and then flung itself at his feet, filling his shoes with milk. Tom has met a man called Greswolde-Williams, who has got a very big property in British East Africa and has asked us to stay there. [*I realized later that every farm in Kenya is always said to be 'very big', even if it is only a few hundred acres.*] It is kind of him, considering he doesn't know us. We've got thirty-six hours of the Bay in front of us. 7 p.m.: Tom says we have been several miles out of our course to look for that ship, but there is no sign of her, so she must have sunk. She was a small English ship.

31 OCTOBER

Today I was on deck by 8.30, and it was the warmest, sweetest morning imaginable. We are off Portugal. I noticed a very faint scent in the wind, which Tom says is the 'gumcistus'. It is wonderful, after a couple of days of freezing wind, to come into this warmth and sunshine, balmy as the best English spring day. We spend the time sunning in deck chairs. What a heavenly, lazy life.

1 NOVEMBER

We have turned east into the Mediterranean, and passed Gibraltar at five this morning. All day we have been steaming along the coast of Spain, in a blue, ripply sea. The coast is all mountains and some are snow-capped. I saw a school of dolphins jumping.

5 NOVEMBER

At 6.30 this morning we passed Malta. Tom made me get up to see it. It looked like a Turner painting – the sea was glassy, and out of a rose-coloured mist climbed spires and domes.

7 NOVEMBER

Reached Port Said this morning, and went ashore. Onto the ship swarmed what appeared to be hundreds of little black devils wearing rags. They ran up and down gangways, with baskets of coal on their heads, looking like a picture of Dante's *Inferno.* Then a conjurer appeared.

"Gully, gully, gully, you watch me ladies and gentlemen. You hold this, Lord Kitchener, Queen Mary, you take this two bob in your hand. You close him and turn him over. I not touch you, I stand right away over here. I take your two shillin' from you without touch you. Then I keep him – so? Now you blow on your shut hand – you feel the florin? You sure got him? Yes? Now say "Go".'

The victim says 'Go!'

'Now look in your hand, you, Queen Mary.'

Sure enough there are two lead weights there, and the man tips the two shillings off his fez!

'Lord Kitchener, you sure you got two shillin' in your hand? *I* think you got little chicken in your coat. You no feel him? Sure?'

'Lord Kitchener' begins to wriggle, and at last pulls the tiny yellow chicken out of his coat, while the money in his hand has also changed into two weights!

At last we got on shore and walked about the town, past people of every kind of nationality – unshaven Greeks with villainous eyes, Italians, half-castes, Turks, Lascars, French sailors, Arabs and English soldiers. The native police wear white drill uniform and white fezzes with handkerchiefs hanging down the back. Port Said, from a distance, looks like Tilbury, with tall chimneys and spirals of smoke. But the buildings are quite fine – domed roofs, low, cool-looking, all painted white with green shutters. We stopped at Simon Artz, where you can get everything under the sun, and then had lunch at the Casino – moderate food but in a good position, looking onto the beach and the statue of de Lesseps, who made the Suez Canal. Everyone has blossomed into topees or terias [*broad-brimmed felt hats*]. Several men wear tussore or white suits, and shorts.

After lunch Mello and I drove round the Arab quarter – narrow streets where the houses lean to meet each other, dirt, that hot, dry smell which is the smell of the East, countless children; Nubian goats, tall old men, native girls in odd European clothes, and married women veiled from head to foot in black, with a short, heavy gold tube about three inches long on their foreheads, so that all you can see is a pair of velvety black eyes; dancing girls and prostitutes, leaning out of windows from houses which look as if you could push them down, with unveiled faces, fat, heavy and badly made up, smiling and beckoning to the men.

We got back and had tea in some café where a man told my fortune, and said I had brought luck to my master, '. . . no much monies, but you master very pleased with you, give you much silk and fine dresses, never quarrel or beat you. You very kind to all poor people, give much baksheesh.' So I baksheeshed him, and Mello and I ran like hares for the boat. We came through the Canal at night – everything was perfectly still and you could just see a flat stretch of desert, looking mysterious. Now and again a little Arab rowing boat appeared alongside; the men sang quavery Arab songs very softly.

8 NOVEMBER

This morning we reached the end of the Canal, stopping for an hour to unload cargo. The sea was clear, dazzling green-blue, and just in front of us were the Iron Mountains; during the war we had sent men up to hold them from the Turks. The soil is hard as iron – it gets blazing hot in the sun, and the wretched men got their feet so terribly blistered and burnt that some of them died. The mountains are a reddish sand colour; they look cruel.

A lovely little yacht went round and round the ship with two handsome

English boys in her. She was a real beauty and very fast. They came straight up to the ship and then swung round and skimmed alongside. They waved and beckoned us to go for a sail. I should have loved it!

Now we are in the Red Sea with a following wind, but it's not hot enough for me.

10 NOVEMBER

The last two days the heat has grown. Everything is hot – face creams, cold water, tiles and woodwork – and everyone drips. The cabins are suffocating. Last night I slept outside, where they have opened part of the ship and put up a balcony rail. Many people sleep on deck now. The starlit nights and the dawns are lovely.

At 4.15 this afternoon we reached Port Sudan. This place is a piece of flat desert, surrounded by mountains with jagged crests, red and forbidding. On one side of the harbour is the European quarter. We drew up alongside the wharf where there were crowds of every sort of native: tall, fat, light-skinned, oily; carefully dressed Egyptians in tarbooshes; Arabs in jackets, trousers and turbans; tall, lean, elegant negroes with shoulders thrown back. Big hands, thin legs, skins that are black, blacker than coal, blue-black. Some have shaven heads, others have a mass of fuzzy, not woolly, hair. [*These are a Sudanese tribe, once called by our troops 'Fuzzy-Wuzzies'. Kipling wrote a poem about them, praising their fighting powers.*] They wear a sack fastened somehow round their middle. They can't *talk* to each other – they *shout* and wave their arms.

Tom and John and Mello bathed. I don't like Tom's bathing here – there are sharks and barracuda.

11 NOVEMBER

Shoals of flying fish jump right out of the water and look very pretty, flashing in the sun. This evening there was a dance at the hotel, to which some of us went in fancy dress. It was great fun and the band was very good. On the steps of the verandah there was a crowd of Sudanese natives – pitch-black men in white robes and turbans leaning forward and watching us as we gyrated in our strange and indecent European dances.

The natives are very mixed. The Fuzzy-Wuzzies I like so much are a tribe who live in the hills, very proud and fierce and independent, and don't come down much to work. They are handsome, tall men with Arab features and thick hair standing out all over their heads.

It has been extremely hot today – the temperature is about ninety-three in the shade, but the air is so heavy. I met some of the English inhabitants and said I wanted a ride, so some nice lad is lending me his pony and coming with me on another, and I have borrowed some slacks.

12 NOVEMBER

At 5.30 this morning I got up and dressed for a splendid ride. I had a little brown Sudanese pony called Pongo. These ponies have nice shoulders and legs, quarters like a giraffe and iron mouths. We went through the native quarter, where the huts are built of packing cases, sacking and reeds, and mostly furnished with kerosene tins. The women are pitch-black, unveiled and swathed in orange, red and crimson robes. They smile the whole time, so you see across these inky faces a shining white bar of teeth. I saw one particularly splendid Fuzzy in white robes and carrying a huge curved scimitar, and another stalking along at the head of a long string of camels. Beyond this flat stretch of desert are the hills, all veiled in a sandy mist today – it is going to be hot. The whole desert is covered with bones of animals that have died here, and there are fat, heavy vultures flapping about everywhere. But the English have created what they always create everywhere they go – a golf course, racecourse and tennis courts. The English overseas are wonderfully enterprising, and never allow bad conditions to get them down.

We came back to breakfast at the hotel where I created a sensation by appearing in slacks. Apparently it hadn't been done before. After breakfast they played the gramophone, all the tunes from England, and we felt slightly homesick.

13 NOVEMBER

At noon today we said goodbye to little Port Sudan and steamed out. As we passed a Canadian freighter, a man on her deck started playing the bagpipes and I nearly wept. What a place to hear the pipes! They were played in honour of our chief engineer, who comes from Mull, and the piper was the same man who had played the Canadians over the top at Vimy Ridge. He was even playing the same pipes. We listened to them growing fainter and fainter, until they died away in the distance, and we were on the open sea once more.

The water over the coral reef is very dark green, shot with pale green, blue, purple and mauve, full of light and always changing.

Tom has spent most of his time shark fishing, but never caught one, though we saw several one night, slipping around in the garbage from the ship.

15 NOVEMBER

Today we passed an island off the Arabian coast called Perim. It's a dreary place – bare, barren, brown, not a tree or a shrub, a small Arab village and a smaller European settlement. There is oil here and a huge tank with 'The Petrol Company Limited' written on it, which looks slightly incongruous.

The Arabs can keep Arabia – so everyone on board feels. Of all depressing-looking countries, this is the worst. Nothing but absolutely barren mountains, very high and jagged. That is all there is to be seen. They look like the spines on a dragon's back. But the country inland is quite fertile.

At 7 p.m. we reached Aden. It looked lovely, because it was night and all the lights in the town glimmered in a semi-circle, climbing up the hills. Then little boats came out, each with a flickering light burning in it, and Somalis trying to sell us cigarettes. 'I say! I say! Cigarette, mister? Three Castles? I say! Baskets? I say! Ostrich feather? I say!'

We got on shore and went to the club for drinks. It was cool this evening, but this is one of the hottest places on earth. The temperature in summer sometimes reached 130 Fahrenheit and the whole place is built on and cut out of rock – the roads aren't *made*, they're just rock hewn more or less smooth. I wanted to see the large wells called 'tanks' which some people say were built by Solomon for the Queen of Sheba, and others say by the Romans. They are the only water supply the place has got. But it was too dark to see. They are vital to the town, as it rains here about once every thirty-two years!

We left at about midnight. This is the last lap. Next stop, Mombasa!

21 NOVEMBER

Last night, being the last on board for most of us, we had quite a good fight in the dining saloon. Walnuts, lumps of sugar and buns are all right, but apples can be dangerous. We finished by dancing, it was all great fun. This morning we came into Kilindini harbour, which is lovely: a very narrow entrance; low land covered with palms and thick green vegetation, rich mauve and red bougainvillaea climbing everywhere and over the bungalows, which were all painted white and red; narrow arms of the sea curling off inland. Then people's boys began to swarm on board, enchanted to see their bwanas again, every black face one large smile. Left by the 3 p.m. train for Nairobi. Keith Caldwell of the Game Department has sent down his own boy, Idi, to look after us. We ran from coconut tree country into rich grassland, then the sun set and in fifteen minutes it was dark.

Our carriage is a joke. One seat runs the length of one side. Above it is a bunk you lower. A cubby-hole opening out of it contains a fixed basin and a primitive tap, and that's all. You have to bring your own pillows (which we didn't), blankets (which we didn't), soap, glasses and towels. But it wasn't so bad, and not nearly so cold as we expected. On Kilimanjaro in the sunrise the snow flashes pink and white. We ran through a large reserve; the animals just stand close to the line staring at the train. We saw a lot of game, but very little variety – zebra, Thompson's gazelle, Grant's, wildebeest and kongoni. The Athi plain is vast, covered with short, yellowish grass. It's a heavenly country, so happy and full of sun. The natives by the track touch their foreheads and scramble for oranges thrown to them and laugh all the time.

Reached Nairobi, found Keith and went to the Norfolk Hotel, which is primitive in some ways but quite nice on the whole. Two boys appeared – Ahbid, a Swahili, for Tom, and Ali, a Somali, for me. We met our hunter, Baron Blixen, who is a 'character' and great fun. We had left poor John and Mello at Kilindini to struggle with the stores, but as we shan't get them for a fortnight, we're going on a short safari first, to the Kedong Valley.

Every sort of conveyance passes here, cars, motorbikes, ox-wagons, with all the oxen trying to leave the work to someone else, mule carts, riding-horses and rickshaws. At night parties of natives sit round a fire, talking endlessly. Keith took us to his house where we met Lady Northey, beautiful and charming, the wife of the Governor, also her daughter, Mrs Martin, and Mr Martin. Lady Northey is a South African, from a famous Dutch family. She is a lively person, and has, it is said, been known to dance a pas seule on a table.

24 NOVEMBER

I was at home to most of the tradesmen of Nairobi all the morning, buying stuff on Lady N's advice, she has been so kind. Lunched with Keith at Muthaiga Club, an attractive place some way out. Vim Hervey, who came down from her brother's farm 200 miles away specially to see us, met me yesterday. She is a darling, and it is wonderful seeing her again. After lunch we went to Government House to see the menagerie, very interesting indeed; two lions in thoroughly bad tempers, having their lunch, some lion cubs, several leopards, one of them very kindly allowed me to rub his back, but you can't touch his head, he mauled his boy the other day; a young buffalo; monkeys, a bush-baby with charming manners, some buck and a young zebra.

Then K. took us out on the plains in his Hupmobile. We left the road and went straight across country, up and over the railway embankment, down into a dry river-bed, scrambling out the other side over flat rocks and banks of sand. He drove us into a herd of Impala; they leapt high into the air, jumping across and across each other, the prettiest and most graceful things in Africa, I'm sure.

25 NOVEMBER

John, Mello and Joseph arrived today, they have had an awful time at Mombasa, getting the stuff through. The stores won't be up for ages, but the guns and ammunition are here.

I dined at Muthaiga Club, good food and amusing people. I met a very nice General Baker-Kerr, he has a place near Mt Elgon. The dancing was fun to a K.A.R. [*King's African Rifles*] native band, who played very well. They can't read music at all, and have to be taught, by ear, every note.

26 NOVEMBER

Today we started off for the camp. Drove sixty miles along the main road, which mostly consists of two cart ruts with rocks, pig-holes about four foot round, and narrow rivers. Lunched at Greswolde-Williams's farm, looking across a vast, yellow valley. The house is backed with the sort of hills you see in the South of France, except that these contain buffalo, snakes and other wildlife. Then on and on, over more astounding country, till, after dark, we left even this apology for a road and came a few hundred yards through long yellow grass to the camp.

It looked fascinating, with fires crackling everywhere, all our tents set up, all the boys, black and shining, wearing red blankets, and Blickie doing the perfect host. I went round with him to the different fires, and saw the boys having their suppers (one black pot, full of a mess like soup – mealie and porridge mixed). Then came bath, pyjamas and a delicious dinner. We sat by the fire and toasted our toes while a boy came and sang to the native violin, a katanda, made like a bow with a hollow red bowl, open both ends, and played with a stick like an arrow. Then bed, and the heavenly sound sleep that the open air brings.

27 NOVEMBER

Arose at 5 a.m., struck camp after breakfast, and started in three parties of two each for the next camp, collecting food *en route* with rifles. I got a bird the size of a small turkey [*a greater bustard*] which will be good at dinner tonight. He was over a hundred yards away, and the gun bearer was quite pleased with me.

Now we are in camp on a little hill, overlooking this vast plain, very tired and happy. There is a great affair about the water. It all has to be brought here, and is as black as a Swahili. But we wash more or less clean and drink milk the Masai have sent us. After dinner we sit round the fire and play the gramophone. The plain looks mysterious and dim, and now and then a jackal screeches. I am quite sure this is the only life for me.

28 NOVEMBER

Tom went off on his own, and Blickie took charge of us. It is so well organized. We have all got nice mules to ride, and when there is anything to shoot, one of us gets off and follows Blickie, who just walks alongside the game until we are near enough, then he walks straight on while we take our shot. I got a really beautiful head, a Grant's gazelle. The horn measured twenty-five inches; it may be a record.

At last we reached luncheon, a delicious place under great trees where our dining tent had been set up with chairs and a table. Even my bed and pillow were ready for an afternoon rest. We had a first-class meal cooked on the spot, and then rested for the whole hot afternoon. Two Masai and two Wandorobo have attached themselves to the camp temporarily. They sat under a tree at the lunch place, watching us with unmoving eyes. The Wandorobo are the oldest inhabitants of this part of Africa. Very small and graceful, living in the forests on honey and game, until the Kikuyu arrived and drove them away. The Masai smear their bodies with castor oil (from the shrub which grows here) and red mud, so that they shine red, and their hair is a mass of tiny, frizzy corkscrews. The huge lobes of their ears are carved out and look like very large ear-rings. Their almost classical features are a cross between Egyptian and Jewish types – in fact one man who has studied them and their habits says they are the remnants of the biblical tribe which got lost. Their clothes consist of a belt hung with a short sword, a little club perhaps a foot long, and a very tiny thin blanket, which blows about in the wind. They carry long spears which they throw short distances with great force, with which they can kill lions. They are a tall, brave, elegant and aristocratic race, utterly different from all the others, who fear them.

It started to rain. In between the heavy showers we got home, but Tom fairly caught it. When at last he arrived he was dripping and shining and bursting with triumph, having killed a lot of stuff including a wart-hog. Soon two porters appeared, having been chased off the wart-hog by two lions and two lionesses. They were so terrified that they just flung down their loads and legged it for camp! Can't blame them.

We shall get those lions soon, with any luck.

29 NOVEMBER

Got a note from Blickie, who had gone out with Tom and Mello at about 4 a.m. to say we were all going to sit up in *bomas [hides]* tonight. There are worse places than a *boma*, I must say. It is as wide as a tent, sunk about two foot deep and built of *leleshwa* leaves, which smell delicious. Shaped like a little house, it has a waterproof sheet over the top, covered with leaves. We had our three mattresses and all the blankets; the door was blocked with thorns and covered with sacking, and there were three tiny windows to shoot through.

The others had seen eight lions this morning, so after lunch we arranged a beat up the ravine. We went ahead and sat in the grass patiently, without speaking or smoking for two and a half hours, but saw nothing at all. David, our excellent Cape Coloured head boy, peered into a thicket and told John a big black-maned lion was there. John couldn't see a single thing; it was pitch-black inside the thicket, and while he was straining his eyes the lion and lioness slinked out the other side. A Masai, who had not seen them go out, stepped into the thicket and plunged about with his spear to drive them out. It makes one feel rather a fool to think of the guns and ammunition and fuss we have when we're after a lion, and these Masai have nothing but their spears and are absolutely fearless!

We had dinner and then started off for the *bomas*. Less than ten minutes after we had settled down we heard the grunting roar and the padding feet of a lion just outside the *boma*. Tom was to have first shot, so I crouched on my mattress with my fingers in my ears. There was a roar and a glare of light which filled the *boma*, and then we saw that the lioness had dropped like a stone where she stood. Tom was wild with excitement. All the boys say the lioness is the biggest they've ever seen. (They always say that!)

30 NOVEMBER

I slept all day and tonight we went again to the *boma*. We settled down and waited, but there was no sign or sound so we went to sleep. Then, towards dawn, Tom woke me up and I looked out of the window and saw two lionesses feeding on our kill. They were very nervous, took a mouthful, then flung up their heads and watched us. They saw my face in the *boma* and in a second had vanished. Then we heard a good deal of roaring – the husband, I suppose, telling his two wives they were fools. In a minute back they came. It was difficult to see, as there was no moon and no dawn. At last I saw a big-maned head lift up and look at me. I aimed at it as well as I could, and fired. He dropped, then we saw him raise his head and Blickie seized the rifle from me, but he dropped again and never moved. We gave him ten minutes, then went out and looked at him; he was quite dead, with a bullet through his brain. The sun got up, and the boys came over, all grins and joy. He is a big old lion, with not a very good mane. But I feel very triumphant.

1 DECEMBER

We are returning to the main camp now. Before dinner the natives gave an *ngoma*, a dance, in honour of the deaths of the lions. We stood by the fire and they came slowly up, crouching, stamping and roaring in rhythm, making the sound of a lion. Each boy carried a stick or a piece of *leleshwa*. They moved round and round us; and then I found that my thoughtful Juma had brought a chair for me, in which I gratefully sat. Instantly the boys rushed up, lifted me and the chair on their shoulders and carried me round in triumph, one holding my hand all the time, shaking it up and down. They went round with the same lifting movement, shouting and roaring and grunting and shaking their sticks. When they put me down there was another rush, and I shook hands with everybody. Then it was the others' turn.

After that each tribe started a dance of its own. The Kikuyu boys in a small ring, jumping up and down, while one clapped in time; the Tanganyika boys, very tall and well-built, in a long line, also jumping up and down, while every now and then one would leap forward, twist and leap back again.

But the best of all was a small group of Wakamba. They crouched in a ring, stepping in perfect time, shimmying and clapping their hands. One would spring out, twist and roll and fling himself backwards, curving his whole body, then rush back to his place, and the ring of quivering shoulders and stamping feet closed in again. The firelight flickered and flared, lighting the whole wild scene.

3 DECEMBER

Left Weke camp today and started off for the hills and the buffalo. We had lunch at the foot of the hills, and then rode up and up. The soil is sand, covered with layers of ash from all these volcanic hills. We reached the top, having come up two thousand feet, and saw a marvellous view with the whole plain spread wide below us to the far hills. The vegetation up here is quite different. Instead of yellow grass and groves of thorn trees, where two thorns grow out of a black ball full of black ants, the grass here is green, and there are large, dark trees from which hang creepers and pale flowers.

A storm blew up and broke just as the boys had pitched one tent, and we all crowded in and played the gramophone. It was very quaint to hear the little thing struggling through the crashing, roaring thunder, while lightning forked into the hills. A pile of natives crowded into the flies at one end of the tent, trying to keep fairly dry, and in the verandah were four Wandorobo squatting on their heels, with their little bits of blanket round their shoulders and their spears stuck up outside (so nice for lightning) and their swords and bows and arrows stuck in their bead belts, watching Blickie with adoring eyes. This is their country, but they all know and love him.

4 DECEMBER

Arose this morning at the ghastly hour of three, and after a very quick breakfast started off for the buffalo. It was murderously cold, and my fingers and toes froze to the reins and stirrups. But it also looked very wonderful and mysterious, with a bright, cold moon lighting our line of mules, gun bearers, saices [*grooms*], and our little Wandorobo guide moving silently ahead, slipping between branches and over twigs and round trees without a sound. In the forest it was very dark, with splashes of moonlight here and there. We emerged from the trees now and then, into little plains. Still we went on, for over an hour; then quite suddenly the dawn broke, and – not every minute, but every second – the light grew, until, in a very short time, the sun was up. We separated, Tom going up one hill, Mello and Joseph up another, and Blickie and I in the centre.

Later we found Mello and Joseph, who had been wandering about, they said, in the middle of a large herd of buffalo but never got a shot at them. We have now sent out Wandorobo scouts to mark down the various herds, since, as one of the old Wandorobo said, 'It is madness to take a white man to *find* the buffalo – they hear him while he is still the other side of the plain!'

6 DECEMBER

We moved camp a short way to a lovely site, all trees and grass. Had an unsuccessful buffalo drive this morning, and walked for miles with John and Blickie up a hill where, from the top, we saw five cows and a big bull, but they must have winded John's after-lunch cocktail for they tossed up their heads and went crashing away. When we went back to camp we found Tom quivering with excitement, and Kongoni, his elderly gun bearer (who doesn't know his own age, but is certain he is more than seven) looking quite pale. Tom had fired at a young bull, and was tracking him, when he suddenly charged out of nowhere. Kongoni threw himself flat on the ground between Tom and the buffalo, and Tom fired at the buff with the 470 and killed him. Poor old Kongoni says he has had many escapes, but that was the narrowest; and he has a new god – Tom's 470!

8 DECEMBER

We left this camp today and felt quite sad at saying goodbye to our little Wandorobo friend, Joribi, who looks magnificent, small though he is, works splendidly, and is extremely nice.

We had an extraordinary ride down steps a foot or two deep in the side of the hill, across a river (very shallow) and up the other side of the gorge, till we came down to the plains again. We stopped for lunch under a thorn tree, and were immediately attacked by the strangest insects: colossal ants and spiders, and horrid things exactly like bits of grass, with about four legs each side, which crawled everywhere, up our trousers and down our necks, and lifted their tails into the air like scorpions. There were praying mantises too, who jumped onto our helmets or the food and held their little front legs up and looked pious. It was the most awful meal I have ever had, and I was thankful to get away from the beastly place.

We are camped now on the plain under a little hill, with a fine view out to the gorge on one side, and the hills we have just left on the other. A boy came in from Kijabi this evening with news of a Masai rising at Endalele, which is in the hills about one and a half miles from our first camp. They have killed an Indian.

9 DECEMBER

We rode out to the gorge today. It is a strange place, and has the excellent name of Hell's Gates. The plain narrows into great cliffs two or three hundred feet high, all rock where vultures and hundreds of swallows nest, and the pass is choked with rich vegetation. We saw a place where sulphur steam rises out of cracks in the ground. It was a real Rider Haggard scene, with these immense cliffs, the big trees and thick bush; and the clouds of steam shooting out of the rock, blowing here and there. The ground below is red and stony, and plants are withered. While we were on our way to lunch it began to rain. It rained like all the bath taps in the world turned on, and when we tried to have lunch, the food swam in the plates, which were overflowing with water, the chairs became lakes, the water cascaded off the table and we couldn't see the cliffs 200 feet away, the other side of the gorge. Then the cliffs we stood under began to crumble and we decided it would be nicer to drown than be squashed by a ton of stone, so we started home. We passed a spot where part of the cliff had slipped, trees were uprooted and great stones had rolled into the valley. Fifteen minutes after we left the sun came out, and dried everything, while away over the hills lightning forked and clouds were inky with rain.

We got a note from Mr Agate [*a South African based at Kijabi*] (Tom had gone there to shoot bongo) to say that the Masai are really making trouble; they have now killed several Indians and two *askaris*, and the King's African Rifles are on their way to Endalele now. He told us to keep near the gorge or move up to Kijabi. This is a bad business for the Masai and we are very sorry about it. They are so brave and, like buffalo, when they get excited or threatened they fight instead of giving in. They haven't a chance against machine guns. They have been much provoked by other tribes and by the government trying to stop some of their less desirable habits, such as spear-blooding. I'm sure they were not frightened, but furiously angry. Also Diana Broughton's party, which was coming through the Masai Reserve, where we are now, down to Tanganyika, will probably go north to the Guasso Nyero where we are bound and may get first shots at the game there.

10 DECEMBER

Started today for Kijabi and trekked along an endless mud track for twenty-four hours. We started at 7 a.m., and got in at 4 p.m., taking an hour at lunchtime, so it wasn't bad going. At the station was Tom, who hadn't gone after bongo as his Wandorobo hadn't turned up. Two lion cubs came out of the cage and rolled about and played with me like kittens. It is quite comfortable in the waiting rooms, but there are fleas and stranger things which bit me all over, though I never saw one. The food here is good too.

Mr Agate has been extremely kind, helping us in every possible way.

11 DECEMBER

It rains and rains, worse than Scotland. We got onto the 6 a.m. train and came to Nairobi, leaving Tom at Kijabi. Rain is unusual this time of year, as it should be the dry season between the big and little rains.

In the Norfolk Hotel I found a boy Keith has got for me to replace Juma, who has not been satisfactory. I told Hamise, the new boy, to come back in the evening, and asked Blickie to catch the offending Juma and sack him before the other arrived. To my horror, when I came in to dress I found both boys lying in wait in the passage. I hadn't the faintest idea what to say to Juma, but Blickie did it quite simply. I heard him say 'Memsahib doesn't want *you*, she wants *you*.'

Exit Juma! The last I saw of him was the poor old thing wandering out of the hotel with a stick under one arm and a bundle of clothes under the other, looking rather lost.

16 DECEMBER

The safari has started for the north. Tom and I were motored to Thika by Keith today. In spite of his lurid description of the road – endless motors, clouds of dust, telegraph poles, motor-bus service, etc. – we saw none of these horrors. We joined the safari and went on.

17 DECEMBER

Camped at Fort Hall, where the Assistant District Commissioner proved his hospitality by refusing to help us in any way whatever, and firmly refusing to let us have any firewood, or to let the jailors, who were close by, with nothing to do, get us any. We got on quite well without his help, however, and managed to have one or two fires – Mininguishi, our head-man, is a friend of the jailors.

I have started wearing shorts and will have a lovely time breaking my knees in. I find them easier to run away in than trousers!

18 DECEMBER

Got away at 6.45., and safaried fifteen miles between breakfast and lunch to a place overlooking the Tana Plains, south to blue hills, and north to Kenya with its two peaks of snow. We were made welcome by the local Kikuyu chief, Ngondo, a friend of Blickie's: a very handsome, stately old man with masses of bracelets, rings and ear-rings, who shook hands with us all, and at once sent out boys to watch for buffalo, to bring us firewood and milk. And, having heard us mention casually that the bananas at the last store were not good, to bring us bananas tomorrow morning – all as presents. What price the British ADC at Fort Hall?

One of these curious men, with his hair in dozens of short plaits sticking up all over his head, came grinning to Blickie and said he knew him. Blickie told him he seemed to remember his ugly face, and it seems that some years ago, when B. was camping here, seventy-five porters ran away and the big chief (not Ngondo) sent this man with some Kikuyu, to act as porters and do everything for him. He had a very narrow chain on which were hung bits of hardened wood – his charms. One against lions and two against tummy troubles, two against toothache, one against snakebite, and then a very precious one, so that when he says his prayers to Muungu, he should get what he wants. He must have been the local witchdoctor. The government has made this business illegal and tries to catch them, but the natives protect them out of fear.

19 DECEMBER

Blickie's friends come for miles to visit him, and sit round the fire with their spears stuck upright in the ground. Ngondo brought us his two wives, one very sweet. The names the boys have given us are quaint. Tom is Mkubwa, the boss. Blickie is known all over Kenya as Wahoga, the man who is first in one place and then in another – the wanderer in fact. John is called Tumbo, fat one, also Mzei, old one, and they have decided he is my father! Joseph is Kidogo, little one – he is the same height as the others but a servant (they know at once) – and Mello is Kikono, the man with bent arms, as he always walks about with his hands on his hips. As I am the only woman I haven't been promoted to a nickname, just Memsahib.

25 DECEMBER

Christmas Day. We have done a fine trek today. Twenty miles, up and down almost perpendicular hills, and I walked for five and a half hours. I'm very pleased with myself. We got into camp at a place called Kochi and had a marvellous Christmas evening in a tent decorated with leaves and bright red flowers, the two lamps hanging on a rope which was twisted round with smilax, and a Xmas tree covered in snow from the medicine chest! We had a wonderful dinner, with a perfectly good plum pudding swimming in lighted brandy.

27 DECEMBER

Reached Meru today. The boys asked us to stay with them as they wanted to swagger in all together. Tom and the rest didn't think much of this, and went on ahead, so Blickie and I stayed with them, and made a triumphant entry, with the oryx horn blowing, with singing and dancing, and all the sticks beating on the loads in time. This is only a tiny place with a K.A.R. Station of 10 whites, a hospital the size of a hen house, and a few Indian dukas. It is the last station in the north, and the boys think it's a superb city.

There is a bad posho [*food*] shortage. Last night they had none, as we had run out, but they behaved very well and came on today with empty tummies. But to our horror the Indians here told us there is none to be got, as 1,000 loads were bad and have been condemned by the Doctor; the K.A.R. have bought up 2,000 loads, and there is no more. This evening I was sitting by the saice's fire, when I heard no end of a row. Wandered round with the head-man, and there, outside the gate of our camp (which has a little fence round it), were 20 or 30 boys, all howling and yelling for posho, while the old Askari stood guard inside the gate with his empty rifle (he has no cartridges) on his shoulder. Then did Mininguishi show the strength of an ox and the guile of a serpent. They didn't touch me, but crowded round him, yelling, but when he lifted his enormous hands as if he was going to hit them, they shrank away. Then he talked to them like a diplomat, and explained that if they eat all the posho given them for three days, in two days, that was their business and not 'Bwana Wahoga's business – wasn't it?'

They saw that and when he told them they would get posho tonight (which I thought optimistic of him) they said Msuri, good, and went off satisfied.

Blickie meanwhile persuaded the Indian – an old friend of his – to sell us 15 loads, enough for three days, so they had their feed tonight, and after all their savagery in the afternoon, were as happy as children.

But the situation is very bad, as there is not nearly enough food for the K.A.R., alone as it is, and everybody is going short. We had a dramatic conference this evening in the tiny mess-hut – Blickie and the others sitting round the table, while our enormous Mininguishi, two or three saices, and an Indian merchant discussed the whole thing; and Ahbdi held a lamp and listened. A quite good idea seems to be to scrap a lot of the boys and go with donkeys, which cost nothing to feed, and are the same price to buy as one boy's load of posho for a month.

28 DECEMBER

It rained in the night, coming down in torrents, in bucketfuls; making a noise on the tents like a hundred small drums, falling in blinding sheets. It doesn't look as if we shall get away today. You can hardly stand up on the road and the tents are soaked, and will be too heavy to carry. We spent nearly the whole morning in the Indian *duka*, where the Indians were very kind and hospitable, giving us tea, biscuits, cigarettes and making me a present of a very nice box of chocolates. I can't think why everyone hates the Indians so, and boycotts them. They have always been very nice to us and are no worse cheats than other people.

31 DECEMBER

The most ghastly thing has happened – Tom has broken his right thigh! He was running after some birds, not looking at the ground, when he caught his toe on a stone, and fell, twisting the whole leg under him. B. and I had gone in the other direction after zebra when Tom's *saice* cantered up, saying the bwana had fallen and the gun bearer had sent him to find us.

Tom was lying on the ground with his head in Kongoni's lap, one arm waving in the air, shouting and groaning with agony. We could do nothing for him except sit on the ground with his head in my lap while Blickie held his hand. There was no morphia in the first aid box, and the medicine chest was at Isiolo with the safari. We sent out boys for it and the doctor and sat there with poor Tom, who grew whiter every moment, with sunken eyes and blue lips. At last the medicine chest arrived and he swallowed two morphia tablets which relieved him a tiny bit. Some boys arrived and a tent was put over him; and at about 5.30 p.m. the doctor came – not the Isiolo one but a man who was staying there a couple of nights on his way to Abyssinia.

The doc had brought splints and chloroform and bandages, and with half an hour of daylight and one lamp started with the operation. Tom took the chloroform as badly as he could, fighting and gasping. He was worn out, and while they pulled the broken leg out and put the splints on his pulse and breathing grew weaker and weaker. At one moment I could feel nothing, and I thought he had gone. I was in a state of cold terror and the doc was frightened too. He pushed Tom's chest hard; he gave a half-groan and, after a second or two, started breathing again – but oh, so faintly! We got him onto a bed, lying on the boys' blankets and covered with our coats, and he came to very slowly.

The others had gone to the camp at Isiolo, and we sat down on the ground and ate the two beastly birds which had broken Tom's leg. We had sent to Isiolo for more boys with blankets, water, tea, etc., and expected them out by about 9 p.m. but they didn't come . . . and didn't come. The boys that were left – about six – went down one after another to wait and show them where we were. We had hardly any water left for Tom, the only lamp was very nearly out of paraffin, and still no boys came. Tom began to wake up and was very sick. But at about 12.30 or 1 a.m. four blessed little lights appeared. I lay down on the ground and fell fast asleep, but Blickie never closed his eyes and looked after Tom all night.

Counterbalancing such amazing bad luck was extraordinary good luck. A simple fracture. It happened a few yards from the main road – such as it is

Genesta at 15 – her age when these Diaries begin

Genesta and friends dance around the maypole at Kitlands. Her mother, Sarah Heath, is on the left

Right: Genesta (aged 5) with her grandfather, Admiral Sir Leopold Heath (aged 90 and holding May ribbons)

Below: Genesta leads a donkey on a road near Cannes. Her mother is on the left

Genesta with her pony Primrose – a painting by W. Symonds

Admiral Sir Leopold
Heath with Genesta's
cousin Fred Heath and
brother Griggs in the
background

Right: Genesta with
Admiral Sir Herbert
Heath, her father
Cuthbert Heath and
Dmitri Tsokoff, first
Minister Plenipotentiary
of Bulgaria

– when it might have been in the Lorian swamp. We have got a very good doctor on the spot. Meru is only seventeen miles away. And Keith is arriving tomorrow.

1923

1 JANUARY

What a New Year's Day! Tom's leg is now suspended in the air from a stay, and fixed over a pulley made of a reel of cotton and a nail fixed to a heavy sandbag. This will pull the leg out, and lessen the chances of shortening. He is not in nearly such pain now, and has got a little more colour. But the plaster is glued to his foot and the weight often gives him hell, and has to be moved.

2 JANUARY

Dr Burkett arrived today, having been driven the two hundred odd miles in nineteen hours. He was very much impressed with the way the leg had been set, but says he must have Tom down at Nairobi. So now the idea is to keep him here for five more days, then take him to Isiolo for five days, then fetch him by ambulance to Nairobi.

5 JANUARY

Tom is a good deal better in every way, though he has very bad pain indeed from the glue on his foot. It was changed again this morning, and the foot was red and raw. He has not had a proper night's sleep since it happened a week ago today.

Blickie is trying his hardest to prevent Tom being taken into Isiolo. It seems such a useless, tiring and frightening journey for him. B. saved him before from being taken to Meru, the day after the accident, and will work it again now, I hope.

6 JANUARY

In the middle of the night, amid much stage whispering and a loud chorus from the doc's dogs, some boys arrived from Meru. They brought a charming letter from the District Commissioner, Mr Weekes, who is sending fruit etc., and a wire from Burkett, saying they are coming to fetch Tom on Monday. The boys have been set to make a road from the main road to Tom's tent.

7 JANUARY

Blickie and Mello departed to the hills in search of elephant this morning; John arrived a good while later and went off in another direction for some shooting. We have paid off ninety-one boys, and are going to do the safari mostly with donkeys. It will be cheaper; but I felt rather sad as they all started off for Nairobi. Two boxes of Tom's went with them and there was trouble about carrying them. No. 1 boy, the porter who marches ahead of the rest and is supposed to set a good example, refused, and so did the other two who were left behind. Blick had gone by this time, so the doc and I solemnly made a list of the offenders' names. I saw one of them having splinters cut out of his hand with a knife, so I did the Good Samaritan trick and got them out for him with tweezers.

'Refuse now?' I said.

'No, memsahib.'

'Then go, fool!' (I must say I think Swahili looks very theatrical and ridiculous translated.) And off they went.

8 JANUARY

Dr Burkett and Fisher and a spare driver arrived in a lorry converted into a fine ambulance; and as it has been raining more than the roads will stand (which is nothing) they started early. Tom was carried into the car, padded in every direction, and driven very carefully down our 'drive' to the main road. Blickie arrived five minutes before he left. He had come twenty-six miles in under four hours, which is good going. Tom was very glad to see him and say goodbye. Some other people who came to say goodbye were a herd of zebra and oryx, who crossed the plain four or five hundred yards away. Tom was thrilled, and more upset because he couldn't shoot them than at the idea of the journey.

Tom wants me to stay with the safari and fill my licence, as we have paid so much. This is the end of this stony camp. And, although it has been such a disastrous place, I can't help loving it; partly because of the wonderful view, over a plain so unbroken that it looks like the sea, to hills ranged all round the horizon. One night I saw the snow on Mount Kenya alight in the moonlight, like a dream.

The doc goes to Meru tomorrow, and his last deed of kindness to me was to pull out a tooth which has been worrying me a lot. I only plucked up courage in the last two minutes of daylight, and sat in a chair (with an interested audience of boys!) while Blickie held my head. The doc seized the tooth and out it came, almost without a pang!

9 JANUARY

Blickie started off at three this morning, back to Mello and the elephants. I packed off Tom's boy, Ahbdi, down to Nairobi to join him, and started for Isiolo. Had quite a good stalk after a wretched zebra on the way, and got him. The porters love the meat I shoot for them.

Just before dark Blick and Mello appeared. Blick has now done eighty miles in thirty hours; and this time walked the last thirty miles, as his mule was tired!

12 JANUARY

B. and I went off early to try for a lion which was roaring a few yards from camp. The Nandi trackers spotted him, but when we got to the place he had gone, and we saw nothing but his spoor. We are camped about half a mile away from the Guasso Njcro river, as this is malarial mosquito country and we don't want our porters to go sick. It is extremely hot here. One drips and drips, and the glare from the earth, which is white, doesn't help.

This is a pretty camp under big thorn trees. I went for a stroll with my gun and the dog Mac has lent me, an adorable mongrel called Siolo, to look at the flaming sunset; and when it darkened I started home. Then I saw Kongoni and Juma [*not the Juma who was sacked*] looking for me, and when they reached me they said it was *mbaya sana* (very bad) for me to go out alone, that I might have trodden on a lion's tail at any moment – in fact, I got a good scolding. They escorted me home, one on cither side. So that's the end of any lonely strolls!

14 JANUARY

Moved camp to another pretty place, seven miles down the river. Blick and I went out, and first met a rhino. We went quite close to him and took several photos, while he stood there, rather puzzled, and not knowing what to do. At last we walked backwards, as from the presence of royalty, and left him having a glorious roll in the dust, heaving over from side to side with his fat, stubby legs in the air.

29 JANUARY

We have moved camp twice and are now in the heart of elephant country! We are on the north bank of the river, and should pick Blickie up soon, they left a couple of days ago. But I wanted to try for my elephant now, so decided to go on a flying camp of my own with David, Kongoni, Juma, three porters, and Fara with two mules. We started about 5.30 p.m., went back a short way, and up a little hill, where we ought to have been above the elephants' wind. But the elephants also decided that was the very hill they wanted to feed on, and up they came, the wind straight from us to them. They were trumpeting angrily, their tummies rumbling like thunder. It was almost pitch dark, about 7 p.m., with the moon just over the half and not properly up. They were under fifty yards away, so we discreetly retired to the next hill, where they presently followed us on their way to the river. They climbed our hill some way behind, but got near again, so Juma went out and shouted at them rudely in Swahili. 'We know we're strangers here and this is your ground, but we're going to sleep here and we've got three guns, so get out! The case can come on tomorrow, but you're not wanted here tonight, so go down and have a good drink and come back in the morning.'

We heard a female trumpeting to her husband: 'Come along my dear, we'd much better not stay here,' and off they all went. I rolled up in my blankets and tried to forget the stones I was lying on. It was very lovely; with the moon hanging serenely in the indigo sky, and the stars blazing – like a queen and her court. In the distance we heard the elephants rumbling, crashing trees as they went, and sometimes a lion roared or leopard grunted. We had no fire, of course, and as the moon got brighter, we could see the elephant quite well, though not enough to pick out a big tusker. I went to sleep at last.

30 JANUARY

David woke me about 4 a.m., and below us in the valley a herd of females and totos (calves) were moving slowly along, on their way back to the hills. As soon as it was light enough we started off in their tracks, and then came a real hard day. We went from 6.30 till 11, and stopped for lunch on top of a steep little hill which gave a tremendous view all round. There I made out an elephant a long way away, who disappeared in the trees; and David even saw someone on a mule, whom he thought might be John. They ought to join us today, as it is four days since they left. At 12.30 off we went again, in the murderous sun, and not a flicker of breeze, the air perfectly still and swimming with heat. Poor old Kongoni and Juma walked and walked, through thorn, scrub and bush, over dry, sandy river beds and stones with never a sign of elephant, except for a lot of tracks. As David said, 'I have known so many gentlemen after elephant, and they always say he is a *hell* of an animal to get! You will excuse me, memsahib, I hope!'

I shared cigarettes and the water with them, they were far too polite to ask. Suddenly we saw Blickie's safari on the main road – there is actually a motor road on this side of the river, a broad sandy track on which a car can, at least, move. B's boys said B. had started out at four this morning, and they didn't know where he had gone, and that John was in front. This road goes to Kittermaster camp, and eventually to Merti. We left the road and returned to our camp, getting here at 5.30 p.m. to find no sign of either Blickie or John!

We sent out three boys and an askari and told them to go to Kittermaster and not to come back without the Bwanas; firing signal shots as they went. We were all pretty tired, having done nearly thirty miles today, and I had a delicious bath and got into pyjamas for dinner.

But before dinner the boys came back, having fired three shots and heard an answer of two, they refused to go any further, and the askari (policeman) came back with them. I told them what I thought of them and promised each one ten kiboko (whips) which is the least they deserve for being such cowards; then I jumped into my clothes and started off with David; Jumbe the askari; and my medical dresser-boy, Masodi, as gun bearer. He is a real little sportsman, and offered to come of his own accord. I went behind Mello's tent not wanting to be stopped; some boys saw me and said, 'Where are you going to at this hour, memsahib?' I said, 'Ah, that's my affair.'

It was only 7.30, but there was a good moon, and we went a fair pace. Juma the gun bearer joined us after a bit. A big bull buffalo galloped past a few yards away, and David sent a shot after him. After about an hour and a half Masodi spotted a light, and when we reached it, there was John, asleep on a bedstead with no blankets, beside a big fire, with ten or eleven boys. They said Blickie had gone on to a camp five hours away, but David wouldn't let me go, as we had no blankets or anything and he felt responsible. We sent on Jumbe and the Boran guide and an interpreter. I was very anxious. God knows where Blickie has got to, he doesn't know this country at all. He had no food and only one Boran and one gun bearer with him. Although he is the toughest, hardest man in East Africa, he isn't super-human and there he is, having started at four this morning, hunting everywhere for our camp. He thinks we're in front, it's too dark for him to see tracks and he is getting further and further away from us.

There was nothing for it but to come back, so we did, bringing John and his camp. He told me that their camp was charged by elephant, eight of them, screaming with rage, trunks up and ears flapping; they were both nearly killed, but Blickie ran across them and got the right side of the wind just in time! A cow in front was bearing down on John, and Blick shot her through the head and killed her.

31 JANUARY

David came into my tent this morning glowing with pride. 'Here is the Baron, memsahib! He has walked those Borans and the men and the mule tired, and here he is, on foot, alone, carrying his gun! Ah memsahib! I have known many gentlemen, yes, many; but there is not one like my boss anywhere!'

B. has done an amazing trek from the elephant camp to Kittermaster;

his mule was sick, so he trotted on foot all the way. (It took John eleven hours to get there, so it must be 33 miles.) There B. saw no tracks of ours, so he crossed the river and went right back, *past this camp!* to our last camp, about six or seven miles back. Slept on the ground and started this morning to chase us, trotting again, when he suddenly found us. He missed us yesterday because the trees hide everything. Everyone is delighted he is back; David said, 'I have been a sick man, memsahib, but now he is back I am well again!'

4 FEBRUARY

Last night, when I was asleep, I was woken by the report of a gun and then heard trees crashing down. I jumped out of bed and hauled on mosquito boots, meaning to wake Blickie, as it didn't sound as if it could be anything else but elephants coming to raid the camp.

Masodi rushed into my tent: 'Memsahib! Where's your gun? The elephants are coming!' But it was only an old rhino after all that, and John had fired a shot to frighten the camp, as a rag. He frightened the boys all right! All the porters had fled except Masodi, who had come straight to me. He said, 'I heard the elephants coming, and thought – they will go straight for the memsahib's tent. All the porters have gone and she may be killed. *Hai zuru!* (never mind) I will die near her!' I was very touched and thought it wonderful of him, though *he* probably thought it wiser to be near a gun!

Today has been perfect, the best day for a long time. It gets sweltering hot in camp, so I came down to the river to bathe. Blickie, who thinks of everything, had his tent put up *in the water*. So while the others laughed at the idea, and sat sweating and cursing the heat up in camp, we were as cool as fish – Blickie in a chair and me in the water, which was as warm as bathwater.

It is just six o'clock and the sun is setting. The river laps past me, the doves are cooing in the palm trees, everything is peaceful and exquisitely calm. Africa looks so soothing and inviting – but there are crocodiles in the rivers, scorpions in the fallen palm branches, lion and elephant and buffalo in the bush. Masodi has just been out to see me, scolded me for not having a gun, and has gone back to fetch it.

7 FEBRUARY

John and Joseph are back, so today we all went out together. Found tracks of a large herd of buffalo. They led us straight away from the river through the thickest thorn bush, stuff in which you can only see ten yards round you. It is all a monotonous grey colour and simply endless, oceans of it! Towards four o'clock we came to a small clearing in which was a swamp with running water – one of these curious little rivers which run underground and occasionally come to the surface. The whole place was pitted with buffalo tracks and several big lion tracks. We saw nothing to shoot, and I was tired enough to do a mild faint.

We decided to stay the night, though we had no food except a few small potatoes, some tea, a tin of milk and a little sugar. Still, it was too late and too far to go back, so we looked for a camping place. Then we suddenly saw a camel, curving his neck and looking at us in disgust down his supercilious nose! That meant men, and sure enough there they were, camped under a tree. A Boran family: a tall, splendid-looking man, his wife, two babies with very fat tummies and very thin legs, his two servants, two dogs, a puppy and a few sheep. Very dignified, he came forward and shook hands, and spoke in Swahili. As I suppose perhaps one Boran out of a hundred knows Swahili, this was wonderful luck. He said every single one of his cattle had died of rinderpest, and he was moving with what sheep he had left, about eight or ten, and his family, and there was no milk for his children. It was rather awful to think of this poor man losing almost everything he possessed at one blow.

We asked him for a sheep, which he said he couldn't spare. Then Blickie said that if he would give us one sheep we would give him two from a *manyiata* (village) not far off. Kongoni rose to the situation like a diplomat – gurgling round him with his soft voice, bending and bowing and waving his arms. In the end the Boran said to Blickie: 'You are my father and I am your child. If you want my sheep then they are all yours – but if you say you will give me two sheep for one of mine, that is very nice of you!'

So the sheep was caught and killed and we had a splendid meal, sitting on the ground round the fire while all the stars came blazing out and we heard buffalo crashing around us.

On my return from safari I found a huge pile of letters, mail from home and letters from Tom. He had a trying journey to Nairobi, but arrived all right, though full of morphia. The leg is broken very badly in two places, they have plated it and it is going on well now. He's had his old malaria again, but is better, though very worried about money – so am I, unless Father helps us, I can't imagine where it's coming from! The home letters are full of news of babies – doing splendidly – and fog, rain and hunting. The more I hear of England the more thankful I am to be out here.

If a boy behaves badly here, some people give him kiboko (whip). Blickie never does that, but just tells him to get back to Nairobi. Next day the boy is crawling about begging to be forgiven and allowed to stop with us.

The day Blick was lost, with a gun bearer called Macau and a Boran, he walked the mule to pieces, changed Borans four times, and at last lay down, with the boys, and made a little fire. B. thought he heard the gramophone, and listened hard. Then he found it was a goat. There were only him and Macau and the mule now, so he said to Macau: 'Come on, that must be a manyiata (a Masai village); we'll go there!' 'No,' said Macau, 'what's the use? We will only break our legs in the dark, on these stones.' 'All right,' said B., 'you stay here, keep the gun and I'll go on alone.' At that, Macau got up, they went together and found the manyiata, where they slept the night.

Next morning Macau said to Blickie: 'I love you now!'

'Very nice of you, but why?'

'I love you because I know you are a *man*. The boys always said so, but now I know it!'

'Why *now*?' asked Blickie.

'Because when we first stopped, and you heard a goat, you wanted to go on, but I didn't. So you said stay. But I did not want you to go on alone, so I came too, and we came to the manyiata, and now I have had some milk to drink! So now I love you!'

11 FEBRUARY

Mello decided to stay out another night, so Joseph went to join him. We three went on a flying camp after elephant or buffalo last night. It was very delicious; I love sleeping without a tent. But the elephants came and screamed and rumbled at us in the middle of the night, and we put on boots and got the rifles and waited. The wind was bad, straight from us to them, but after a while they wandered away, with a few farewell tummy rumbles. At daybreak we went out to look for game, but saw only tracks.

The camp was flooded with Borans, who came to sell sheep and be doctored. They gave me a sheep for having doctored them. I was after one of the old chief's ivory bracelets, but it was nothing doing.

Late in the evening Mello and Joseph turned up. Mello was very upset about the camp being moved, and at having to come on another six or seven miles. I'm afraid he was not predestined for safari, nor the mildest kind of roughing it.

The Borans were very funny with the gramophone. They crouched round, amazed, and they especially liked Caruso's song from *Pagliacci*. They hid their faces and screamed with laughter at it.

14 FEBRUARY

Blickie put it to us that we could either take a chance for buffalo, who had certainly been in the swamp this morning, and risk the safari not arriving, in which case we should have to sleep Buri, as the natives call it – which means without food or blankets or anything at all – or give up the buffalo and trek back to meet the safari. I didn't mind sleeping buri, and wanted to try for the buffalo. John, in a very legal manner, conveyed that he didn't think there was much chance for the buffalo, and he couldn't face the idea of sleeping buri. Mello thought the same, so we said farewell to them and went off to the swamp. If they won't face a little discomfort for the sake of the buffalo – that's their affair.

We left them sitting in a sad little heap round the tree, and reached the swamp in a short storm of rain. Stalked round the swamp and came to hoof marks. Then – there they were, perhaps a dozen of them, feeding under the trees. We saw a big bull, about 150 yards away, and I fired and got him in the right place – high on the shoulder. They all galloped away, and Blickie, Juma and I ran after them. The trees ended, they stood still in the open, not knowing which way to turn. I tried to get another shot, but they moved. Blickie fired, we heard the bullet strike, and ran forward into the open. They turned our way, saw us, and charged. Juma yelled, 'They're coming! They're coming!' and rushed for the only tree. When we reached it, I thought I would stand behind it and blaze at them, Blickie said, 'Get up the tree! Get up! Get up!' So up I went – I think it was a record climb! Juma had my gun and it wasn't a moment to be asking questions, so I stood there on a branch, half-way up the tree, helpless and furious, but hoping Juma would fire. The herd came straight at us, looking splendid, and Blick shot as they came. He shot so fast, every bullet striking, that they turned aside – but they passed within ten or fifteen yards of us. With the last bullet he shot the leading bull in the neck. He fell at once, but Blickie was already running after the others with an empty gun in his hand, while I slithered down the tree. When we reached him we found my bullet in his shoulder – it must have gone straight into his heart, and yet he galloped three or four hundred yards!

20 FEBRUARY

The safari came to an end eventually. We reached Nairobi red with dust, tired but triumphant. Tom was almost well again, so we started making preparations to go home. Saying goodbye to the porters, gun bearers and the good dog Siolo (who went to a good home) was very hard, for we had all become such friends.

[*Re-reading this in the 1980s I am shocked at the amount of killing I did. Of course, it was the fashion in those days. The person who influenced people's attitudes for the better was King Edward VIII – then Prince of Wales. He hated hunting and killing, and managed to make photographing wild animals fashionable.*]

1923–24

As my diaries of Abyssinia and Somaliland were probably burnt, I will try to remember what I can of them. My marriage had been under a lot of strain and finally Tom Farquhar had left me to marry someone to whom he had once been engaged.

I wanted to return to Kenya, but *en route* had the idea of going to Abyssinia. So I left the ship at Aden, got visas, money and so on and found a tiny boat going to Djibouti in French Somaliland. It was a rough trip. I slept on deck as the cabin was stifling, and I did not much like the look of an over-helpful Indian passenger, so stayed near the bridge.

Djibouti was dreadful, hot and dreary; all the French and their children were pale and bored and had not found anything to do with themselves – totally unlike English colonials, who at once have polo, clubs, swimming, sailing, attractive houses, and so on. When I was taken for a drive to see the sights, I was shown the coal heap where the ships refuelled!

I bought a train ticket for Addis Ababa – the name means the New Flower – the capital of Abyssinia. I also hired a Somali boy named Yasin. On the first day the train crept along through dreadful country, all lava rock, and stopped in the station at night as the locals used to rob and murder people travelling at night. Next day the scenery was better – greener, more wooded, with one or two lakes. I slept in a station rest-house again. The natives here were tall, handsome and ferocious; they had white bands round their foreheads stuck with feathers – one for each person they had killed, my Somali said. Next day there was much better country, and we got to Addis at last. I booked into a pretty primitive hotel, but it was the only one for white people. I found Yasin sleeping outside my door, as he trusted no one not to bother me.

I met all the diplomats; the Americans were especially kind. I had a mule on which to ride to dinner parties. The mule boy ran in front with a lantern and a long stick, with which he whacked a way through the crowds.

Here they have law suits in the streets and can call any passer-by to be judge. They tried to call me but, knowing no Amharic, I escaped. For theft one hand is cut off; you never see anyone with no hands at all!

The ruler is Empress Julie, the great Menelik's daughter. She married several times; her last husband got bored and took to the hills, so now she is alone. I was presented, and found a fat, dignified woman about sixty years old; she gave me very sweet champagne, and biscuits with currants in them.

I asked permission to travel to Somaliland, and this was reluctantly given.

At night the smell of burning eucalyptus drenched the air. When Menelik built Addis Ababa he made everyone plant eucalyptus trees in order to drain the swamps, remove mosquitoes and provide firewood. This they have done ever since. His name is still all-powerful. To call attention, make way in a crowd or stop a fight, you only have to say: *'Ba Menelik.'*

All transport in Addis is by pony, mule or cart; there is one car, belonging to a *ras* (prince). Hawashi (Abyssinian) men wear long white robes and a thin, large white cloth called a *shamma* over their shoulders. They are fairly tall, and have regular features and fine eyes, but none of the real beauty and panache of the fierce Somalis – their mortal enemies.

After a couple of weeks here I started on the next trip, to Somaliland. Before leaving Addis I was warned not to carry any money on the trek, as there were roving bands of natives, called Shifta, who attacked and robbed travellers. With great kindness, Indian shopkeepers supplied me with all I needed for the journey, and I arranged to pay in Aden. They were most generous.

Yasin had got an extra boy in Aden, a very handsome and well-mannered person about twelve years old. We three went by train to Dirredawa, where the local Indian had been told to get my safari together – mules, food (money I did not carry because of the *shiftas* tents and several ancient soldiers, besides a pony for me and a mule for Yasin.

The Indians were charming – they sent messages ahead to other Indians to supply me, gave me meals, and trusted me completely to repay them when I returned to Aden. The British have a good reputation.

The start was chaotic. A mule with the saucepans and kettles on his back reared straight up on end and flung himself down sideways, smashing the lot. 'Oh devil and son of Satan!' screamed Yasin – I found my Arabic was coming along nicely. The other mules jibbed, kicked, bit, fell down and rolled on their loads. It was hilarious. At long last we were organized, and set forth. We had to get to Harar before dark.

I rode a bit, then walked – formidable mountains rose before us, and very soon my ancient bodyguards were so worn out that they had to take turns riding my pony and Yasin's mule. Being out of training I got very tired plodding up the tiny, rocky tracks on those endless mountains.

I took a gun from a guard, broke it and looked down the barrel – it was clogged with dirt. Their impressive-looking bandoliers were full of cartridges which did not fit the guns.

We met two men fighting with their long staves. They stopped for us, drew aside and bowed politely to me. I was riding now, and bowed back. As we went on, they started fighting again.

Many hours later, footsore and very tired, we came to the great walls of Harar, an old, old town which Somalis and Hawashi have been fighting over through the ages. We walked along narrow, dark streets to the British

Consulate; the Consul and his wife were infinitely kind, took me in, fed me, looked after my safari and the animals. I fell into bed and slept.

While I was in Harar there was a holy day for the Abyssinians. Crowds of several hundred milled about the streets, mostly drunk, chanting prayers in which their priests led them. They had huge, endless feasts, and they danced and sang and yelled for many hours. The local *ras* and his wife were coming to dinner, and I did my best to dress up and tidy my awful face and wild hair. At dusk the rain came down. Etiquette forbade the *ras* and his wife to be seen out together, so she, poor lady, had to leave their house first, with her attendants, on their mules, and plunge into the dripping night; then wait under a tree until her husband and his guards passed her and rode to the Consul's house. They all had very thick, heavy cloaks with hoods, so they did not suffer too badly. We had a rather strange meal – talking was difficult as I knew no Amharic, but we managed with smiles and bits of English. The din outside was terrific, but the house's immensely thick walls kept it fairly quiet. The *ras*'s wife was plump and pretty in her white *shamma*, head veil and heaps of necklaces.

Next day off we went again, heading for Somaliland. The Consul had lent me a rifle, which I was to leave with the officers at Upper Sheikh when we got there. We soon left the mountains and came to semi-desert, flat, sandy, scrubby country. We were aiming for Jigjigga, the first town in Somaliland. Now we were among the Somalis: very tall, very black, elegant people with large eyes and classical features. Even today, after a lifetime of travels, I still think they are the most beautiful race I've ever seen. The men wore turbans, untidily balanced on their splendid heads, and robes of a sort. The married women hid their hair under white scarves; they wore several petticoats, all of different colours, under a gaudy skirt, and some bright-coloured stuff around their shoulders. The unmarried girls were exquisite, with large, dark eyes and clouds of dark, wavy hair – no tight frizzes for them, they were uttely non-negroid. They herded the flocks of camels, running like gazelles after straying animals.

When we rode into Jigjigga various officials appeared to look over us and my papers. I had not asked the British Governor of Somaliland for permission to come, as I was sure he would refuse. I met him later – he scolded me, then forgave me, and I apologised and said how sorry I was, which was not true.

Now I exchanged our horse and mule for camels. My own riding camel had a native saddle – just a sack to sit on with wooden cross trees in front of you, round which you wrapped your legs. Next day we went on, through the monotonous thorn-scrub country. When it was time to dismount I found my knees had seized up, burnt by the wind, and my legs were bleeding because of the rough sack. They hurt a lot, but eventually I was able to unbend my knees and stand up. I covered my legs with Pond's cold cream, and this hurt even more; but the bleeding stopped and the grazes healed as if by magic. In a few days I was quite used to this type of saddle.

At one village I called on an old *hadji* – a Moslem who had been to Mecca and wore a green turban. He told me stories of the Mad Mullah's war, and of when Lord Delamere [*who became leader of the Kenyan settlers*] came to this village. He said D. gave a reward to all the Somalis who came and salaamed to him, so they came in crowds. Hadji Mussa was charming and gave me a long narrow piece of Somali cloth, woven with silver, which I still have in England.

This safari took some time and I was blissfully happy – on my own, with fairly wild natives (they eat grass for breakfast), half a dozen camels, Yasin and the little boy doing all they could to make me comfortable. Yasin taught me quite a bit of Arabic, and I learnt their social customs from an Arabic grammar I had. Always use the right hand when eating. Drink the coffee three times round from the one communal coffee cup. Shake the cup three times when you don't want any more. Never speak first if you are on a horse and meet someone on a camel, as he is above you. Above all, never point the sole of your foot at anyone – this is a gross breach of manners; the best way, if sitting on the ground, is to tuck your feet under you.

Soon we were in Galla country, and took great care not to step on their grass, for I had been warned in Addis that, if you do, they might kill you. They seemed friendly enough to me, and very surprised to see a young white woman with camels, camel boys and two Somali boys travelling through this wild country.

Now, in the 1980s, those rough, stony tracks on which I crossed the mountains have become motor roads, as it was through here that the British advanced to drive the Italians out of Abyssinia in the Second World War. I would not like to go back and see its wildness tamed.

Some days later I was met by a detachment of dazzlingly smart Somali Camel Corps soldiers, so with much regret bade farewell to my porters and camels and went on, riding astride on a fast camel with a proper sheepskin-covered saddle. This was most luxurious. We proceeded towards Upper Sheikh, but I had been living on camel's milk, which made me ill, and I could not ride much further. So a soldier went on ahead on a fast camel, and next day a doctor arrived in a car and took me to the camp at Upper Sheikh. Yasin and the boy came with the camels, guarding my things.

At Sheikh there were seven white people all told, counting me, besides a few RAF officers and men with their planes. I was back in civilization, and it was good to be clean, comfortable and properly fed. I made friends with a pilot called Gibbons, who took me up in his plane. As it was quite forbidden to take up civilians I wore a mechanic's outfit, and everyone looked the other way. We flew round for a while, and then the engine stopped. I was petrified, but Gibbons had stopped it on purpose because of the noise, and he wanted to talk. Would I like to loop the loop? I said no – I only wanted to come down. So we did – I never thought then that I should learn to fly and do mild aerobatics myself, and adore it!

One night, after a good dinner, a camel race was arranged, in the dark, between a visiting District Officer and me. I was wearing yellow silk pyjamas, which I rather fancied. A course was marked out, lined on both sides with highly amused Somalis, who of course had never before seen an English memsahib in yellow pyjamas racing a camel against an English sahib, at night. After the 'off' I shot ahead. By now I knew exactly where to kick the camel with my bare heels, and how to yell at him. There were howls of encouragement all the way, and even now I can remember Yasin screaming at my camel to gallop faster – which it did. Yasin was dancing up and down with excitement, and clapping – dear Yasin. He was so hoarse he nearly lost his voice completely. As we galloped past the post he rushed at me, seizing my hands when I got off and bowing. I won because the other jockey must have pulled his mount.

The Somalis are very violent people, 'at the mercy of their emotions', as Thor Heyerdahl said of sharks. Quite fearless, utterly loyal, fiery-tempered and unpredictable, they have been called 'the Irish of Africa'. I was told a story about one of the numerous risings against the British, when a mob of hysterical Somalis, armed with guns, rushed the officers' quarters. One officer begged to be allowed to go out and speak to them, as he knew them well and loved them. Very reluctantly he was allowed to go, and as he stepped onto the verandah he was instantly shot dead. Many Somalis then burst into tears and said they never meant to kill him.

Eventually I had to leave Upper Sheikh and join some people motoring down to the coast. A marvellous road, built by the Royal Engineers, wound up, over, and down through the mountains. At last we were in the baking heat of Lower Sheikh – a hive of industry compared to miserable Djibouti.

Here there were people, drinks and parties. I had said a sad farewell to Yasin and the boy, given them large baksheesh and received many flattering remarks, thanks and blessings – all of which did not prevent Yasin from stealing my beautiful hunting knife.

I reached Nairobi at last and was met by Boy Long, a man I had met before in Kenya and with whom I was very much in love. We married soon afterwards. He was manager for Lord Delamere. I think he was the handsomest man I have ever seen, with infinite charm but 'difficult'.

Life with Boy was electric. The best times were when we went to the sheep farm at Laikipia, which was run rather haphazardly. There was always trouble – sheep stolen or missing or sick or dead.

We received great hospitality from the few settlers who lived on these big ranches, in their charming, comfortable stone houses, filled with old furniture, family portraits, silver and ornaments, good servants, boiling hot baths and wonderful cooks.

Sometimes the bath boiler was in the principal bedroom. When the boy came with early tea he also lit the fire for the bathwater in the tank outside, so the rooms were warm even though outside it might have been freezing.

The herders clustered round their fires, swathed in blankets and drinking a first gourd of hot milk laced with ginger. When the sun came up, animals and people thawed to life.

During these years I experienced sometimes fun and happiness, sometimes misery and fear; and a good deal of pain from my not very strong heart. I used to get nasty heart attacks which ended in a violent pain, as my heart stopped completely for a second or so before bumping – as it were – into gear again. Living perpetually at six thousand feet and spending hours on horseback every day did not help. I learnt to fly – not very well, but it was exciting and took no energy. I travelled a little, always alone.

Some years later Father gave me the money to buy Nderit, the neighbouring farm to Soysambu. The name means the land between the rivers. A great plain runs south and north down the middle, between two rivers, and ending on the shores of Lake Nakuru.

The very blue waters of this lake are usually covered with bright pink flamingoes – someone once counted nearly a million of them. They march to and fro all day, feeding on the green algae growing just below the lake's surface. When the lake dries up in time of drought they go elsewhere; they also leave if too much rain raises the level of the lake, so that the algae becomes too deep for the birds to get at it. They flight at dusk, weaving long skeins across the pink and lemon sunset sky, clattering and chattering all the time – one of the loveliest sights in the world. Sir Philip Sassoon visited us once and described the flamingoes as 'a scarlet scarf, flung around the lake'.

We bought the cattle that went with the farm – a fairly scrubby lot; got some goodish bulls, and improved the breed. We had about seventy horses, fifteen for farm work and the rest to sell, for polo and racing. Many people came to stay, and on the whole life was good and certainly great fun.

The house, entirely designed by me, had an L-shaped drawing room, fifty feet by forty; a verandah seventy feet long, carpeted all the way; two very big bedrooms – one with a fireplace in it; a sleeping verandah, bathrooms and one smaller bedroom. The house was built round a patio, with flowers and a small fountain (later on a snake was found to be living here, but not for long). The big dining room had a specially made table to seat twenty-five. Our servants wore dark red *kanzus* (long robes), gold-embroidered Arab waistcoats and crimson turbans. For big parties the two house girls came in, also in dark red *kanzus* and Masai necklaces and bracelets. A smaller guest house was built outside.

The grey stone house looked across a plain to a forest of scented acacia thorn trees, and beyond this forest stand the hills of the Mau, about ten thousand feet above sea level. Every day, when the sun rose behind the stables, the cliffs of the Mau caught the early shafts of light and turned bright scarlet. This was a sight which always enchanted me and which I have never forgotten.

The horses had a big paddock to themselves; only the two stallions, the riding horses and near-to-foaling mares lived in stables. Both stallions' sires had been English Derby winners. They were beautiful, gentle creatures. All the stable boys were Kikuyu – Mau Mau to a man, as we discovered later when the troubles began. I managed to get rid of them, and the Masai took over the stables, the house and all the other farm work except the wagon-driving, which was done by very strong, very black people from Victoria Nyanza, called Jaluo. This tribe made good policemen and soldiers and were very anti-Mau Mau.

Two ancient Masai dames decided they would groom the stallions. I took them, laughing their heads off, up the hill to the stable. The first stallion stood quite still as they entered his box, but they smelt different from the people he was used to; he craned his head round, ears pricked and gazed at them. I thought he looked surprised, but that must have been my imagination. He stood like a rock, as one grasped his mane and the other his tail, still laughing, talking to him in Masai and sometimes singing in their harsh monotonous voices, as they do to cows when milking them. He seemed to like it. They groomed him perfectly; I showed them how to lift his feet and clean them. In half an hour his toilet was complete and they went on to the other stallion, still laughing, chattering and singing.

We rode for hours every morning; several dogs came too. They chased, in vain, all the buck they saw. The buck went prancing off, stiff-legged, teasing the dogs who raced after them. When they got closer, the buck seemed to slip into top gear and in seconds were far away. Besides the cattle and horses, the farm carried a lot of game. Gazelle, waterbuck, eland, hippo, hyrax, zebra, impala, leopard, jackal, the specially charming little bat-eared foxes who lived in burrows and came out to gaze at us in curiosity, and buffalo, who stayed in the forest from which we tried (in vain) to dislodge them. But they did us no harm and none of our cattle got east coast fever, which buffalo are said to carry – a dread disease against which the cattle had been dipped and inoculated.

Just before dawn the Kavirondo crane cried out to each other: a mournful, haunting sound, soon to be lost in the clatter of legs, the chatter of beaks and the beat of wings of the huge flocks of flamingo returning from their long, mysterious night flights. The Masai said they fly about at night in order to keep warm. When the sun showed over the horizon you knew it was six o'clock, and in came the early morning cup of tea. Then there was a burst of birdsong. So many different sorts of birds, all calling, singing and twittering together, in what to me seemed like a birds' Te Deum of thanks for a night safely passed – though, of course, they were only defining their own territories. Soon it was time to visit the herds.

Two or three horses, groomed and gleaming, appeared and we left the house with its bright garden to canter across the plain. There stood a tall Masai herdsman, leaning on his spear, wrapped in a cloak of red cotton, while a young boy (in Masai called 'the dirty one', because he does the menial jobs) brought the lordly herder his gourd of fresh milk – warmed up, sometimes, by the addition of scraps of ginger. Herds of zebra and gazelle grazed at a respectful distance, undisturbed by the riders but watching the dogs. A small flock of Kavirondo crane, with their smart black and blue feathers and their beautiful golden head-dresses, bowed and danced to each other in a unique, graceful aerial ballet. I am told they mate for life. Sometimes, among the courting birds, you see one lonely one – a sad sight.

We rode slowly through the grazing herd of about two hundred cows, their bulls running with them; the dogs kept their distance, for cattle will attack them if they come too near. The herder has already counted his herd, so if any beasts were sick or missing steps could be taken at once to help. Some cattle strayed at night to go to the lake and lick salt on the shore. Sometimes they were harassed by predators. We went from one herd to another and into the forest, where two white native Boran bulls were running wild. They were bored with their cows, had taken to the forest and would charge intruders.

Lions were discouraged from visiting the farm, being undesirable companions for cattle; but once there was a plague of wild dogs, which are deadly. They hunt cleverly, making a shrill whistling sound which panics the herd. The cattle bunch together and begin to run – three or four dogs give chase. They do not go very fast but they never tire, and as the cattle outdistance them and stop the first hunters fall back while others take over. The cattle start galloping again, the dogs closing on them, until the weary cattle fail. Then the dogs leap at their udders, pulling the animals down and tearing at them until they die. The only way to save the cattle was to sit up all night at the time of the full moon near the remnants of the diminished herd. When you heard that sinister whistling you would go as silently as possible, nearer and nearer to the sounds, until you could see the pack by the light of the moon. Then you shot, and might be able to kill one or two dogs before the rest melted away into the dark bush. They would not return to that herd, and they seemed only to hunt cattle when the moon was full – at other times they must have lived on game. They would probably try for another herd, not too far away, so you might have a few sleepless, moonlit nights until the pack had gone completely.

Near the lake there was a small dam where a family of hippo lived. The dogs barked at them, which annoyed them. The big bulls lifted their heavy heads, grunting furiously; the tiny, ungainly calves climbed onto the dams' wide backs, slipped off and climbed up again, the cows protesting in vain. If some newly arrived dog, unused to hippo on a farm, ran into the water, the hippo charged at once, jaws wide open and big teeth shining. The dog would learn his lesson and never try again. I often took visitors to the hippo pool, and they were enchanted. Waterbuck stood among the reeds growing on the lake shore and gazed quietly at us with their soft, dark eyes; they are dark grey with smart white shirt-fronts, like waiters.

After about three hours, and having seen five or six herds of the several thousand cattle on the farm, it was time to go home for breakfast. We rode through villages where ill-bred dogs rushed, yelling, at our house dogs which trotted quietly beside the horses in silent dignity.

We went through the lucerne paddock. This was just below a dam and near a well, so the lucerne – grown in small, square plots intersected by small channels – was always watered as in the Hadramout, where, by irrigation, they get forty or fifty crops of feed a year on one and a half inches of rain. This resulted, for us, in a crop being ready to cut every two weeks instead of taking over a month. Lucerne was taken to the stables and the milking places by wagons drawn by teams of eight or ten matched oxen. Wagons did all the carting needed on the farm – there was only one tractor, used for ploughing or emergencies. The Jaluo wagon drivers had a small boy to help them, whose job was to lead the animals at the head of the team. He was called Shika Kamba (Hold-the-Rope). Forest buck would joyfully graze on the lucerne, and I put a Jaluo on to keep the buck away. One day I rode down to the paddock and found no Jaluo but only his dog, sitting beside his hat. The dog kept flying at intruders and was a better guard than his master. The work oxen all had names, and their drivers talked to them a good deal.

There were quite a lot of snakes on the farm, including black spitting cobras who spit poison at the eye and never miss; then they hurl themselves at their enemy and strike – it is an agonizing way to die. There were also puff adders, whose poison is not so painful, but just as lethal; grass snakes (quite harmless); small black night adders; mambas, pythons and others.

After breakfast came office work and sometimes medicine for the natives, consultations with the elders of the tribes, conversations with visiting Masai and with the gardening ladies (Masai again), news that one of the wells' machinery had struck work – the manager and the carpenter would have to go and fix it.

After lunch was siesta time when the whole farm drowsed: cattle, game and humans alike. Then, in the evening, out again, on foot or horseback or by car, until the magic moment when the sun went down. There was half an hour of twilight, when the flamingoes took to the air in long, graceful skeins of birds, flighting across the sky in their thousands. Little spots of fire appeared here and there in the dusk – the herders' cooking fires. Our own log fire blazed in the drawing room and the dogs subsided before it with deep, contented sighs. The cats lay among the dogs, all friends.

Once a month the cattle were counted, five or six thousand of them. This took all day and was a hot and tiring job. We had half a dozen Masai with us, including headmen. There was a break in the middle of the morning, when everyone drank quantities of orange squash. Sometimes there was a miscount; then the herd was brought back, driven past one by one and recounted, slowly and even more carefully.

Christmas was always a jolly affair. The harness of the work oxen (who did as short a day's work as possible) was decorated with scarlet aloe flowers and the lovely red lily which grew wild in the forest. More were stuck in the drivers' hats. Every child on the farm was given a bag of sweets. Bullocks were killed to feed everyone. At night there was a big bonfire. Young Masai herders from neighbouring farms arrived, their bodies and manes of hair shining with bright red mud and their long, beautiful spears gleaming like silver. Our Masai, young and old, had also bedecked themselves. A great proportion of Masai are Protestant Christians; they are the only Kenyan tribe I know who have not had their manners and traditions changed by contact with Protestant teachings. Dancing went on for hours, the women and girls joining in, jumping up and down, their breasts, copper necklaces and beaded ornaments bouncing. They sang their monotonous tribal songs in accompaniment. At last the bonfire died down, and the visitors went to their friends' huts where they were regaled with Christmas beer and meat. Finally they trooped off, our own people went to sleep and silence enveloped the farm, broken now and then by jackals' howls, hippos' grunts and the voices of night birds. They speak quietly: I only once heard a Masai raise his voice in anger.

We sometimes went on safari in two vans strengthened against bumps and stones with extra springs. Besides ourselves we had two Masai who took it in turns to drive the second car, in which they slept at night. We saw endless game, some of it fairly tame; in the morning we sometimes found lion tracks passing our tent on their way to water. They never bothered us, nor we them; except one night when a pride of nine half-grown cubs spent hours frolicking in the camp, pulling the clothes and towels off the tent ropes, knocking the travelling fridge off its stand, scattering food and saucepans from the 'kitchen' camp, and finally going to sleep, grouped round the lavatory hut, a few yards away. The Masai guard had to be forcibly restrained from jumping out of the van and attacking the pride with his spear and club. They would probably have run away, but you never know – and, anyhow, what a pity to frighten them.

We went to various Masai villages, very far from roads and tourists, camping outside the villages because of the flies. Here we were visited by 'the blind, the halt and the maimed' for medicine, which it was my job to dispense. Masses of children, very quiet and polite, came with their elders. We all sat round the fire and talked of the cattle, the lions, the weather and the initiation ceremonies, some of which we saw – and very tough they were. One very handsome old Masai described to us, in perfect mime, how he had driven a prowling lion away from his herd, threatening him with his spear, running and shouting at him. The Masai are fearless – lions are not. Those evenings round the campfire, among these handsome, dignified and aristocratic people who knew a good deal about us and the farm because our Masai had 'spun yarns', were almost the best moments of the safaris.

In the mountain forest, behind the farm, was a tribe of smiths. They are taboo to the other natives, who will not approach them, speak to them, nor allow their shadows to fall on them. Now and then we visited them. In a small clearing they had a fire, surrounded by stones. Here they forged the short swords and long, elegant spears carried by the Masai, Samburu and other tribes living in this dangerous lion country. Since no native I knew would have any contact with them, I could not imagine how the commerce took place. They speak Swahili and displayed towards us the usual charming manners of 'wild' Africans. We liked them, but our Masai driver, an intelligent and enterprising lad, born on the farm, of the family of our head-man, would not go near them; he said they were very bad people.

On the farm there was a tunnel, about five miles long and fifteen feet deep. Here the Masai, when attacked, used to hide their cattle and women, but many young girls would stay above ground, egging on their boyfriend warriors to the fight. A very old Masai friend of mine told me she had watched such battles. When Evelyn Waugh came to stay he was very intrigued by the tunnel and wanted to explore it. Carrying quantities of a strong rope we drove over there and told the Masai what our visitor wanted to do. They were horrified, warning us of the pythons and other deadly animals which were bound to be living in the tunnel. But nothing would stop Evelyn – we fixed the rope round his body, below his shoulders, and down he went, spinning like a spider, for about fifteen feet, holding a torch and a panga. He walked a short way up the dark recess and then the Masai insisted on getting him back, so he was reluctantly lifted to the surface, having seen nothing exciting, but gaining a justified reputation for dauntless courage.

Some of our porters on the 1923 safari were Wakamba – this tribe are extremely acrobatic dancers and file their teeth; when I asked why, the other tribesmen said perhaps it was because they ate men! They are also clever snake charmers. Once one of the manager's houses on the farm became so infested with puff adders, night adders and cobras that the District Commissioner at the village of Machakos, the marketplace for the Wakamba, very kindly agreed to send an experienced snake charmer to get rid of them. All the Masai villages near that house asked that he might visit them too, and we thought he might as well also go up to the stables, five miles away. The head manager, a dour Scot who lived near the big house, disapproved of the whole thing.

In due course the snake charmer arrived – an old man wearing a shirt and shorts, rather tattered, a battered hat and a necklace of tiny gourds round his neck. These contained juices and powders which killed snakes; our expert had been all the way to Mombasa to get these drugs. His father and grandfather had been snake charmers too; he himself had the most courtly manners, and gave me a little wooden carving of a Wakamba warrior.

He laid his charms all round the house, and put out saucers of milk, which cobras love. He told me that, if I saw a cobra drinking the milk, I was to move away very quietly and fetch him. I never saw a cobra at the milk, and I never saw another snake in that area. The stables were all snake-proofed, and even the Scottish manager finally succumbed – though still jeering at the idea – and allowed charms to be placed round his own house.

The Wakamba are excellent herders and trustworthy, brave and faithful servants. In an old book about Kenya I read that once a large tribe of cannibals with filed teeth appeared in southern Africa and *ate* their way up the coast until they reached Malindi. The men of Malindi, great fighters, attacked them. There was a fierce battle which the cannibals lost, and their survivors fled inland and were seen no more. I often wondered about the Wakamba and their sharpened teeth.

1928

Between 1924 and 1928 I did not keep a diary, but was fully occupied with building up the farm at Nderit, racing and occasional trips back to Anstie. My son Robin was born in this period, a half-brother for Heather and Callum.

The pioneers of Kenya had left their home-lands for various reasons, some for their country's good, some for domestic unhappiness – most from a sense of adventure, and among these I had many friends. Lord Delamere was the leader of the Europeans. He was wise, brave, and possessed a great charm, and a wit which could be, and sometimes was, biting. His beautiful first wife, the daughter of the Earl of Enniskillen, faithfully followed his safaris and helped him establish a home which, though not luxurious, was the first to create certain standards of living and of European culture in a wild and beautiful, exciting and enticing land which was not without its dangers. She died quite young. His two brothers-in-law, Galbraith and Berkeley Cole acquired huge tracts of empty, fertile country where they established houses, cattle and sheep. Ewart Grogan, a handsome Irish man living in South Africa, agreed to walk from the Cape to Cairo, surveying a route for a possible railway which Cecil Rhodes wished to build. His beautiful fiancee met him in Cairo, they married, made their home in Kenya, and founded a remarkably good-looking, clever and hardworking family.

Denys Finch-Hatton, of the Winchelsea family, a famous white hunter and one of the central figures in *Out of Africa*, was a delightful companion, witty and charming – he was also extremely strong, and once lifted a small, elderly Ford car out of a muddy ditch, setting it on its wheels again. He could tear in half a double pack of cards. His love affair with Baroness Blixen is now well known – they were both kind, civilized, clever and gifted people. Tanya (that was her real name, not Karen) Blixen was very special – brave, beautiful, and clever; a true friend and loved by all who knew her – she had a sad life, but wrote some remarkable books, after emigrating to America. I knew her very well for many years, and, like all my friends, was devoted to her. Her father, Isak Dineson, was an author, and her brother, Tommy, won the VC while serving in Hitler's war with the Canadian Army. Tommy was a great gentleman.

Lord Francis Scott, of the Buccleugh family, was one of the builders of Kenya. He and his beautiful wife entertained a lot in their big house. His niece, Lady Alice Scott, married Prince Henry, Duke of Gloucester. The natives called her memsaab Maua, the Flower Lady, and indeed, she did look like a beautiful gentle flower.

Lord Erroll, handsome and amusing, was another of my friends. Silver Jane, a pilot, was the first woman to fly solo from England to Kenya. She had a silver coloured plane and a silver flying suit. Beryl Markham flew solo from East to West over the Atlantic establishing several records. She had a special gift for horses, and a rather long and complicated native name meaning 'The one who never falls off a horse'.

There were many, many others in our circle of friends, mostly hard-working stock farmers, who loved Kenya and their natives; Kenya was, in those days, a 'happy ship'.

17 JUNE

I've had two lovely peaceful days here at Anstie with Father. Today we went over the kennels which he has built on land he bought for the Surrey Union Hunt. There are some very good hounds there in splendid condition. Farmer, the huntsman, is rightly proud of them.

Some are going to Aldershot for the show. Father has improved the pack out of all knowledge since he became Master of the Hunt. Farmer burst into praise for him all the way from the kennels to the car. I agreed with every word he said, but found it almost embarrassing.

25 JUNE

On board *Rajputana, en route* Port Said: I had a beastly journey in a couchette (doing it cheap but never again) with two men who were extremely kind. In the night a party of drunken sailors went roaring and singing down the corridor, trying (hopefully) the doors of the carriages. Ours, at any rate, was locked! One of my stable companions lent £12 to a complete stranger who vanished with it. Poor little chap was fearfully upset.

In Marseilles the gendarmes are protected from the dangerous heat and inhabitants by white topees, dark glasses, huge revolvers *and* batons! They stand about under the trees looking rather sheepish.

We are due at Port Said tomorrow, Tuesday; we were hung up by fog just out of Marseilles and lost a certain amount of time, but are making up for it now.

29 JUNE

Jerusalem, Allenby Hotel. Just arrived. The journey this morning was through the most barren and desolate-looking country – pale rocky hills, terraced, though I saw nothing growing. What a dreadful trek it must have been for the poor Virgin Mary and the Baby, through those hot white hills!

I have been nearly killed with sightseeing. I had to take a guide and first went to Bethlehem where I saw the spot where Our Lord was born, the spot on which stood His manger, silver stars, silver images, silver saints, Greek altars, Armenian altars, RC altars, the spot on which they yearly fight, the spot from which the shepherds saw the star, the hole down which it disappeared, and a cemetery. Back to Jerusalem; there I saw the Mount of Olives, the garden in which Judas cast away the thirty pieces of silver, the olive tree from which he hung himself, a footprint of Our Lord, the spot from which He wept over Jerusalem, the damage caused by the last earthquake, the dome of the Mosque of Omar, the roof of the building near which stood the courts Our Lord was judged in, and at last, at last, a quarter of an hour's glory – the sunset.

Even the guide couldn't spoil it, though he still couldn't stop talking. The lights came twinkling on, one by one, as dusk crept over the city and across the Dead Sea. The mountains of Moab changed from fierce hot red to violent smoky grey to a great dark wall.

30 JUNE

The hotel people tried to persuade me to follow in the footsteps of all the other tourists, through Nazareth and Tiberias to Haifa; but I think I might murder the guide if I have to do any more sightseeing. So I went (*still* with Tewfik, the guide) over the mountains of Moab and into Transjordan. What a drive and what country! Hot white mountains, fearful gorges and chasms, heaped masses of brown hills, outcrops of rock, and the road winds for four hours.

We passed a wedding party on their way to fetch the bride; a half circle of chanting, bowing Arabs moved forward led by the bridegroom, who danced wildly in front of them, going backwards, brandishing a walking stick. Behind the men came the bridegroom's children, on mules covered with flowers, and behind them the women. At last we arrived at the top of the mountains of Moab: high desert country with tufts of grass growing here and there. One or two Bedouin, long guns slung across their shoulders, herded flocks of splendid sheep and good goats. Sometimes we passed a Bedouin encampment, a few dark tents very low and close to the ground. At last arrived at Amman at a typical Greek pub; personnel consists of proprietor and Georges – waiter, housemaid, bath-boy, boots, all in one. But he got through his duties all right by missing them all out except waiting.

I saw one of the Englishmen here and he very kindly gave me a letter to the officer commanding the Transjordania Frontier Force at Jerka [*British troops were stationed in the country at this time*]. So I went there after lunch. Waving my letter I marched into the second-in-command's office and in five minutes we found a mutual friend in Kenya – Crewe-Reade! He was so kind; took me round half the three hundred horses, nearly all pure Arab and in perfect condition. Jerka is on the edge of the desert; red hills, rolling to the horizon in front of it and all around except where the road goes to Amman.

I met Major Shute, the OC, later; everyone was so kind and very interested in Kenya. There is a Circassian village below the camp; the rank and file of the Frontier Force is composed of Circassians [*light-skinned, blue-eyed people originally from southern Russia*]. It is odd to see a Russian peasant walking about Arabia, dressed in high astrakhan cap, long dark coat belted at the waist and soft, half-length boots. The Circassians have been here a long time; there is a belt of their villages all along this country.

1 JULY

How I would love to trek in this country. The drive back last night should have been so wonderful, all the desert misty in the moonlight; but it was ruined by being hurtled along in a shut car with nothing to look at but the back of the fat Tewfik.

2 JULY

Back to Jerusalem today. On the way I photographed a fine Bedouin with his sheep and goats and children. I gave them some money which they didn't expect or want, but were glad to have. The pretty little Bedouin girls have straggly hair and tattooed faces and long dark blue clothes. The sheep have long fleeces – hair, not wool, white and fine.

The Dead Sea is just an ordinary-looking inland sea with a fresh breeze blowing off it. The correct thing to do is to bathe in it, but I did not bother. The Jordan valley is hot, being 1400 feet below sea-level (according to Tewfik). *How* guides ruin atmosphere! But one's got to have them for the first time, at any rate, to keep beggars and other guides away.

In the Mosque of Omar it went something like this: 'This mosque, lady, is built on the site of Solomon's temple. You see great paving all round.'

(We're crossing it, so presumably I can see it.) 'We enter by this door, here, lady. You see stone on which Abraham tried to sacrifice his son. Here, lady, you see supposed footprint of Mohammed. Here, lady, you see supposed fingerprints of Angel Gabriel. If you will look up . . . if you will now step this way . . .' etc. etc.

It is a glorious place, dark and still – some beautiful mosaic work which has been defaced, great shining pillars, curious carved brass screens round the rock which were put there by the crusaders when it was a church. I wanted to go there again alone, but hadn't time.

The Jews' Wailing Wall is very interesting; a narrow street with a thick mass of worshippers, men one end and women another, chanting age-old songs, mourning for the Captivities (two thousand years ago!), rocking to and fro, beating their heads against the wall, kissing it; then walking up and down murmuring prayers. Old women, all shawls, young women in tawdry jewels, babies in arms, men of every age and description, priests with long robes and large fur-edged caps and hungry, lethal fleas. Too late I found the weapon against fleas: a few drops of *eau-de-cologne*.

8 OCTOBER

Kenya. We've had an invasion by wild dogs which ate nineteen cattle in a week before we defeated them. Today the Delameres brought the Prince of Wales [*later King Edward VIII*] to lunch. He is staying with them, which is a great honour. He is the easiest person in the world to get on with, once he's out of the public eye; cheerful and amusing and apparently entirely unselfconscious.

9 OCTOBER

Today Boy had to go to Gilgil early to arrange the reception HRH was going to hold after golf. It was in the club dance *banda* with all Gilgil and Elmenteita standing in stiff clumps against the walls while HRH and Lord D. went round and talked; and what he finds to say to them all I can't imagine. Of course, he does it marvellously. Margaret Collier distinguished herself by trying to make him shake hands with her dog – boy!

1930

15 MARCH

I have had to leave Kenya again and take Heather [*my daughter*] to England.
When we passed Aden all the hills were covered in green – an amazing

95

sight! No one in our ship, not even Grogan or Mr Bulpit [*one of Kenya's veterans*] had ever seen it before. Where has the seed hidden and kept alive all these years; perhaps centuries? The ship's carpenter said to Mrs Wybrandts, 'We shan't be able to sing "the barren rocks of Aden" no more – it'll 'ave to be "Coom inter the garden, Maud"!'

8 APRIL

Father met me at Marseilles with Admiral Candy, the captain of his yacht, *Anne of Anstie*. They had a fearful passage through the Bay of Biscay, and were all sick except the steward, who was too frightened! All the crew are ex-naval men; some have been in destroyers for fourteen years without a qualm of a gulp – but the *Anne* defeated them!

We went one day to San Remo – and what a grand feeling it is to put to sea in your own ship, go anywhere, stop anywhere, do anything you like. She bucks about in the smallest sea like a fresh horse – she seems almost alive.

30 MAY

Luxor. Started on a camel at 5.30 this morning, with a boy on a donkey, and another unlucky one on foot; he had to run all the way. We went first to the Temple of Karnak, where I sat in the hall of pillars, absorbed in their huge, towering, ancient monuments. Complete silence except for the myriad birds who flutter and twitter about in the great court where who knows what grand and mysterious ceremonies took place in the days of the Pharaohs. At last I went back to the camel, and we started for the Coptic monastery. My lazy camel shuffled along, grumbling, at the slowest jog-trot. We went through acres of cultivated fields, growing maize and other food stuffs – I saw bundles of lucerne on donkeys' backs, but none growing.

Then on again into the desert, over the ridges and through the gullies, and at last I left my camel and the boy and walked up a hill and sat there alone, looking at the red cliffs and the waste of stones and sand – and the desert seemed wonderful. I forgot the time and myself and everything till the boy came clumping up the hill to look for me, thinking I was lost. Then we went to the Coptic monastery, passing a funeral party on the way, the mourners walking to and fro and wailing. In the cool and simple monastery – said to be eighteen hundred years old – I rested on a native bed during the midday heat until it was time to go. Back to the hotel by four o'clock, tired and stiff – I have not ridden a camel since Somaliland, six years ago!

31 MAY

All night mosquitoes and sandflies feasted on me so that I had very little sleep and got up at 5.30, covered in bites from head to foot. Across the Nile by boat to where a pony and a donkey were waiting for me and the boy. We took the tamarisk-bordered road for the Valley of the Kings. Then turned off up a white, hot, winding path which goes on and on through tremendous red cliffs; a grand and desolate place, towering pinnacles and walls of rock, great boulders scattered everywhere, no living thing to be seen. At the Place of the Tombs I got off and an old man came and took me into the tomb of Rameses I; we went down lighted by two candles into the bowels of the earth, in almost complete darkness. Every inch of every wall is covered in frescoes depicting the history of the King, and the great pillars supporting the roof bear large pictures of Rameses with various gods. Most of the mummies and their treasures have gone to Cairo, and the tombs are empty. Each one rambles about with many chambers and alcoves; every inch is decorated. What a work carried out by patient and cunning hands how many thousands of years ago!

The second tomb has a platform running across a great pit, which made me shiver. Again every part of the wall was covered in decoration, the colours as bright and fresh now, I suppose, as when they were first put on. The same utter darkness and the same curious underground smell everywhere. I was glad to get back to the light.

The boy insisted on my seeing one more burial place on the way home; that of a queen, where lines of red arches are built against a wall of red rock. The frescoes have been mutilated; the guide said by her brother, who was angry because sometimes she wore a ceremonial beard and liked to pass as a man, and 'went with' another brother. I thought Egyptian rulers always married their sisters, but I was tired, and it all sounded very complicated.

One of the most extraordinary things I saw today – or ever – was a snake charmer; he was jogging along on a donkey with his small son behind him and we said 'Good morning' to each other; and he said 'Snake charmer'. I thought it might be interesting and got off my pony (with a heart-whirr which passed off, thank heavens) and the old man walked about praying and calling in a loud voice – then dived his hand into the dust and straw on the road and picked out a scorpion! This he brought close to me to show me the sting in the tail; he held it and turned it about for a while, and finally let it go. Then he went to a wall full of cracks and holes, still talking loudly. Presently he saw something in a hole and called and prayed insistently and loudly, telling the snake to come out. I saw a small yellow head darting about in the hole; the charmer still talked and the snake seemed to hear him and listen. He put his hand into the hole, snatched it out and went on talking. This happened three times; at last he thrust in his hand again and whipped out a struggling snake by the tail and threw it on the ground. The snake rustled away but he caught it and held it behind the head and gently pressed its body, talking all the while and quietening it. The snake was bewildered and angry at first; it reared up and spread its hood, but did not try to strike. At last it became quite quiet and the charmer put it round his neck, but always held it behind the head. He had two snakes and wanted to put them round my arms. Scared as I was, I let him, while he held their bodies. Then the old man wanted to put them round my neck, but that was beyond me. A snake's body is warm and dry, and moves wonderfully in your hand.

The old man at last went away with the snake draped round his neck. Poor little frightened snake; they are no worse than other animals, really – though I dread them and they fill me with horror. They are beautiful when they move, and pitifully frightened when caught, like any other wild thing. It is uncanny how these charmers speak certain words from the Koran to call any wild snake from its home, and the snake *must* obey. They say it is hereditary, and that they had the power over snakes and other reptiles given them by a certain Sultan Suleiman very long ago. Sultan Suleiman is really King Solomon, who knew animal languages and is the sort of patron saint of snake charmers. More or less tame snakes such as the Indians keep and play to I can understand, but this African affair is a mystery.

1 JUNE

Last night I went on the Nile in a little sailing boat; it was exquisite – soft, cool air and peace.

The hotel manager told me of a snake charmer called Moussa, and I sent for him this evening. We walked to a small, enclosed garden, and there he took off most of his clothes to show me he had no snakes up his sleeve, and then walked along the narrow paths calling them. Again and again I heard '*Sa'i'd, Suleiman*' ('Help me, Solomon') and '*Sita*'. He said, 'No snakes here' (they smell them), and walked on; then he stopped by some dry, fallen palm branches. The chanting changed to a quick, imperative tone and he beat on the ground with his stick: '*Sa'i'd, Suleiman! Sa'i'd, Suleiman!*' I saw a coil among the branches; in flashed his hand and he stood up holding a large and very angry cobra. It bit him and there was blood on his arm, but it had no effect on him at all. He put the cobra on the ground, where it moved about with outspread hood and darting tongue; several times it dived away into the bushes, but Moussa caught it, brought it back and slung it round his neck. 'Moussa grandfather of snake, snake no hurt Moussa!'

Then he put it on the ground and . . . hypnotized it? I suppose so. He spoke some words, beat the ground beside it, and left it. It remained absolutely motionless. I said, 'Wake it up!' Moussa spoke again, and instantly it was moving about with its hood up and its tongue darting. He spoke again and it became still. Mustapha (the boy) photographed us.

Then he found a scorpion and let it strike at his thumb three or four times – it too had no effect on him. Later he found another snake; very long – three or four feet – with a yellow belly and dust-coloured back. It bit him savagely again and again, whipping about in his hand and striking at everything within reach.

We took the two snakes out into the road where the light was good, and Moussa spoke to them until they were quite still; only the smaller snake's head moved a little. Here another photograph was taken. I have never seen anything like it before. The odd thing is that I *could* hold them – I dread snakes, and yet I didn't mind. It was a most amazing experience.

This evening I went again on the Nile; the young moon hung in a sea of rose pink clouds; the sky was orange, amber, pale green, violet; the great cliffs stark and black. The water went whispering past the boat; complete silence, complete peace. Tomorrow I go; but I must come back: 'He who drinks the waters of the Nile will always return.'

2 JUNE

I went to the Colossi of Memnon, which stand in fields of maize and roots; and then to another temple, beautiful and lonely.

These people have bad manners – quite unintentional, but it infuriates me. All the children and most of the grown-ups anywhere near Luxor ask for baksheesh; a result of tourism. All peasants have natural manners; but of course nothing spoils them so quickly as crowds of casual trippers.

3 JUNE

Cairo. Staying at the Continental; comfortable and expensive, though the food might be better – it is quite good, but not the best.

Went to the Museum and saw the things found in Tutankhamun's tomb. What luxury and beauty; where has all that art and skill gone? Such jewels, such lavish use of gold. I saw many mummies and was so sorry for them; taken from their own peaceful and splendid resting places and laid in rows on shelves for anyone to stare at. There is a grand statue of Amenophis II with an impressive hatchet face, full of strength and power.

I visited the pyramids and the Sphinx later. Hoardings and trippers, screaming women bumping about on camels in pain and misery. Photographers and fortune tellers. But nothing can disturb the serene dignity of the mysterious Sphinx.

16 JUNE

Back in Mombasa.

1931

Zanzibar. I got here on the 13th in the *Ayamonte*, a boat of 500 tons with an English captain and mate. The boat was perfectly clean, but the heat below and the continuous smell of curry, natives, engine oil and hot iron nearly defeated me. However I was not sick. We arrived on a lovely still evening, with the low-lying, wooded shore glowing in the sunset, the lighthouse pricking through the darkness and strings of lights glittering round the harbour. I was met by Harry Stedman [*who was, many years later, hacked to death by the Mau Mau*], who has asked some friends of his to put me up; people are so kind here.

Each day he has taken me out somewhere – first to Chukwani, to bathe. The palace was built by Seyyid Ali, and a hundred yards in front, just across the bay, stands a little pavilion built for one of his wives, a beautiful Circassian. There are some fine old baths of various sizes with endless little rooms and niches; the walls delicately grooved and the high ceilings domed.

To Marahubi, the Lily-pond Palace – most lovely! Huge pillars stand about, outlining the old terraces; there are stone-edged pools, full of purple water lilies. The sea whispers beside the walls. A dream of a place. Everything is in ruins: creepers with enormous leaves grow up the walls, trees flourish everywhere. It was built by Seyyid Bargash, the ruler of Zanzibar, the islands and the coast. While my grandfather, Sir Leopold Heath, was stationed in Zanzibar, hunting slavers' ships, Seyyid Bargash gave him a knife in a beautiful sheath, for his '*youngest* son', my father. I still have it.

At Mbweni there is a haunted house, built by Sir John Kirk and afterwards lived in by Miss Thackeray, a missionary. She built a small church, and is buried in the churchyard. Near the church are some huts where live a few very old people, brought over, they told me, in slave ships as children. When I found this village the old people were delighted to see me and I was regaled with coconut milk while they clustered round and chattered. They kept the little church swept, clean and cared for; their families are buried in the graveyard. They were all Christians, and enchanting.

I went to the Museum and saw letters and account books of Livingstone's and the great drums of the Mweni Mkuu, who were the ancient rulers of the island before the Arabs of Oman came. The Mweni Mkuu claimed to be descended from those Persians who first settled here many centuries ago. The drums are about four feet high, carved from a single tree trunk, and finely decorated all over. The skins have been taken off; before this was done the drums used to beat, it is said, by themselves, three days before the death of any Sultan; and during the bombardment of Zanzibar by the British in the 1890s they sounded all the time.

Very beautiful china was sent to the Sultans from time to time by the Emperors of China, with whom there was a steady trade.

I went today to see the haunted palace at Dunga; it is just a heap of ruins surrounded by a broken-down wall. A row of police huts with red tin roofs has been built just in front of it, so that it is almost impossible to see anything of the ruins. They say the mortar for the gate posts of the old house was mixed with human blood – this makes a house lucky. Behind one of the walls was found a well half full of human skeletons.

Dr Spurrier, the museum curator, told me that he had slept there once, as a dare, and woke to see a dark figure in a burnous, with the hood up, sitting reading at a table. It dissolved after a while and reappeared in another part of the room, where it stayed a few moments before disappearing completely. Another ghost seen there is a woman in black followed by a large black dog. The Mweni Mkuu who built the house was a very cruel man with complete power over his subjects and slaves.

19 SEPTEMBER

I've been wandering about old Zanzibar town. The streets twist and turn among the tall white houses and are so narrow in some places that there is only room for one person to walk along them at a time. Sometimes you come upon an old graveyard, or a walled-in garden. And the bazaar! Here are tiny booths selling vegetables and chillies, curries, papuri cakes, beads, kekoys and bits of jewellery. A blacksmith's shop is dark and smoky. A pawnbroker sells amber, chests, old coats and trousers; a silversmith charm cases, bangles, rings, incense sprayers, copper and brass jars, jugs, trays and coffee pots. Everywhere filthy children tumble under your feet and beautiful white Muscat donkeys carrying loads trot by. The coffee seller walks along with his large brass jug in one hand, jingling two cups in a rhythm. There are many Muscat Arabs with huge, floppy turbans. They wear long kanzus and belts with big curved knives in splendid silver scabbards. They are small men, almost white, bearded, handsome and aloof. They seem too free and savage for tame Zanzibar.

22 SEPTEMBER

Pemba – 'The Green Isle'. Harry had to come here on business and very kindly allowed me to come too. The shore of the bay stretches around, blue with morning mist, and tacking across the harbour go the dhows and fishing boats with their sails bellying. The District Officer did some telephoning, and as a result I motored north for some miles; then, at the appointed place, found a charming white donkey with a Pemba native, and off I went into the forest alone! The divine feeling of wandering away on new paths, in country I've never seen before, with no one to talk, and only a native going in front to show the way; perfect quiet and peace. The forest is very lovely, with groves of clove trees and palms; big mango trees, sometimes making an avenue along the track; little hills and little valleys, a few native huts, the ground swept clean all round, and charming, well-mannered people, all smiles and greetings.

After a time we came to Pujini, to the ruins of the fortress built several centuries ago by a chief they call Mkame Mdume – he who milks males – notorious for his frightful cruelty. He had the stone to build Pujini brought from several miles away, forcing the porters to shuffle along the ground on their buttocks, carrying the stones on their heads. Not long ago a man sitting in the ruins saw a line of ghostly porters carrying their loads up the steps to the central square. I saw no ghosties, but the place is very eerie, dark and silent. In immensely thick walls you can see where the old china plates used to be that were let into the stones for decoration. People have dug them out and stolen them – I wouldn't dare! The jungle has grown up all round, and most of the buildings have disappeared under creepers and bushes. There are two old wells with flights of steps going down to them – one, I believe, was the subterranean chamber of one of Mkame Mdume's wives. The sea once came up to the walls, but now it is nearly an hour's walk away.

On the way back some kind natives gave me a drink from a coconut, and very welcome it was.

At last we came out onto the main road, and there was the car, so I had to say goodbye to Hamisi the donkey, and the boy, and go on to Weti where the ship was.

23 SEPTEMBER

Left Weti for Wesha. We landed on a white beach, and walked about three miles, through bush and over sandflats and plains of short grass, to a place where mangroves grow in the sea. Here we had to wade, with clouds of starving mosquitoes feasting on us, till we came to a ruined castle with fine tombs beside it and the usual great encircling walls. In the sea the boys picked up two beads, which might have come from Persia a thousand years ago!

28 SEPTEMBER

Back in Zanzibar. I've had several rides, and went once to the house at Mbweni. I visited the church and found some of the very old women who

Right: Genesta's parents, Sarah and
Cuthbert Heath, in 1904
Cuthbert Heath on the grouse moors in
Scotland

Right: Sarah Caroline Gore Heath
(née Gambier) – a portrait by Paul
Chabas

The opening meet of the Surrey Union Foxhounds at Anstie Grange. The top picture shows Cuthbert Heath with the hounds

Genesta with her parents

Right: Genesta as a nurse at Anstie

Below: Archery at Anstie during the First World War. Genesta is on the left

Patients at Anstie. Cuthbert Heath stands in the centre

Right: The Anstie
ambulance

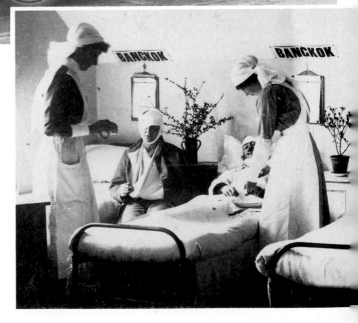

Above: Leopold Heath with
machine-gun section, Surrey
Yeomanry

Right: Nursing at Hill Hospital,
Farnham. Doreen Gore-Brown is
on the left and Genesta on the
right

had been brought over in slave ships so long ago they can hardly remember it. They were so sweet, making a little 'reverence', between a bow and a curtsey, telling me their names with great pride – Marion and Laura and others; one was sweeping out the church and another sweeping the path. A charming old man held my pony; the place is like a little village in England full of very old people, but black instead of white.

The church is lovely inside, dim and peaceful. The churches here are beautiful in a simple way. The cathedral was built by Bishop Steere and his freed slaves on the site of the old slave market; the altar stands on the spot once occupied by the whipping-post. This church at Mbweni has a graveyard where all the old slaves, freed and baptized, were buried, and the few survivors sit quietly in the sun waiting till their turn comes.

In front of the house of Mbweni is an old tree to whose trunk is fastened a slave yoke with the chain still attached. The yoke was a piece of forked wood, as thick as a man's leg, which slaves, captured by other tribes and sold to Arab slavers, wore round their necks during the long, agonizing trek to the coast.

On a spit of land above the sea is the ruin of a Portuguese chapel, inside which is a flat stone where nowadays witchdoctors put their charms and spells. The very best and most expensive witchdoctors on the whole east coast are trained on the island of Pemba.

I am sorry to say goodbye to lovely Zanzibar, but so very glad to be going home! Today I leave for Nairobi.

14 NOVEMBER

Lord Delamere died yesterday, Friday the 13th, at Loresho, his house outside Nairobi. A grand fighter and a fine diplomat, he made Kenya and kept it going through every difficulty. We shall miss him terribly in every way. He was buried today at Soysambu. The Masai have always revered Delamere, and a great many of them came to his funeral carrying spears and shining from head to toe with red mud. The elders wore karosses [*skin cloaks*] and carried sticks, to show their age and dignity.

1932

12 MARCH

Travels. After a beastly night in the train we arrived at Kisumu, *en route* for a holiday in England, to catch the Imperial Airways machine tomorrow.

13 MARCH

We left in the flying boat at 1.15, roaring through the water – a lift, and you are soaring over it. The trees and houses shrink away, and you fly steadily along at 5000 feet with the world at your feet. I must say Uganda looks a most unalluring place – red earth and thick bush, a sort of banana country. The lake [*Victoria*] is spattered with islands. We landed at Kampala for lunch (there wasn't enough to eat), and flew off again. The country changed to scrubby bush and in time we reached the Nile, passing along over its shining ribbon, into more desert. We reached Juba at 5.45, very weary. The seats are comfortable, and the cabin steward looks after you beautifully, taking endless trouble, but the noise and vibration are tiring. There was a nice little hotel at Juba, and two lion cubs tumbling about on the hot sand.

14 MARCH

Took off in a different plane at 5.45 as a spectacular dawn was breaking, and flew over miles of green sudd [*floating plant life*] and small herds of elephant, coming down at Malakae at 10.15 to eat eggs and bacon in the shade of a tin hut and in whirling clouds of dust. This is Shilluk country; they are rather like Masai, but with goat-hair coiffures, spears and tattoos. We left Malakae at 11.15, flying over more miles of sand and bush to Kosti, where we lay hot and exhausted in the shade of a mud hut, smoking (it's not allowed in the machine) and panting. Away again at 3.15 and reached Khartoum at 5.30, almost too tired to think. Here there is a good hotel and a certain degree of civilization.

15 MARCH

Off to the aerodrome and away at 5.45 into the sunrise. Over flat grey deserts, the engine going worse and worse, one tired propeller barely turning, flames and sparks shooting out of the exhaust. We limped into Atbara at 8.15 a.m. and had breakfast while they disconnected one cylinder. Away again at 9.45. But in a quarter of an hour we turned round and came back to Atbara, and there found very many things wrong. So we sat and waited, while the captain and crew sweated and worked.

16 MARCH

A message came last night to say we needn't start till five, and in the middle of the night our splendid pilot had walked all the way back here, having worked on the engine all day long, to tell us he couldn't get the trouble right and we might not get away at all today. So we must go by train to catch our boat at Wadi Halfa. I'm not sorry; I get less air-minded every hour – very tired, and not too brave.

17 MARCH

Left last night in a good sleeper, arrived at Wadi Halfa in the morning, and boarded the little steamer. Presently we were sailing down the Nile between black mountains; belts of cultivation; rocky hills crowned with ancient castles, Nubian, Byzantine, and Roman; mud villages, temples, statues and acacia groves.

At night we tied up at Abu Simbel, a temple running back deep into the rock, the entrance guarded by four magnificent statues of Rameses II. The temple ends in a lovely shrine, and the altar is a block of stone which once every year is touched by the sun; round the walls sit guardian gods and kings. [*Many years later the Aswan Dam was built here, and the entire temple, with·its statues, was rebuilt in a higher place.*]

20 MARCH

I took Boy to Karnak, but it had been ruined for me – a trolley line runs through the Hall of Pillars, and the place rings with the voices of guides and Americans. All the lovely peace and silence I found here before have gone, and all the dignity and grandeur too. But last time I was here it was midsummer, and far too hot for tourists. The Temple of Luxor was a little better, and as we sat there in the evening the sun set, while a priest called the muezzin from a minaret outside the temple walls.

21 MARCH

We crossed the Nile and went to the Colossus of Memphis. Boy was delighted with the wheat and barley, and the waterwheel method of irrigation, but the temples meant nothing to him.

On the Nile this evening in a small boat, peace and beauty, golden water, the distant hills in a golden haze, palms in silhouette, and, against the grey Libyan hills, two white sails like the wings of a bird.

AUGUST

Holiday nearly over, money all gone! We've bought about fifteen beasts, mostly Guernseys; met lots of charming people, done some racing and had a grand time. We went on our last night to see Martin Johnson's film *Congorilla*, part of which he made on Nderit. It is excellent and our flamingoes look most lovely.

27 AUGUST

Back on the farm again. We flew from London to Paris, found the train and installed ourselves for the long journey to Brindisi. We left on the night of the 17th and woke up next day in Switzerland. At Milan we were allowed out for lunch; the food was excellent. All the food and tips are provided by Imperial Airways, which makes everything very easy; you merely say, '*Je suis un voyageur Impérial*' and the best of everything is yours, without the usual forest of outstretched hands.

At last we reached Brindisi, and I had a bath provided by Imperial Airways, which really thinks of everything! After breakfast we went to the seaplane which was lying in the harbour, only too thankful to get into a clean aeroplane once more! The train journey certainly gives one a taste for flying. Our cameras were locked up going over Brindisi in case we should want to take photos of the horrible place and [*Mussolini's*] fortifications! In due course we were flying over Greece; the hills looked bare, brown and scrubby – not the sort of place which would be chosen to live in by nymphs and satyrs with any taste. At Alexandria we got into a train again, and arrived at Cairo tired, dirty, and cross.

At Cairo we changed to an Argosy, very old and shaky. We met Donald Drew, who had been private pilot to Loewenstein, and was piloting the machine L. disappeared from, over the North Sea. A mystery which has never been solved. L. was a multi-millionaire, he had his enemies. Drew and a grand old prospector called Battling Johnson shared a carriage from Milan to Brindisi, Drew, watching the moon rising over the sea, said to Johnson – 'Look at that, did you ever see anything so lovely?' Johnson heaved a big sigh and said, 'Yes, lovely; just like Blackpool!'

After further delays we finally arrived back at Nderit, and I thought I'd never seen anything so lovely as the lake, or so charming as the house. I heard later the servants were so worried at our non-appearance that they had asked the police to try to find out where we were, and what had happened.

1933

JANUARY

At sea in the German ship *Usambara*, second class, very comfortable; and oh, how cheap! As we left the quay, people were given paper streamers to throw; with loud and hearty cries they threw them to the people on shore. The band on deck played martial tunes. Everyone called 'Goodbye' and '*Auf wiedersehen*' – and nothing happened. This lasted for a quarter of an hour before we finally got away.

I am going to Aden, and from there will take whatever steamer the gods will send to take me for a good trip somewhere – perhaps to Abyssinia again.

Today I heard a high and piping voice say, 'This is a naice ship. There is a taitled lady in the third class, and a taitled lady in the second class'!

8 FEBRUARY

My luck! At Aden I was told that the interior of Abyssinia is so disturbed and the people so out of hand that I should never be allowed to travel there; so I picked up all my luggage and trailed back on board again till Port Sudan, and thought I'd either try to get a boat to Jeddah from there, or else go on to Suez and trek to my dreamed-of Petra, that 'rose-red city half as old as time'.

It was, of course, too good to be true. I got cables from the farm to say poor Boy is ill and I must go home! So now I shall go from Port Sudan to Khartoum and fly back on Tuesday.

Yesterday I went for a heavenly ride in the desert, on a camel, with a wild fuzzy-wuzzy [*Sudanese native*] on another. The air was so still, and the wind smelt of sand and sea. The alluring red hills are too far away to reach in two hours. The fuzzy made me stop while he slid off his camel and said his prayers – why can't we say ours as unselfconsciously as that?

This morning I went to see Suakin – an amazing place, huge and deserted in great encircling mud walls. Large crumbling houses with Turkish lattice windows. Suakin proper is on an island; you go over the bridge and find yourself facing a high white wall in which is set a gateway with two old guns on either side. The town is rambling and twisty – lovely windows and doors, some fine buildings, many roofless, and hardly a soul there. There are no white people at all, and very few natives. An Indian showed me over the house which was Kitchener's – with large rooms overlooking the sea. Leave for Khartoum tonight.

Khartoum. That was a nice journey from Port Sudan – twenty-five hours at about 12 m.p.h. in the train, through flat, empty desert all the way! We went through the hills at night, so couldn't see them. Not much food and not much sleep.

I found General Butler at the Grand, who was very kind. The next evening I went in the Butlers' launch to Omdurman, to pick him up after polo, and then down the river (all golden ripples) until we came to General Gordon's boat, the one which carried his last dispatches to the relief party; she is kept just as she was, with a high, old-fashioned funnel, the decks protected with fortified sleepers.

Nothing exciting happened in the flight next day, except that we came down to one lonely elephant in the sudd who splashed away, then suddenly turned, spread his ears and glared up at us. He'd have charged us if he could, although he was frightened. Brave old elephant.

Boy, recovered, met me at Nairobi. We had flown over the farm and circled the house. Thrills for everyone; I could see Robin waving a curtain at us. It is lovely to be back.

19 MARCH

We started at seven one morning from the farm for a riding safari. Our horses, Juanita and Too Soon, were very full of themselves in the cold morning air.

We rode across country; the car went by road, and miraculously found us every night. It had the driver, Kebe; two *saices* to look after the horses; food and a few spare clothes. No tents; we either stayed with friends or slept out. The boys slept in the car – much safer than us. When we reached the camp each night, a big fire, *leleshwa* leaves beds, sherry and dinner were all ready for us.

The second evening I caught a trout, which we ate for breakfast today at 6 a.m. *What* a good trout, cooked perfectly by the versatile Kebe. We left this place of thorns, and rode through the freezing dawn across the lovely plains, frightening dozens of herds of zebra, ostriches, kongoni, waterbuck and one staid old warthog. There are caves here in which Kikuyu used to sleep until one night lions found and killed them. The plains were lovely in the morning sun as we rode along, passing the head of Ol Boloset lake till we came to a belt of trees under the mountains.

Then down to the plain where years ago the Purgo Masai killed most of the Damatt Masai. We stopped for an hour or two with Pat Ward, then on towards Ndaragua. Just before you cross the Lolmerigo there is a clump of olive trees, and here the Purgo caught the last survivors of the fleeing Damatt, and finished them off. Our camp is in a dell on the slopes of Ndaragua, sheltered and charming.

Oh what a night. It began with us sitting peacefully by the fire with books, cigarettes, sherry and gramophone. But then both horses broke their halters and ran away, and after being caught ran away again!

The following day we left early, riding over very dull country, mostly black cotton soil full of deep cracks. The hill we were aiming for never seemed to come any closer and we crawled along, hot and tired. At last we reached the Adairs' house; they have a fine view up the Ngobit Valley to Satima. Hundreds of feet below winds the road, and you feel on top of the world.

23 MARCH

Next day to the old, lovely camp with the snows of Kenya showing between two hills, the river below and the hills behind us, fresh green grass, a herd of heifers moving slowly past, cropping and munching, a great fire and a bed of leaves, stars gleaming, crickets cheeping and a hyrax croaking – what more could anyone want?

25 MARCH

The hills seemed very close as we rode over the soft grass among big trees beside the river. Then slowly climbed till the valley was below us, green and soft, shaded with big acacia trees, with here and there the pink of a Cape chestnut.

The trees continued onto the plain and gave us their shade as we rode. The whole of the Delamere land is now grazed by Kikuyu squatters.

A few days later we reached someone's kind and hospitable house. [*Travelling haphazardly in Kenya in the old days, anyone could go to any house and receive instant hospitality. Native servants were delighted to welcome people – guest rooms were always kept ready, and our boys entertained by our host's servants.*] There we all rested, including the horses and the boys. When we moved on, it was over plains of black whistling thorn where red colobus monkeys lived and played in the few trees, and there was endless game, all harmless – buck and zebra, giraffe and ostriches. An enchanted journey. At one point we had to cross a river on a narrow bridge. The first person got safely over, leading his horse, and I started on foot, leading mine – but suddenly she slipped and fell off the bridge into the river! She seemed to turn a somersault in mid-air before my horrified eyes, but landed on her feet and had a long, long drink. At last she emerged from the water and came quietly to hand. I climbed onto the soaking saddle and on we went.

Next day, down a lovely forest road, then over the river till we stopped under a tree for a rest. There we met the car, and devoured a large tin of strawberries with cream and sugar.

On we went, crossing another river, and got off for another rest, under a marvellous tree, but unfortunately every insect in Kenya also thought it was a marvellous tree, so the rest was not as peaceful as it might have been. On again for many more miles, and my poor horse got very tired. At last we reached Freddie Guest's house – oh, luxury! A bath and a soft bed to sleep in.

Next morning we started off again for Silver Jane's, at Timau. Silver Jane was the first woman to fly solo from England to Kenya; she has a silver plane and a silver suit.

We lunched on a river and slept till three o'clock, then rode on up through a dark and lovely forest till we came to Silver Jane's house, a two-storeyed cottage with a glorious view of Mount Kenya which looks so close you feel you might walk to the snow.

28 MARCH

Rested yesterday morning, and started off in the afternoon for the Loldaika Hills. All through that wild, hot, thorny country we never saw a head of game, though there are always rhino and buffalo there. We camped in the forest close to the river, below Macdonagh's house; it is heavenly – so quiet, and full of birds.

29 MARCH

Next day, on to Nanyuki. The horses were put into the club stables. During the night buffalo passed within fifty yards of our camp, and I never woke. Kebe never called us, though he saw them.

30 MARCH

We rode as far away from Nanyuki as we could to camp, and came to a plateau under the Loldaikas – a perfectly beautiful place! Nothing more heavenly than camping at night, sleeping on a bed of leaves near a great fire, with the stars overhead and the wind on your face.

Next day we rode to Narro Moru station and put the horses on a truck. This was the end of our safari. It has been so lovely – we got so fit and so did the horses.

JUNE

In May I sailed again in the *Usambara* for Suez, hoping to find a ship there to take me to Tor, in Sinai, from where I could get to Petra. As we got into harbour at Port Tewfik a terrific sandstorm met us, and the whole sky and air darkened to the colour of a London fog. The shore boats were unable to come out as the sea was now fairly rough, and for two hours we waited while the air slowly cleared and the sea calmed down. The Cook's agent had so many people to look after doing the Suez–Cairo–Port Said trip that he completely forgot me, and the barge went off without me. But the agent's boat was still waiting, and in that I finally got ashore, and, with the agent's help, through Customs.

Next day I found there was no boat to Tor until 7 June. This was too long to wait. The alternative was to try to get to Aqaba, further from Suez but much closer to Petra. There seemed to be two alternatives: to pay the ship to deviate, or to go by car. I found that the first course would cost £100, and the second about £60. On Monday I got a taxi and went to Cairo; I thought it would be easier to fix things there, and also more amusing. Needless to say, the taxi broke down. The driver opened the bonnet and beat the engine with his fist, but a car came down the road and a charming young man got out and talked to me while his driver dealt with the car, and in no time we were going again. The road goes through flat desert all the way, most uninteresting; and in two and a half hours I was at the Continental in Cairo. There I got hold of Wing Commander Measures, a director of Imperial Airways, who said I had better come up to the Heliopolis House Hotel, which is not so 'international'. That evening I went there and dined with him and some other English people. After dinner we went to the flat of Squadron-Leader Markham, a famous and wonderful flyer, and saw Mr Carrol, of Misr airworks. Everything was arranged for me to fly to Aqaba for £20 any day I liked; it made me feel very grand to have an aeroplane and a pilot at my disposal! The next day was spent shopping, making arrangements with the Consul, and moving my things to the hotel.

It is fascinating to sit on the terrace here and watch the RAF machines practise night flying, roaring overhead through the darkness with only their three lights showing. Measures said that one of the IA machines is going to England about the end of the month via North Africa, Sicily, the Alps and France, and all for the fare of the straight ordinary route. It is a *marvellous* chance, and I jumped at it.

Everything is arranged now for my flight to Aqaba, and I hope to start tomorrow morning with a pilot named Mahony.

2 JUNE

Wing Commander Measures came with me to the aerodrome, and there I had tea with brandy in it to steady me! The Moth is very comfortable with a large swing chair and cabin in front for me and my luggage, or two people.

We flew in the direction of the Gulf of Aqaba, passing over small flocks of anything-but-air-minded goats, and some camels who haughtily took no notice of us. Then we were flying over the most savage, jagged mountains, black and red, with fearful gorges and chasms cut in them. And suddenly a lovely scene was before us – these wild, rocky, fearful mountains, piled peak behind peak against the sky, with their feet in the water of a dark blue sea, the deepest, most lovely blue, patched with vivid green and purple. A small fishing village full of palm trees runs down to the edge of the Gulf, and all around stand the red mountains with their black shadows and crevasses.

We came down at this lovely place, sat under the wing and waited for something to happen. Across the desert came a solitary shabby figure, with the inevitable gun across its shoulders. This turned out to be an Arab policeman who squatted under the wing with us and let forth a flow of gargling language punctuated by spits. We gathered there were no Englishmen there; only Arab soldiers or police at the camp across the bay. In spite of all my prayers, Mahony absolutely refused to leave me there unless there was an Englishman. So there we sat, M. with a funny little hat on his head and a bit of cigarette in his mouth, getting very cross, me hot and disap-

111

pointed and looking even odder, and our Arab spitting and being voluble.

In the end we flew over the other camp, but there was nothing white there, so we went on to Ma'an, and in no time were there – an oasis of trees, shrubs and fruit, growing in the mud-built native village. The aerodrome and Transjordanian Frontier Force barracks are some way from the village; as we landed, people came out to meet us. We had lunch in the RAF mess, and I tried to find out what would be a good route to take for a nice trip. Everyone said 'motor' would be quickest, but I wanted to go slowly and I loathe cars. So in the end we all went out to see Captain Domville, the Intelligence Officer, who was extremely kind and promised to find a 'nice trip' for me.

3 JUNE

I spent last night in a hotel reeking of garlic and Greeks, dirt on the floor, on the tables and chairs, on the beds – everywhere. All night bedbugs and fleas feasted on me, and in the morning I had bites in serried ranks all over my arms, neck, legs, even on the soles of my feet; and I appeared to have sat on some bugs too! Mad with rage and itching, I left the beastly place, and went to show my wounds to the Transjordanian Frontier Force officers. Captain Revney and Captain O'Flynn were shocked at my unhappy state and asked me to stay with them. O'Flynn lent me his pony – fat and fresh and pleased with my weight. We had quite a bumpy ride to Domville's house. D. had got a friend of his there, a Sheikh; the route they suggested will take about a fortnight, and I shall see lots of beautiful, interesting things. They will arrange camels and escort, and people have lent me a tent, net, bath, etc. How lucky I am to find such kind people everywhere.

4 JUNE

I left Ma'an with Captain O'Flynn and my servant, Mahmoud, for Petra. We drove for one and a half hours then came to the police post of Wadi Musa; where O'Flynn left. Here we got ponies and rode down the hill till we were alongside the Ain Musa, the stream that Moses created by striking the rock (several other streams in Transjordan also claim this distinction).

Following this we came to the north of the Suk, that marvellous gorge which is the only approach to Petra. High up along the walls are the old aqueducts which carried the water, and at intervals there are small niches cut in the rock, often decorated with fine sculpturing. Many tombs line the walls; perhaps the small niches were for shrines or food offerings. Or perhaps to prop ladders against? How else could one get to the tombs? The walls of the gorge tower twelve hundred feet up, and the way is narrow and eerie; the air is still, and here and there an oleander bush blooms. When

Petra was a live city her warriors watched and guarded the way through the gorge, night and day, while others listened at the lesser ravines.

The people of Petra, the Nabateans, were tall, lean and warlike. Sometimes they imported foreign sculptors and artists, and the results are seen in the exquisite coronals, leaves, wreathed flowers and other decorations on the walls of the tombs. At the end of the gorge you suddenly come on the façade of the Treasury, at one time used as a temple to Isis. Here men prayed for protection before setting out for some desert journey; and here they gave thanks for their safe return. The pillars with their delicate coronels carved in the pink rock are a marvel of loveliness. High in the rock is a statue of the goddess Isis standing within an exquisitely decorated, rounded shrine and flanked by two winged figures. Many powerful tribes tried in vain to break into Petra, some got as far as the city itself but the Nabateans always managed to drive them away. They kept their own city and their own religion intact.

In the end, the Emperor Trajan took Petra by treachery. The district round Petra became a Roman province, and many Nabateans settled in Palmyra. Finally Bedouin tribes swept away the last defences and looted what was left of the city, probably massacring the remaining inhabitants. Petra was deserted and forgotten.

The Nabateans had a cult of the dead. I can see no traces of living houses except the Beit el Bint (House of the Girl), said by the Arabs to have been built by one of the Pharaohs. It has a few walls but no roof. Among the ridges – in fact everywhere – are Nabatean tombs, some just holes in the ground with no decoration; some as splendid as palaces with pillars, statues, carved flights of steps and beautiful sculptures. The Nabateans, it seems, believed that the body has many souls, one of which will remain close to its former body as guardian; they would also help to guard the storehouses of treasures. The Nabateans thought their ghostly army had driven back early invasions by the Romans and Macedonians. The tribesmen lived side by side with the dead, and under their protection.

Last night I camped in the ruins of the Beit el Bint. It was a tall building, with the remains of fine sculptures still on the walls. The moon shone down on rocks and ruins and lit up the grand façades of the tombs.

5 JUNE

There are six RAF men camped across the valley, and this morning they came over to see if I was all right. Three of them decided to go with me to the Great Place of Sacrifice. It was an hour's walk, they said, but it took us two. The path winds up a steep mountain face; in places the ancient steps are worn away, and we scrambled over loose rocks, up high boulders, along old paths not six inches wide with chasms yawning below – luckily these bits of track were only three or four feet long. One of the men helped me on, and often I had to stop with a pumping heart and no breath left. It certainly was a trial for me, and probably for them too, as I went so slowly and stopped so often. At last we came to a plateau on which were two obelisks; these contained the spirits of heathen gods, and might be the 'groves' which the Israelites were forbidden to approach. One more climb and we came out on the Great Place of Sacrifice, where on the large paved summit stands a slab of stone; on one side three steps rise to the sacrificial stone, which has a circle in the centre and a channel cut down the side to carry the blood away.

Coming down was a slithery job, but not exhausting like the climb up, though when we arrived back at the men's camp I was dead tired. However, mugs and mugs of black tea soon put me right, and we all became great friends. They were charming, and gave me things they swore they didn't want – frying pan, marmalade, etc. I must find out what they would like and send them a nice present. They all went off at two o'clock, trudging through the sand with their packs on ponies behind them, and now I am really quite alone with the servant, Mahmoud, the guide and a Circassian policeman, who I think is inclined to be rather cheeky.

This evening we went up a narrow rocky gorge with towering sides, and after a short climb came to some graves where all the poor bones have been tossed about – jackals perhaps? At the head of the gorge is another magnificent tomb with two lions carved into the rock, the portico and arch richly decorated. The distant hills are shrouded in a sandy veil tonight; the lovely colour has gone.

6 JUNE

Very early I set off for Ed-Deir, the convent. Another fearful climb! In some places you just catch hold of a rock above and haul yourself up. Halfway up we went along a rocky ledge and came to the 'baths', small hollows in the rock with caves behind them. The water drips down the side of the cliff, dark green creepers and ferns cling to the wall, and one oleander bush blooms brightly.

The convent has a marvellous façade, with designs on the capitals of the pillars. It stands on a small plateau cut out of the rock. Within is nothing! One small room with a few niches – but I think the interior decorations were mostly paintings, as you can see traces of them here and there; also the entire ceiling and walls are covered in chisel marks.

This is the last of Petra for me. My pony arrived; everything was loaded onto the men and the pack ponies, and off we went past all the carved tombs; past the lovely Temple of Isis – and I caught myself very nearly praying there for a safe journey, but I thought as a Christian it was not quite the thing. Up the twilit gorge with its still, oppressive air and its flaming oleanders, till we were at Wadi Musa. The Arab officer was most kind, gave me tea and biscuits and helped to get the camels loaded.

At last we started; I felt wonderful, quite independent with my little caravan of six camels, two men and Mahmoud. We went up and down hill after hill of this curious stony country speckled with little shrubs which the camels eat. We passed small communities of people, and said to them 'Peace be upon you', and received the answer 'And on you be peace.' After some time Mahmoud rode up to me and said that the camel boys knew of a spring about one hour's ride away, and suggested we should camp there the night, instead of trying to make Shobak in one day. So on we went hopefully for two good hours. Then I said, 'Where is your spring?' and the camel boys said, 'About two more hours' away,' and I said '!!!——!?! . . . !!???——!!' etc. But in English, not Arabic. So Mahmoud and I rode on, I being almost ready to fall off by now, till we came to the crest of a hill and I said firmly, 'Here we sleep.' But looking across the valley we saw a small town on a small hill, and Mahmoud said, 'There is Shobak.' I thought we'd better go on there, but first we waited for the camel boys, who assured us it was not Shobak!

Then Mahmoud suggested we should ride on down the valley to a lovely place he knew, and I had the pleasure of telling him that he knew nothing, and the camel boys knew nothing, and we would sleep where we were, as I said. It is so bitterly cold that I am in bed in all my clothes with all the blankets on *and* a hot water bottle!

7 JUNE

I found last night I had a bit of a temperature, so three aspirins and brandy and hot water made my dinner. I slept for about thirteen and a half hours, and still had a slight temperature, but was well enough to go on. We had a long, weary ride; my camel is a brute – she is lazy and hates everything except eating. At last we came to Shobak, and the excellent Mahmoud who is *never* right, and understands nothing, of course took the wrong road. It became a track hardly fit for goats, along which I walked up the side of a precipitous hill. I could hardly breathe, and stopped again and again, sitting on the ground and trying not to look at the drop below.

At last I got there, Mahmoud having taken the two riding camels round the road. I scrambled over a breach in the wall. I found a door before me, knocked on it and said 'Open.' A woman came to the other side, peered through the cracks, saw me and rushed away screaming. Then the door was wrenched open and a dirty, hairy, unshaven, half-dressed policeman stood there waving a stick at me. I said, 'I am the English Sitt, where is the officer?' He said he was the officer, but he did not look fit to clean cowhouses. We went in and found his howling wife falling about all over the floor. I was angry by this time, and asked where the camel road was. He took me along wall edges and through narrow passages, and suddenly a slimy-looking fellow ran out of a house speaking English. I was very glad to find someone who could understand me. He had been a Petra guide and knew a lot about the place. He also gave me a curious meal to eat: fried eggs and a large, thin piece of bread rather like a pancake to look at and a boot to taste – at least I suppose a boot might taste so. You break off and fold a small piece of bread and pick up the egg with it, and put it in your mouth – if you are lucky – or down your shirt front. I made haste to tell my friend that we owned three thousand cattle and fifty horses. I find this makes a glorious impression!

The first castle crowning the hill was built by the Romans when they conquered Arabia; but in time the Arabs took possession and the place was almost entirely rebuilt. Then the crusaders stormed Kerak, the principal city of the district, whereupon Shobak capitulated with the other cities and was occupied for about seventy years. They built more houses and strengthened the walls.

The countryside is barren, glaring and monotonous; a few trees grow at the foot of the mountain in the valley, but the empty desert stretches all around. And I thought of the bored, lonely and homesick women of the crusaders, condemned to pass their lives in this dreary spot, far from the dark forests, rushing streams, flowers, friends and all the joys of Europe.

I was invited into the house of another Arab policeman and seated among a crowd of dirty, hospitable women and still dirtier children. I drank coffee and tried to make conversation. With the dozen words of Arabic I know, it's not too easy! The soldier wanted his children photographed but absolutely refused to let me take a picture of his pretty wife, with her slanting, shining black eyes and tattooed face. There was a terrific scrubbing and combing, clean clothes, clean faces (not bodies), the asker [*policeman*] put on his uniform, and they grouped themselves tastefully against a wall. Then my conceited friend wanted his picture taken, which meant that I had no film left to take the wonderful old gateway, the only entrance to Shobak.

We walked down the hill and went to look at the baths built by the pre-Roman inhabitants called Ana-Kaiyin, a tribe whose king was so tall that he is said to have taken a fish from the sea, hundreds of miles away, and held it up to the sun to fry. The baths are quite ordinary, and not worth the walk. On the return journey we did some more goat-jumping, climbing up and down walls, up and down hills, and finally walking a mile along a crumbling six-inch track halfway up the precipitous hill, which gave me the shivers.

I am now entertaining a party in my tent: Sheikh Mukbil Aboula Hai, his son Ali and all his friends! This Sheikh's father was the not-too-heroic central figure in the last siege of Shobak. Ibrahim Pasha, the grandfather of King Fu'ad, attacked Shobak, captured the Sheikh and ordered the defenders to open the gates. He said that as they had no water they had better surrender at once. But the Arabs descended the hundred-foot well in the centre of the town and, bringing up buckets of water, poured them on the heads of the besieging army to prove that they were well supplied. This infuriated Ibrahim, who brought the captured Sheikh to the front, tied him to a cannon's mouth, and said that if the gates were not opened he would blow him into the town. The Sheikh cried: 'Open the gates! I am your Sheikh and you must obey me!' So the gates were opened, and the son of this hero sits now at my feet, having been well fed on Ryvita, butter and marmalade.

He asked me to go and have supper with him, but I tried to convey my exhaustion and said I must rest. My Petra guide had said he would kill a sheep for me and I knew what that would mean: a succulent mass of insides would be presented to me, and on the top would be the very choicest morsel for the honoured guest – one or even two eyes. Next time, when I have learnt the Arabic for it, I shall say it is against my religion even to look at a sheep's eyes.

I had one lucky moment. Feeling very dry, I told Mahmoud to bring me some water; before drinking I said, 'May I?' to the Sheikh, thinking it was rather rude to drink first. He was *enchanted*, and said I had spoken good words; the water was his, inherited from his forefathers, and I was quite right to ask his permission before drinking.

Petra then said, 'I tell you a good true story.' A Dutch Jew wished to visit one of the many holy Moslem cities. He took with him an escort of soldiers, and gave out he was a Mohammedan. He passed slowly through the country until he was nearly at his destination, when a large party of Bedouin came out and forbade him the road. 'But I am Moslem,' he said, 'I want to pray in your city.'

'You know the fashion of the Jews, lady?' Petra went on. 'They take down him clothes and they see he no Moslem, and they kill him.'

A pretty story.

8 JUNE

In the night I woke up and saw a camel's behind wedged comfortably in the tent flap. I feel well protected! They really are rather touching creatures, the way they slowly turn their long necks about looking for their friends.

I got away at about nine this morning, having got up at five. They have no idea of hurrying – perhaps it's against their law or their dignity. Although I cooked my own breakfast they never attempted to take the tent down. Petra arrived, and I've let myself in for giving him a revolver; *most* annoying, as he is the last person I want to give such a good present to. But he gave me lunch yesterday, and milk and butter, and money is out of the question, and I won't be indebted. It is maddening but unavoidable, I'm afraid.

To get on to the Tafilah road we had to go about six miles in the wrong direction, round the gorge and craggy hills which surround Shobak. We had a long ride today and I'm not really in very good form. I still have the frightful cold, all day my head aches, and my temperature is 100°. It goes up a little at night and down in the morning. My lips are black and peeling and my legs rubbed raw by the camel's rough skin and the sacks they put over it. I must try to bandage them tomorrow. I took Mahmoud's camel and, though he goes well, his hump caused me agony! If only my legs didn't hurt so I should be quite happy.

After about four hours we reached a tree – the only one, I believe, in the district; and here I slept. The country is flat, with a deep valley on the west. In time we came to more mountains, but rolling, not too steep. A party of Arabs tossing chaff stopped us and said, 'You must drink coffee here.' I tried to say I had to go on, but my camel settled everything by giving one deep roar and suddenly lying down. So into the tent we went; a red rug was spread on the floor, and on this I sat, taking care that the soles of my feet should point at no one and remembering to take the cup with my right hand and not to ask for less or more than three helpings. A filthy child was placed on my lap, and her beaming father assured me that she was now mine, and I must take her to England. Truly, the hospitality of the Arabs is great! But they were charming and kind to me, and when I salaamed them before going there was a chorus of 'Peace be upon you.'

Quite soon we came to the top of the hill and camped on a ridge overlooking the valley. An old man came to us, embraced Mahmoud and invited us to his house, but I managed to refuse. He and I went through the ritual of 'Peace be upon you.'

'And on you be peace.'

'How are you?'

'Well, praise be to God. And you?'

'Well, praise be to God.'

They are a leisured, very courteous people, but I wish they were a bit cleaner. Heaven knows what will happen to me after drinking out of their cups and holding their children! Temperature 101.

9 JUNE

Temperature this morning down to 99. I had to wake Mahmoud up to give me tea, so we were late again getting away. We rode through pretty, green country with outcrops of rocks, springs and streams here and there, and a certain amount of cultivation. Then more fearful, craggy mountains on every side, down which we crept and crawled. I was 'weary, weary, and full of pain', but enjoying it for all that. The scenery is so grand with the white rocks and blue, mauve and rosy gold backgrounds.

Tafilah sits alluringly on the side of a hill, and the road winds away, but we got there at last and down to the police post – only to find it was Friday and a holiday and the officer was in his house. So up the hill I toiled again, and the policeman hammered on the door, and in time a small, dirty boy peered out at us. We went into the sitting room, which was hung with photographs of Arabs dressed variously as soldiers and Westernized Oriental Gentlemen – rows of chairs lined the walls – armchairs with comfortable white linen seats, and sofas; a few iron ones stood humbly near the door. The Zabit strode in looking very smart, having leaped into his clothes, the policeman saluted, and I thought what a contrast to Shobak! Dear Domville had telephoned and ordered the horses, and everything was ready. I had rung up Ma'an from the post office, and heard there was a wire to say the Avro leaves for England on 24 June. So that cuts my trip short quite a bit, but it can't be helped.

I asked to see the Zabit's wife and was taken into the bedroom and presented to her, a charming, pretty girl with dark brown hair, a pearl-white skin and pink cheeks. She was nursing a pretty baby, and the room was full of children of all sizes and in various states of filth, some apparently spotlessly clean (her own) and others quite dreadful. I was enchanted to find anyone who looked so sweet and clean; she is a Turk from Istanbul. The Zabit has two other wives and eight children; most of them live in this house and make the poor girl's life absolute hell.

We talked as best we could; I trotted out the usual old thing about a husband and children. They made me lie on the bed, and the girl gently covered me with a sheet; they gave me eau-de-cologne for my headache and left me to sleep. I could not sleep, what with the headache and thinking of the trip and all, but someone came and shut the door and I lay there for hours. Then I had to eat something. Mahmoud had vanished, and my camels not arrived, but I found the family in a back room. There seemed to be dozens by this time: sisters and half-relations, servants and babies were everywhere. They asked me if I would eat and I accepted as politely as I could. An enormous feast was spread before me – a delicious parsley and rice soup, then eggs and meat, then a sort of meat cake and finally some bitter junket. I was very afraid of offending them, but I told the girl I only ate one or two eggs and some biscuits every day, and I think she understood.

Then back to the sitting room where I started to write, but in no time two Arab ladies came in, one speaking extremely good English. They are the wife and daughter of the Governor. The mother, a Circassian, looks a perfect aristocrat; the daughter is a very good-looking and intelligent girl. In time more ladies came in; no two were dressed alike. One was a tall, heavy, dark Arab woman tattooed all over her face, in a flowing silken cloak edged with red. On her head was a thick band of red woven with silver and bound with two rows of coins, one silver and one gold. She sailed down the room and, after kissing our hands, touched her forehead with them, then seated herself all over a chair and smiled at me, displaying two beautiful gold teeth. That headdress fascinated me, with its rich jingling coins. The tattooing is a pretty terrible business: seven needles are tied together and the face is stabbed with them, and while the blood runs ink is rubbed in.

Some of the women suckled their babies, and the noise grew and grew. One old thing with bright henna hair sat on the floor and shouted; she wanted me to take her photograph as a genuine antique. Our poor, pretty hostess sat on an iron chair getting whiter and whiter; she has a sort of sickness which gives her a headache, and I gave her some aspirin. In the evening the Hamuds and I left and went down to their charming house, with a real tree and some flowers growing in tins in the courtyard.

My clothes arrived and I had a most glorious wash and changed into a frock, just to show that I did have some respectable clothes. My face is too awful, though! There was another party here. These women have nothing at all to do, so from noon onwards they spend the day visiting each other's houses, where they sit around the walls in rows drinking coffee, tea and water.

The different types are so interesting. Some of the women had the typical long sloe eyes and heavy face of the Arab, while others had sunken, wistful eyes and sad mouths, and one had a funny, turned-up nose and gay eyes. There was a heavy Kurdish woman, with thick features and stupid eyes; a short, red-haired, grey-eyed one of Circassian blood; and another with a thin wicked face, cruel eyes and a mouth like a shark's. This one is the fourth and latest wife of the richest man in the district; she behaves like a slave-driver to the children of the other wives. They are treated worse than servants – beaten and kicked, and fed only on a little olive oil and bread. When the husband comes back from his travels bringing presents for this woman, the other children carry the loads to her house, well knowing that there will be nothing for them. That is the way of Arab men. They worship the latest wife and immediately turn cruel to the former ones. This woman, being the fourth, can have no legal successors; but one of the others might die, or the man might take a concubine; then her reign will be over.

My hostess, the charming Circassian lady, was superseded by her own servant. No wonder Miriam Hamud, who is intelligent and was educated at the American School in Beirut, refuses to marry. She tells me that if a man so much as says that he loves a girl, she would probably be killed, and the same if a girl said she loved someone. No question of their having misbehaved themselves – it is only that the Arabs think it is shameful for men and women to love each other, and the girls must be given in pre-arranged marriages, after which they never set eyes on any other man than their husband, father, brothers and sons. Miriam is a most remarkable girl: she is only eighteen, yet she runs a school here in Tafileh and has fifty pupils, most of them older than herself. She teaches hygiene, reading, literature, sewing, handicrafts, geography, etc. She showed me some of the sewing they had done – lovely, careful work, all based on designs drawn by her out of her head. She will probably end up as the leader of a feminist movement for freedom for the women of Transjordania, and a very good thing too – the lot of the Transjordanian women is hard and sad, and Miriam is so intelligent and advanced in everything.

The shark-woman's mother is a stately, beautiful old lady; she has taken a great fancy to me, as I resemble a niece of hers. She held my face and we kissed. Then she took off her black overskirt, veiled her head in white muslin and prostrated herself beside me saying her prayers. She prays on my *keffiyeh* [*headcloth*] that it may be blessed. She says Hammam is not too safe a place to go to alone, so I have arranged to take two soldiers with me, and I'm sure her prayers will go with me.

10 JUNE

Last night there was a party – what a party! All my friends arrived after dinner, more and more of them with their sleepy children, till the place was full of howls and chatter. Gradually the children were made into bundles and laid under the long seat which runs round the room, and then the girl with the funny face and turned-up nose, a Damascene, began to play the oudd – a large mandolin. It has five or six sets of double strings and is struck with a thin pick, the left hand touching the strings. She played extremely well and fast, and after a good deal of coy hesitation was persuaded to sing. She twanged through her nose, first on one side, then on another; it sounded rather like a French taxi-horn but was received with great applause. After more coyness, she got up and danced round the small space – still playing the oudd.

Then a local girl danced an Aqaba dance, shaking her tummy and shoulders, shimmying, moving her head from side to side, slinging herself on her knees and leaning over backwards in front of someone for a kiss.

Another Aqaba dancer caused shrieks of joy. She stood in front of one woman and moved her body spasmodically, singing a verse of some very vulgar song, I am sure.

Then the heavy Arab woman from Irbut, when I had gone over and begged her to dance and lifted her to her feet, did a lovely, graceful dance with two handkerchiefs, waving them round, over her head and down to the ground in a continuous circular movement, moving her legs and swinging her body in the same rhythm. She looked magnificent with her long robes swinging and her coins jangling.

The old women pestered me to show them an English dance, but it was frightfully difficult without a partner. So I did a sort of charleston till I was thoroughly blown, and they all flew at me and said they'd no idea any Englishwoman had such a supple body. This was an exaggeration, of course.

After the party I had great difficulty with my bed, as I couldn't make out if I was supposed to sleep on or under the very thick cover; there were no sheets. I tried sleeping under, and was boiled, so I slept on top, but discovered this morning that it was definitely meant to stay tidy and not to be slept on – that was a pity, but it was too late to worry about it. I was ready to go at six, but I was forced to stay for breakfast, which I couldn't eat, to Miriam's horror. They are all much too kind, and if I ate one quarter of what they set before me I should very soon be a physical wreck. For breakfast there were hard-boiled eggs, fried eggs, and olives soaked in oil; some small, dark dried fruit in oil, bread, a sort of cucumber, and pats of junket. I simply could not face it. After long farewells, embraces, thanks on both sides and photographs, I got away, really sorry to leave these charming people but delighted to be on the move again. Miriam gave me two pieces of cut onyx turned up by a native plough, possibly very early Greek [*I have them still in 1986, mounted on a pin*]. It was now about 8.30.

I am riding horses instead of camels – oh, the relief! Mine is a curious creature, extremely thin but with good paces. She wears a soft, comfortable but very small native saddle, stirrups I can only get my toes into, and a lovely halter covered in shells, but no bit! My asker is on a prancy, showy, good-looking dark chestnut, and Mahmoud sits on top of a burdened mule. The pack ponies were late, of course, so we started without them. We rode up and down steep hills, seeing a lot of cultivation and great sheets of barley swaying in the wind. After a time the asker and I changed horses, and riding this smart, game little animal was a real joy. We are bound for Hammam, and the people say I am the very first white woman to go there, which is very lucky but probably not true.

Presently we left the road and turned towards a deep valley. The country got wilder and more magnificent, the path became the merest trail, and in time we began to ride down the side of a fearful mountain, I should think well over a thousand feet high, on a tiny track about a foot wide, with a sheer drop below us to the bottom of the wadi. I was so scared I felt faint and quivery inside, but it had to be done, so I carefully guided the pony, giving him his head but holding him together, for he is not a mule, and he is shod, which makes him slip on stones. The sides looked crumbly too, but it was no good fussing; only I simply couldn't look over the edge, and pulled my *keffiyeh* forward over my face to hide it from me. It must have taken three-quarters of an hour to get down this awful place, and at the bottom I got off and rested.

We were now on the floor of the valley, where a thin green stream wandered about and the huge brown mountains shut you in on every side. Sheets of barley were growing, and flocks of black goats and sheep, with some white ones, were grazing the short grass. In time we came to the grass shelter of the Sheikh, a fine old man with a grand head and kind face, and here we sat while they offered me my share of a large dish of bread and oil. I had one mouthful out of the spoon to be polite, but I couldn't face any more and pleaded my headache. Mahmoud and the asker went at it, and in three minutes the whole mess had disappeared. After that we rode for an hour or two down the valley till we came to the head of a fearful, wonderful gorge. On one bank is a stone aqueduct leading to a tower. This leads down to another larger, square building, from which another aqueduct leads into the gorge itself. Thus the hill water is brought down to irrigate the crops, which look like sorghum.

I notice graves everywhere, many in the fields. I suppose the spirits help to guard the crops. There are caves in all the rocky places, some partially closed in front with small stone walls.

We rode round the edge of this wadi and now seemed to be in another world, with mountains towering on every side and hemming us in, and great cliffs and masses of rock flung around. Cascades of green appeared now and then down a mountainside, showing where a spring bubbled, and there were sheets of loose stones where there had been a landslide; fearful cracks in the ground reached down, they said, to the floor of the wadi. In the distance a brown, hot haze veiled the brown, arid heights.

It was near here that some Germans found, long ago, a golden calf – a relic of what dead faith practised in this wild, awful country? Did the Israelites pass this way? Or was it the idol of older people? I only heard of this calf by chance; I know nothing of the details.

When I looked into the depths of the valley and realized that we had to ride down there, I was consumed with terror again. But with the asker leading we began the hour-long descent of a practically sheer precipice – the path, if you could call it a path, had S-turns in it every few yards. Each turning was on the brink, and there was barely room for a horse to turn his body round – sometimes one foot would slip on a stone, but they always recovered themselves. Below was just the sheer wall of rock, with crags jutting out here and there. I had to urge my pony, who was frightened too, now. In the end we all got off, and then the chestnut would not budge. The mule boy came and took him from me, and after a good deal of shouting and a blow or two he started his slithering descent again. We began to get nearer the bottom, but it was still more than I could do to look over the edge. At last we were at a cave only a few feet from the bottom where I rested.

When I went on again I found we were in a sort of Garden of Eden; a clear brown stream ran down the valley, edged with reeds, grass, feathery green trees and oleander. Here and there water gushed out of the fern-hung rock, and the sound of its continuous murmuring, the birdsong and rustle of leaves was delicious. Here there are two baths, one used now by the men, and one by the women. They say these baths were made for Solomon – and the place is called Hammam Sleman bin Daud, meaning the Baths of Solomon, the son of David. To reach them he must have come *up* the valley, from the Dead Sea end. The men's bath looks like a natural pool, with ferns drooping from the rock which partly overhangs it. It is large enough to swim in but the water is extremely hot, for this attractive stream, with its patches of scarlet and others of clear green, contains boiling water. The women's bath is smaller – I think hand-made. The water has been diverted into it in a deep channel – deepened, of course, by at least three thousand years of running water. There are small niches, possibly for lamps, and steps lead down to it. I saw what looks like writing on the walls, but half submerged. An old woman in Tafilah told me that people used to come here and make sacrifice in thanksgiving for recovery from an illness. In the old days they rubbed henna upon a rock, but now they probably sacrifice a goat. High up in the cliff on one side I could see a cave dwelling with an entrance leading through to another room. The path which must have led to it has entirely disappeared; it must be thousands of years old.

11 JUNE

My servant Mahmoud really is most unreliable. I've just remembered a perfect Mahmoudism, too good to forget. Yesterday when I was in the hakim's house and wanted to change I sent a message quite clearly to say I wanted the three boxes of clothes. In time there arrived the iron, and three tins of baked beans!

12 JUNE

We've had a marvellous journey today; up an apparently endless mountain, at the top I saw a great valley below us, full of round, craggy, rocky, brown hills of every shape and size. The road wound on and on – it was always the same narrow rough track. On one mountaintop is the ruin of a small house where the Turks had an outpost [*in the First World War*]. As far as I could make out from M. they were all killed, but whether murdered for their money before the war or killed in the fighting I don't know.

At the foot of this long mountain there was a small stream with a little cultivation on the edges and clumps of oleander here and there. Then we began the climb up. I would never have believed that any animal could get up that mountainside. The path got steeper and narrower; often the ponies had to step from one stone to another, and they stopped again and again. At the very top the gradient must have been 1 in 2; then the track levelled out again and ran between two walls of rough rock. The wide valley below was full of tumbled rocks and savage hills, deep gorges and high cliffs; all were brown and barren except for the little stream which wandered away down the wadi, a thin, dark green line with the pink of oleanders showing faintly now and then.

We cantered on ahead of the mules and in half an hour were at Masar, a picturesque little town of mud and stone with large herds of camels grazing close by, and here and there a horse tied; men tossing chaff, a slow caravan of camels moving along a path, horsemen riding about the streets, and women with tattooed faces in dirty black robes.

The policemen were perfectly charming to me, sat me down and gave me tea. I tried to telephone Fernie at Ma'an, but it was nearly impossible to hear each other till the operator stepped in, so to speak, and repeated our words to each other, ending up with an invitation from the operator to me to go and drink tea with him if I should be near his town! Very hospitable.

I remember a number of sights from this morning. A fat, terribly worried hen partridge rushing down the track in front of me with her scattering brood, all cheeping and hurtling through the air a short way and then running along the ground. She managed to hide herself and them in the end. Then a bird exactly like an owl, a pale fawn colour with darker speckles, light rings round his eyes and a round head. He was sitting on a stone gazing at me, every now and then quickly moving his body up – then down; at last flying swiftly away with a flight like a parrot's, sometimes closing his wings for a moment while his body shot on through the air, looking like a small shell. He should have been asleep at this hour, unless there are daylight owls. A deep, quiet glen, green and peaceful, running into the fold of the hills, with birds singing and a little breeze moving the air. A great tumbled mass of red-brown rock, like a giant's fallen castle, towers still standing, huge blocks lying on the ground. The deep blue of the Dead Sea just glimpsed on our left, between two hot brown mountain ranges. The immense wall of the Wad Lakusi mountains towering into the sky above us, seven thousand feet high with the flat tableland at the top, an apparently unclimbable wall – and yet we came up it. And a vast, coal-black hill, Jebal Hami el Hassa, astoundingly set in the middle of the brown mountains; with peaks and crevasses and shoals of black stones lying at its foot; five black, sharp-pointed, spear-like crags standing one by one behind each other, the smallest in front.

These people are taller and finer-looking than the others I have seen.

I feel perfectly fit now. My temperature has been normal for days, and marvellous Pond's cold cream has cured my grazed legs – in one night they were 100 per cent better, and all the sores on my body where I got rubbed by the camel saddle are healed. Even my face is recovering. It's absolutely miraculous the way it has healed me, and it stops the sandfly bites from itching. I have learned to keep the *keffiyeh* over my nose and mouth all the time. It keeps the sun from blistering me, but it's very hot.

15 JUNE

After riding for two hours through rolling barley country and then down a winding wadi we came to Kerak, a mighty walled fortress on an almost unclimbable hill. The walls are broken down in many places, but at one time they enclosed the whole plateau and the big town. Many nationalities meet in Kerak. Greek Orthodox priests with their tall black hats, curved outward at the top of the crown, and knotted hair, work in the oldest Christian church of all. There are also Roman Catholic priests and nuns, and here and there you see fair or red-haired people, still showing their crusader blood. (In parts of Jerusalem I saw native women wearing tall peaked medieval hats, with long veils flowing from the back, relics of the Crusader invasions.)

I am in a mission house with Mr and Mrs Ward. I realize how lucky I have been to come through this wild country without any trouble, but Domville would never have let me go alone if there had been any danger. And yet three months ago robbers stopped sixteen cars going from Kerak to Amman and stripped the people of all they had! I don't understand it. Probably the sight of my asker guard put them off. We asked about the Turks' outpost in Wadi Hessa. They built it there because it commanded a view over the valley on every side, but the time came when the Arabs surrounded the outpost, which was entirely cut off from all help. The soldiers were murdered and the house partially destroyed; 'murder' by these people usually means 'tortured to death'.

This is what Ward told me about the history of Kerak. The first fortifications were built by the Moabites about 2000 BC. When David was suffering persecution at the hands of Saul, his parents fled to Kerak for protection, but the treacherous people murdered them and David swore that he would be avenged on the city. His day came; he conquered the Moabites, forcing them to pay tribute. Later the Moabites grew stronger again, and an alliance of three kings was formed against them. The Moabites put up a fine resistance against the enemy armies, but they were forced back while their country was laid waste. The survivors retreated to their last defence. In his despair the Moabite King Mesha took his eldest son, who should have succeeded to his throne, and on the north wall of the city, in full view of the besieging hosts, sacrificed him as a burnt offering to his god Chemosh. The horrified Israelites withdrew from the siege, and Mesha in his triumph set up the Stone of Moab in the heart of the city, recording his victory and the names of the prisoner chieftains.

Many centuries later Kerak became the fief of the wild crusader Reginald of Châtillon-sur-Mer, on his release by the Moslems after fifteen years' imprisonment. After endless exploits of courage and callousness, including an ill-fated attempt to seize Mecca, he was captured after the battle of Hattin and killed by Saladin in his tent. Kerak, however, still held out against the rising tide of Islamic victories, but at last surrendered in 1188, when the garrison were starving. After Saladin had finished dividing the country among his friends and relations he took Kerak for himself, for it was then a beautiful and powerful city, with orchards and large flocks of camels, sheep and goats, set on a hill which commanded the caravan routes going to Petra and Cairo, Damascus and Baghdad.

Later again Kerak was used as a dower city to which deposed Sultans of Egypt could retire. In 1893 a Turkish garrison was established in the city, which once more became the capital of a large district under Syrian rule. It remained so until taken by the British during the First World War.

In the evening I went over the castle with Mr Ward. A wide deep fosse had been dug by the Turks between the castle and the town to guard against surprise attacks by the inhabitants. The walls are colossally thick, and the face of the hill was paved with large, thick stones, so that it was absolutely impossible to storm the castle. The walls are niched, the arches running in a V shape to the arrow slits, so that the whole countryside is overlooked. The immense view over the hills to the Dead Sea is a wonderful sight. There are seven storeys in this building; no way has been found into the lower rooms, which may contain treasure. Jars of gold coins have been found in the upper rooms, and it is known that the surrounding tribes and chieftains kept their treasure here, just as they brought in their people and animals during local wars.

The rooms are immense – a hundred feet long or more; some were stables, some living rooms. Air shafts run up to the roof, and a little light comes through the deep-set arrow slits. This castle had secret entrances, and as each new power held it these were destroyed and fresh ones made.

I had a most interesting evening with the missionaries. When we got back to the house we found an old German missionary called Liebler, on his way to Ma'an. These people live an entirely different life from anything I have yet seen; they cook the local food in their own way, and the result is very good, but unlike anything I have eaten before. Old Liebler told us wonderful stories of a missionary called Reidhal, who is now on his way to Germany by donkey. This man penetrated far south of a long wadi till he was in the heart of the wildest country among the most savage people. When they realized that he was going to try to convert them from their religion they seized him and put him in prison. After a time they decided to put him to death and the executioner advanced towards him with his long sword. But the people between him and the executioner saw a man dressed in white standing before Reidhal, and the executioner fled in terror. After this he was released. He himself had not seen the man in white.

14 JULY

I left my kind friends this morning to go to Amman. Mahmoud has suddenly become polite and efficient – because there are white men about, I suppose! I paid him off. I was *delighted* to get rid of him.

There was only one car and that was taken, so I had to go by bus. It was an endless, agonizing journey. I ached and ached, and there was no room to move. The driver chattered without ceasing, gesturing with one hand while he steered the bus with the other. Every now and then he spat on the floor between his feet. Every hour or so we stopped and drank tea and uncreased ourselves.

Clouds of white dust enveloped the bus at times and poured through the open windows upon us. I could have wept with pain and misery. After nearly six hours of this hell we reached Amman, and I am now staying at the clean and orderly Philadelphia Hotel.

15 JULY

I went by car to Madaba, and there, in the old Rumm church, is a great mosaic map of the country made by the Greeks. People say it is the oldest map in the world, but I doubt that. At one time it covered the whole floor of the church, but most of it was destroyed by the Persians. The sturdy old priest, with his high black hat and hair in a knot behind (as they say Christ wore his), would not let me photograph it for less than £1 – which was too much.

A man dressed in western clothes took me to a poor house on the floor of which was another mosaic, nearly all destroyed, in a deep room which was once a temple. We went to yet another house, and there in an unused room, also a former temple, was a glorious mosaic in perfect condition showing lions, antelope, hares, buffalo, and in two corners the crowned heads of women. Very few people see these houses and I was extremely lucky to fall in with this man.

How luxuriously the Greeks must have lived in this country! Now everything is in ruins. When the Moslems over-ran the country after the Roman settlement they destroyed everything which bore a likeness to any human being. I wonder why the mosaic at Madaba with the two queens was not destroyed? Perhaps they never found it? Or perhaps they were content to cover it with whitewash – though this was not likely, as everywhere else the mosaics have been wrecked.

19 JULY

There are some fine ruins in Amman – a fortress on the hilltop, within which is a church laid out in the shape of a cross. In the thickness of the wall a winding stair climbs for a few yards. At the top we found a broken-down niche, and lying in the dust one small bone. I wondered if someone had been walled up there and left to die. Here and there are the cannon used by the Turks against us in the 1914 war.

One day I went to Jerash, which lies in really pretty country, among olive- and pine-covered hills. The fine old entrance gate is still there and beyond is the stadium; further on many rows of lovely pillars are still standing. There is a temple to Zeus and another to Artemis, the guardian of the city. The place was inhabited not by Greeks but by Greco-civilized Orientals. A long paved street, showing the wheel marks of chariots, runs through the town; beside it were shops and temples. Later the Christians came, built some fine churches and converted some mosques. Here every year was repeated the miracle of the water that Christ turned into wine: out of a certain fountain in the cathedral wine flowed. This cathedral was built on the site of the temple to the infant Dionysus, so it is likely that the priests, unable to root out the pagan ceremonies, converted them into the Christian miracle. I saw some fine mosaics taken up from the church floors and now in the gallery of inscriptions.

Now I am in the train nearing Cairo, having got up at four o'clock this morning and left Amman at five. I am tired, and we are not due in till 10.30. It is curious moving in stages towards civilization. Starting with an aeroplane, the most modern of all, I have used the progressive means of travelling through the ages. First with camels, then mules, then a little faster on ponies; then the frightful bus, after that motor cars, and now a train. I hope to finish up by flying to England.

1934

24 JUNE

Travels again. I have had several days in Cairo, but never managed to see the Mohammed Ali mosque. I could have seen it yesterday, but that was Friday and you can't get into a mosque on the Moslems' holy day.

Today I rushed about wildly packing and saying goodbye; then I got on board the Avro 10, which is going almost straight to England. I am the only passenger so far. We flew away from Cairo over dark crimson lakes full of some chemical substance which colours them; then over dreary grey desert, with nothing to look at – I slept. At Mersa Matruh we came down for fuel and two more passengers. Now we had the sea on our right: deep, deep blue with purple streaks and bright green patches, and if you look down you can see the rocks through the water.

At Tobruk [*Libya*] we were in Italian territory and they sealed up our cameras – as if anyone in their senses would want to take pictures of this frightful country! At last we reached Benghazi, where we sleep tonight; it is a fairly large and rather pretentious town, with fine big buildings and lots of Italian officers marching about and clicking their heels. The hotel is not at all bad, considering where we are. The native soldiers are very fine-looking people, black, tall and lean, with narrow heads and handsome faces. They wear immense fezzes cocked on one side, and rather good uniforms. Captain

Mollard, our pilot, and I went for a bathe. There are rafts and boats, a terrace for drinks, swarthy young men swimming and fat women in terrible beach suits.

25 JUNE

Called at 4.30 this morning with no tea. At 6.30 we took off. Again desert country on our left and the sea on our right. We came down at Sirte and Tripoli for petrol, and from Tripoli flew northwards over the sea for two and a half hours (which had its thrills in a machine that is not a seaplane) till we came to the brown, stony island of Malta.

It is an interesting drive to the town of Valetta, through brown fields ringed with stone walls. Little cream-coloured houses stand under great crusader castles, set in the huge old walls. In the town, little cobbled streets run up and down to the sea. The women wear immense black capes with huge hoods. They are descended partly from an original Mediterranean race and partly from their Arab conquerors, and the language is an ancient Mediterranean one slightly influenced by Arabic.

26 JUNE

On to the aerodrome at six o'clock; I am beginning to feel the lack of sleep. As we waited, machine after machine was wheeled out of the hangars till there were thirty-two of them lined up in rows of five with their propellers turning and their engines roaring: small, powerful naval machines with large engines and small wings. Every now and then one took off and flew to her aircraft carrier, settling down to be carried away tomorrow when the fleet sails. The commander allowed me to take a photo 'not for journalistic purposes'. It was a magnificent and thrilling sight.

The ground here is very short and we only just scraped over the top of the hangar, clearing it by ten feet – rather too exciting.

Soon we were over Sicily and landed at Catania, where the Customs searched our boxes – thank heavens they just missed my cartridges! If they'd found them there would have been serious trouble. The authorities kept us here for two hours – it was infuriating, but I made friends with some charming boys in the Italian Air Force who took us to the mess and gave us coffee. Then we came back and sat under the wing and talked away in the most curious mixture of French, Italian and German. It is rather strange to be in Europe, sitting on grass instead of sand, and with white people everywhere.

At last the police let Mollard go. We took off beautifully, waving goodbye, and flew past the Straits of Messina up the coast of Italy – fine, mountainous country, terraced and cultivated, with small, red-roofed villages clinging to every eminence, large farmhouses, wild, jagged hills on the right and always on our left, the green and purple sea. Here and there clouds lay below us, and our shadow passed over the country.

We came to Vesuvius, flying low over it, and as we passed she belched forth a great column of pink smoke. Although my camera was sealed, I edged the string off the case and took a photo, then put it all back again. In a few minutes we were on the Naples landing ground and surrounded with officers. The nearer we get to civilization the taller, smarter and cleaner the Italian officers get!

28 JUNE

This is the last day, and I am really sorry the trip will be over so soon. I've made friends with Bourne, the wireless man; he lets me sit with the receiver on my head, listening to screaming Italians. Once he was in a bad accident, one of Imperial Airways' few tragedies. His machine crashed on a night landing and burst into flames; he and the mechanic were flung out of the open cockpit, their clothes soaked with petrol but otherwise unhurt. The door jammed and the passengers were trapped in the burning machine, so the mechanic rushed into the flames to try to get them out. His clothes immediately caught fire and he burnt like a torch, but by rolling on the ground and with Bourne's help he managed to extinguish the flames. They had to stand by and listen to the passengers burning, and when it was over they struggled up the hill to where there was a building. There, people went to get help while Bourne and the burnt mechanic sat on the verandah. Of course the mechanic had had a terrible shock and was horribly burnt; people came at last and took him away to hospital, but he died. Bourne stuck to his job, but he does not like night landings now.

We flew over Paris, circling the Eiffel Tower and going low over Notre Dame, and landed at Le Bourget for lunch. Over the north of France, then the Channel and England with green, wooded country, hedges, straggling fields and glorious great houses in their gardens. We made a smooth landing at Croydon, and this is the end of my trip. Oh, it is heavenly to see England again.

1935

20 MAY

I left Nairobi five days ago for Iraq. There doesn't seem to be much Haroun al Raschid about Baghdad; one wide street, which was pushed through the town during the war to let our guns go through, and off this a good many

131

narrow, dusty native lanes. There are some mosques, one with lovely blue faïence domes – but we are not allowed in.

Stayed here three days, shopping and making arrangements for my trip. A Mr Macpherson, who knows Kurdistan well, says it is very beautiful, wild and hilly country. But the part I would have liked to go to is closed as there is fighting in the southern deserts, and these northern tribes might possibly get out of hand if they hear of the rebels' successes. The war is quite serious, especially for the oil people; Ur and some other stations have been evacuated and the tribes are having a grand time looting. The Arab children make holes in the oil pipes and light the oil. But one tragedy happened – mistaking it for an Iraqi machine, tribesmen shot down a British plane and murdered the pilot and mechanic. Abject apologies from the Sheikh, who said they didn't know the difference between British and Iraqi machines. But that does not bring the men back. If the Sheikh had to pay a really big fine, he would punish the villagers, and such an outrage would not happen again. The authorities say I must not leave the roads – but I might see about that when I get there.

Off by car to Mosul. The first part of the drive was fun. Kurds dress in the gayest colours: baggy trousers, blue or patchwork, thick chequered fantastic waistcoats, broad scarlet sashes, huge turbans piled on top of their heads; and some have immense straw hats, the crowns covered apparently with grass or fur. They carry thick, crooked walking sticks, and a number have guns. They are fine-looking people with clean-cut faces and hard, proud, fierce expressions.

They graze herds of white, long-woolled, fat-tailed sheep; their horses are quite good but their cows are miseries. Their dogs are white, long-haired, curly-tailed, like Samoyeds, big as Alsatians – not cowed, but friendly and fairly clean. We drove through miles of barley. The pack animals on the road would stop to guzzle it before being driven on. Oil wells here and there on the edge of the sandy hills, some of them burning. Villages are built of mud, each with its spired mosque. Came through two deep rivers where the water was over the mudguard and over my bedding (strapped on behind), until I finally got onto a ferry. Mosul seemed very far away; I began to ache.

21 MAY

Started at last. After a good deal of shopping and arrangements, made with the help of Mr Condopoulos, the ROC agent, I was allowed to go for a trip, provided I take a police escort and sleep near a police post every night. I was delighted to get away from Mosul. I have an Assyrian boy in the most awful clothes – tweed coat, breeches, golf stockings and homburg hat; his name is Faris.

Motored for about two hours, passing Kordofan and other humps which are all ruins of once grand cities, dead now and decently buried by the kind earth, to a spot beyond Ain Sifni. There I found mules, policemen and horses.

I rode along a gay little stream under big plane trees to the shrine of Sheikh Adi, the place of the Yezidi devil-worshippers. There are many buildings and a tiny bazaar. At the door of the tomb is a big black stone snake; taking off your shoes, you step over the threshold into a dark place, smelling damp and sounding of dripping water. We went from room to room under low arches, always stepping over, and never on, the thresholds, until we came to the tomb of the Sheikh, shrouded in a dirty black curtain which the guardian kissed.

This lovely air is scented, dry and exhilarating; we came right into the mountains, all covered in scrub oak, and rode round them and up and down them. The people looked at me with more surprise than pleasure, quite naturally. My asker kept on trying to talk, or rather yell, at me in Kurdish, Turkish and Arabic. Artrush, a tiny village on a hilltop, is this night's stop. On arrival they shut me up in a smelly little room with bars on the windows and sofas round the walls. All the people sat about staring, but being perfectly kind and trying to talk. It was very embarrassing and it seemed like hours until the mules came. Then, with great difficulty, I persuaded them to let me put up my tent outside the village; and here I am, on the windiest hilltop in Kurdistan, but on my own! Being devil-worshippers, the Yezidis hate blue (the colour of Heaven), and my mule boys of today all have red turbans. I have sentries spitting away and guarding me all night.

Awoke at dawn to the crowing of myriads of cocks in the village. People soon began to pass as close to my tent as they dared, to see the show.

The mountains are piled all round us. My escort is now one very fat policeman on a mule, and Faris on a mule, and I'm on a horse (of sorts). Also I have two wild-looking and tireless mountaineers as guides. The track is almost invisible in places. The hills have got steeper and the air thinner. We passed some mountain villages, each house built from stone to stone, and all on different levels, so that one person's roof was another person's verandah. From their rooftops, they stared down at us. Nobody spoke, and they barely answered when I greeted them. Though none of these women is veiled, they cast their eyes down when strangers are about, until they have gone.

Faris told me he was born in the mountains, but out of the eighteen men in his village he was now the only survivor, all the others having been killed by the Turks. He escaped – I don't know how. He says, 'If I see one snake and he not hitting me I leave him alone, but if he coming for me I killing him. Same with mans. I see one mans trying to shoot me, I shoot him quick first.' Very sound.

We arrived at a third village, Christian this time, but Iraqi Christian, not Assyrian – which is why they are still there. I was taken to meet the patriarch, a venerable, white-haired old priest whose hand everyone kissed but me.

133

His tiny church was quite dark inside, with a few oleographs of the Holy Family on the walls – the village has been there for about two hundred years.

We crossed the motor road to Amadia and went through an exquisite gorge, all grey boulders shaded by tall oak trees, with springs running under our feet and falling down the cliffs. It was a rough track, but so beautiful. My mule kept trying to fall down – a pretence, of course. Mules never fall.

We were camped outside the village of Darawa when, to my astonishment, a venerable old gentleman in European clothes, hat and all, with a pink face and light hazel eyes, advanced and spoke in English. He is a famous Presbyterian priest, Kasha Kina Gabriel. On hearing I was a Protestant he announced that I was his sister. His brother is about six feet six tall, with bright red hair and light green eyes; wearing a shirt and breeches, and in his Iraqi cleft black hat, he looks for all the world like a caricature of a Scotsman even to his ears sticking out! The patriarch was born in the Hakkiari mountains, the ancient home of the Assyrians, and says his family is fair and tall because they are descended from some of Alexander's Greek soldiers – it may easily be true. He took me to his hovel where, covered in flies, we conversed and drank tea. He had brought the survivors of his village here twelve years ago. They have lived here ever since but expect soon to be moved to Syria. He is a plausible old man but all that white beard may hide a bad face. Poor Faris hates him, and says 'Good tongue, bad heart.' I suppose I shall hear all about it tomorrow.

24 MAY

I had no fewer than eight guards last night, making more noise than a chorus of lovesick cats, spitting and yelling at each other and thinking they were whispering. Then my tame fleas got busy; what appetites they have got! By 4.30 I was very wide awake and presently the camp awoke and we all started to get up. It is incredibly difficult to get a bed, a box, myself, a basin and some elbow room into a 60 lb tent, so washing gets sketchier every day. The old patriarch appeared, everyone shook hands, I took everybody's photo and at last we got off.

The highlight of today was a valley. Oh, such a scented highland valley, where a large herd of sheep and goats grazed, herded by two Assyrian shepherds in huge sheepskin coats, their guns sticking out behind; and on their heads the ancient cone-shaped hat found in the oldest Assyrian sculptures. Two immense white dogs roared at us to go away, but were quieted by their masters. When I dismounted the sheep ran to me, sniffing my legs and licking my hands, asking for salt. They were friendly and spoilt and used to being petted. The shepherd called one of the goats by name; it came to him at once and put its head down to have its ears scratched. He said they cut the long, clotted white hair off the sheep and goats twice a

1922

Oct.
27.

On board S.S. Haardi—, en route to
British East Africa. Our party
consists of Tom & me, John Rawe,
Mello van Reichersberg Verslays, his
invaluable valet Joseph, & Blixen, who
is our white hunter, & whom we
pick up in Nairobi. We had a
tremendous send-off from Liverpool St.,
several people came to say good-bye,
& I had masses of flowers, which are
now all over my cabin & our
dining-room table. This is a funny
little ship, only 9000 tons, but
she doesn't roll too much. The crew
are nearly all Lascars, with silent
feet & grave faces. The white crew
are charming. They apparently have
dances every night "more or less —
everything except sleep" the chief
steward said! Mello & I danced
this evening to a gramophone, but

Above: A page from
Genesta's Diaries

Right: Feeling at home
in Kenya

Right: Genesta with baby gorilla, later sent to an
American zoo where she died of a broken heart

Below: On safari – hacking our way
through

The safari in camp

Left: Denys Finch-Hatton beside his plane

Below: Denys's plane taking off

HRH the Prince of Wales in Kenya in 1929, with 'Boy' Long (left) and Lord Delamere (right)

Right: Blickie with Genesta

Below: Blickie in camp

Below: Jos *et son amie*

Genesta with Joss Erroll and his wife Mary

year, and the women spin and weave it into cloth for the clothes they wear.

Then on for Amadia. We went along a stony, white track to a hot, glaring valley and then started to climb, looking up now and then to the town above us, in its natural wall of rock, where people stood and stared down looking immensely superior. The path became a series of steps, so steep and rough that nothing but a mule could climb it; then we passed a walled spring and entered the city through a huge, ancient arched gateway with iron doors.

What a fortress this place was! We rode through the main street in complete silence, eyed by a savage-looking lot of Kurds with knives stuck through their belts. An old man came to us and said, 'You can't go to the rest house – there is a "big man" staying there.' Faris and the policeman said they didn't care; they would take me there and the 'big man' could go elsewhere.

On we plodded – at last they brought me to a filthy hovel, smelling of every sort of dirt, where five or six beds, all used, stood round the walls and several filthy men and women got up and stared. I was in despair. Stranded in this awful place with nowhere to put up my tent unless it went on someone's roof! 'This is all right,' said the policeman. 'There are some sick people in this room but this one, next door, is empty.'

I went out into the street and didn't know what to do next. Visions of the comfort and cleanliness of Nderit assailed me. Then someone said I was wanted on the telephone! It was just like a dream. I was taken into a large old building and there was a telegraph office with a clerk in a grey suit. My caller was Mr Condopoulos, but the clerk called him 'Annas Effendi'. I talked to him for quite a while before realizing who he was. Then in came a fair man in a tidy suit, speaking good English and better French, who introduced himself as the doctor. All my troubles vanished. We sent the mules and boys down the hill to the rest house and I went to drink tea with the doctor and his nice Syrian wife.

'I have five daughters and no son,' said the doctor sadly.

'Well,' I said, 'there's heaps of time.' The wife looked rather pleased.

25 MAY

Up the hill to the town early, and to the doctor's house. His name is Dr Ferid Alexander Meshak; his ancestors came from Corfu several generations ago and settled, as British subjects, in Syria. He and his wife and I all walked out to see the sights. I think they felt the going, rather, as they don't usually take much exercise. They were both in the Sudan for some years, and pine to return. Their house here consists of a courtyard and two rooms, one where they and the children sleep and one where they live, eat and spend all day. The poor wife, coming here from a big modern house in Khartoum, told me that when she saw this place she sat down and cried.

No cupboards, no bathroom, and what the house agents call the usual offices were very Kurdish.

I went to luncheon with the Governor, a man of noble family whose wife, also high-born, came in and talked to us. She was dressed in her best, and very impressive, wearing an immense black turban with tassels here and there, and loops of double gold chains hung with gold coins and set with coral and turquoise. Round her throat, tight under the chin, was a row of gold balls, and slung across one shoulder down to her waist was a gold chain hung with charms and charm holders. Her dress was of flowered silk, as were her full trousers; her coat was of purple and silver woven stuff, very full and long, open in front. She was a very grand-looking lady, and all the glass necklaces and bracelets she wore among the gold ones couldn't spoil the effect.

The lady disappeared when lunch arrived. A smaller table was brought in laden with different sorts of food, with a huge dish of rice in the middle. We had some sort of sour milk and water to drink – very nasty. Later on, Madame Ferid and I went to the lady's boudoir where we took off our shoes and sat on cushions round the wall; the floor was covered with very fine carpets. There sit the wife of the Governor, her two children and her sister-in-law all day long, drinking tea. When other ladies come to see them, they talk scandal and drink more tea. And that is all they have to do with their lives until they die.

Back in his house the doctor told me the story of Amadia. The arches in the huge gateway we had passed through were made by the early Assyrians; one of them has verses of the Koran carved round it in Persian characters, some worn away but a number still there. The spelling is incorrect, which seems as if the carving was done by a Christian Assyrian who didn't know the Koran. Below the gateway are three niches in the wall, where you can just see the traces of carvings of men holding spears.

The town's ancient name was Ashab. When the Assyrians had their great Empire, from the fall of Ur in 2000 BC until the sack and complete destruction of their capital, Nineveh, in 606 BC, they probably ruled the surrounding district from Ashab. Then the Medes and Persians drove westwards, and the Assyrians' power was smashed – but their survivors, who took to the hills, continued for many centuries to live in their mountain villages and to hold the fortress city of Ashab. At last, however, the Persians managed to take Ashab, and held it until the eighth century AD, when Moslem Kurds drove them out. Because of these two conquests the population was very mixed.

The Kurds, who were nominally under the rule of the Caliphs of Baghdad, were just as savage and independent then as they are now. They ruled Ashab and the district in a feudal way, the Agahs being practically all-powerful. Even so they wanted to be entirely autonomous and rebelled against the Caliphs again and again, sallying out of their fortresses and swarming down the mountains to waste and burn the Arab country. At last a strong expedition was sent against them from Mosul, under the Emir Ama-ud-Din-Junghit. After what must have been a terrific fight he stormed the citadel and razed the town to the ground. When he rebuilt it he called it after himself – Amadia, the town of Ama-ud-Din. This history was written by a Greek from Byzantium, who became a Moslem and wrote of these things only eighty years after they happened. Dr Ferid had found one of his books and gave me these notes from a translation.

Until the fall of the Arab Empire in the fifteenth century Amadia remained under the government of Mosul. Then the seat of government shifted to Constantinople and Amadia returned to its feudal state, nominally under Turkish rule but in reality in the power of two or three families of local Agahs, who were for ever quarrelling amongst themselves and fighting the neighbouring tribes. Very few Assyrians lived now in their old city; nearly all had become farmers in the surrounding country and were used by the Kurds as builders, blacksmiths and artisans. In the succeeding centuries no changes came to Amadia; the Kurds' jealousy and hatred of each other were only exceeded by their fanatical loathing of Christians. But the Assyrians, too, were formidable fighters when the need arose, and their courage and stamina were greater than that of the Kurds. Should the surrounding villagers be in any real trouble there was no doubt that down from their high mountains would come thousands of Assyrian fighting men, delighted at the chance of a battle with their hereditary enemies.

In the eighteenth century a Kurd of the Rowandez district cast covetous eyes at this rich and strong hill town, and by treachery got inside the city walls, sacked the town and massacred most of the population. Having become master of the place he determined that no treachery should be his own undoing, so he built a citadel and sank several wells at a point where the cliff drops sheer for several hundred feet to the valley below.

This Agah was succeeded by six of his descendants, of whom Sultan Hussein was the strongest and best; he built the tall minaret tower beside the old citadel, several mosques and even some schools.

One hundred years after the invasion of the Rowandez Sheikhs the town was again beseiged by a Pasha from Mosul, and over-run after bloody fighting. A Turkish governor was installed, but power came quickly into the hands of the Agahs who ruled and robbed the people in the ancestral way.

One more century passed and the invading army this time was Russian. A large body of troops had reached Dashtazé on the Great Zab river, only seven hours' march from Amadia. But the river was swollen, so crossing was impossible and no reinforcements arrived. Soon the Russians were surrounded by Kurdish tribesmen and, though the invaders fought well, very few escaped.

The Kurdish Kingdom collapsed in 1918 and again the local families enjoyed a period of power, but this time their rule only lasted a year. In

1919, when the British occupied the town and district, some order was brought to the turbulent country – though not before four British adminis-trators had been besieged and three of them murdered. Then, after an inefficient local Governor had been sacked, the angry and humiliated man made overtures to the neighbouring Zebar Kurds and agreed with their Sheikh to attack the town at night. They, as ever, gained entry through treachery, and in the typical Kurdish manner sacked the bazaar, killing everyone they could catch. But this time the citadel was being properly defended by British soldiers. The fighting raged with heavy loss of life all that night and all the next day. By nightfall on the second day the defenders' position was desperate, but help came from the hills. The Assyrians, hastily arming themselves, rushed joyfully down from their mountain villages, longing for another fight with the Kurds. The Kurds, hearing of their approach, bolted.

Since then the town has been governed by Iraqi officials under orders from their own government. But though the fanatical anti-Christian feeling has to a certain extent died down, it has by no means disappeared; and here, as in the rest of the country, the Christians and Jews exist on sufferance and lead rather precarious lives.

Nothing remains of the old Assyrian fortifications except the great carved gateways with their immense iron-covered doors. The old citadel, now the seraglio [harem], was rebuilt. Over the arch is an eagle, carved in stone, holding in his claws the heads of two entwined snakes. This very ancient carving may be early Assyrian. Near the citadel of the Rowandez Sultan is a depression in the ground in which lie the remains of an old temple. Small pillars stand round at regular intervals; and set in the wall above the ground is an arched recess and what might have been an altar. The temple was possibly Persian, and used for sun worship.

28 MAY

Looking for a nice place to camp we got further and further away from Kani Masi. We lost our way, nearly shot a big snake, nearly climbed over the frontier into Turkey, nearly camped on a Sheikh's tomb, and finally pitched the minute and really dreadful little tent just outside the village on the public footpath.

Tomorrow night's dinner was clucking about the back door of my tent, tied to a piece of string. Faris's voice: 'Lady sahib, chicken him inside him tent?'

'No.'

'Jesus Christ, him run away with him lamp string!'

Both policemen organized a search, and soon the chicken was brought back under arrest.

Tukerr is a Kurdish village: they don't seem to have the same respect for money as the Assyrians. The head-man brought onions and butter as presents, and chickens are cheaper here. He also brought me a bouquet of four little pink rosebuds tied together with grass. I said to Faris, 'How very nice of him – very good Kurdi.'

'Yes, all same as dog.'

'There are many very good dogs.'

Faris wouldn't argue. All he said was, 'Werry good, lady sahib.'

[*Soon after I got to Kenya after the Kurdish trip, I wrote an article for the local paper and then got a letter from the English Commandant of the Nairobi prison, who said he had been one of four men in beleaguered Amadia in 1919. They had drawn lots to decide who should ride out to the nearest British post for help. He won and managed to get through the sleeping Kurds' lines and ride like mad all through the night to the British lines. The British rushed to the rescue but were too late. All they found were the mutilated remains of the three British officers.*]

29 MAY

6 a.m. Still at Tukerr. My bed is getting very tired. It came in half on one side before we got to Amadia, and was mended there with a piece of bright green leather. Now it has given way on the other side, and every time I moved last night there was an ominous rending sound. The village head-man brought me another lovely bouquet of roses with the most heavenly scent. I haven't been 'bunched' like this for years.

1 p.m. Chelki. The head-man saw us on our way, and then we toiled round mountains for hours. My camp is just above the Khabur river, which goes roaring past over rapids.

2 p.m. Terrific lot of talk with one of the villagers about how to cross the river. Quite impossible here, very swift, nothing could stand up in it, not even a hippo. The villager, Faris and my policeman yelled at each other, *fortissimo, crescendo*, and at last the yokel said that five and a half hours' walk up the river there was a bridge, but it was very thin and not at all strong – fifty yards long, and bounced up and down as you walked over it. It was made of plaited osiers over a row of long tree trunks about as thick as poplars. That is quite definitely beyond me (Faris was glad to hear this, as he says he couldn't cross it either), so we were stuck. When I ask Faris's advice about something all he will say is: 'As you like him, lady'; very polite and quite useless. More yelling. Then the villager said of course there was a raft, ferry or ship, which would take mules and everything, quite close in the next village. Why hadn't he said so sooner? He thought I'd prefer the bridge.

Why do I travel? I get hot, exhausted, burnt about the face, frightfully thin. I get covered in fleas, and all the sandflies and mosquitoes in the district come and graze on me. I have to ride mules, which I loathe, or walk, which makes my heart bump. I eat the most awful food and drink the most

139

awful tea. If I lie down in the shade the sun goes swiftly round the tree until it is shining right on me.

But I see views, people, places I never imagined existed; I learn new customs and hear old history. Sometimes I am wonderfully lucky and see something very few white people have seen before. I make friends with servants, soldiers and odd, charming people in remote villages. I get hard and strong, my mind opens out and becomes more receptive. Birds sing new tunes to me and I smell new scents. And for a short time I'm not only independent but completely responsible for my own safety, which is a grand feeling. I shed the aura of civilization and become quite a different person. And everywhere I go makes me love Kenya more!

But I do make the most awful gaffes. I have just discovered that I drove away the village patriarch when we first arrived in Chelki. A large crowd of villagers sat on the bank just above where I was trying to rest and started spitting and yelling at each other, so I told them to go away. One was the patriarch. They all wear the same sort of rags and have the same sort of faces; it's really impossible for an outsider to tell t'other from which.

There is an ancient church here, nearly at the top of a rocky hill; I've just been up to see it with my two policemen. Built onto a huge rock, it has narrow holes or slits up and down the wall. It is of roughly squared stones mortared together, and must have had two storeys. On one side there are double arches one above the other, rather like very big chimney arches, and a hollow beneath the lower arch – filled, now, with rubbish. On one corner stone is a cross in a circle, like the one I saw at Petra.

There is a very small door placed in the middle of one wall, shut with a six-inch-thick wooden door bolted with iron. Over the doorway is another cross, encircled; round it is a snake and above, to one side, what looks like the sun. Outside the main building, which has a flat roof of stone slabs supporting a foot of earth and stone, are the ruins of another enclosure, about fifteen tombstones and regular rows of holes in the ground, which might at one time have held pillars – six on one side, but the others are difficult to count. Some have been filled up and some used as fireplaces. Then there is a small wall with an archway in it, and, just outside, a big square tomb – a marvellous place to be buried, with the Khabur roaring below and the mountains all round. This place might be any age and now I do want the patriarch to tell me its history, if he can, and if he will come. I climbed the hill at the back and found another graveyard and behind that another big tomb. Then up and up till I seemed to be on top of the world. I could see for miles, range after range of mountains and the Khabur twisting beneath me, bright silver.

Later the 'Patri' came and drank tea; we were very polite to each other. He could not tell me much about the church, which is of unknown age. The story goes that as the man who built it sat on the high rocks there he lost sight of his little son, and prayed: 'God, give me back my son and I will build a mosque here.' After two days the man found the child, but he was dead. He built the mosque and buried the little boy there. Later it became a Christian church, and is so still. It might be a thousand years old or more. Some of its tombs are very ancient, and I'm told that in the last twenty years no outsider has seen the church but one other Englishman and me.

A lot of trouble about crossing the river tomorrow. A policeman has just come back from the village to say that the ferry crossing is too dangerous and I must go by the bridge. But that is worse, for I *know* I should lose my head and fall in; I'm helpless at a height. I said I would ask for men to build new rafts. I simply can't go back to Amadia, but it does sound discouraging, not to say dangerous.

30 MAY

Left camp late, as usual, and rode to the village where the raft was supposed to be. Of course, it wasn't there. The river roared along looking most dangerous, and everyone yelled. Foreseeing a long wait, I rode back to investigate a cave I had seen below the old church. High up in a tall rock was a squared door, not the usual rounded cave entrance. Inside was a space about ten feet square, and a ledge ran round three feet from the ground; there were three niches cut in the three walls – seats, altars, or light holders?

There must have been a prehistoric settlement here, for over the other side of the river there are two crude drawings in the rock, one apparently an antelope with five horns but only two legs, and one a four-legged creature of unknown species wearing a large hat. Further down is another squared doorway in a tall grey rock; and all about are huge tumbled heaps of stones, once a township of some sort.

When I got back to the village, no raft of course. After more yelling it was said that the men on the other side would appear, with raft, at a fine place for crossing a little further down. Reached the place; the river was just as swift here and very much deeper – fifty yards wide at least. It looked extremely dangerous.

Then two men appeared on the far bank and started to make the raft; it was to be of four or five poles, tied with ropes and covered with thin sticks. It would take two or three hours to make and we should spend the rest of the day getting ourselves across – if we succeeded. Denha, one of my policemen, said he knew the way to a big bridge on the main road, which meant three days' trek to Zakho instead of two. So I thought we'd give up the raft idea and go on as fast as we could – Faris on a shabby-looking, very good mule, me on a flashy-looking white animal which could barely walk and certainly not canter, and Denha on a donkey on which he slipped from side to side, being apparently no horseman. Faris, without stirrups, went hell-for-leather up and down the mountains; he can certainly ride. The track was almost invisible, the gradient 1 in 2 or 3, up and down which we crawled (F. miles ahead always), resting now and then, and bumping along on the flat; each climb took at least an hour. It was certainly exhausting work, but much worse for the mules.

At last we went down the last hillside and reached Déhé, a filthy, smelly little village of the worst sort. I lay under a tree and tried to rest when suddenly a voice said: 'Good morning, lady. You suttinly are far from civilization. I am the son of the village head-man. Anything I can do for you, you're perfectly welcome. Yes, mam, I been in America since I was eight and came here three years ago. Yes, mam.'

I *was* surprised; and looking round I found dozens of villagers and myriads of children sitting comfortably on the ground staring at me. More arrived every second. The chap took me away from my tree to the gorge, talking all the time. 'During the troubles two years ago, night and day my rifle never left my hands nor I never stopped guarding the gorge. Yes, mam. We were only thirty rifles here and surrounded with Kurdi armies, but they never dared attack us. Yes, mam. This was a vurry old city. See them big stones there? They were all houses time of Nineveh. Yes, mam. Then Genghis Khan and his army came through here, but he never took Déhé and he went up to the top of the Tyari mountains and all of his army he had only ten men left – the Assyrians had killed the lot. Yes, mam. Course, that's only hearsay handed down from father to son. The Kurdi destroyed some of the neighbouring villages, but they never got Déhé – I been all over the place. I was in Norway, wasn't doing nothin' at all. I had one thousand pounds in gold I brought from Russia. Yes, mam. Our church was built by disciples of St Thomas two hundred years before Mohammed was born. There's a heap of old towers all around there, where they found ancient coins from time to time. This ain't much of a city to bring you to, but plenty come here. Yes, mam.'

At the gorge I found I had to camp on the site of his summer house. It looked nice enough with the towering rocks on either hand and an icy stream rushing past, but every puff of wind blew sand about. Soon his womenfolk brought me luncheon on a tray: eggs, milk, tea, Kurdish butter and very good, paper-thin Assyrian chapattis. He said that while I was in his village I must eat his food. But though I asked for supper at six and he rushed away to bring it, nothing more happened and at last, in despair, I went to bed empty. Out came the fleas. Fast as I caught one, another hopped happily about having a good feed. I lay on the hard sand, too tired to sleep, every hour or so flea-hunting with the torch and the Flit. By midnight I'd caught six. Then just as I was going to sleep there was a lot of clattering by my head and there sat the guard, not two feet away, chatting and smoking abominable cigarettes. I shouted for Faris, who at last dislodged them. Then another flea came out and gorged – it was extremely hot and now and then there was a breath of air which covered me with dirty sand and dust. I think it was truly the worst night I've ever spent.

31 MAY

I woke at 4.30 after two or three hours' sleep and dressed very quickly – no washing, no breakfast – wanting to go as fast and far as possible from this horrible and even sinister place.

In an hour and a half we reached the Khabur again, meaning definitely to cross by raft. Though just as swift and deep here, it's not quite so wide. After the inevitable wait, while all the villagers sat in a circle and chattered, the raft was brought. It consisted of half a dozen gourds tied with rope in a circle about the size of a tyre! So I bribed a chap to go across and take a wire to Zakho for Boy and with a deep sigh of relief started off for the main road bridge, once more two days away, they say. Everyone was delighted we weren't going to try to cross on the gourds; Denha touched his forehead and said 'Thank you', and Faris said 'Not for one tousand dinars' would he have tried it.

Very hot trek today, from 6.30 to 3 p.m. We've left the mountains behind and are now in the foothills – soft, rolling country, good soil, lots of barley, grass and trees, but very hot. The people must be peculiar. When Denha went on to the village the other asker stayed behind with Faris and me; otherwise, he said, we might get shot. But I think he was just being self-important.

Zakho Hill is now in sight, and said to be only six hours away. I do hope to heaven that's true. I'm terribly tired and don't feel well, but that may be lack of sleep and food and a lot of hard exercise. I must be mad to leave home. What a garden of Eden Kenya is and what a *perfect* home I've got there, and it will be at least six weeks before I get back!

1 JUNE

The fleas came out again like a covey of partridges last night, in spite of my bed of grass being in the open. After an exciting two-hour hunt I got six, but two more got away. However, the starry sky was lovely and in the end I slept quite well, though awakened every little while by strange insects exploring me. There are more insects in Iraq to the square inch than in any other place in the world.

We got away at six, and bustled along till eight o'clock when we came to a village. Only four hours more, I thought. But there, asleep right in our path, was the loveliest, fattest, fluffiest white puppy with grey patches round the eyes and one or two grey markings. I was undone! I got off, stalked it, scratched its tummy, picked it up and fell in love with it. The poor owner, who wanted to keep it because it was a bitch, had to give way in the end and let me have her. I promised him half a dinar (about ten shillings) for the loan of his brother as guide to Zakho (six hours away, they now say) and the pup. So off we went again; the half-blind, half-gaga, very ancient and

143

unspeakably dirty brother crawled along, tugging my mule, and I carried the pup in my arms and tried to keep the sun off her. It got hotter and hotter. And then hotter still.

As we went forward, Zakho retreated. Now and then we stopped to rest, and the poor, panting little puppy drank water feverishly out of my hand. She struggled and scratched me and turned round and round, and I ached and sweated and got sore, and I thought we should both die before we got to Zakho. The glare off the white stones was blinding; the only trees were four feet high – there was no shade anywhere. Sometimes a puff of wind came and scorched us. My lips felt as if they had been cut with a knife – and still we crawled on. I told Faris to hurry my mule along, so he beat it till it kicked and jolted me all through. I said, 'Don't make it kick,' so he left it alone and on we crept. Then we came to an ancient arched bridge and the old ghoul dragging my mule said, 'There is a woman buried in that hole under that arch, and a few years ago her hand hung out, but it has gone now.'

To add to our joys, during the day we lost Denha; he stopped to drink and never came back to us. We waited a long time; then I told Faris to ride back to the top of the hill and shout. 'How you say if I got killed?' said Faris, rather to my surprise, and went off expecting to be shot at any moment. I believe he was actually right and that the Kurds in this bit of country are really bad. However, I followed him on foot and found both him and Denha (who had lost the road), so all was well.

At last we actually crossed the Khabur on the bridge and got to Zakho, where I went straight to the doctor's house. I was all in; we had been going ten hours, for eight of which I had carried the pup. The doctor gave me and Lakri (the puppy) tea and biscuits and cocoa. I recovered quite soon, as I usually do. Then we went to the rest house which seems clean, cool, quiet and nice; it is above the dam on the river, which makes a lovely noise. The doctor had just come in from a shooting case, and when he left me at the rest house was called away to another. They certainly are gunmen here.

I got two cables from Boy, to my greatest delight. They were apparently getting worried about me in Baghdad and Mosul as I was late, but I was unable to communicate until yesterday; it wasn't my fault.

I had a *bath* this evening, in an old tin one, but nevertheless a bath – and my last flea died by drowning. I still remember Lakri's first bath. She had a thick mat of fleas under her coat and Faris bought a cake of carbolic soap in the bazaar, with which I scrubbed her all over. Dead fleas cascaded from her and an hour later she was entirely flealess.

3 JUNE

The old bridge I saw is apparently about eight hundred years old; there was a big city here then, and even earlier, but its history is not known, except that Alexander passed this way. Otherwise I suppose the story is the usual one of battle, treachery and sudden death – in fact it still is, what with three shootings this week. The Zaimakhan's office is one of the more modern buildings, being only about four hundred years old. The present town was built centuries ago by a Jew called Zakho; and that is all I know about it. When the bridge was being built, there was trouble with the river, then in spate. The ruler prayed to Allah, promising to sacrifice the first person who crossed it. It was his beloved only little daughter who came running across, and it was her hand which I had been told hung from the bridge.

After endless delays, arguing, bargaining, running backwards downhill instead of forwards up it etc., we got started, in the oldest car in the world, for Mosul. She boiled all the way and did not answer to the steering wheel. Bits came adrift now and then, and with the heat of the engine my feet nearly caught fire sitting in the front carrying Lakri. The wind covered me in hot dust. I would really rather do eight hours on a horse than four hours (which is what it took us to reach Mosul) in a car.

Near Dohuk, we said goodbye to Denha Daniel. He has been very good. I gave him a good baksheesh and my flea-ridden coat, with which he was delighted. It is very warm and I don't suppose he minds fleas.

6 JUNE

There are more smells and noises in Mosul than it's possible to believe. Every other shop has a wireless or a gramophone going, or both at once. The smells are indescribable, composed of human beings, old food, hot dust, dung, coffee, dirty clothes, meat, horses, bad water, dirt and human beings again. In the afternoon a very hot wind blows dust over and through the town, and everything shakes in a haze of heat; the electric fans throw a wave of hot air on you as you lie on the bed, sweating.

I went to Jonah's tomb yesterday. It is a beautiful place and to my astonishment perfectly clean, quiet and dignified. After the usual blackmail (take off your shoes – 'baksheesh' – 'Here's two hundred fils' – 'Give four hundred' – 'No' – Put on your shoes – 'Or ri, two, come in.') we entered a long stone passage. High in the wall is an arch set with old tiles of an exquisite blue-green. You look through a grille at the tomb, and a hump of dark stuff covers what I suppose is the coffin. On one side hangs the sword of a swordfish – the one which swallowed Jonah – and a short time ago they had a saucer and a little bit of soap with which he washed himself while travelling along in the fish's tummy!

19 JULY

Lakri and I stayed in Mosul four or five days. It was 110° in the shade every day. Going out very early in the morning one did get a little air, but it was hardly worth breathing, even then.

Once Colonel and Mrs Allen and I went to Erbil, the Arbela of Alexander's time, said to be the oldest continuously inhabited city in the world. It is so ancient that it has grown up out of the desert, fresh houses always being built on the debris of the old ones, until it looks like a cake on a plate. It is now about two hundred feet above the desert floor.

The entrance to Erbil is a huge, fine archway; within, narrow streets flanked by tall houses of mud bricks twist and turn, running about in every direction. The moment we got out of the car we were mobbed by scores of children. They ran around us, trod on us, screeched at us, posed for photographs, pawed our clothes and begged. Two men took pity on us and tried to get rid of them, throwing stones and trying to hit them with sticks, but that was just part of the game, and the delighted children dodged about, screeching louder.

Now and then one of the huge old wooden doors opened a crack and a woman peered through. They were beautiful and very richly dressed: strings of gold coins hung round their necks, and on their heads they wore hard black fezzes covered in gauzy handkerchiefs and jingling with gold coins. We got few glimpses of them – the moment they saw the camera or Colonel Allen they shut the doors.

20 JULY

They were harvesting barley. The men here wear big straw sun-hats crowned with bunches of feathers. They move along in line, men and women reaping and working hard. At intervals stand small fortified towers, guarding the crops. One group of workers was being supervised by the farmer on horseback, his two dogs sitting beside the horse. It was all very peaceful and bucolic.

Mrs Allen and I went shopping, with Mr Condopoulos. I lost my head over a pair of diamond ear-rings and paid £8 for them (I think they were worth more), then repented and gave them back, losing ten shillings on the deal. I bought three beautiful long narrow carpets, such as I have seen in the women's rooms running round the walls. They are about three feet wide and twenty feet long; I only paid £11 for the three, but it took a great combined effort to get them at that price.

Lakri has been a terrific success with everyone who sees her; she prances about looking like a white woolly toy. Right up to the evening before I left I didn't know if I could take her into Kenya or not; then when I had the cable to say I could, it was too late to get her a fiancé. She missed Denha to begin with and ran hopefully after every policeman she saw, sniffing at their heels. She soon became obedient, though rather rude about the house.

The relaxations here are polo (two or three a side) and swimming in the RAF pool, which is walled off from the public eye by a barrier of old petrol tins, cut open and nailed together. Not very pretty. From the top of the diving board there is a fine view (when there is no dust storm) of unlimited flat scrubby desert and fields in one direction; in another the mounds which once were Nineveh and behind them those alluring, deceitful mountains, looking so quiet and grand. But really I don't wonder that people who have to pass their lives in Baghdad and Mosul look upon the hills as cool, beautiful promises of paradise.

The houses here are bearable; that is all. People carry their precious, beloved rugs about so that the floors are always well-dressed. They also try to grow flowers, pathetically enough, in petrol tins – and from a distance there are quite bright patches of colour. But Mosul smells and Mosul sounds and Mosul dust penetrate everywhere. However, these people get used to them and are brave and uncomplaining. I come here fresh from Kenya, and spoilt, with a critical eye; and I thank God I don't have to live here.

I couldn't make up my mind which way to go to England – I tried Imperial Airways, but there was no plane until the 18th from Baghdad. Then there was the 'Stamboul Train'. This meant five days in the train, plus at least two in Istanbul, because it would be criminal to go through it without stopping; apart from the big extra expense, I had really had had enough of Eastern cities. So I decided to go by train and car through Syria and pick up a boat at Beirut. Up to the last minute I couldn't make up my mind about Lakri, and then suddenly realized I *couldn't* leave her behind, and trusted to Providence to help me put her on the road to Kenya.

A convoy of six cars gathered at the hotel. We were due to leave at 1.30 and did quite well for Iraq, getting away about three. Lakri and I and a man were in the last and oldest car. It was so lovely to be on the road again, and actually leaving Mosul behind; it seemed too good to be true. It was. In ten minutes we reached a petrol station where all the cars filled up for the trip. This took over an hour.

In the fields at fairly regular intervals were large humps like old barrows. My companion (who has been here for years) said these were prehistoric landmarks, or perhaps harvest forts, and stretched all the way to China. In the mountains to the south of the road was the only other colony of Yezidi I heard of: mysterious people with their fallen-in faces and turned-up noses, and their aloofness and their devil worship.

We got to Beirut after ten and a half hours of pure hell, and I staggered out of the car aching in every bone. I had tidied my face up but my clothes were disreputable, and Lakri was white again – with dust. It was heaven to be in a large, pretty room with a grand bathroom and a lovely view across the harbour, twinkling with the lights of hundreds of little boats, to the lighted town beyond.

We stayed here two days and Lakri put on weight by the hour; she also had a proper shampoo from a delighted hotel coiffeur. We took a hot and dusty drive over stony, glaring and unimpressive hills (the mighty Lebanon) to Baalbek. I understood I had to have a guide, so I gave him my coat to hold and told him not to dare come near me unless I called, and then not to speak unless I told him to. Then I went off alone with Lakri, and sat among the pillars and arches and tried to dream of the past, as I have so often done. But Baalbek eluded me; there seemed no spirit of gracious dead beauty hovering over the carved stones; the grandeur and pride of Karnak, and the exquisite delicacy and loneliness of Petra were missing.

The wretched guide, feeling humiliated, insisted on leading me to the Temple of Mercury (or Bacchus); here on the arch is some lovely and intricate carving, but nothing really impressive.

I went into the little museum and saw a white plaster model of Baalbek as it was two or three thousand years ago. This was really beautiful – the layout was gigantic and the pillars and temples magnificent. But it has all gone; the glories of Baalbek now are an encircling iron railing, several picture postcard booths and some depressed-looking guides. This really was a waste of money and a day; I wished I had gone to Damascus instead.

I tried to book a seat in an aeroplane here, but no one could tell me anything. So I got on an Italian ship and set sail for Alexandria. Lakri was very interested in all the new smells and the new motion; she had a lovely new kennel made for her by her devoted admirer, the hotel hall porter. She vamped the cabin steward and stewardess at once; they gave her huge meals of unsuitable food, and sat on the floor playing with her instead of doing their work. I took her for walks on the top deck and the wireless officer came and talked to us. Fearful strain between England and Italy over the Abyssinian situation [*Mussolini was to invade in October*]. The Italian press has been spreading the most absurd lies, such as a concentration of eight thousand troops on the northern Frontier of Kenya (there are eighty there, permanently); British advisers to the Emperor of Abyssinia (there are also French, Swedish, Belgian and others), a British tutor for his son (he is not British), and God knows what else. They also bitterly attack Anthony Eden, who is only doing his utmost to avoid war. However in spite of all this the (Italian) wireless officer was very nice to us, and in twenty-four hours we arrived in Alexandria.

Now I was practically in England, and anyhow I knew many people here. I went straight to the telephone when I got into the hotel and tried a number of friends, all airways pilots. All away and so I was still alone. Not even the Imperial Airways clerk was there (a boy called Lee-Warner, from Bletchingley in Surrey, near Anstie).

There was nothing for it but to get into another Italian ship and crawl to Brindisi, where Lakri and I parted. She was shut in her kennel and carried away to the station, yelping with rage and despair and trying to bite her way out. She had a beastly long train journey before her, and several hours' wait in some burning hot station in the middle of the day. However, they telephoned the next day from Port Said to say she had arrived, was very well and everyone had stopped work and was playing with her. Now she goes by Union Castle to Kenya, where she has six months' quarantine.

[*In due course Lakri emerged from quarantine. She had grown into a beauty – her coat was thick and white, all but the grey rings round her eyes. She was loving, clever and polite. She rode with me, leaping through the long grass and never leaving me to hunt. Her inherited instincts were to guard, not to destroy – I never had a dog I loved better.*]

1936

29 AUGUST

France, on the way to Spain. After worrying a good many people, I got a vague letter from the *Evening Standard* which might be misconstrued into saying I was their war correspondent. I also got four letters to correspondents through Patrick Balfour, who couldn't have been more kind and helpful.

In the aeroplane I got that happy, soaring, invulnerable feeling I always get when I start off for somewhere on my own. But I soon got deflated as the anti-typhoid injection in my leg took a hold. I nearly fainted from pure pain at Le Bourget, and spent the next five hours in the most exquisite torture crawling about on the arms of various taxi drivers and people from Cook's, and feeling like an old hag at Bournemouth. At last I was able to get into the sleeper, and that was better.

Next day at Pau, all pain gone, I wandered about wondering how on earth to get to Spain, till the *concierge* rang up the best hotel in Hendaye [*the border town*] and found that the *Times* man was there. So I stepped into the train again and stepped out at Hendaye, where I found Mr Steere and Mr Rice of the *Morning Post*.

Very exercised in my mind over the family of the waiter at Pau – one wife and five children in San Sebastian and the poor man is frantic to get them out. I said I'd try, but don't quite see what to do. Rice did say he might come to San Sebastian with me. I can just see him nursing smelly Spanish babies, supposing I *can* get them out! Me too! Even funnier.

Here in this hotel you can hear the boom and rattle of artillery; everyone looks rather suppressed and strained, to my imaginative eyes. A waiter told me all the roads, houses etc. round San Sebastian were mined, '*et si les rebelles avancent . . . pouf! . . . tout ça s'enterra! Et j'en ai vu des réfugiés, moi, arrivés en maillot de mer, qui avaient traversé à la nage à la pointe là.*'

I got a taxi, and the driver said he would take me to Biriatout for 60 francs. The hotel *concierge* looked pompous and said I was risking my life, and no one liked that road. The driver was extremely unprepossessing – as fat as a hippo, bleary, beery, scrubby, slightly bearded, he rolled in his seat, his eye leered (quite unintentionally) and in a real gin voice he told me of the awful dangers we were facing.

We went to the station, where I announced I was a journalist and said I wanted a pass. Impossible: Mr Chadwick of the *Evening Standard* had taken one. I said he was *Daily Express*, but that annoyed the chap so I hurriedly said of course I'd made a mistake. He said one paper, one pass, was the rule, but just as I was beginning to wilt with disappointment he gave three large shrugs and signed my pass. We started forth. A *gendarme* wearing a steel helmet looked at it, then at us, sadly and said: '*Passez – à votre risque et péril.*' But we went on, my Falstaff leering happily at me and saying: '*Du moment que j'ai une cavalière courageuse!*' He gave me a small cushion to hold against my face. We stopped at Béhobie, where people were hiding behind houses watching the fighting, while every now and then spent bullets whistled overhead. I borrowed some field glasses off a man and could see soldiers lying behind sandbags, shooting.

Further on we saw a well defended farmhouse where a lot of shooting was going on. Falstaff was terribly pleased: '*Voyez, madame – voyez l'embuscade! Ils tirent dessus d'en-haut – c'est fort dangereux ici, vous savez. Allez – marchons!*'

At Biriatout there was a crowd of people, mostly journalists, standing on the terrace watching the fighting. Decided to stay the night; *la patronne* found me a room. The firing never ceases; they are fighting below us in the valley, not two hundred yards away. Machine guns break into a vicious rattle, then they seem to draw a snarling breath and have a short rest before starting again. Rifles go crack-crack-crack; lots of the bullets scream away in the distance – very bad shooting, I think. The people here are terrified of aerial bombardment; a bomb has already fallen on a roof. A peasant girl wanted to return to Béhobie, which is about two kilometres down the mountain path; she said bullets were continually dropping against the walls and doors there. At sunset there was a short lull, and then we heard the soldiers singing. Their voices rose up to us from the valley in long, sad notes; and then the firing broke out again.

The children play pelota; the guns crash and boom; old women sit about knitting; the lovely old church tolls its bell; there is a crackle of machine gun fire, someone turns on a radio and you hear swing music. Later the moonlight pours softly down while Spaniards go on trying to kill each other; from the crest of every hill come regular flashes followed seconds later by loud thuds.

30 AUGUST

The firing never stopped for more than a few minutes all night long; I awoke at 4.30 and went out about 6.30. Exquisite morning, with mountains piled all round us, their crests lit in the sunrise. I went into the church where there was an early service, then walked through the meadows behind. Nothing could have been more peaceful and beautiful; the air smelt of frost and the things which grow in hills. It might have been Scotland. I looked back – a long line of soldiers was moving up the hillside to a house above them. Then an aeroplane appeared, frightening the villagers badly; it circled in the sky and there was an explosion. No aim was possible at that height – the bombs might have fallen anywhere.

I talked to some Frenchmen who had crossed the mountains from St Jean de Luz; after a while three of them and I went down the little track to the road which runs beside the river. Just across the stream was Spain, and there were half a dozen soldiers drinking in the river. I called to them first in English and then in French; one of them knew French. After a while I waded over and talked to them. They were pleasant boys, about twenty to twenty-five years old; dressed in dark blue dungarees. They were well armed, with heaps of ammunition, and had plenty of food. They were quite happy and their morale was good. Seeing all was safe and I wasn't being shot or captured, some time later two of the Frenchmen followed. They told the boy who could speak French that there were definitely two spies at Biriatout making signals, and said they had better tell their chief. At last we had to leave them, shaking hands with them all warmly and wishing them the best of luck.

I panted up the hill again and came face to face with two *gendarmes* who hadn't, thank goodness, seen me. I hid my wet legs and dripping skirt and sat on a wall talking to a poor girl who was in a state of dithering nerves over the aerial bombing, until the *gendarmes* had moved on.

Came back to Hendaye later, and rushed to Cibours to see the French Ambassador to Spain for permission to go to San Sebastian; absolutely refused. I wrote down all the details about the waiter's family, and begged him to help them. Then to the Spanish Consul – gone till Monday. Then to the frontier bridges; the French allowed my driver and me to walk over to the Spanish end, where I begged in vain for a pass to go to San Sebastian. Tomorrow I might try again, they said. These men were dirty and shabby and didn't fill me with trust and confidence like the other lot did.

Jean, the driver, is a grand chap, the son (I think) of bleary old Falstaff. His taxi was hit twice by ricocheting bullets last night when he came to Biriatout with my camera; but he didn't care. He's game for anything and I think is panting to go to San Sebastian. The Basques are lovely people, proud and gay and charming, with courtly manners. Everyone is so friendly, and under these conditions you just talk to anybody, instead of staring coldly the other way.

31 AUGUST

Yesterday I returned to Hendaye and motored up to Béhobie in the evening with Andrew Rice, an American woman and a Canadian pianist named

Jimmy Campbell (a fantastic player, with a devil in every finger). Rice pulled the American woman's leg and suggested she should go up to Biriatout (the road is under fire occasionally).

Would she? She would not! Hadn't she three children and a husband dependent on her, and though God knew she wasn't afraid, it wasn't fair to them or her hundreds of friends – etc. etc. While she was protesting I went down to the bridge and had a talk to the *gendarmes*, watching the big gun firing; a burst of scarlet stars – crash – pause – burst of stars – crash. Rifles cracked at intervals and now and then we heard the bullets whine – but as Rice says, you never hear the one that hits you. Had great jokes with the *gendarmes* and we were getting on famously when the *douanier* appeared and ordered me to 'circulate' as it was dangerous (how they love that word!) to *stoppér*.

I returned to the car where the American woman was still giving tongue but on a lower note, and we shot away to the safety of the road at the back of Hendaye. About midnight a heavily laden lorry roared past us up the hill, undoubtedly carrying ammunition to Irun. Train loads and lorry loads go in nightly; obviously the *gendarmes* have orders to let them pass. If we had waited a bit longer at Béhobie we might have seen it – though probably we should have been sent away before it arrived. People say that gun parts, ammunition and food go in every night, and Fascist watchers on the roads can't stop them. Meanwhile Blum [*the French Premier*], whose son is manager of an arms factory in Russia, is inaugurating a non-intervention policy, by which every nation pledges itself not to send help of any kind to either side. Thus everyone is happy. The governments all make *beaux gestes*; the arms manufacturers are making money, and both sides get supplies. That is how wars are made to last a long time, so that more people are killed, more buildings destroyed, and more money is made by the arms manufacturers.

Today to St Jean de Luz, to try to reach Pampluna. The Insurgent [*Franco's forces – the Nationalists*] publicity agent's office is in a mysterious little house on a hill just outside the town. A carload of journalists goes to Pampluna and Burgos every day. I waited two and a half hours but was told I could not go today – '*Mais demain, peut être.*'

Several of us were in the porch when we were suddenly bundled inside a room, and a man whispered to me that he believed one of the Spanish princes was there. After a time I went out. The room opposite was in darkness; two men were sitting on the bed with their backs to the door, which was open.

I talked to a Yugoslav journalist; he was terribly thin, unshaven and haggard, and looked miserably poor. He spoke very bitterly of rich people and of religion, said there was no God – how could there be when there was war, poverty and misery everywhere? I was desperately sorry for him. I *know* there is God, but how can *I* talk when I have every comfort and happiness that life can give one? He was unhappy and lost, with nothing to hold onto, and I couldn't help him. We walked down to the town, and I pretended to be fearfully poor too. He offered me something to eat, but I refused. It was all very fine pretending to be poor, but I felt rather a cad. Our values are so wrong. When I think of the money one spends on clothes, food, decorating one's house and so on, it seems utterly insane. I am far, far happier and have much more fun going about like this, on the loose and in the rough; meeting strange, interesting and often very charming people in perfect camaraderie; and eating when and where I can. I suppose I'd hate it if I wasn't in a position just to open a door and step into the other life again. But at present this is heaven to me.

I had a good laugh on myself today, at eleven o'clock and again at 11.20 a.m., when we heard some loud reports. Everyone (I was in the Press Bureau) jumped and said: 'What's that?' I thought it might be a ship firing across another ship's bows to halt and search her – it might be an 'international incident' – it might be anything! Hours later, after endless inquiries, I discovered it was the starting signal for the Sunday game of Pelota.

I returned to Hendaye in the bus and heard there had been tragedy at Biriatout – bombs dropped on the village and a girl killed. Rice couldn't get through on the telephone, so I got a taxi and went up the hill. I stopped on the way to photograph the gallant old fighting train which lost its battle against the Insurgent tank last Wednesday, and retired to safety round a corner. I asked the *gendarmes* if I could take a photo; the reply was the inevitable *'A votre risque et péril.'* I must say I did feel a qualm as I walked down that very exposed bit of road to the corner; but for the three or four minutes it took me to get there and back there was a lull in the firing.

At Biriatout we found the rumour about the girl was completely untrue, thank God; and the telephone was cut because it is Sunday! My driver discovered that an escaped rebel soldier had been found hiding on a farm, and was being taken to Hendaye. He arrived in a car, crouching behind several other men. He was a thin, exhausted, miserable-looking rat. At first he was delighted with the large crowd who peered at him, and with the publicity, and then he suddenly began to wilt and look white and done in. People said he would probably go to the Front Populaire – Government troops – to fight, but I think all he wants is a quiet time. They say there are spies all along this hillside.

Just heard a big battle starts tonight, at 8 p.m. It's seven now. The firing is hotting up and we can see men moving into fresh positions. They have been working on the trenches, making them deeper, and two tanks, looking like battle-of-flowers cars with their camouflage of green branches, have moved down the road. The troops sing and sing: *'España! España!'* The sound of their voices drifts up the hill to us. They sing every night, but this evening more than ever; extra wine ration, I should think! They are in very strong positions – some in a wood almost at the top of the hill, others in a wooded gully. They move up the hillside in groups of ten or fifteen. There is a Red Cross station on the road, and when aeroplanes come over they run to fetch the flag and spread it out. The big gun at Béhobie bridge hasn't got the range right, thank God – its shells burst on a hillside beyond the last line of trenches. We hear a great boom, then whizz . . . goes the shell. We see the men lined up and waiting; it passes over their heads and explodes with a splendid crash on the hillside five hundred yards beyond them.

7.45: hot rifle and machine gun fire. Mr Steere not back yet; they were supposed to get back long before this. 8.15: firing practically stopped. For supper?

Everyone is getting nervy. People quarrel loudly over nothing at all, and the women in the *auberge* shriek with hysterical laughter at the slightest thing. One was idiotic enough to wave a handkerchief to the men across the river; we stopped her. We are not allowed to eat or drink on the edge of the terrace, as they think that the flash of glasses, knives etc. might attract fire. While I was watching through Woodhall's glasses the men on the other side saw me, and one raised his arm as a salute or signal, but I thought it better not to wave.

About 9 p.m. I walked down the road to the next inn, wondering where Mr Steere was, and came upon an old man who was astonished to see me and obviously regarded me as a spy. I asked him if there was an inn here; he said vaguely that he thought there was a little bar, but didn't know its name! People are getting more and more cautious in what they say until they get rather tight; then they scream their opinions at each other. I don't think there will be a revolution; I think there might be a civil war! It strikes me there is just as much Fascism as Communism. A strong Democratic Government is probably the only solution, though where its strength is to come from God knows – except from a dictator, and *they* are pretty dangerous; there aren't many Dolfusses.

It was quiet all night; I came back to Hendaye with Steere, but hardly slept at all out of pure excitement. I honestly believe that all that shelling and firing is setting up air currents which *do* affect the nerves; everyone seems full of electricity – I know I am! Something has come alive in me; I'm simply tingling with life and eagerness – I don't see how I shall ever settle to normal life again.

I'm trying for Pampluna again today; how I *pray* I shall get in! The scenery here is so gloriously beautiful. Mountains tower all round us, green and forested, and the distant ones have a mauve haze over them; at sunset each crest catches fire, and then you see that each crest is fortified with a redoubt – and you are back in the war again.

31 AUGUST

I got to Burgos! Press cars, owner-driven, run every day between St Jean de Luz and Burgos, the seat of the provisional National Government – in other words, the rebels. The Yugoslav journalist I was talking to yesterday (so poor and tattered) turned up very well dressed, with a very small and expensive camera hung round his neck – he no longer looked like a starving tramp. There was also a French boy called de Girondes in the car. Our driver was named Macaya; he had, he said, once led a fleet of racing cars at a Brussels *tournée*, and he drove like a devil – the speedometer danced between 90 and 115 k.p.m. [*60–70 m.p.h.*] We tore through the most glorious mountainous, wooded scenery, leaning round corners, skidding round precipices, till I got all air-minded again and the Yugoslav clutched at his seat, pale with fear.

At Véra, in Navarre, we mounted the traditional red and yellow flag, the Royalist flag of Spain. Lorry after lorry passed us on the road, some crowded with singing soldiers to whom the driver gave the Fascist salute, some weighed down with ammunition, some loaded with livestock and others with flour and provisions, all going up to the Irun front. Everywhere the enthusiasm was splendid – the same spirit of patriotism animates everyone, from the children cheering and waving at us to the sturdy old farmers armed with antique rifles, guarding the roads and interrogating passing cars. Everyone felt excited and important, but it was not easy to guess which side they were on.

Pampluna was crowded with soldiers; now and then they sing choruses and the last words are always '*España! España!*' Draped across the balconies are long strips of cloth bearing the words 'For God, for King, for Country'. There are several distinct parties: Nationalists, Legionnaires, Carlists in scarlet berets and Fascists in dark blue (more of these than any others) – they sit apart from each other in the cafés, and I wonder what form of government they will evolve after all this business is over (they *must* win) and how the Carlists will settle down under, say, a Fascist Government? At present they are all fighting loyally side by side to throw the Communist–Anarchists out of Spain – but what next?

A few women wore Red Cross armlets, while most of the children and some young girls were dressed in dark blue Fascist uniform. The Insurgents have no 'fighting women', which is against their idea of what is right and seemly. But their women are doing secretarial work, nursing, etc., though a great many are obviously doing nothing but sitting in the cafés all day long indulging in the national sport of conversation. The noise is deafening. They talk unceasingly and apparently aimlessly, just like Arabs.

As there was no room for me in the press car I had to go on to Burgos by train, so I spent another five hours wandering in Pampluna and watching the people. Rifles, still with paper sticking to them, are stacked against the pillars of the cafés. Priests move about among the soldiers. Everyone wears the red and gold ribbon, and religious medals or crucifixes.

I found I had not nearly enough money, or I would have hired a car to go to Burgos. I had brought 500 francs, equal to about £5 – plenty, I thought, for two nights in a cheap country like Spain. But here I only got 45 pesetas for 100 francs, and the car would have cost 200 pesetas, so the train was the only method of progression, and second class at that. The journey took six and a half hours – and what a journey! I was put into the first train by the kind old hotel porter; the carriage was full of ceaselessly chattering peasants. After crawling along for some hours we reached the terminus, and waited endlessly on the platform for the next train.

Not knowing a syllable of Spanish all I could do was to show my ticket and ask 'Burgos?' in inquiring tones. The next train left in the dark; I sat in a wooden compartment full of peasants and soldiers. They were all very intrigued to find a woman travelling alone, and clustered round screaming questions. I just shook my head and said *'Inglese'*. Two Civil Guards appeared (they are a cross between a policeman and a soldier; rifles; khaki uniforms; curiously bent – almost tricorne – hard, black, shiny hats). They asked lots of questions and looked at my passport and the press letter. I had no official pass – no one had told me to get one. They went away. I went to sleep. Presently a police officer appeared – same performance. I fell asleep again, sitting upright on the wooden seat. Someone shook me by the shoulder, looked at the passport and the letter and examined the bottle of Evian I had brought. I hadn't any luggage. They kept on asking me questions which I could not answer. Some time later it happened again – then again – then again.

By the time we got to Burgos, at half past twelve at night, I was exhausted, and realized I was in a rather stupid positon, with not enough money, no proper papers, and not a word of Spanish. Two Civil Guards were standing by the corridor door, quite obviously waiting for me; one jumped out of the train in front of me and hurried down the platform. The other followed me. I got out, looked about, and there was the angelic Yugoslav, Maurice Kabillo, waiting for me in the middle of the night with a hotel porter! I was so thankful to see him I nearly burst into tears, and was still shaking both his hands when a plain-clothes man walked up, showed his badge and said I was to follow him. We went to his office, where Kabillo explained why I was in the train and why I had no special pass; and we were allowed to go. We walked for nearly half an hour through the dark town; no light anywhere – there is a curfew. On either side walked an armed man; the shadows were full of them. Kabillo tried to keep in the moonlight, but we were continually walked into the shadows. Our escort was extremely chatty and Kabillo talked away, gave them cigarettes, made all the friendly conversation he could. Every now and then two fresh men joined us and the others stayed behind. Still we walked and walked. At last we reached the hotel; the escort waited to see us inside the doors, and then Kabillo turned to me with a great sigh of relief. What a godsend for me to meet such a thoroughly good, kind and competent man just when I needed him.

2 SEPTEMBER

Kabillo and I went to the Press Bureau. Here all the pressmen wait for news, and as communiqués come in, the journalists are allowed to send reports to their various papers.

A very good-looking young man in khaki, with a red and gold holy medal on his chest, came and talked to me in utterly perfect English. His name was Pablo Merry del Val, and his father had been Spanish Ambassador in England for years. [*My husband Claud told me, years later, that they had been at Eton together*] In a few minutes, just as I was telling him about all the interrogations in the train, a slip of paper was brought to him.

'They're after you already!' he said.

'What will they do?'

'I don't know. You'll have to see Captain Aquilèra, the military chief here, and he'll ask you some questions. You probably won't get any news. Come out with me now and I'll show you where the bombs fell yesterday.' I asked if Kabillo could come too as he had been so decent to me.

Four bombs fell on Burgos yesterday, two near the moat and two right on the hospital. The first two killed no one – miraculously since large holes were torn in the side of a house and a bedroom was completely wrecked. Stones weighing at least 200 lb flew through the air and landed forty yards away, stout iron girders were struck and twisted double, and thick wooden doors were smashed to pieces.

But the hospital has suffered badly; all the wounded were rewounded, and four people were killed. In one of the rooms was found a man's jacket, torn and bloody, containing an arm. In the mortuary, which is just a heap of debris, the body of a soldier who had died of his wounds lay on a bier; two of his relations were praying beside it. Most of the windows are smashed – broken glass flew into the wards and buried itself in the walls. The operating theatre is a wreck, although the circular light over the table was not touched.

As the hospital is on the outskirts of the town, and has a water tank in the middle of its courtyard, it is easily recognizable from the air. The people here think the bombing was done on purpose to terrify them. The bombers arrived half an hour after the last of the Burgos planes had gone out, so there must have been espionage of some sort.

Outside in the street the funeral cortège of the four dead men was drawn up. A large crowd lined the route, silent and orderly, tears running down their faces, and their arms raised in the Fascist salute. Merry del Val stood with his arm raised, and so did I. Column after column of soldiers passed; they are all volunteers but they marched smartly and looked like trained troops. It was very moving to see the four plain black hearses, drawn by black horses with tall black plumes on their heads, waiting in line while their escort of soldiers marched by.

When we got back to the National Junta I was taken to see Captain Aquilèra. He was a goodish-looking, grey-haired man of about fifty, who spoke perfect English, having been at school at Stonyhurst. He glared savagely at me, said my press letter 'didn't mean a thing', which was true, asked why I hadn't got proper passes, said he hated women in Burgos and that I was being a damned nuisance. I said his office at St Jean de Luz should not have let me in, and Macaya ought to have had the decency to tell me to get a pass at Pampluna, and not just left me there, knowing I had very little money and no Spanish.

'Well,' said Aquilèra, 'the quicker you get out of here the better I'll be pleased.'

'Then you'll have to send me out in your press car. I've got to go tomorrow anyway.'

'There's no "got" about it,' said Aquilèra angrily. 'We can perfectly well keep you here.'

'Yes – you can,' I said, seeing things for the first time in quite a different light.

'Where's Rice, anyway? I've got a good story for him and I want him.'

'He's at Hendaye,' I said. Then very humbly, 'Is there anything I can do for you?'

'*Not a thing*,' he replied, slowly and emphatically.

Then he told me to go to my hotel and stay there until he'd made up his mind what to do with me. I went upstairs again, considerably shaken, and found Merry del Val. He looked at me and laughed.

'Well – are you going to be shot?'

'I don't know,' I answered truthfully. 'He doesn't believe me. *You* believe I'm speaking the truth, don't you?'

'Yes, I believe you,' he said, not looking at me, but I knew he did. It was a great shock to find a man like Aquilèra who firmly believed I was lying. Merry del Val took away my camera and films, then he drove me back to the hotel. He was very nice but entirely non-committal.

I went to my room and thought hard, and the situation didn't look so funny. I was certainly suspect. I had terribly little money and absolutely no means whatever of getting any or of communicating with people unless they allowed me to. I went to the hotel office and explained that I couldn't afford the *en pension* rate of 20 pesetas a day, and said I would eat *à la carte*. I ordered one egg and a long 'bread' for luncheon in my room, as I knew from the way people looked at me they all knew I was suspect, and I didn't like it. I went and spoke to Kabillo, who was in the dining room. I was nearly in tears, and he was very upset and begged me to have luncheon with him, or anyway something to drink; but I wouldn't because I thought I couldn't sponge on him until I knew if I had enough money to stand him a drink.

I went back to my room and ate my egg and bread, saving some of the bread, and then I regret to say I burst into tears. I was definitely not scared for myself. I imagined quite clearly that the ridiculous situation might come to a very Spanish conclusion, and I might be quietly shot – 'an accident' – but I was frantic when I thought of the feelings of the family. I felt strung-up – something heavy and dangerous was hanging over me, and it made me cry. It was beastly sitting alone in that room with nothing to look at or read or do, and not knowing in the least what was going to happen next. I had no clothes, no luggage, nothing but my little face-box and a toothbrush and paste, and a bit of soap the hall porter at Pampluna had given me.

I lay on the bed and then walked about the room for six hours. I wrote a letter to Rice saying I was detained, and asking him to send telegrams to Patrick Balfour, Father and my maid – the two last merely saying I wouldn't be home as soon as I expected. I wrote an article, and then there wasn't anything else to do. I also wrote to a friend of mine, a member of the Royal Family, but the letter was confiscated, I was told later. But it made an impression on the authorities, who began to think I was all right and just stupid.

Then in the evening the waiter came and said I was wanted downstairs. I went to the hall, and there was Aquilèra. He took me into the manager's office and we talked. He was quite different – charming, kind and sympathetic. He asked what I was really doing there. I said I'd told him; I was writing articles which I hoped the *Evening Standard* would take. Then I asked him straight out if he thought I was a spy.

'No, no, certainly not,' said he, hurriedly. He seemed slightly embarrassed.

In the end he said he would arrange for me to go the next day, and meanwhile I could 'fool around the town'. I was so relieved that I burst into tears again. He gave me a cigarette and waited a minute, giving me a curious piece of advice. 'You shouldn't go in for this sort of work,' he said, 'you can't do it.' We parted amicably and off I went, only too thankful to be able to walk out of doors again. I saw at once that I was being followed, but that didn't worry me. I found my way to the exquisite cathedral and sat in the peaceful courtyard for a long time, looking at the hundreds of beautifully carved figures on the outside of the building.

Then with some difficulty I found my way to the only other decent hotel, where most of the journalists were. There were about twenty of them, mostly English and American; all ages, classes and shapes. They couldn't have been nicer and more friendly to me and to each other. I didn't tell anyone of my little trouble, because it seemed so stupid. They gave me drinks – and did I need them! – and talked newspaper shop, telling each other all their bits of news – 'Here's a story for you' – there didn't seem to be any jealousy or meanness. But all the news they got was censored, and all the telegrams they sent, too, so the endless list of Insurgent victories one hears of doesn't seem necessarily accurate. I heard of English pilots fighting on this side, and of spies and suspects being 'liquidated' (but that was said very quietly), and how difficult it was to get a story. Nothing ever happened here except yesterday's air raid, and there probably wouldn't be another.

After a time I went to the Press Bureau with a very charming middle-aged Irishman on the *Daily Mail* and found Merry del Val, who was pleased that the Irishman was able to give him good news of his cousin in Madrid, whom they thought had been shot. I went back to my hotel (still with my fat shadow trotting along behind), found Kabillo, told him I was all clear, and went and had a drink. Then it was curfew time and all the outside lights went out. I had some dinner – a huge one, actually, which I proudly paid for myself – and then said goodbye to Kabillo and tried to thank him for all his kindness; he has been really marvellous to me. And so to bed.

3 SEPTEMBER

Ready at 7.30 a.m. for the press car to take me to St Jean de Luz; the driver was not Macaya but a much nicer chap called Lopez. We hummed along, but not at that terrific pace. The passengers were a lame colonel going up to the Irun front in command of Moorish troops – he was rather quiet and strained; a very charming woman, Lopez's cousin, whose husband is in Madrid and who was going to St Jean to try to get him out; and a Dutchman, Dr Brouwer, who has been writing books about old Spain and has seen more than enough of the revolt from both sides. At the first police post the Civil Guards poured out and crowded round the car, staring at me; quite evidently they had heard that I was a spy.

In Hendaye I got hold of our Attaché and told him what had happened, and he said I was quite all right now. However, I must certainly not go to San Sebastian, as they would then be certain I was a spy, and I had better be in before dark.

4 SEPTEMBER

At 4.30 a.m. the night porter woke me up in great excitement, saying there had been a terrific explosion and he thought the bridge had been blown up. I went down to the beach opposite Fuenterrabia and found that someone had blown up an ammunition dump in Irun, and a shell had hit the match factory, which was blazing beautifully.

Refugees were crossing from Fuenterrabia as fast as they could get over the water. The splendid Basque fishermen rowed their boats back and forth, crowded with people, and refused payment. It poured with rain, and miserable and frightened groups sat on their poor little bundles, getting soaked. Others were quarrelling with each other; having barely escaped with their lives from the Anarchists in Fuenterrabia, their nerves were strung to breaking point, and they were shouting their political opinions at the tops of their voices and shaking their fists at each other. There were Red Cross men and ambulances waiting under the trees. Some very old people were being carried up the beach; there were also wild-looking *femmes miliciennes*, fighting women, in blue shirts and dungarees, each with a boyfriend carrying her bundle.

I was soaked through, but a charming man gave me a lift back to the hotel. He had been over into Fuenterrabia to see what was happening. The troops had evacuated it, and the Anarchists were doing what they liked. They were overturning and burning cars, sacking the shops, pulling the shop people out and shooting them. I saw a young man, pale as death, who had just got across. He was the Marquis de Villa Casa; he had lost his family in the crowd, but hoped to find them at the hotel. Someone gave him money, and someone else took him to the hotel, which was becoming more and more crowded with refugees of all sorts. All the French were utterly good to them. I saw a very, very old, frail and beautiful lady, with an exquisite black lace scarf over her head, walking slowly along escorted by a young boy and girl; following them came a servant carrying a baby.

At the Irun–Hendaye bridge there were the most pathetic scenes. Groups of women sat in the road, clutching their children and their little bundles. Every now and then the big gun hidden in the trees on the outskirts of Irun bellowed, and spat a shell. Then the poor refugees jumped and cowered, shaking with fear, tears of terror and exhaustion running down their faces. You heard the shell whistling overhead; a fountain of earth and stones leaped into the air beneath the fort of San Martia (it is a fortified church, really), there was a roar which made the air shake, and the women jumped and wept again.

A sturdy little boy of two stood in the middle of the road with his fists in his eyes, crying bitterly because he could not go home. A very old lady, dazed and dumb, carefully dressed and wearing a black band round her forehead, followed her family over the bridge. Two men with a barrow went to and fro all day long, bringing their friends' belongings. More fighting women came over, hot, excited, impatient, with wild eyes and tossing hair; one clasped her old mother in her arms – the old woman looked scared and bewildered. The fighting women are not formed into separate regiments but fight side by side with the men.

Deserting Government troops came over, shot at by their comrades. One was followed by his dog. There were excited arguments with the French *gendarmes*, who searched and disarmed them. The police post was full of rifles, revolvers and cartridge clips; behind a pillar of the bridge was a mountain of hand grenades made from piping. A soldier mounted guard over it and no one was allowed near, since a dropped cigarette would have blown us all sky-high.

The deserters were in every stage of demoralization – their nerve had gone and they only wanted to get out of it. Some were in uniform; dark blue shirt and trousers, scarlet neckerchief and steel helmet. One wore his

161

national dress – a large straw hat, black and shiny, loose shirt and waistcoat with baggy trousers tucked into high boots.

The refugees told me that for days on end parties of them have been held up at the Spanish end of the bridge. They have slept on the ground, afraid to return to their houses in case the barrier should be lifted in their absence and they should miss their chance of crossing the bridge. The spaces under the arches are crowded with people who fled there when the bombers came over. A crippled old man of eighty-four was carried there by his relations six days ago, and has been there ever since. I bought large jars of coffee, and with two Basque men took them round to the oldest and most frightened refugees. They were so thankful and got some colour into their grey, drawn faces.

A rumour went about that a bomber had been forced down. There was the wildest joy among the women and a screaming mob of them rushed to the spot, only longing to tear the pilot to pieces with their teeth. When they found there was no aeroplane and no potential victim, they wept with disappointment.

Besides the human beings, livestock and cars came over the bridge. Farmers brought their cows, each one carrying her load of fodder – on top of one bale of clover were two fat puppies. And there were donkeys and dogs and mules. At first the animals were sent back, for fear of bringing disease, but later on the guards let them pass. Farm carts were drawn by cows wearing on their heads great mats of fur to keep the sun and flies off.

A fleet of brand-new cars came over, towed by a lorry. They belonged to a garage and the proprietor was evacuating them before the mob got at them. There were several private cars covered with slogans in red paint: FAI for Federación Anarchistica Iberia; UHP, Unión Hermanos (brothers) Proletarios; UGT, Unión General Trabajos (workers); CNT, Confederación Nacional Trabajadoros. They were not allowed in until the slogans had been effaced, and the owners were frantically scrubbing at them with petrol and knives. Some of the cars were sent back, as the paint would not come off.

At 3.30 San Marial fell. The defenders fought till the last round and the commandant, the last man out, was wounded as he left. My fat Ramundo took him to Bayonne hospital. The Insurgents left the fort empty, and shells from the Irun gun burst harmlessly round it for the rest of the day.

I went to Béhobie where there was a great sense of strain and danger. A few people crouched behind doors watching the fighting. Anyone moving about the streets ran, bent double. Bullets whizzed overhead, now and then hitting the walls, while some dropped in the street. Two *gendarmes* were wounded at the police post last night, and another badly hit in the head today.

I watched the fighting five hundred yards away. Men were resting in the shelter of a farmhouse; others lined a wall – firing – ducking – firing again.

One crouched on the ground, obviously wounded. I took two photos, but it was such a long way away that I don't think they will be much good. Ramundo hid in a café – he is such a large target!

Back at the Hendaye bridge we saw a bomber come over. As soon as they heard the hum the poor refugees burst into tears again and crouched against the walls, forgetting that they were safe in France. A big biplane came into sight, circled, and dropped two bombs near the Irun gun. The gun was silent. The machine circled again and dropped two more, on the hill. The next two bombs dropped at the other end of the town. No bombs were dropped in or near the centre of the town. As the bomber was making her fourth circle three fast little fighting machines rose into the air and attacked her like angry wasps. Looking like a big bird mobbed by small ones the bomber flew away. Meanwhile a large French police plane had appeared and flew up and down the invisible aerial frontier, saying 'Keep off France'.

Soon the Irun gun started firing again, just to show there was no harm done.

In Spain arrests are continually going on in the towns; people are taken into the fields, shot and buried not very deeply. They have such a spy complex at Burgos, I found, because they have so many bogus correspondents and naturally they have to be careful. I got off because my letter was so very vague that it just could not have been meant as a shield, and also because Kapillo had spoken up for me and my letter to Alice [*Duchess of*] Gloucester helped a lot.

I heard a story about a foreign journalist who appeared in the Press Bureau and asked some pertinent questions here and there; within a few minutes the head of the motor transport, a most suspicious man, had spotted him. Another journalist who had seen more than enough of that sort of thing and knew what was coming tried to give him a hint – 'Go, quick, while you can' – but he was too late. Someone beckoned the man outside; the other followed at once, but the man was being held by two Civil Guards. He was terror-stricken – he too, knew what was coming. They took him into the field and shot him.

I heard of someone taking an evening walk in the fields and coming upon the bodies of an old peasant and a young boy, propped against the wall, looking quite peaceful. Someone else stepped on a hand which stuck through the stones. Yet another group came across a party of six soldiers surrounding a bewildered, terrified peasant boy, who stared dumbly, with the eyes of a frightened cow. The group marched on, and three minutes later there was a volley followed by a shriek which died away . . .

I really don't think I should have disappeared in the fields, though I believe one of them was in favour of it. But both sides are killing mercilessly – one side shoots, the other tortures. '*Arracher entre deux charrettes*', Brouwer told me, is one way of dealing with spies in the Red lines.

163

5 SEPTEMBER

There was a fairly quiet night, but today Irun is in flames. The Anarchists know they can't hold the town much longer, but they will leave nothing for the Insurgents. The station is packed with refugees, who hardly have room to sit down. I thought of giving them coffee, but it seemed hopeless because there were so many. They fill every café and doorway and the roadway too. They are not allowed on the bridge; only journalists are.

I saw Lopez in the crowd. He was delighted when the soldier turned me back (because my pass was out of date) and rather crestfallen when I got a new one from the permit issuer. He took it, and read it very carefully, and asked if I had been into Irun. (Incidentally I am still being watched; the same man is always at the next table or close beside me wherever I go.) Hundreds of Guardes Mobiles have been rushed here in lorries; they look fine men and quite well disciplined. At the bridgehead was a large crowd of journalists, including some of my friends from Burgos, and young de Girondes, and a Colonel Ferron of the Red Cross and his brother. Everyone said, 'You must not go any further, it is very dangerous.' How they do love saying that! The Civil said, '*Passez à votre risque et péril.*' It is a formula. But then they look the other way and one moves forward. It was intensely exciting and I was stimulated, tingling. I climbed on the bridge parapet and every whizz of a bullet gave me a new thrill. I was told to get down. Colonel Ferron lent me his glasses; I could see the last defenders of Irun, a hundred yards away at the bridge-end.

A padded lorry went to and fro bringing refugees; with it went a young Belgian journalist, helping the refugees and picking up stories. I would have loved to go, but didn't dare; as the British Attaché had said, 'Don't go over to the Red Lines and don't be out after dark.' I knew that he, at least, was talking sense.

The Insurgents were hidden in the maze below the bridge; they were quite invisible as targets, and so were the Red defenders, who were in and behind the Customs house. But no Mediterranean can have a gun in his hands and ammunition in his pocket and resist the temptation to make a noise; for that reason the firing was incessant. And as none of the soldiers can shoot properly, it was very wild – more bullets came over the middle of the bridge at the French end than at the Spanish end. The stone was chipped everywhere, and bullets clanged all the time against the iron bridge just beside the stone one.

Some of the refugees, who must have been pretty well mad with fear, tried to run across the railway bridge instead of waiting for the lorry. An old woman fell, and lay perfectly still.

'*Elle ne bouge plus!*' said Ferron, watching through his glasses.

But suddenly she scrambled to her feet and ran the rest of the way, arriving almost dead of exhaustion and fear.

Under a parapet of mattresses sat a herd of journalists and photographers, having the time of their lives. Andrew Rice was in the lee of a café, with a long loaf in one hand and a pencil in the other, writing like one possessed and now and then having a bite at his bread.

Young Jean, Ramundo's 'second', came to me and said, 'The Reds shot 512 hostages today between 1.30 and 2.30. I know it's true because two friends of mine saw it happen. They are fishermen; they got across and are hiding now in the cellars below my house. Five hundred and twelve they killed!'

I flew off for Andrew Rice and George Steere, who questioned Jean, but they weren't prepared to send the story back to their papers unless they were convinced it was true. Everyone said something different. Some refugees said all had been shot, others that all had escaped; one or two went a bit further and said some of the hostages had been burnt. Although this was a real scoop I didn't dare send it to the *Standard* without being sure.

Meanwhile Irun flamed as more and more houses were fired. First the rich quarter, a monumental pyre! The big gun still roared, machine guns rattled and snarled, and rifles cracked unceasingly. All the time I was there I never saw a single casualty, thank God; the sufferers in this war are the civilian population. Hundreds, probably thousands, have been shot – as spies, as capitalists, on any excuse.

Later on, the fifteen men in the Customs house decided to give the journalists a show. They hung some mattresses over the parapet, put chairs beside them, and fired short volleys into the maize. I should say for certain they never hit anyone, as we could see the maize too, and the attackers were perfectly hidden. There were fast volleys in reply; people scuttled behind the police post.

Having given their show, the Red soldiers returned to the Customs house. At intervals deserters and refugees raced over the bridge, bent double. Two men ran across, each clutching a tiny girl; one fell, and our hearts stopped beating, but he picked himself up again and came on, child and all. Two days later his photo was in several papers, headed 'An heroic exploit'. His name was given too, saying he had rescued the child under heavy fire. The man carrying the other child, who got over first, did not get a word of praise.

A white-haired Scottish journalist created a sensation by walking quietly over the bridge at his own pace. Everyone said: 'My God! Look at that type there! He is mad!' I was so pleased to say: 'Not at all! He is British – he does not wish to hurry himself.'

Colonel Ferron came to me in the evening and said, 'This is the truth about the hostages. Thirty were shot. The rest escaped.' Still I did not dare send it to the *Standard*; but eventually we knew it was true, and I was the first to know.

At 7 p.m. three Red soldiers ran over the bridge and shouted for their comrades who had deserted. They came out of the police post and there was a fierce argument, the fighters urging them to return and the deserters screaming that they would not. The French police put an end to it by hustling the deserters back into the post and sending the fighters away. It was a fantastic scene!

That was the end – and the end for me of the most exciting week I ever had; crammed with feeling, adventure, fantastic circumstances; thrills, complete fearlessness (I who can't face a riding jump!), wonderful friendliness from perfect strangers, camaraderie and kindness from everyone to everyone, which I saw all round me and experienced myself. In the height of the firing, human nature among the non-combatants was at its very best. Café people fed thousands of refugees free, the hotels took them in, the Government escorted them; there was no thieving, expensive cameras and field glasses were left lying about and never touched; everyone was sympathetic, kind and brave. Five thousand refugees and two thousand deserters came over in two days; all were cared for.

Ferron very kindly came to the station to see me off. I was very sorry indeed to say goodbye to everyone and go.

1937

22 MARCH

En route Johannesburg. We have flown for hours over miles of empty Africa. I wonder what answer we can give to the Germans when they say 'You have got this land, are you using it?' except 'Yes – as our air route.'

Dodoma. Lunch. A little patch of civilization in the bush – some Greek traders and a couple of other Europeans. Then over more wild, empty country – forest and swamp, where the few natives have probably never seen a white man.

Mbeya – night stop at a lush green valley in the mountains. The sharp crest of Mount Mbeya is ten thousand feet high, and beyond this range are the Lapa goldfields. Tough-looking miners in the bar with their tough-looking wives, some of the men talented drinkers, some with tight mouths and defeated-looking eyes; carefully dressed in white shirts and grey trousers, the women in clean but shapeless dresses, the ambitious ones with pathetically badly made-up faces – smudgy lips and pink paint on top of sallow, unhealthy skins. A silent old Scotsman called Dave, standing quietly by himself and drinking away. The bartender was a hard, disappointed man, glad of a job but hating the place.

I said, 'Your mountains are splendid.'

'Prison walls!' he answered. They go to Dar-es-Salaam for their gay

Above and right: The train to Addis Ababa on the first expedition, with blind beggar and local belle

Below: Moussa the snake-charmer with Genesta

Above: On the trek through Transjordania, 1933. Genesta rides her camel with a native saddle, and with her legs wrapped around two sticks

Right: A camel with a liver!

Below: A chance to relax in camp

Above: The stark landscape of the Wadi of the Baths of Solomon

Left: Genesta relaxes at the Baths

Below: Genesta's bedroom!

Right: The Sheikh of Shobak (left) in Genesta's tent, with entourage, luggage and water-bottle

Below: Time to break camp

The Avro 10 in which Genesta
returned to England

times. Nairobi sounds to them a new Paris, but too expensive. Night after night they say the bar is empty; even the people from the planes don't always come.

Charming Mrs Menzies, the owner of the pub, put on a fresh frock and some make-up, in our pilot Dudley's honour. The Station Superintendent, Edwards, is clever; he thinks and reads a lot, knows German perfectly and French a bit. They have a lonely and boring time, the people in these outposts, except for the two southbound weekly planes – the northbound ones only stop for a few minutes. The barman and another man brought us back to the rest house; we all had some more drinks and everyone got quite gay – but it was pathetic, really.

23 MARCH

People came to see us off. Dave is a passenger sitting dumb and lumpy beside one of the three Indians who are returning from Mecca.

Eighty miles south is the lonely little landing ground of Isoka, just a clearing in the bush kept up by natives and occasionally glanced at by a white man from the outpost of Fife, twenty miles away.

The native villages are far apart, and each one is ruled by a chief. Below us is the red thread of the road which Hopley and Englebrecht raced over by car from Nairobi to Jo'burg. Forest and swamp for miles lie under a thin layer of fleecy clouds.

Mpika. Breakfast. Passed over Stewart Gore Browne's exquisite home, a village in itself, set above a lake in wooded hills. Oranges and coffee grow here; the houses are beautifully designed and built and the shooting is splendid. Their nearest neighbours are the District Commissioner and the Station Superintendent at Mpika, fifty miles away. Mpika is charming. When I went to have a wash all I found was a man's bedroom with three good guns and two fine buffalo heads on the bed. The Station Superintendent has turned himself into a white hunter.

11.15. We have just passed over another farm! Its nearest town is Broken Hill, one hundred miles away. A forlorn white house stands on the main road, hoping for the cars which hardly ever pass.

Lusaka. A widely spread town, each house far from its neighbour. On the aerodrome were the fittest-looking men I have seen for a long time; hatless, brown and full of life. But it's not my sort of country – they can't keep horses because of African horse sickness.

Salisbury. Large and pretentious. Meikles Hotel, where we stop tonight, is old, famous, ugly and second-rate, exactly like a 'commercial and family' hotel near the railway in some small town in England where they give you at every meal 'a cut off the joint and two veg.' In the 'lounge' there were groups of oldish women all with precisely the same expressions – thin, wizened faces, thin, down-turned mouths and spectacles. Their clothes were shapeless and tasteless but the more dashing ones had flowers in their hats. I know that type so well! Conscientious, good mothers, faithful wives. They have fixed ideas of their own, and insist on their rights.

24 MARCH

Bulawayo and breakfast. A scattered, unimpressive town. Now we are over the famous Matopos range, a wild heap of rocky mountains where Cecil Rhodes is buried.

Johannesburg is a huge, smart place surrounded with what looks like rubbish heaps which someone has forgotten to sweep away. These are mine dumps. Hiding among them are clusters of tall chimneys overhung by a sad pall of smoke. A most striking weird landscape, unbeautiful, but with a personality of its own. People here are always in a hurry. The streets are full of hurrying crowds of all classes, races and colours, but all charmingly kind to me when I asked the way to places; nice manners and friendly smiles. Johannesburg is like an adolescent boy bounding with vitality and spirits, who can't be bothered yet with art or music – but that will come in time and then it will be a beautiful place.

28 MARCH

It has all been great fun and very interesting. Dudley Travers, the pilot, took me to the races yesterday, where we had a grand time but lost our money. Such wealth everywhere compared to Kenya! Small races worth £250, big ones £2,000 – magnificent equipment and organization.

29 MARCH

A friend took me to Robinson Deep, the oldest mine on the Rand [*the gold-mining district, properly called the Witwatersrand*], and handed me over to the manager. There was a continuous noise of machinery clashing, of whistles, and trolleys running along on rails to empty their loads on the dumps; and there was a sad canopy of smoke hanging over the tall chimneys.

I put on a pair of blue dungarees, had a cloth tied round my head and, dithering with fear, went into the small iron cage with a boy called Davidson, who was to show me round. Four other men got in, the gates were shut, some bells rang, somebody whistled and we moved downwards, slowly for a few seconds then shooting down at the rate of two thousand feet a minute while the skip rattled and banged and crashed and shook like an earthquake. I was terrified, and thankful for the small glow of light which appeared now and then when one of the men drew on his cigarette. After two endless minutes we stopped at four thousand feet down, crossed to another skip and started again. This shaft was newer and the skip moved quite smoothly. They are run on steel hawsers which are examined every day.

At six thousand feet we got out into a maze of tall, wide tunnels, electrically lit, hot and wet and full of noise. Glistening with sweat, natives ran behind trucks pushing them along the lines and whistling warnings. A drill started up with a noise like a machine gun and made me jump; trucks tipped over and shot their cargo of ore down a shaft with a terrific din.

The precious reef is between two and two and a half feet wide and 8500 feet thick, though they might go down still deeper (the Crown Mine is 13,500 feet deep). It is mottled with quartz. All day long they drill holes in it, which they then fill with dynamite. At 3 p.m. they begin to blow them off, starting at the top and working downwards. Visitors hardly ever go below six thousand feet because of the danger of heatstroke; even the natives collapse with it. As we got nearer the workings, the tunnels got smaller, wetter and hotter. There was no light except from our naked lamp, the tunnel was low and narrow, there was water everywhere and dead, eerie silence.

After a time we heard the voices of miners working beyond the rock. We could not get to them as Davidson, peering into black depths with loose rubble underfoot, said it was too crumbly and dangerous and he would not take me – to my vast relief. I felt very scared and rather trapped, though very interested. When we returned to the main tunnels, the noise and traffic and people everywhere seemed like Piccadilly.

Davidson told me about the mine. One hundred and ten thousand tons of ore rock are taken out every month. It goes crashing and tumbling down its shafts to the lowest skips which lift it to the surface for crushing. Three thousand natives and five hundred white men are at work in this shaft of the mine, in eight-hour shifts. Young men like Davidson, keen and clever, still go to university lectures most evenings, studying for the managers' exam. He is also going to start flying soon. He says mining is a man's life and he would not change it for any other. You get used to the danger, he said, though never to the heat and depth, and miners still get TB.

30 MARCH

Away early to catch the Durban plane. A three-engined Junkers of South African Airways, crew of eight, crowded but comfortable. We flew over flat plains full of homesteads and cultivation, then orange groves, then the foothills of the Drakensberg Mountains, with the line of jagged crests on our right and below us larger, more scattered farms – beef and sheep country with little dorps [*very small townships*] here and there – over some clouds, over the Valley of a Thousand Hills, over the suburbs of Durban, then over the sea, after which we circled and landed at Durban. A pretty town as towns go, the famous rickshaw boys dressed up in feathers, bells and coloured rags, wearing on their heads towering decorations of feathers and buffalo horns.

1 APRIL

Pietermaritzburg is about the size of Nairobi but their shops are not tempting. This is the land of tin roofs. We have them in Kenyan townships because we simply can't afford tiles, but still regard them as an evil stopgap, to be altered as soon as possible; here they are an accepted permanency.

I got a taxi and drove out to a Zulu kraal. The road was bad, the scenery good, and the Zulus utterly unimpressive – rather under-sized, dark brown men dressed in European rags. The women, however, wore native clothes and ornaments; their hair is done in a high crown distended at the top and plastered with red mud, and they don't look so shabby as the men. Photos – baksheesh – presents, and a cup of native beer to drink: very mild, quite pleasant and full of hairs. They make it by chewing up a small seed and spitting it into a calabash – I was told afterwards.

Took the train to Cedarville, East Griqualand.

2 APRIL

Tommy Pope and his two daughters met me early this morning. This is a real little dorp, just the sort one reads about – a straggling collection of houses midway between village and town. The country is exquisite, freshly green after the rains, and the hills are streaked with silver waterfalls; clear streams run through the valleys and springs ooze through the grass in marshy patches. This is a tamed country; there are no wild animals. Tommy's house he described as a 'dog-box'; it is very tiny and simple with no attempt at embellishment but the atmosphere is warm, friendly and hospitable. It feels like a Kenyan house.

3 APRIL

Charlie Chaplin's cousin, no less, came to dinner last night and made us all laugh! He is a very dark, tough-looking man with a handsome wife. He and the other guest told me tales of the old days (always the best days); he acted his stories, which were exciting and funny. Towards the end of the evening the women disappeared into another room and drank tea and coffee. I, not knowing the custom, stayed put with the men and was rewarded with a brandy nightcap. This Cape brandy is a good, clean drink and I'm going to introduce it into Kenya.

4 APRIL

This was a splendid day. We motored into the Drakensberg Mountains up to eight thousand feet, past the tiny frontier fort and into Basutoland. Crowds of Basutos were on the road, some mounted, and all wearing gay red blankets. The women wore twisted round their heads scarves of all colours and at all angles – as bright as flowers. Hills and mountains towered all round us, while the valleys at our feet had sheer cliffsides and running streams – slabs of wet rock glistened in the sun. Beyond the Orange river the serrated crests of the Drakensbergs stabbed at the sky, dark purple in the evening light. It was so wild and beautiful I could hardly bear to leave, but at last we had to turn back to the plains, the farms and the tamed country.

5 APRIL

This is my last day; I have been looking at cattle. Chaplin has got a really magnificent herd of Friesians. His average on 78 cows in milk is 312 lb butter fat per head per year, 8830 lb milk, milking for 290 days. His best cow milked for 410 days and gave 531 lb butter fat. His sheep shear 7½ to 8 lb wool yearly, but his top price was only 16d per pound as against our 19d. The best sheep in the district shear 11 lb wool a year, which fetches 18d a pound. The top wool price in the district is 21d.

Why aren't these people millionaires with the prices they get? Is it farming or is it just them? Their overheads can't be high – Chaplin has one manager, poor fences, and poor buildings except for the milking shed, which is a fine, big one. But they have to feed heavily all through the winter as they are sometimes under snow and sometimes frost-struck.

7 APRIL

12.30 p.m. We are eleven thousand feet above the world, bumping among big clouds, on the way home. I hope the weather will be smoother further on – I don't know what the wireless says, but the clouds look thick ahead. What is fear based on? Partly on health, I believe. Flying nearly always frightens me; there is not much fresh air in the cabins, and I get tired. Yet on the Hendaye bridge, where bullets passed so close to me, I was wildly excited, marvellously fit, standing up on the parapet over the hand grenade dump, revelling in every burst of machine gun fire and the crackle of shooting – especially as I did not see *one* casualty. The aim was wild.

'*Vous n'avez pas peur, madame?*' said some French soldiers to me, and I answered quite sincerely and happily: '*Non. D'ailleurs nous sommes tous dans les mains de Dieu.*' I was convinced I was safe – but I did not mind even if I was not.

8 APRIL

A very quiet and almost uneventful flight. The events were: one engine refused to start, one wheel nearly caught fire on landing, one other engine refused to start, and we hit a bird while landing somewhere and tore the fabric off the machine, which had to be repaired before we could go on. But at last there were the beloved Ngong Hills, and there was Boy waiting for me on the aerodrome. And my little trip is over and there's no place like Kenya.

1938

SEPTEMBER

I was in England and not well. This was the Crisis week, and I was in hospital in Portland Place while Chamberlain flew back and forth between England and Germany, trying to arrange a last-minute settlement. Tension, and a feeling not of fear but of sorrow, was growing in England. Fanned by the press, sympathy with the Czechs roared into a flame. And yet there was no war spirit or hatred of the Germans such as I remember in 1914.

We felt war was inevitable. Cavalry rode through the streets, Hyde Park was dotted with guns, and searchlights reached skywards. Unemployed men were brought from the 'distressed areas' in Scotland and Wales to dig trenches in the parks, as air raid shelters. They would have been quite useless, but perhaps people felt comforted.

Women enrolled for various duties and millions of gas masks were prepared. The barrage balloon people worked feverishly, trying to prepare their defences in time, while over the wireless came warnings to shipping of 'obstacles' to be encountered in the North Sea. My doctor came to me in hospital, late at night, in uniform. A few days later certain hospitals were prepared for half a million casualties, the results of the first expected air raid. Someone was given the job of disposing of the seventy thousand anticipated corpses. At night the Communists held demonstrations, chanting 'Stop Hitler, Save Peace' and 'Stand by Czechoslovakia'.

A British Expeditionary Force was ready to dash across the Channel. All sorts of conflicting rumours came of the states of the air forces – our own and that of the other side. Ken Waller [*my flying instructor*] and others patrolled over London all night long. The churches were full, day and night; people prayed as never before. Special services were held and a great wave of spiritual feeling swept the country. Meanwhile the unhappy Czechs turned miserably this way and that, vainly looking for help.

My own problem was how to get home and even whether to try, for I did not know if our people in Kenya would come back here or fight there. All Imperial Airways lines were booked up. I got out of hospital on Wednesday, the Crisis day. That night the first air raid was expected. I got a gas mask, but was still too sick to do anything but creep about. Everyone else worked frantically.

Next day there was great tension and strain: people were ready for anything, but still hoping against hope for peace. There was no personal cowardice, but an infinitely sad realization of what war would mean for the men in our armed forces; for the non-combatants, the wives and families; and for the beauty and culture which it has taken the world so long to build up.

On Thursday posters with the one word 'Peace' were splashed all over London. The relief was indescribable, but the Czechs were heartbroken. They had braced themselves for an annihilating war, for supreme sacrifice and glorious death with the eyes of the world upon them – but all they got was the most crushing anticlimax. They were torn to pieces without a shot being fired; all in a few hours they lost some of their own people, their industries and their line of expensive and impregnable forts. [*The Sudetanland (German-speaking, and a major industrial region) was ceded to Germany, and other frontier adjustments made in favour of Poland and Hungary.*]

The next day my maid Bowman and I went to see Chamberlain's return. The crowds in Downing Street were terrific, and while we waited in the rain for hours the people sang old marching songs, hymns and 'Land of Hope and Glory'. When at last he arrived there was a wild rush for his car and roars of cheers, and when he and his wife appeared at a window the houses seemed to rock with the noise. The shy, tongue-tied British went crazy, and some men were in tears – 'God bless you, Neville! God Bless Mrs Chamberlain! God bless our King and Queen,' they sang and shouted. At last he held out his hand for silence, spoke a few words and told us to go home. 'God Save the King' was sung, and then the people went away. I have always thought that it was thanks to Chamberlain's physical (he hated flying) and moral courage that we had one year in which to build up our defences.

Later I went to Westminster Abbey, but of all those thousands who had been praying for peace, only fifty or so were kneeling by the Tomb of the Unknown Warrior. But those few were in deadly earnest, many of them weeping. There were sailors, soldiers, airmen, nurses, businessmen, shop assistants and foreign tourists.

Lots of people said, 'Disgraceful – we should have fought.' It's too soon yet to tell who was right. But peace is preserved, we are becoming stronger, and we shan't be nearly caught unawares again; the Czechs are still alive, as are millions of other people who would by now be dead, and trade will recover in a few days. There has been a strong spiritual revival, which perhaps is the greatest good that has come out of this turmoil of fear, anger and patriotism; and the greatest safeguard of all for the future.

NOVEMBER

[*I felt I had to see what was* going on *in Europe.*]

I came to Cologne by air. Leaving my family and friends was a wrench. It is all good discipline, like going up alone for a spin – which, to date, is my high spot of fear. I've met some grand people this time – a very mixed bunch indeed!

Jacques Balsan: a pilot since 1900, and holder of balloon licence No. 7. He flew on most pioneer flights and invented a new kind of parachute. He gave me his altimeter – '*Il est vieux, mais quand même son coeur ne bat pas trop fort dans les altitudes*' – it has been thirty-eight years in the air. He was married to Consuelo, the former Duchess of Marlborough.

Don Taylor Smith: painter, publisher, writer, aerobatic pilot, owner of a collection of Chinese treasures and some photographs of Chinese executions – beheadings and stranglings – which he took himself at great risk. I don't know how he got out of there alive.

Wence Torr, in Rome: student, writer, satirist, diplomat, kind and sarcastic, with a penetrating mind, brother of Rosita Forbes, the famous traveller.

Daniel Wolkonsky, in Venice: White Russian prince, no passport, no home, no work, but perpetually and cheerfully moving from one small job to another. Great fun, good friend, witty and never downcast.

The policeman who arrested my car and then got me off a charge by saying how ill I was. We used to have great talks while he was on duty.

Joey, Paddy, Ben, Buddy and Sam from the East End of London – all Jews, great friends. And there was Judah who was mixed up in dog racing, but he did something against etiquette in one of the pubs, and couldn't go back there, so I only saw him once. The other three men were tailors for the cheapest shops and sometimes for Petticoat Lane . . .

Well, here I am in Cologne. It is sunny and dry and cold. There were anti-Jewish riots here, and all over Germany, four days ago. Their shops were looted and burnt, everything smashed, their synagogue burnt out. The riots started in the morning, but when the police appeared, very much later, they instantly stopped. The shops are boarded up and plastered with swastika signs.

The cathedral was packed for High Mass on Sunday. I don't know how the religious persecution works, but there are many nuns and Dominican monks and other 'religious' walking about the streets.

The population is peppered with uniforms – of soldiers, youth leaders, police and young girls from the working camps. Even the motorcyclists in from the country for the day have got themselves up to look semi-military, with their black leather jackets, helmets and goggles fixed on their foreheads.

The wearing of uniform demands a serious demeanour and a military manner; it appears to be *infra dig.* to laugh or joke when you are dressed by the state. Germans are addicted to dressing up in warlike costumes.

13 NOVEMBER

Leipzig. My second-class carriage is extremely comfortable and clean. There is no restaurant car, but a steward brings tea, coffee and cakes at intervals. A uniformed woman pays frequent visits to the loo, tidying and cleaning.

Nothing is wasted in Germany. Razor blades and old toothpaste tubes are saved; iron railings are torn up and replaced by concrete ones. '*L'état, c'est moi,*' said Louis XIV. And nothing – no opinion, no deed – must be allowed which might hinder the progress of the conception of the State.

The people are friendly towards us, deeply grateful to Chamberlain. 'We are so thankful to him. That is a good man,' they say with quiet fervour; and they have been utterly friendly and helpful to me, despite the 'wave of anti-British feeling' which our press said was sweeping Germany. But towards the Jews they are completely merciless. It doesn't matter where they go or what happens to them, the other Germans say, but they must be got rid of at once, and for ever.

14 NOVEMBER

Dresden. Climbing out of a third-class carriage encumbered with three bags and one box – all my luggage for two months – I spoke to the porter about a clean, cheap hotel. He took me to the Hoeritz, where I have a very nice room with hot and cold water and three lights, for 3.50 marks a day. This is OK. The chambermaid is all kind heart and politics.

'We must have our colonies back [*taken from Germany after the First World War*]. It is only right. We must have wool for our winter clothes. We are poor and cannot afford English material.'

They all say the same thing. 'Our Leader! Ah! What a man – we love him dearly. Our papers say you foreigners hate us – why do you? What terrible things you are doing to the Arabs! [*The British plan for the establishment of separate Arab and Jewish states in Palestine, then under British mandate, was unacceptable to the Arabs; terrorism was rife at this time.*] We just want a prosperous and safe Germany, our own people, in our own Reich. We only hate the Jews. We will burn their shops and their synagogues if they stay. We want to be friends with you – we like the English.'

There are 'Ludendorff' shops in each town selling anti-Christian books with the most horrific dust covers – blood, dripping daggers, a church soaked in human gore, kneeling men fervently kissing a Pope's hand, a naked woman on a rack being tortured by gloating priests.

15 NOVEMBER

I walked the streets for hours. Pirow, the South African minister, madly anti-British, is due in Berlin tomorrow. The papers are giving him a terrific write-up: 'This still-young man, lion hunter, first-class pilot with a spirit of adventure, successful, the most talked-of minister in the British Empire(!) – independent and popular . . . He is of German origin, went to school in Germany, has a German wife. It is believed that the Colonial Question will be solved in a spirit of goodwill.' On the next page, in blazing headlines: 'British Barbarity in Palestine. Many houses blown up' etc. etc. Goodwill? Yet despite their press the people are charming, gentle, kind and warm-hearted. But this is Saxony – not Prussia.

After trailing around Dresden alone in the bitter cold, visiting the lovely old baroque palace, revolted by the gross, coarse Rubens and Jordaens nudes and delighted with the beautiful Van Dyck portraits and some of the gentle, dreamy landscapes, I got back to the hotel and said I was fed up with my own company – could someone come out with me that night?

The hotel people, hospitable, and anxious that I should enjoy myself, produced an air force escort – an observer, the soul of correctness and formality, with courtly manners. Struggling bi-lingually we managed to understand each other, went to the cabaret, danced and drank a bottle of very good white wine. It was the greatest fun. After the cabaret we went downstairs to a beer hall, where four Sudeten *Backfische* [*young girls*] were rocking back and forth over their concertinas, and the jammed mass of gloriously cheerful people, all workers, got a little tight, linked arms, swayed to the music and sang *Volkslieder*.

The air was dense with smoke, and the walls rocked with singing and laughter and noise. Everyone talked to anyone who was near enough to hear; strangers came and talked to me, patiently.

They also seemed to forget politics and the stiffness of their uniforms and the difficulties of modern life. I wish the diplomats could go to that beer hall . . .!

16 NOVEMBER

Third-class all-wooden carriage, a one-and-a-half-hour trip to a place called Haida for 2 marks. No one could call that dear! We left the fields and found the Elbe, moving quietly along its valley between steep, forested, rock-crowned hills. Logs were floating down the river – logging is one of the main industries.

A young man talked to me; my German is coming along. He had been a reserve officer in the Czech army, but because he was of German origin the Czechs had promised him every sort of trouble in the event of war: 'We'll see to it that you and your pals get killed first.' He said his people,

Sudetenland Germans, had been miserably unhappy for twenty years [*before this time the area had been part of the Austro-Hungarian Empire, and Czechoslovakia did not exist*], allowed no privileges, no promotion, and told they were not Germans but Czechs.

'We want colonies because we must have wool to make our own clothes,' he said, like the chambermaid in Dresden. 'But best would be a trade agreement. No war! No one wants that. Everyone dead, babies and women, and nothing gained. If only we can have wool, iron, bread and safety, we want no more. You don't trust us, we know that! It is the papers who make trouble between us.'

At Bodenbach little boys were lined up, drilling opposite the station. 'SS men,' he said disapprovingly. He took my bags into a restaurant and we had coffee. Then he carried them back again to the bus, and packed me in. The time he spent looking after me must have made him about an hour late.

At every stop we disgorged peasants and filled up with others. Trade was evidently booming and it was the cheerfullest bus ride I've ever had. Everyone cracked jokes and rocked with laughter, sat one on top of each other and pulled the conductor's leg. Everyone was fat and well-fed and bursting with spirits. There was a conference about me. Would the conductor see I got off safely at Haida? I didn't understand German. Would he help me? The very old peasant women, with their heads tied up in shawls and colossal baskets on their backs, were just as jolly as anyone else – they were helped about or hoisted in and out by the young ones.

At Haida it was dark and wet and bitterly cold. There were no porters and no cars. The driver and conductor searched about but found no one to carry my bags the ten-minute walk to the hotel. So they abandoned their bus and the waiting passengers (very few now, luckily) and carried them themselves. We padded along through the mud and the dark, talking as well as we could. When we reached the hotel they were astonished and quite overcome because I tipped them. They shook hands warmly and wished me a happy journey, and I said '*Grüss Gott*' to them! (No *'Heil Hitler!'* for me!).

17 NOVEMBER

This Sudeten country is booming now, after five years of depression. The restaurants and cafés and hotels are full to bursting, and I was lucky to find a room. It is a fine room – two windows, two beds, two down quilts (thank heaven), running water and bedside light – 4 marks a night.

The changeover from Czech independence to German domination must have been painful. The Czech soldiers had no petrol to enable them to get away, and no bread to eat. German civilians gave them food and helped them. The electricity was cut off and food was very hard to get. It is a mercy that it all happened while the weather was warm.

I went to the glass shop owned by Hantiche & Co. – lovely Bohemian

177

glass, in beautiful colours and of the very best designs: stuff that you see in Asprey's and is bought by the very, very rich. Four or five hundred years ago the peasants in the forest began making glass with wood as fuel. At the end of the seventeenth century the factories started, burning coal instead of wood; and the peasant workers had to give up. Gradually they left the forests, came into the towns and took jobs in the factories, and some of the families have been here ever since. But others stayed in the forests, still making glass. Hantiche's factory employs two hundred men who get free housing, coal and electric light.

They told me that once there were twenty glass factories here; now there are only seven.

18 NOVEMBER

Young Kurt Hantiche borrowed a car and drove me out to the famous Czech 'Maginot Line'. These forts are strung along the German–Czech frontier in three strands, each strand consisting of three lines of forts each two hundred yards apart. The walls of each tiny fort [*similar to the pillboxes erected in England at this time*] are six inches thick, made of concrete reinforced with metal. The machine gun aperture is minute: there is only room to turn a gun a limited distance to either side. It would be quite easy to walk right up to any one of these forts, in line with the blank walls, and lob a hand grenade in at the gun hole. It wouldn't blow the fort down, but it would destroy the aperture, the gun and probably the man behind the gun. Each fort was meant to hold three soldiers and their provisions for quite a long time, and during the Crisis week they did so. Besides the forts the frontier was held with a double line of barbed wire.

The treble line of defence was certainly strong, but those forts, dotted along that thick forest vulnerable both from the ground and from the air, seemed to me the weakest part of the whole thing, as well as the most expensive. The Czechs said the forts would be utterly useless to Germany; they would probably be destroyed and the concrete used to build houses.

We left the main road and drove along a potholed, splashy track behind the hills, through some farms. The countryside is enchanting – the hills dark with fir forest, villages sprawled about, houses dotted one by one on the grass and not stuck each to another down a street. Each man has his own bit of land in the valley. There are no hedges to separate the various fields, but some are ploughed and some are grass, and they are all of different patterns, like a patchwork quilt, so you can see where one man's land begins and another's ends. They use cows in the wagons and ploughs as well as oxen and a few horses. The farmers work very hard in the summer, but have an easy time in winter when the houses (padded with thatch and wood chips) are deep in snow and there is no work to be done in the fields.

19 NOVEMBER

Up at 5.30 to go to Karlsbad. Packed into the train by some students, and passed half an hour among the youths and maidens going to school – fat, pink and bursting with giggling good spirits. I've got quite used to travelling 'hard', third class.

After much wandering I had an excellent meal for 1.35 marks, then went to the biggest hotel for coffee. It was full of German government officials, come to put things in order. They looked fat and coarse, and had rolls of fat on the *backs* of their necks.

The Czech waiter told me the same story they all tell. If they had been allowed to keep their own language and have equal rights with the others they would never have wanted to change, but they weren't and they couldn't bear it.

At the movies tonight I saw a film which shook me. It was of Hitler at Nuremberg, reviewing the troops. There they were, miles of them, solid phalanxes of fearless and unimaginative robots. Line after line of aeroplanes in perfect formation, a cavalcade of tanks and armoured cars, cavalry, guns, anti-aircraft guns and sailors.

No wonder the Führer looks proud and satisfied. The people adore him – they really worship him. Of course he had the material ready to hand, for the Germans have always been orderly and disciplined and have always loved being trained and drilled and ordered about. But things were chaotic until his party got the power, since when he has given the German people a superb army, air force and civil airline; security, prosperity and power; increased their coal and food supplies from the days when the grates were empty and bread was queued for to the present state of central heating and plenty. Found petrol for them, guns, munitions and ships; added several millions of people to the population, besides dozens of flourishing industries; and fed their emotions on what to them takes the place of love affairs to us – banners, standards, badges, slogans, organizations, military gestures and capitalized patriotism. Hitler is certainly clever and a *devil*.

There is the most terrific Hitler cult here. The streets are draped with crimson swastika banners, and the shop windows and car windscreens are obscured with little red flags. In hotels you see the slogan: 'Our greeting is "Heil Hitler" ', and so it is – every person entering a bus or train, a café or shop, utters these un-harmonious words, accompanied by the gesture a trained seal makes with his flipper when hoping for a fish.

His picture, surrounded by wreaths of gold or silver paper, or of fading leaves, is in every window. In a book shop or a picture shop, or even surrounded by knives and razors and metalware, it doesn't look so bad, but embowered among vegetables or hair tonic or nestling among women's woollen undies it does look rather odd. One picture was framed in a lavatory seat – very suitable, I thought.

Like all converts, these people are more passionately pro the new cult than are the old hands.

21 NOVEMBER

Two hours in Eger, a grey, drab townlet where everyone looked pinched and cold. In the train people were saying, 'Our Führer has conquered more than Alexander or Julius Caesar or Napoleon, and without shedding a drop of blood.'

Marienbad – even more dark and gloomy. In a cheap café I listened to the BBC four o'clock news, with a few pangs of homesickness. It said Pirow was going to Berchtesgaden, so I think I will go there too and hope for an interview.

22 NOVEMBER

Motored through the countryside. Farming is bad. The soil is poor, but more could be done with it. All these plains should be under proper cultivation, instead of bits and pieces, some badly neglected and all belonging to different people. Perhaps this will be changed.

I have now embarked on a foul journey, third class to Munich, arriving there at 11.30 p.m. and leaving for Berchtesgaden at 7 a.m. I only hope I find Pirov at the end of it.

A most charming Czech boy talked to me in the train; he was despondent about the future. I still can't believe that these people want anything but peace and prosperity. Any other goal seems so stupid. But no one knows what the leaders want – perhaps they don't know themselves. Perhaps they have an atavistic longing for power, which can only be achieved with money or by force. Then you have a faith and devotion which positively welcomes privations, since they are 'all in a good cause'. It is also possible that Germans are masochists.

23 NOVEMBER

Munich at midnight. Too exhausted to think about going on early, so I found a small hotel and slept. Later I found that Pirov only starts for here this afternoon, so that's very lucky for me. I bought some peasant clothes – they are so lovely I couldn't resist them. Then I walked about for hours till I could stand the cold no longer.

People are being fed with 'The Jews want a war', so perhaps that's the first whisper of propaganda for the placing of future war guilt. I know nothing of politics, but these thick-headed, brave, gullible, easily led and devoted people are such a menace that it makes my blood run cold to think of what might happen. They are gentle and warm-hearted and kind individually, with beautiful manners, and they've been wonderful to me, but their inflexibility and brutality in politics are terrifying.

25 NOVEMBER

I saw Pirov this evening, after several hours' wait at his hotel. He thought I was the press, at first, and kept off, though when he did come and talk he was charming. But he looked very grave. We only talked about Kenya – nothing that really mattered. This sort of person can always turn on a certain charm – like a 'con-man'. It doesn't mean a thing.

27 NOVEMBER

Left Munich at 8 a.m. yesterday morning for Prague. Eger station was full of soldiers, because there is an artillery regiment stationed here. I was in the large part of the third class, three back-to-back benches. A battered old Irishman returning from his first visit home for fifty years sat beside me; he has worked at Brno for fifteen years.

The Customs and passport people passed us Britishers through without a word, but they spent a long time with the peasants. Many of them were very poor. With babies and bundles, baskets and sausages, some of them looked more like ill-kept animals than people. There were Poles and Slovaks and people from the Hungarian border. Near us was a family who had been in France for eight years, working on the land. They said food was getting dearer and dearer and so they were going back to the mother's farm near Bratislava, where they had four acres of land and could grow wheat to make bread and feed themselves. They had been in the train for twenty-four hours and had another night and a day to go; the tiny girl of three was good, and very quiet, but white with tiredness, and so was her fifteen-year-old sister. They had hardly any food. I gave them some of my sandwiches and chocolate, and money to buy more. They didn't even know if the farm was still theirs or if it had been taken from them by the Hungarians.

By the time I got to Prague I was done in with the cold, and felt rather sick. In the hotel I went to the *Damen* – though outdoors, it was water, not earth, and was perfectly clean.

The old brown-tiled roofs of the city cluster together below the hill, insouciant and countrified, like a large village.

With Douglas Reed, author of *Insanity Fair*, this evening, also Michael Hogan, late of Kenya, now of Palestine, whom I walked into by the hotel porter's bureau. That's part of the fun of travelling – you never know what old friend you will meet next.

Reed thinks Tanganyika [*formerly a German colony*] will be quietly given back in order to avoid a nasty bit of trouble. Czechoslovakia is being

181

swallowed, next comes Hungary, then Romania, then bits of the British Empire.

Hogan said Palestine is a mess which could be cleared up in a few days. Perfectly innocent villagers are held responsible for bandits' raids. The best houses are blown up – houses belonging to respectable, fairly rich Arabs who didn't encourage and could not control either the bandits or their own village lads. Villagers sometimes fought off the bandits, caught and shot their leaders, then asked for British troops to protect them. But when they found we could only send troops for one night they said, 'You go home, we'll be on the safe side and make our peace with the bandits.'

I went out later with one of my oldest friends, a Czech [*Prince Max Lobkovitz, one-time Czech Ambassador to London*]. Two-thirds of his property has been left on the 'other side'. A quiet boycott is already starting here of some of the wine and mineral water which is produced on his land. The place he was brought up in, and where his ancestors have lived for three hundred years, the estate offices and buildings, the vineyards and farms and peasants, all belong to the Germans now. It is not legal, but as he will be killed if he returns he cannot arrange for the rents and revenue to be paid to him, so that is what it amounts to.

28 NOVEMBER

This must be one of the most unhappy cities in the world. It is crowded with refugees; besides the Jews there are Czech, Slovaks, Germans and people from all the border countries. One hundred thousand Czechs have left their homes; all these people are crowded into Prague, without work or money or food, except what they are given by private people and a few charitable organizations. I went over the Czech hostel, 180 people sleep there every night, though there are beds only for 72. Even those beds are only straw-filled mattresses laid on the floor. The rest sleep on boards, with whatever blankets they have got. Sitting on benches round the walls are people who have never thought about politics and probably never heard of Hitler. They have been caught up and smashed in the Nazi machine . . . driven away from their small homes, and the streets and villages in which they have passed all their lives, and which were all the world they ever knew. They have lost everything except their lives, and not all have stayed alive, since some have been killed, and some have killed themselves.

All the survivors have now are little bundles and tin boxes with a few belongings – everything they possessed, except what they brought away, is now lost. They sit there with white faces and staring eyes, dumb and hopeless and miserable, with nothing to do and nowhere to go, waiting for someone to help them.

4 DECEMBER

A bitter, iron-bound, cold day. I went over the Host Horov bridge, with its ranks of old statues on either side, and into the old town. There in a café I unfroze my inside a little with a hot coffee, and my aching toes in the warm air. Then up hundreds of winding steps to the old palace to await Hacha, the new President.

The Jews are in a terrible way. The sixteen thousand who were in German territory after 10 October 1938 (the date of the changeover in the Sudetenland), and thus suddenly became German citizens, are not allowed to work. They must either live on their relations for ever, or go to some other country (almost impossible now), or die of starvation. Without work, police permission to stay is not easy to get; many will be deported to Germany and almost certainly end up in the concentration camps.

Somehow work must be found for the fugitive Czechs, and for the Germans who came into this country. Industries are lost over on the 'other side', big export and import businesses have broken down, and everything has to begin all over again.

Worst of all, I thought, are the families who have been wrenched apart. The family life of Jews, specially, is very close-knit. They sit close together in the same room and talk, and several generations live in the same house because they can't bear to be separated. Now many families are broken up and have lost touch. People search frantically, begging for news from anyone who might know something about their lost ones. Their little savings, accumulated over years, have gone in getting their relations out of German territory and bringing them into Prague – they take great risks to get them over, and many people have been shot trying to cross the frontier at night.

I went to a village on the frontier and met a man who has rescued over a hundred people – a real Scarlet Pimpernel. He was short and tough, with a thin face, a broken nose and straight eyes – a quick thinker and a brave man. In the No Man's Land between Czechoslovakia and Germany thirteen people are living in a camp. They have one small shelter with a canvas roof and straw on the floor, where ten of them sleep, and a tiny gipsy caravan for the other three. There are, among others, a man of eighty-eight with a long pipe forever in his mouth, and an old lady of seventy-five, with bright eyes and the sweetest smile. When we arrived they came to meet us, so glad to see someone from the outside world, asking for news of their relations and if there was any chance of their being given permission to go into Czechoslovakia. They are 'stateless' people, whose nationality changed when the frontiers were altered in the last war, and so humble, obscure and ignorant that they never thought of asking for passports or papers. Suddenly they found their world had fallen to bits around them. They were driven from their homes, not allowed to enter Czechoslovakia, sent backwards and forwards from one frontier to the other, on foot, for days at a time, and at last collapsed in No Man's Land, unable to go any further, absolutely helpless. Many died, and some babies were born out in the fields, in the cold and the mud. They made camps for themselves and stayed where they were, and there seems no hope of their getting out unless some organization can help them.

They were fine-looking people, steady and calm. They said they didn't want food or clothes or anything – but to be free. Local peasants sent them food. So they sit, day after day, with nothing to do and nowhere to go and the winter coming on, when first it will rain and the roof will leak and the straw will be wet and muddy and the fire won't burn, and later it will snow and this shelter will be half buried and the cold will eat into them and the lucky ones will die.

There were other refugees, eight in a room, the women crying, the men staring at the floor. They were likely to be sent back and to a concentration camp unless they could get to Prague. They had no money, and all they possessed were two vanloads of furniture which were not allowed over the frontier. They had even pulled bits of linoleum from the floor and scraps of sheep's fleeces and stuffed them into the vans. We returned here the next day, fictitiously bought the furniture, put the people in the train and shipped the whole lot to Prague. I don't know if they ever got there, or were allowed into the country.

The broken hearts and broken lives, the agony and misery and homesickness, the fear and bewilderment have to be seen to be believed. There is so much to do, and I can do so very little in the short time I am here. All this tragedy has been caused entirely by Hitler.

8 DECEMBER

For the last three days I have tried to get away, but something always happened. Now I am in the train *en route* for Prešov and Mukachevo.

Yesterday I tried to do something, and failed, which I shall regret all my life. I started out with a Czech friend named Prachner, and a driver, in a car for the frontier village, dropped Prachner and continued over the other side. The Czech officials, let us through with smiles and salutes; the Germans were very chilling and military. We went into the bureau, where snappy voices barked questions at the chauffeur; at last they said we could go. Two kilometres further on a police car overhauled us, and a furious young man, with a fat face and cruel eyes, full of self-importance, cursed the chauffeur for not getting permission from the police and the military, and then came back with us. One felt he longed to poke his new revolver in someone's ribs and really show his authority.

At last we reached the village I was bound for. Two Jews came out of their house, the last of the family to be removed from the home they have lived in for 250 years. Their farm and horses and furniture and pictures have all to be left behind, though they may get them later – or they may not. The villagers are very fond of this family and have done all they could to help them and will take care of their things. But the next pogrom will be – probably literally – the death of them.

Back we went; we passed the Germans easily, with a lot of nice smiles, and handshakes and good wishes from a friendly young sentry, and then came in the twilight to the Czech frontier. And there we stuck. Nothing I could say would make them let us pass; polite as they were, they would not let the Jews through – Prague was already terribly overcrowded. So, very frustrated and downcast, we returned to the Germans. The sentry was sorry and kind. '*Mein liebes Fräulein* – I would help you but it's not us, it's the Czechs! You must come inside again, I am sorry.'

The boxes were opened, their clothes and mattresses searched. Everyone barked and snapped and looked ferocious. The police officer in the next room was even more ferocious and the plain clothes man upstairs positively cold with threatening authority. 'Why didn't you say you were going to get two Jews?' he barked at me. 'I helped you get your car through and now you have done this.'

'You mustn't speak so fast – I can't understand you,' I said.

'You'll understand all right when I've done with you!' he roared. He banged the table. '*Why didn't you tell me?*'

'I know very little German. You must speak more slowly,' I said. If you are quiet enough and pig-headed enough it usually works.

So, despite the audience whom he wanted to instruct in the art of interrogation, he had to speak slowly, and I answered.

'You never asked me why I was going. If you had asked me I'd have told you. Now *you* tell *me* – why didn't you ask me?'

He sidestepped this and said, 'You should have told me.' Then suddenly he got angry. 'Come here!' he said, and flung open the door of a room containing a table, a chair and a rifle. A motherly and apologetic old lady appeared.

'Take off your clothes,' said the man. 'How do I know you're not carrying money out of the country for these two Jews?'

I wasn't really angry, because I realized that if you go around with Jews and no proper papers you are asking for it. But I said, 'This is very wrong of you, and I shall tell the English Legation. I've been through Germany and travelled a lot, and always found good treatment up to now. I shan't forget this.'

They were rather upset. 'It's not our fault. We have to do our work.'

'I know it's not your fault, but what sort of a government have you got!'

They went out and I stripped to the combies.

'That's enough – that's enough,' said the old dame. 'If you wore stays I would have to have them, but this will do.'

'*Gott sei dank ich bin so schlank*' [*Thank God I am so thin*], I said in the best

German rhyming manner – and hopped about, freezing and shouting: '*Schnell! Schnell! Ich bin kalt!*' until she reappeared with my searched clothes.

A brand-new young Gestapo recruit, very correct, came with us in the car. He had a sensitive face, but was doing his best to harden up as quickly as possible.

I said, 'What were you doing before you did this – a student? You look like a student.'

'Yes, I was.'

'Well,' I said, 'try not to get too hard. These people are pitiable, nothing else.'

'The Jews are terribly bad people,' he said.

'Not all. There are bad Germans and Jews and English and French, and many good Jews who have now lost everything.'

He would hardly speak to me because of another Gestapo officer sitting in front. He was full of the excitement of the regime and the importance of his new job.

'Where will they sleep?' I asked him.

'With the police,' he said.

'Please, please try to get them into a *Gasthaus*. I will pay for them. Please do this, it can't hurt the *Regierung [government]*, and they will be so sad and afraid in a police station all night. Both are old, and one is ill – please do try to help me.'

After a pause he said, with the same correct and military firmness, 'I will try.'

So in the end we left them with money and great mugs of beer and kind people round them in a *Gasthaus*, and there they can stay till 3 p.m. today, unless I can get their permits first.

On the way back the young man said, with great difficulty, 'I admire you.'

I said, 'Promise my Jews will be all right.'

And he said, 'On my honour,' and we shook hands on it and I drove to the village, very crestfallen. I thought and thought, but could envisage no way of getting them over the frontier except through the fields round the guards, and of course that was out of the question.

So back to Prague we went, I half asleep and very tired and ashamed of myself for failing. Prachner sang Wagner . . .

My friends came to see me off and I nearly wept. Partings are horrid. Almost the last thing I saw in Prague was the birthday gathering of a very, very poor refugee Jewish family round an old lady of eighty. We brought her the most beautiful crimson and white cream cake, and some nougat; and when she saw her cake all she could do was to cry. The relations crowded round her, kissing her and holding her hand, and crying for their homes and their families and their friends who were not with them, and the others who had killed themselves. Such heartbreak! For such political madness.

Prague and all that is now behind me. I can only pray that the people I have tried to help *will* be helped, and all that this nation has suffered will be wiped out at last. [*Czechoslovakia was freed when we won the war, but alas for those luckless, brave people, they are now under the Russians.*]

Twelve hours in the train, third-class sleeper, three berths but I had it all to myself. It was clean and comfortable. I am going to the Ukraine.

9 DECEMBER

Prešov. Breakfast in the station restaurant. Soldiers, gypsies, peasants in bright bunchy petticoats and top boots, with bright cloths over their heads. Then the bus, which was packed full and very hot. We climbed through beautiful, wooded country and rolling hills which became higher and higher, reaching up to the snowy mountains behind them until we were on top of the world. Here we waited for the second bus with a panorama of forests and rivers, backed by the grand mountains, spreading all round. It was twilight and very still, and the air smelt of snow and was cold and pure. In the dark we arrived at Perečin, the bus terminus, where a smaller bus would take the others to Khust and me to Svalyava. A kind young soldier carried my bags and made himself agreeable with the unfailing hospitality I've found everywhere.

We stood about in the dark and the cold, wet mud, and at last heard that there would be no bus till next day, and that there was nowhere to sleep since the town was overflowing with soldiers back from the frontier. My soldier set out to find me somewhere, and at last got two compartments in a second-class, empty train for me and a tired, sick and anxious old lady who had been travelling for a whole week from the Ukraine and was nearly exhausted.

There was no light and no heat, but the heat was alleged to be coming. The old lady's son and his young friend and I set forth for the café, without a common language between us except a very few words of French. I wanted candles and matches for the train and some coffee, but had no means of asking for them. The café was very small and smoky, full of shouting men drinking coffee and white wine.

I told a police officer who spoke German what I wanted and he helped me; we talked, and he asked to see my passport. We had some coffee and bread, but there was no butter and I hadn't enough money to buy meat. Everyone stared at me, with the usual intense curiosity.

The police officer came over and said a friend was going in a car to Svalyava and would take me; I thought he meant in the morning, but after he had gone I was told he meant that night. I felt this was rash, but thought I'd chance it. We waited and waited, but the boys wouldn't leave me. The man never came back, but two obvious plain clothes policemen suggested it was better to go and sleep; then they walked one on each side of me to the train. I guessed they were secret police when they let the boys carry my three bags without offering to help. They smoothly detached me from the train and my fellow passengers and shepherded me into a room on the station, where it was: 'Please sit down. Will the *gnädige Frau* smoke? You can sleep here, but we would like to ask you a few questions first.'

The usual interrogation followed; I am getting quite used to being 'suspect'. Ages later a soldier appeared, speaking alleged French, and we went over the whole thing all over again. Why was I going to *Russia*? And then where and why. And then he said he'd explain the situation to me, but added, 'You had better sleep now. In the morning we will resume our debate.' But I thought I'd rather know the worst at once. However, I persuaded him at last that I wanted to go to Mukachevo and not to Khust, which is an important military town full of soldiers. Then they went out and I got between the black blankets in all my clothes except my frock and boots, and in spite of the soldiers and people talking just outside all night, and occasional trains which awoke me, I slept.

10 DECEMBER

Today yet another interrogator appeared, speaking English – not another soldier, but a cheerful young man with a sense of humour, and the atmosphere cleared at once. He is shortly going to Johannesburg to buy skins for Bata, the shoe people, and I made a date to meet him for a drink in Mombasa.

He took me to a peasant's house, one of the rich ones, where five people live in two rooms, growing during the summer enough food (mostly maize for bread) for the winter, and weaving coarse linen which they embroider most beautifully with coloured wools. We went up the hillside a little and sat on a log, and for a few moments there was silence and peace and mountain air and I felt rested.

His orderly now appeared accompanied by an old gnome with a fur cap and a hook nose and an American accent, and off we went again, between the mules and carts and soldiers, to his cottage. Here there was a guest room spotlessly clean (much to my surprise), with two big bunchy beds and holy pictures round the walls.

Then we visited a Jewish shoemaker's house. The man, dirty and surly, lay on the bed; a pretty old lady took us into a room which was miserably poor, hot and smelly. Their daughter had plucked eyebrows, a smirk and a gold tooth. She was a bride. We saw the newly-weds' room with its beautiful new furniture, *à la* Maples' bridal suite, which must have cost an absolute packet.

The soldier left me writing, sitting on a heap of logs beside a small fire, out of doors, with empty trucks round me and the mountains behind. A pretty incongruous setting.

Over lunch he said he had found a lift for me, and as it was still early I was very glad of it – but no more night travelling for me. So off I went in a military lorry, sitting in the front seat with a handsome young officer and a driver, and forty singing Ruthenian troops behind, in a convoy of twenty-four bound for Svalyava. The country is gorgeous – rolling, forested hills rise up to the snow mountains and broad rivers run through the valleys – but the fields are miserably poor. They have cultivated a little up the hillsides, but they can't have much to live on. The peasants are the most miserable people, white-faced, sick, bare-legged, utterly poor; many are syphilitic and half-witted. TB raged through here lately, and syphilis was brought, after the First World War, by the soldiers' women from the small towns. I've never seen such miserable, sickening poverty before.

The drive was hair-raising. We climbed over a mountain range, round hairpin bends on a muddy road, always changing gear just too late on the corners, so that the officer hung onto the brake for dear life and the engine roared while the lorry slipped backwards.

This poor boy's father returned rich from America and bought 1,560,000 kroner worth of property in what was Czechoslovakia. Then it suddenly became Hungary [*under the terms of the Munich Agreement*], and the old man was kicked out and had to leave all he had behind. Compensation is in the air, where it will probably remain. The new frontiers mean that miles of fertile plains now belong to Hungary, so that food for the utterly poor peasants who live in the mountains and forest must now be brought from Moravia, five hundred miles away. The troops, who have been stationed here for some time, have eaten nearly everything there was, and there's very little left for the people. Some of the mountain villages are six miles' walk away from the nearest township, up and down hill; they are cut off from the world, and though they have winter food they can't get any medicine or drugs.

Over two hundred thousand Slovaks are now in Hungarian territory and some fine old towns like Uzhgorod, once the capital of Ruthenia, and Lavice, Zvolen and Košice have been taken into Hungarian territory. In the north they have lost coal mines and iron works, now taken by Poland.

The officer took me to the station and explained that I wanted to go to Mukachevo, and there was some talk of getting a taxi at once. But I'm rather off tackling frontiers at night, especially as one of the detectives at Perečin had said, in a hinting sort of way, 'It's much better to travel by day than by night.' The next question was where to sleep. Eventually someone said, 'Would the *gnädige Frau* step upstairs?' and again I was following a strange man up strange, bare stairs, at night. And then into a strange, bare room where an official sat at a desk and stared at me hard and wondered what the hell I was up to there, at this hour, with a much-visaed passport and only three small bags for luggage. We went through the familiar exchanges.

'Please sit down. Will the *gnädige Frau* smoke? Please, what are you doing here?'

And again I explained, in my miserable scrap of German, that I wanted to see the old Jewish sect in Mukachevo, and that I was not employed by a paper but a freelance journalist, sending articles to my agent in London. And then, where to sleep? By now it was pitch-dark, and nothing would have made me leave for the frontier before dawn.

This official was the station master, and turned out to be one of the most chivalrous, courteous, kind people I've ever met. He went to speak to his wife and came back smiling. They had a spare bed there, in the office, and I could sleep there; they had sent for a friend who spoke perfect English and in the morning I could catch an early train for Mukachevo.

Their friend was the pastor, back from America – a fine, kind and honourable man. We talked a long time and at last I said I must write. I also said I would like to pay for my lodging, but the pastor said he thought that was quite out of the question. After he'd gone my host came back and said I was to pay *nothing* – I was their guest and that was the end of it. They gave me tea with rum, then dinner consisting of meat and potatoes, cakes and mineral water.

This station master had saved his train, family and several coaches from the Germans by simply driving the train away from the town they were in, through the night, to this small town and station, and all his hopes were pinned on the Russians. 'They will save us – we are all Slavs together.'

Up at 6.30 and away at 7.30 in a little country train full of peasants and hunters in green hats and big fur-lined coats and boots and guns. They were going to shoot the weekly stag for food. Someone was put in charge of me; when we reached the frontier village he carried my bags and put me in a *fiacre*, then said '*Küss die Hand*' and bowed his goodbyes. As proud as a peacock I drove past the pedestrians in my carriage, all falling to bits as it was, behind a thin and weary mare, with a tiny, grinning boy for coachman.

11 DECEMBER

In five minutes we were at the frontier, where the Czechs passed me and my luggage out with the utmost courtesy. The coachman carried two bags, and I the other, through the Czech barrier as far as the railway line and ten paces beyond, where he halted – he was not allowed to go any further. There was rather a pause then, while the Hungarian sentry looked through my passport, not sure whether or not to let me through, and not sure whether or not I ought to have a frontier pass. Then a German-speaking man arrived on a bicycle and explained that a British passport needed no visa for Hungary. They let me through. I passed the Customs unsearched, got into another crazy cab driven by a bearded, bundled-up old Jew, and drove away to Mukachevo.

I was taken to meet Rabbi Rabinovitch, the head of the Mukachevo Orthodox Jews. Though he was educated only in Poland and never went to a good school, he is well-read, interested in everything, very intelligent, with a soft voice and a gentle but strong personality. His room was stacked with books, some of them over four hundred years old, saved from Spain when the Jews fled during the Inquisition.

Forty-six per cent of the population of Mukachevo is Jewish, and the rabbi is responsible for twenty thousand souls; like everyone else, he is very worried about the future. The Hitler regime is thrusting its way in here, as in all Hungarian towns; Jews are already losing their existing jobs, being denied other work, and beginning to feel they are in some danger of a pogrom. They are leaving Hungary when they can, just as they are leaving Czechoslovakia. But they don't know how to fulfil their dream of reaching America via England. For this you need papers.

The Rabbi explained that of the fifteen million Jews in the world twelve and a half million are safe, already living in Britain, America, the colonies and free countries such as Belgium, Holland and Scandinavia. But the rest of them, still in central Europe, are in daily danger, and it is only this number for whom some place of safety must be found. One of his secretaries said they could support and look after themselves if only they had some place to go. It shouldn't be difficult to find a place for such a small number.

Back to that dreary hotel for a miserable lunch of uneatable soup, meat, rice and bad pears, which cost 2 marks. There were no vegetables or potatoes to be had. This is a tragically poor city. It was once only a village, but the Czechs poured money into it, built fine iron bridges over the river and streets of new houses. It was becoming fairly prosperous, when, four weeks ago, Hungary took it within her frontiers, and since then everything has been utterly disorganized. The villages have been left in Czechoslovakia, so now the villagers can't bring in their produce and buy clothes and medicines, and the townspeople have lost their market and their food supply.

Something odd has happened to the exchange, too, so that everything costs more. Everyone is pale, scared and poor-looking. Crowds of heart-rendingly miserable, white-faced, diseased children wander about, staring hungrily through the café windows and begging. Their clothes are thin and ragged and their faces peaked or puffy. In a state of utter depression I got into the local bus in the twilight at 4 p.m. and started off for Bargozasz. The bus was full of depressed-looking Jews, townspeople and cheerful Hungarian soldiers, who seemed to exhibit the pleasure of a cat well-fed on another cat's cream.

12 DECEMBER

After a dreary wait in the damp, cold darkness I had a third-class bench in a rattling train to somewhere called Chop – lovely name, and the only one

I could remember – where I was rushed across the lines and suddenly found myself among a lot of rich people in a smart, expensive, rather bumpy, fast electric train bound for Budapest.

Utterly exhausted, I got out at Budapest at 11.30 p.m., failed to change my money and thus to catch the Orient Express, and so I slept the night in the nearest hotel.

13 DECEMBER

I am lapped in luxury in a beautiful second-class carriage, though I've only got a third-class ticket, and I'm all by myself travelling comfortably through the flat Hungarian plains. The soil looks very poor, and I know they have to use large quantities of fertilizers. More and more do I realize how rich, fertile and valuable Kenya is. Now I'm in clover again, at the Russian frontier post of Tiraspol.

After my passport and luggage had been vetted one of the officials took me up to a sitting room, lit the stove (carrying the coals himself), installed me with infinite care and kindness and made me as warm and comfortable as he possibly could. Bless his heart – what a lovely welcome to Soviet Russia I have while I wait for the train.

[*What follows is the Diary I actually kept in Russia.*]

17 DECEMBER

I find I have against my will got into a second-class carriage. It takes me straight to Kiev and avoids a two-hour wait in this bitter weather at some dark station. I shared the couchette with three workmen who were kindness itself, and finding I had very little money and no food, and there was no restaurant car, they stood me tea and bread and apples for breakfast. The country is covered in snow, flat and featureless. I haven't seen any real snow for fourteen years, so this is rather fun. It looks clean and fresh. One of my workmen speaks German, and I told them all about my proposed trip and about Kenya and the farm. I showed them photos and the carriage became full of people, all thrilled by my pictures.

At Kiev a quiet little Intourist guide was waiting for me, complete with taxi, to take me to the hotel, where I have a double room and a washing room.

18 DECEMBER

I went last night to a Ukrainian opera; the singing and the colourful dances were fascinating. The people must be well off, for the seats cost between 10 and 15 roubles (at 24 roubles to £1) and the theatre was full of workers, soldiers, sailors and their lady friends. I have two guides with me – one speaks English and the boy speaks American, which I like to hear. They took me round the old city and showed me a glorious view from a hilltop, with a statue of the first Christian missionary looking across the frozen river Dnieper to the Ukrainian plains beyond – a remarkable sight in an officially anti-Christian country.

What was once the cathedral of Lavra and monastery of St Sophia now houses what is called the Anti-Religious Museum. Prepared for I don't know what, I went round it with the guides. It has been kept just as it was; the golden domes of the cupolas, patched a little with snow, and each topped by a golden cross glittered against the sky in all their ancient beauty.

The magnificence of the interior is beyond description. Many of the huge ikons are of solid silver, painted gold. Catherine the Great gave the monastery a solid silver chandelier weighing 442 lb. The 'Tsar's doors', likewise of silver, beautifully carved and decorated, weigh 185 lb. The altar and communion table too, are all silver, and the little chapels contain heavy ikons of silver gilt. What must be the total value of this treasure house?

The monastery was founded in the eleventh century, for Greek Orthodox monks who were considerable landowners in the region. They also made a handsome income from pilgrims who came to worship their images and doubtful relics, paying their kopeks into the boxes.

When the Tartars conquered and ravaged Kiev the monks at once made friends with them, and by some miracle of tact persuaded them to leave their treasures, their villages and their property alone. The Lithuanians drove the Tartars out, and they also made havoc of the town, but the monks, by now perfect diplomats, allied themselves immediately to the new conquerors, so again St Sophia was untouched.

However, when Kiev was conquered by the Poles it was a different story, for the Poles were Catholics and the Orthodox priests, up against fellow Christians, went to war with them and got the worst of it. The Poles took over St Sophia and the cathedral became Roman Catholic until the Russians, under Tsar Bogdan Khmelnitsky, took the Ukraine back into Russia and re-established the Greek Orthodox Church.

They managed to stay on through the Bolshevik Revolution, though their numbers rapidly diminished from thirteen hundred to forty-eight. The end came in 1930, when there was a mass trial of the remaining monks. One of them was keeping two wives, a nun and a pilgrim. The pilgrim turned sour on him and threatened to denounce him for bigamy, so he cut her up with an axe and dropped her down a well. It all came out at the trial: the monk got ten years' hard labour and the rest were dispersed. They seem to have taken quite kindly to civil life; I am told one is an artist with a large family, and another a book-keeper.

Deep below the church is a labyrinth of catacombs, interspersed here and there with tiny chapels, and a few terrible little caves, once used as dungeons. There are coffins, exposed skeletons, piles of skulls and heaps of bones every few yards.

So this is Kiev – dungeons, cells and skeletons; round, golden domes shining against the snow, piled one above the other, and the immense, breath-taking vista over the Dnieper, with dark crowds hurrying through the streets at night, children on skis and toboggans, and the streets filled with wild music from amplifying radios. A city being reborn, past the first pangs, not yet grown-up.

Groups of uniformed sailors in long, dark, swinging coats and black fur caps were being shown round the Anti-Religious Museum, which contains nothing more anti-religious than the exposure of the fake relics, love charms and miracle-working skeletons of saints dug up now and then from the graveyard by the monks when a new *divertissement* was needed to draw fresh pilgrims and their kopeks.

19 DECEMBER

I went to a fine new movie last night, well acted and photographed; but finding one's way about, specially at night, is a difficult and depressing job.

Saw over a school. The principal was a nice-faced woman of fortyish, with dark hair and gleaming silver teeth. Most people who can afford it have a gold or silver tooth on view, but she had a whole mouthful. The children have a free education. From the age of eight to seventeen or eighteen they attend this school, then on to a university. They learn English or French or German, and science, physics, mathematics, etc.; no more theology or philosophy. Also music and drawing if they are apt. The older children belong to the Pioneer Party of Communist Youth, and the best thing about that, it seems to me, is that they get flying instruction free – or so I am told. Holidays are two weeks for New Year (Christmas does not exist for them), two or three days for state holidays, and two or three months in the summer. There are eight hundred children here and thirty teachers.

One big room was a Lenin–Stalin memorial room, with photos and stories of their lives hanging round the walls, flag-bedecked busts, and a fascinating little model of Stalin's secret printing press, way underground below a cottage. The entrance was down a well in a bucket to just above the water level – first turn to the left down a long tunnel, then up a ladder and first right, and there you were: a 'commodious living apartment' with an upstairs room for sleeping and eating and an office with printing press just below.

The children have a doctor attached to the school, and during the holidays contact with the teachers is maintained by means of visits to their homes, concerts and outings. The school receives 400,000 roubles a year from the state, which covers all expenses. Each child costs about 1800 roubles a year – in English money about £77.

Everything here is staggeringly expensive – 5 roubles for a cinema seat,

15 for an opera seat, 1.75 for a glass of tea and some bread and butter. A shabby little yellow fox fur tie in a window was priced at 260 roubles. I asked a guide what she thought my fur coat, bought in Prague, had cost – about 2000 roubles, she said, whereas it was actually about 200.

The choice of French and English books in the best shop was amusing – *Gulliver's Travels*, *Robinson Crusoe*, *Hiawatha* and propaganda Soviet books translated into English. Incidentally, the schoolchildren get foreign literature; in English they have Scott, Dickens, Upton Sinclair, Hemingway and some 'epic' books like Scott's *Last Journey to the South Pole*, which are specially popular.

20 DECEMBER

This was a really good day, but for the cold. They took me to a collective farm, and now I see how it works. The farm manager came with us – it was good to talk to a countryman again. In no time we were outside the city and driving through the snowy forest; some trees have managed to keep their autumn leaves, and very smart they looked against the white background.

When we went into the first cowhouse I could have wept with homesickness at the sweet, soft smell of cows and hay and milk. The cattle are of mixed breeds: Friesians, the Herefords I have seen elsewhere (this breed runs right through from the Sudetenland), and some called Simenthal, originally from Switzerland, like rather leggy, shaggy, biscuit-coloured shorthorns – only these have long horns. There are about two thousand acres for the stock on this farm (which also grows vegetables, roots, corn and fruit), carrying and winter feeding 150 cows, 170 calves and six bulls. The beasts' winter food is lucerne, beet, bran, hay and corn.

There are forty-eight men and women workers, one to ten cows for milking, cleaning and feeding, and one to ten horses. They milk by hand because this farm has only been going a year, but next year they will have an Alfa-Laval [*milking*] machine (they hope). Ten workers constitute a 'brigade', and each brigade is in the charge of a 'brigadier'. The workers are paid on results except for the brigadier, who gets two days' pay for one day's work. The workers also get housing, food, fuel, light, schooling and hospitals free. There are other rewards too, of the 'birthday honours' type. I saw one woman who for her services to farming has been awarded the highest honour in the Soviet Union. The workers elect their own bosses, and the farm costs 200,000 roubles to run a year, making a net profit of 400,000 roubles.

The snow lies thick over fields and houses, and in deep furrows on the road. Some tough little ponies were nosing it, trying to find grass. There are 147 horses and two stallions here; the best horse was a dappled grey, rather lightly built – a riding stallion, with a great curved neck, a real pulling neck. The others are mostly for farm work – short and hardy, light in front but with good round Percheron quarters. They are bred from Prussian-American or pure Russian stock.

After revelling in the smell and warmth of the cowhouses, and freezing outdoors, we crowded round a stove, eating home-made black bread and drinking a creamy junket while the manager gave me information. The walls were covered with photos of cattle and horses, and with milk production charts – it seemed just like home to me. This bucolic afternoon was the best part of my Russian trip.

21 DECEMBER

To a circus last night; the clowns and acrobats and trick musicians were good, but the animal turns nearly made me cry. Such a frightened, unhappy cat; such an ashamed and miserable Aberdeen terrier, dressed in a skirt, among the troupe of dancing dogs. He wouldn't dance and finally ran away, sneaking through the doors, pursued by a trap-mouthed harpy in blue silk, obviously going to belt him. Such a terrified monkey on a galloping donkey's back, and an equally terrified hare, strapped to the driver's seat of a little cart with the reins strapped to his paws, while two dogs and a goat galloped round at their best speed, pulling the cart. The dogs' tails vanished between their legs during their turns, all bar one frisky, happy little toy, obviously master's darling. The others would probably commit suicide if they knew how. I asked my guide if I could buy the Aberdeen; he said it was quite impossible.

The factory workers leave their children in the factory nursery all day or all week, just as they feel inclined. They have a nice new building in the yard near the factory, housing 102 children aged from two months to four years, and another where they take them up to eight years old. In one room nursing mothers come in from the factory at regular hours to feed their children. The women get four months off for childbirth, at full pay – two before the birth and two after. In one room tiny babies were being given their midday feed of minced meat and mashed potatoes. I am told they also get fruit and vegetables. They were wrapped like cocoons in thick woollen clothes with an outer covering of rough yellow suede, and looked exactly like Egyptian mummies. Others were being carried to an enclosed verandah where they cool off, so to speak, in a temperature of 15° below zero. They stay here for half an hour, or until they cry. They are all examined daily by the woman doctor permanently attached to the nursery, and those who are only slightly sick are nursed here; the others go to the hospital. In the summer the children can go to a sanatorium in the country, if the parents like. All, of course, is paid for by the government.

22 DECEMBER

I visited a hospital. The principal was a charming woman of fiftyish; she and a surgeon showed us round. They are very proud of this hospital, which they told me had the finest therapeutic theatre in the world (the Russians always say that). One thousand two hundred patients and one thousand staff, the whole divided in three departments – surgery, gynaecology and therapeuty. Thirteen different menus to choose from; radio, cinema and magazines to entertain the patients. A famous dietician is attached to the hospital. There is a special theatre for blood transfusions, and a census of people with different blood types is kept. The blood itself can also be kept for two to three days.

The bigger wards have about ten beds, the smaller ones four to six; the patients are looked after, with ten beds to one nurse. Very bad cases have a ward to themselves.

While we were in the blood transfusion theatre a surgeon ran in; his operation was complicated and he wanted advice. Later we stood in the room next to the theatre where a crowd of students clustered round the table. There lay a seven-month-old baby with some bad congestion in its tummy. The surgeon came and explained to me in French what was happening, then returned to his case. They could naturally only give a very light dose of chloroform to such a tiny baby, which never stopped crying. They very politely urged me to join the watching crowd, but I couldn't face it. My coat and boots had snow on them, and I had not been disinfected in any way. But this did not worry the surgeon, who kept coming out to talk to me.

Some of the patients were waiting for their operations; others, with khaki-coloured faces, just getting over them. They showed me a woman with a growth in her neck, and another with an immensely distended stomach, suffering from a disease of the spleen.

Patients walked about the big verandah and sat on each other's beds and gossiped; they seemed looked after. The doctors had their own bathroom, and the patients had theirs. Beside the theatre was the washing room, with a row of basins, 'sterile' water, many nailbrushes and some yellow mottled soap. The nailbrushes lacked some bristles. The therapy room was lined with ray-proof sheeting and operated by women from the next room, as the rays are too powerful for anyone but the actual patients to stand.

In a bread factory I saw workers' clubs belonging to 'the people'. Here they have a library with thirty thousand books; literary lecturers come and talk to the 'toiling masses' (Intourist phrase) and find out what type of literature they prefer. There are groups for music, dancing, singing, reading, acting and every sort of 'culture' they can think of. For some inexplicable reason they are very keen on what they call 'culture', and the state hands certain forms of it to them in large slices.

We went to a musical lecture; the person introducing it told the audience that they must cultivate the musical culture of the Soviet Union, not ignoring that of the old regime and of other countries, that music was a very high form of culture, that the children especially must be encouraged in musical culture, and that the freedom and beauty of the Soviet state were being aptly celebrated by their most cultured musicians and poets. Finally he introduced two very cultured musicians, who sang pieces from *Prince Igor* and a modern opera (warm applause) and then two quick-time modern military tunes, the second called 'Nobody Shall Take Us' (very popular, terrific clapping). Then a girl played a Tchaikovsky violin piece quite beautifully; she was Kiev-born and taught, and I admired her playing and technique.

Tomorrow I leave, having seen quite enough of Kiev.

23 DECEMBER

Goodbye, Kiev – and what a farewell! The train was due to leave at 9 p.m., but every time we telephoned to the station the answer was that it was late and there was no news yet.

Nicholas, my guide – a tall, fair, handsome Siberian – and I and my three little bags drove to the station at last. Carrying the luggage ourselves, we staggered up the icy steps to the huge waiting room, which was packed with workers, soldiers, peasants, be-shawled women carrying cocoon-like babies, poor people in tattered furs and peaked, torn fur caps, rich people in fine fur coats – all carrying their own bundles, bags and luggage, since porters there are none. One or two of the poorest people crawled about on all fours.

At last, defeated by the atmosphere, we fought our way through the silent, dark mass of people and went right out onto the platform, where an icy wind lifted drifts of snow and hurled them over us, and more snow piled up fast underfoot. So we waited inside on the steps, while Nicholas told me funny stories because he thought I was getting depressed.

Nearly two hours late, the train drew in and the crowd poured past us, slithering and slipping on the platform. My feet by now were on fire with the cold. Nicholas found my carriage, put me in it, saw to everything and at last went off. The Intourist guides are first-rate in every way. I've never met better; they are charming, kind and thoughtful, and their manners – for this country – are unique.

24 DECEMBER

Christmas Eve! I wonder if they got my telegrams at home. I spent the night like a sardine in a tin, with three men. We crept through the snow, now and then the train came to a jerky stop and sent wild, despairing cries into the night, like a lost dog howling. I thought it said, 'I can't get through!' and

Genesta in Transjordania with
dagger, koffia and burnous

Left: The moment of peace

Right: Embarkation from East Africa. All the
passengers were winched aboard in a canvas bag
Below: Kurdistan, 1935: the ferry to Mosul

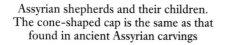

Assyrian shepherds and their children.
The cone-shaped cap is the same as that
found in ancient Assyrian carvings

Right: The very hospitable sheikh of a Kurdish village, flanked by two officials

Above: Lovely Lakri, a dear companion in Kurdistan and later in Kenya, photographed with Assyrian servant

Right: An Assyrian caravan

The bridge at Amadia. Local legend has it that the little daughter of the builder was immured in the middle arch

another train called, 'Here I am' and our train cried, 'Don't leave me!' and the second train suddenly screamed, 'I must go! Farewell!' and our train wailed, 'Goodbye! . . . goodbye!' I have never heard such mournful sounds from trains before. They rang and rang in my ears all through the night.

Oh, if I get home – there will I stay! I've had enough of wandering about in a cold, dark, unfriendly country.

Kharkov. Seven hours late. A smudgy little man met me at the station, but rest was not yet, for an argument started between him, the car driver and some official. They all gesticulated and shouted for about twenty minutes while I sat silently at the back, smoking thin, delicious Russian cigarettes in despair.

In Kiev I was haunted by out-of-work plain clothes detectives, as I was the only tourist in the whole Ukraine. They waited outside my bedroom, followed me down the stairs, sat at nearby tables, thinking they were invisible, and nearly fainted when I said 'Good morning' to them. At last I asked the Intourist lady how much longer they would be with me, and they vanished.

The Intourist hotel seems an improvement on Kiev. There the huge, gaudy place was dark and heavy with the dirt of ages, against which the staff half-heartedly and vainly fought. The dining room was encrusted in gilt paint, very worn and old, with drab little still lifes of various dishes empanelled round the walls. The long, rambling passages were gloomy and foggy, the rooms dark and smelly, and everything was falling down. The food was such as no English servant would condescend to touch, the floors were chipped, the walls were cracked, keys clanged, doors slammed, the bathroom floor was always wet, the lavatories were very Russian and there was never any paper (but if you made a fuss it appeared in your bedroom). Here things are pseudo-modern; the building is newer, lighter, cleaner, the food quite edible, the lavatory more 'cultured', and the bedroom is large and simple.

There is only one tap in my room and it runs melted ice, so the bathwater had to be specially heated for me, but it was a good bath when I got it. I was offered an alluring concert, but first the man was a quarter of an hour late, then there was no ticket. A few moments ago all the lights went out, so now the hotel is in total darkness while the passages ring with loud tones of Slav complaint – I always have an electric torch wherever I go.

25 DECEMBER

Christmas Day. The only thing I wanted was to go to church, and considering all I've heard about free worship in Russia I thought it should not be too difficult. I told yesterday's little man what I wanted and he promised to find out. But today they said in the Intourist Bureau that it was impossible. First, they said, it was too cold, then they said they did not know, and at last the woman said crossly I could find out for myself, if I wanted to go. Later she tried to give me a lecture on 'anti-religion', starting: 'All religions are against the workers' interests.' I told her to keep her opinions to herself, and then discovered that there *are* no churches in the whole of Kharkov.

26 DECEMBER

To the Pioneers' Palace, now a school. Once the nobles' club, it is a long white building looking onto the square. The rooms are large and lovely, the ceilings supported by tall marble pillars. It is very clean, airy and well kept – far better than anything I saw in Kiev. The children are correspondingly better – good-looking, cheerful, clean and healthy.

They have different rooms for different studies, and large, thrilling, expensive toys to play with. In the automobile room was the complete chassis of a car, all the spare parts hung onto the wall for the female teacher to lecture about. There was a tractor in the engine room, and a big model of a public square in the tram room, where you turn on some lights and a couple of trams run round and round – quite useless, but what fun.

In the acroplanc room were dozens of boys of all ages making simple models such as our very young children make, and in the centre was a big model machine made by the boys. On it stood a portrait of the Soviet flyer who did the Moscow–America flight and was killed last week.

In the ballet room was a crowd of eight- and nine-year-old girls, doing infantile ballet steps round a thin, angular woman. At the piano sat another woman furiously frowning, thumping out a tinkly tune: three bars – stop for a lecture – five bars – stop for a lecture – play the whole thing through, start again – stop again – no wonder she looked fed up, scowling at the piano, the dance mistress, the children and us.

Then to the Kharkov picture gallery, still with my guide who clings closer than my conscience, and is nearly as dumb. Here a collection of exquisite Chinese treasures filled me with joy. Gods and goddesses of brass, wood and bronze; fans, screens worked so delicately they looked as though they were painted; china of each period in glazed and glowing colours; ornaments of pearls and jade, pink crystal shrines for household gods and others for ancestors, carved brass and embossed gilt, painted pictures of angry and threatening gods on the walls. There are fine rugs, closely stitched and coloured with vegetable dyes. Delicate china services, groups of exquisite china figures, chairs, bureaux and inlaid dressing-tables were all survivors from the old regime. My guide made a few remarks. Of the rugs she said, 'They are of wool'; in the Chinese rooms she said, 'They are from China'; of the wooden gods she said, 'They are of wood', and finally she sighed and asked: 'At what time will you eat your dinner?'

I could not see a farm here as they said the road was too bad, though there is no snow and the mud must all be frozen over. A favourite excuse, spoken with a kindly smile, is: 'You will be too cold.' This seems to work quite well. They used it about going to church, and about the farm, and I felt the guide was just going to say it again when I asked her to explain the anti-religious photos and caricatures which the children in the Pioneers' Palace were studying; but she said instead, 'You will not be interested.' The anti-religious museums and pictures I have seen seem to be directed not against Christ but against the priests, and are usually Hogarthian drawings of priests gorging, drinking, gambling, torturing, firing guns at the 'toiling masses' or larking about the confessional box with pretty penitents (as one Russian guide described the outdoors people).

I had a two-hour wait at the station. A medical commission from Tiflis in Georgia arrived, frozen, hungry and tired. Their train was eighteen hours late, they had been in it for sixty-six hours, and had run out of food. The wind as well as the snow holds the trains up, so that instead of doing 60 k.p.h. they can only manage 20.

At last my train pulled out for Odessa, and the first step towards home, at 12.30 p.m. – two and a half hours behind scheduled time.

27 DECEMBER

6.30 p.m.: still crawling along, and not due in Odessa now until 1 a.m. Three men and me again in a sardine tin; one of them speaks a little English. The country is white with snow – the trees are decked with it. At the stations children run about pulling tiny toboggans, and sometimes on the roads you see horse sleighs taking the farming people home. There is no sun: just a grey leaden sky and wastes of snow, without a hill to break the landscape, stretching to the horizon.

I have a picture in my mind – several of them – of home . . . Of the chairs under the pepper trees, and the scent of warm earth and fresh-cut grass, the bright green treetops showing just above the edge of the plateau, and then the plain, and the dark forest, and the Mau Mountains rising beyond, painted in misty pastel colours, forests and plains and red cliffs, with dark blue cloud shadows moving slowly across.

Of the trees and the grass, fresh and bright, washed in the rain, with the faint dust haze gone and all the colours vivid and clean.

Of Eburu in the early morning, with clouds lying along the hilltops and halfway down, heavy and grey in the shadowed hills, promising rain; then the sun creeping up the hillside and flooding over the plain, burnishing the grass and painting the trees scarlet. And everywhere the tall, elegant, brave and charming Masai, our best and dearest friends, with their smiling quiet children.

Or the aerodrome – the roar and the rush and the lift of the take-off, then flying low aiming at the fence, then just easing the stick back and up she soars like a lark. And bending her from side to side in figures of eight, or climbing until everything dwindles away from you; the dive and then the lift – swing – pause – and last lovely lift of the loop, or the swing-over, turn, and the screaming, revolving whirl of a spin.

And, from the ground, the blue, folded Ngong Hills, and the great scented plains, with a few dark, shady, wild olive trees, herds of zebra galloping away with their heads up and their tails streaming, wildebeest dark and shaggy, looking at you inquisitively, unafraid. And the silence and the blessed sun and the vastness of it all.

28 DECEMBER

Odessa at midnight. No one to meet me, but a kind-hearted porter took charge, swung my three tiny, very light canvas bags over his shoulder with deep grunts, and set off to look for a taxi.

The Intourist man appeared, but when I asked him why he was so late he just waved the question off. The hotel was a great surprise – large, airy, modern, and almost smell-less. I have a bedside light which turns on and off (even though the plug has been nearly pulled out of the wall, there is still contact enough for the light to work). Also a telephone, and hot and cold water (though in the morning, about bathtime, it is all cold). The place is warm, clean and comfortable, the food is good, the staff smiling. I've noticed that all the waiters are really old, and judging from their out-of-date manners they are survivors from the old regime, unable to forget the customs and courtesy of pre-Revolution days.

This city is *sympathique*, and if it was summer I think I would like it. The streets are wide and the houses of a quiet and charming architecture, not harshly aggressive like Kharkov nor tired and shabby like Kiev. There are tree-filled parks just on the outskirts, and all the pretty little villas which once belonged to merchants have been turned into sanatoriums for tuberculosis and eye cases. And there is the sea! Grey-green and rough, but the first step home for me.

30 DECEMBER

A house which once belonged to the Tolstoy family is now the Professors' Club. 'Professors' are the top grade of teachers, doctors, etc. A musical competition was held there for children: they played their simple little tunes quite well, while the mistress stood smiling steadily on the platform and gave them and us little lectures. The result of making the children perform from an early age is that they have perfect self-confidence in public, and not a trace of stage fright.

I walked out last night along the seafront. Wild music came from the street radio, trains screamed and ships' sirens hooted. There were black puffs of smoke, blue flashes from the trams, port and starboard lights showing in the harbour. It was very dark and cold; there was ice on the ground and a light snow was falling. I thought where had I got myself to, right away here on the edge of the Black Sea, cut off from everyone – for nobody knows where I am. It feels rather strange.

31 DECEMBER

New Year's Eve. At home they were racing yesterday and they will have played polo today. The club aeroplanes will be up all day, and tonight there will be that terrific dance at Muthaiga with the bonfire, everyone singing 'Auld Lang Syne' and kissing each other.

1939

1 JANUARY

New Year's Day, the first I have ever spent away from home and my own people.

Two Danish tourists, 'educators', have arrived, and the three of us sat together on New Year's Eve. The restaurant was packed full of first shyly silent and later an uproariously boisterous crowd.

We got nothing to eat but red caviare and cheese – the waiters were quite overcome by the crowd, and the extra work was more than they could attempt to cope with. Everyone was in day clothes, though the most dashing women had added hats. Every curve and bulge showed under their tight dresses, some so pointedly that I couldn't help wondering if they were artificial. At midnight the lights went out, the band struck up, everyone clapped, '1939' appeared in lighted letters over the bar, the lights went on, people toasted each other, and there we were, in another year. Then all round the room between the tables a lane was cleared along which the people danced.

The Danes were enraptured with Russia. They found the people charming and the system successful, though they did not think as well of the hotel staff as I did. I think they were lying – perhaps afraid I would report them to the KGB if they disparaged Russia. I was equally discreet.

3 JANUARY

The boat for Greece does not now sail till tomorrow! I had everything packed, spreading out the time as much as I could – staying in bed until there was just time enough to dress, to eat the last meal on the food coupon I had saved, and to buy a souvenir for poor, misguided Buddy (my left-wing

East End Jewish tailor friend), and I was looking forward to leaving this country and sailing towards home.

I went to the office, where the manageress smilingly told me that the ship was not sailing on time after all. Still a day and a night here. It's like being in prison. I came back to my dreary little room and lay on the bed and cried.

Communications are always breaking down in this country; trains late, ships not sailing to schedule. There are not nearly enough trams in the streets, and hardly any taxis. I cannot imagine what the air service is like. I tried to get information about civilian flying, but this was refused.

There is nothing to do, no way of passing the time except to sit on the window ledge and look at the harbour and yearn to go. I've finished the book I was reading and haven't enough money to buy another, even if I could find one. The sky is grey and heavy and sad, and the naked little trees are grimy. Heaps of dirty snow are piled along the street. It is too cold and too slippery underfoot to walk out, and anyway there is nowhere to walk to. There are ships in the harbour: pillars of dirty smoke rise slowly from their funnels, and now and then they sound their sirens as though they were laughing at me.

Yesterday the guide took me to the mud bath clinic outside the town. The mud is used for curing rheumatism, arthritis and heart trouble. Between two and three thousand patients come here daily – men in the morning, women in the afternoon. The doctor in charge was the only one I have seen in this country who gave a good impression – he seemed competent and clean, though badly shaven. The clinic is a low, white building set round a tree-filled courtyard with a fountain in the middle; it is on the shores of a lake and in the summer it must be quite pretty.

All the treatments are free. The factories and unions pay 13 per cent of the workers' wages to insurance companies, and in this way all who need medical treatment or a rest in a convalescent home get it free.

I went to the ballet last night hoping to see some really good dancing, but was disappointed and left before the end. The dancing was very mediocre, and not always in time with the music.

At about eleven o'clock some men started to beat and hammer on my door. Very startled, I leaped out of bed, hung onto the handle and shouted: '*Niet! Niet!*' But they stayed there for three or four minutes, shaking the door and roaring at me in Russian. It is not the sort of thing one expects to happen in an ordinary civilized country, but then this is not an ordinary civilized country.

Today I went for a walk. The cold has turned to a damp which is just as penetrating but not quite so painful. I walked down the side-streets and looked into the courtyards of some very poor houses, where the broken windows were mended with bits of wood and paper, and the steps up to the doors were cracked, and rows of dilapidated washing were hanging out to dry. Then I went down hundreds of steps to a street near the docks. Here the buildings were anything but showy, and there were the ships – so near!

Oh, if only I can start tomorrow! They say the delay was caused by the enormous crowd of Greek passengers who are trying to get home. This morning the hall and corridors of the hotel were filled with them and their children, bundles and boxes. They were patiently waiting to start, all dressed to go in their shabby hats and coats. Later, when I came back to my room, they were sadly carrying their things upstairs again, probably just as unhappy and distressed as I was.

4 JANUARY

Goodbye, Russia! For ever, I hope. I am at sea, we have left Odessa's lights behind and are rolling down the Black Sea with a cargo of five or six hundred Greeks on board and a list to starboard.

All day, from twelve o'clock on, I waited to go, while in the office they telephoned again and again to the port; but the answer was always 'Not yet.' They had the Greeks down there from early morning, going through their things, and they kept them waiting in the Customs House all day long. I lay on my bed and dozed, too depressed to go out and walk on the cold terrace and look at that dirty sky and dirty sea and the heaps of dirty snow and the dank, damp washing.

At 5.30 they came for the baggage, and at six I left the hotel. In the Customs House they took out everything I possessed, searched eagerly in an envelope which contained toilet paper (which they hastily and embarrassedly replaced), read my typewritten letters and an article, and were thrilled with the photos. They were perfectly polite, but more thorough on their examination than any other Customs people I have yet met. One Customs man asked, in German, how I liked Russia! *'Interessant,'* I said. He looked rather upset and said it was not *wunderbar? 'Sehr interessant,'* I said.

The ship was in chaos. Greek families and baggage blocked the corridors and sprawled on the stairs. Through the open cabin doors you could see groups of unshaven little men in worn dark coats and collarless, dirty shirts, dark as earwigs, and overflowingly fat women in shawls and shapeless dresses.

They tried to put me into one of these cabins, a four-berther, but I flatly refused and asked for the captain. Much to my surprise I was taken straight to his office and found that he acts as purser as well. Thin and pale, very tired, unshaven and unsmart, he listened to what I had to say and told the sailor who brought me to give me a first-class cabin. So here I am, *installée de luxe* (Russian-style). There are two berths and a sofa, heat which won't turn off, a porthole which won't open, a door which won't lock, a lifebelt but no instructions, and no boat stations allotted. No blankets (not that one needs them). Nothing to be sick into. No bed-light. And the inevitable ancient grime in the washbasin and on the shelf.

But we've started! The Greeks are uproariously happy. Soon they will be devastatingly sick.

Now I can write what I truly think.

This is, to my mind, a very strange country and I'm very glad to be out of it. It may be the system and it may be the people, or a bit of both, but it fills me with fear. I can't remember ever being frightened of a country before. It seemed like an octopus, reaching out to engulf me.

I haven't dared to write freely in case the diary was read and I got into trouble; everything I have written is true, but only half the truth, which just shows what a false impression one can give and yet be honest. In Kiev my room, books and papers were investigated every day, and never put back as they were. I pencilled around my belongings, and the 'investigations' stopped.

12 JANUARY

Mycenae, Greece. No war-worn, homesick warrior of Alexander's army was ever more glad to go back to these shores than I was. Russia has disappeared behind me, I can get off this boat, the sun is shining and I am in touch with Imperial Airways again.

14 JANUARY

Today I left Athens and came to yet another enchanted village, after three and a half hours in a bus. I should be in Alex, repacking, but Greece is so lovely I can't bear to leave it – so damn the luggage.

This village has probably been here for thousands of years. The sea is quite close, the hills stand behind it, and across the valley steep, jagged mountains tower against the dark blue sky. I had supper out of doors, while flocks of turkeys, sheep, donkeys with loads of hay and sticks, some goats, peasants with vegetables, mule carts and ploughing ponies, all came slowly back from different directions, and the village quietly folded itself up for the night.

16 JANUARY

At last I was in the flying boat, homeward-bound. And now I am home again, on the farm. Life is wonderful.

8 MARCH

I had a wire to say that Father was sinking, so I flew back to England. He died at the very moment I reached my brother Griggs' house – just as though he was waiting for me to get back before he was released, Margit said.

When I saw him there was nothing there – only the framework, the

206

covering. The splendid spirit, vital and brave and wise, had gone. And now he seems nearer to me than he has been for two years past, when he sat in a chair or stumbled up and down the garden paths, his body still moving but his mind already half away.

11 MARCH

The tenants and farm people came to say goodbye to Father. They walked quietly up to him, looked at him a moment, and went out.

The memorial service in Coldharbour church was rather splendid. All the neighbours, the villagers, the tenants, the hunt servants were there, all the house servants and some office people. There were only flowers from his garden, and his two banners. His coffin was drawn uphill on a farm cart, by two splendid carthorses, groomed and gleaming.

There was a memorial service in the City; the church was so full that half the people were standing. The Chairman of Lloyd's read the lesson, and a great many City dignitaries were there. Father was one of the most powerful men in the City, and at Lloyd's itself a special meeting was called to pay tribute to him.

My father was a most remarkable man, a genius and a saint, a rare combination. Deafened in his youth, he lost his chance of going into the Royal Navy, for which his Admiral godfather had given him a nomination, which was one way of getting into the navy, in those days. He joined Lloyds Insurance instead, and here his remarkable financial brain came into its own. He would take risks that no other insurer would look at, and in a History of Lloyds some members are quoted as saying, 'Poor young Heath is riding for a fall.'

But poor young Heath never fell – he went from strength to strength, and it was only his deafness which prevented his becoming Chairman of Lloyds. He worshipped my beautiful mother and they really were a striking-looking pair. He helped everyone who was in need, and only regretted, as he once said to me, that none of his kindness and goodness 'cost him' anything personally. At Anstie there were endless parties, children and their parents from the village, tenants and employees, shooting parties, meets of hounds (he was joint master of the Surrey Union hounds) and summer bathing parties in the lovely rhododendron embowered 'Bath Garden', made by my great grandfather. Mother loved entertaining, with her beautiful looks and perfect figure, she was an ornament in the landscape and a born hostess.

Brought up in France (where the Hugenot Gambiers originally came from), she was in Normandy in 1870 when the Germans invaded Paris; there was a flood of French refugees into Normandy, some of them wounded and with terrible tales of the atrocities they said their enemies had committed. Mother never forgot this, and all her life she detested and distrusted the

Germans as a race, though she did, of course, have a very few German friends.

APRIL

Political upheavals follow each other at such a rate that the map of Europe seems to be breaking up all round us. Suddenly in mid-March, without warning, the German armies entered Prague, a few hours after Dr Hacha, the President of Czechoslovakia, had had an interview with Hitler. The people did not fight, having nothing to fight with, but they lined the streets and watched the soldiers going past in deadly silence, except that here and there women booed and jeered, while others wept. The Gestapo got to work at once, and by the evening of the second day had made eight thousand arrests. A concentration camp, the first in the country, was opened, to which five thousand prisoners were sent.

The posters in London were typical. They stood side by side, some saying 'Death of a Nation', 'Czechoslovakia Breaking Up', and others, 'Test Match Reports. England scores a century.' People rushed for the papers, stood in clumps reading the headlines, the sports pages, then folded up their papers and walked quietly on. In tubes and buses the only ones to take any notice of the foreign news were workmen and labourers, who read all the foreign news with set faces and grim mouths – dreaming, perhaps, of that false dawn, Communism.

In the streets groups of East End Jews suddenly appeared, talking loudly in Yiddish, their faces crumpled or stony with misery. All the telephone boxes were full of Jews pouring in coins, sending long-distance calls. These people, trying in vain to get news of their relations who might by now be in German concentration camps, their lives suddenly broken up, were tortured with anxiety. Helplessly roaming the steady, stolid London streets and surrounded by phlegmatic British faces, they were as heart-rending as those other refugees I saw in Prague five months ago.

About two days after Prague was invaded in March, the British public began to realize there was a crisis. The posters were purely political – people talked of conscription and the power of the German and Russian air forces. One party says: 'Chamberlain must go. There won't be any end to this engulfing of Europe until we have someone in power who will act.' Another party says, 'Trust Chamberlain. He'll move when he's ready. In any case, we can't have a split yet.'

When Czechoslovakia had been completely swallowed, people sat back and breathed again and said 'How awful!' The eastern European countries trembled. Romania entered into a trade pact with Germany. The British government tentatively approached Poland, Russia, Greece and Yugoslavia to form a peace pact against aggression. Hardly had they begun than on 22 March the Germans, after one day of German minority agitation in Lithuania and one day of threats, marched into Memel [*on the Baltic coast*], hard on the heels of the retreating Lithuanian army and the panic-stricken, fleeing Jews.

Germany had now established herself pretty successfully round Poland, hemming her in on the north and the south. *Démarches* were made towards Poland, but the Poles are tough. When the Germans arrested several thousand Polish subjects in Germany on some flimsy excuse, the Poles arrested an equal number of Germans, and held onto them until their own nationals were released.

A few days ago a wave of benign sentimentality swept the world on the news of the birth of a son to the lovely Queen Geraldine, the twenty-three-year-old Roman Catholic, Hungarian wife of Zog, romantic Mohammedan King of the romantic mountain country of Albania. This world-wide cradle appeal was a great relief after all the iron and blood and terrorism and Jewish agony and continual crisis. But two days after the baby was born Geraldine and her son were fleeing across the mountains by car, while Zog, in peasant costume, led his tiny army of mountaineers against the Italians who were invading the Albanian ports with guns and planes. Zog gave up after a hopeless fight and joined his Queen. The mountaineers fought on a little longer, and then their resistance collapsed.

14 APRIL

Corfu flashed into the news – an important Greek island with a big deep harbour. The Italians assured us that if we occupied it there would be 'most dangerous reactions'. We told the Italians that we were not going to occupy it, but if anyone else did we would take 'a very grave view indeed'.

Ciano and his Edda [*Mussolini's daughter*] are to become Viceroy and Vicereine of Albania. This, the paper says, is to remove him from the post of Minister for Foreign Affairs, which he has not handled to the entire satisfaction of his father-in-law.

Everyone is preparing for war. British engineers are building barriers across the roads leading out of Gibraltar. The French have manned the Maginot Line, and the Germans the Siegfried Line. German ships sail for Spain. Italian troops pour into Spain – to leave, says Franco, after the Peace Parade [*the Spanish Civil War officially ended on 1 April*]. Spanish troops are concentrating opposite Gibraltar.

2 AUGUST

There was a pause in the threatening and arguing; all quiet politically. Personally, I've had a bad time. Boy has left me for good. He wants to marry someone else's wife. He and his new friend are living together on the farm in Kenya.

Don Taylor-Smith has got a fifty-ton seventy-foot ketch, *Zareba*; my daughter Heather and I have been getting her ready. Two days ago she was decorated, stocked with food, clean from stem to stern, with new plates in the galley and new green sheets on her lovely bunks. She was all ready to go to sea, and so were we, but it seemed quite impossible to find anyone to go with us. We asked everyone we knew, but everyone either had previous dates, or couldn't get away, or they thought it was the most awful idea they'd ever heard of.

On Monday evening Heather and I were sadly wondering if we ever would get started when a little racing boat sailed past us and the two boys waved. We waved back. They put about and asked for matches. We asked them if they would like to come to Marseilles. The end of it was that late last night two tall, dark, handsome and very nice medical students, Gordon and Ian, arrived with their luggage and a black kitten. Today we steamed down the estuary and said goodbye – we hoped for good – to England.

15 AUGUST

Brest. After endless delays and countless tacks across the Channel, we got here. At dawn we came carefully into the estuary with the motors. Soon one began to knock badly, and Don abandoned his hard-earned lunch and went into the engine room; here he sat staring at the works and looking rather like a blond Satan, crouching among his smoky fires contemplating his roasting sinners, wondering whether he should give this soul another turn, or stoke up the fire under that one. The trouble was a broken tappet, but our hearts were in our mouths until we finally crept past the lines of French battleships and dropped anchor inside the port.

26 AUGUST

We were about ten days in Brest getting another crew. First Ian and Gordon left us, as their holiday was nearly over. The health officer, a Corsican called Poggioli who acts as paterfamilias to all yachts, got us a snub-nosed, round-faced Breton sailor called Corentin Gourlasuen, who knows the way, and all the lights, apparently by heart, and who washed first the decks, then the plates, then the galley floor, without even being asked.

Brest is one of the strongest ports in Europe, and holds most of the French fleet. French planes roared overhead all day – they make more noise with less speed than any planes I've ever seen, and when they turn they put the stick hard over and stamp on the rudder and seemingly *bend* round.

We went to Plougastel village on Sunday, where everyone wears native dress and the flocks of women and girls look very demure and clean and rather sweet in their flouncy black skirts, their little plaid neckerchiefs and their tall, plain, starched white caps. The men have big black hats with curly brims and streamers behind, and embroidered, blue cloth waistcoats.

We got a Breton captain named le Duff, and were all ready to sail when another crisis blew up. Germany and Russia have signed a non-aggression pact, to the stupefaction of the whole world, and the Germans naturally say: 'Now for Danzig' [*Poland's only port*].

French reservists have been called up. Roosevelt, the Pope and the Belgian King have made peace appeals; German nationals are leaving England and British nationals are leaving Germany and France. English schools are prepared for evacuation; the French fleet has put to sea, and all the ministers are making long, patriotic speeches. I still hope and pray that peace will remain with us. I feel no price is too high to pay to prevent one or two million men from being killed.

28 AUGUST

We had too little wind, and crept along at about half a knot an hour. It may take me two months to reach Marseilles, there to pick up an aeroplane which left England three and a half hours before. Life is as you take it.

Just now several million people are enduring terrible fears; women for their menfolk, the Poles for their country, Jews for their lives. Millions of pounds are spent in preparation for a war which may yet be averted. Cabinet ministers dash to and fro, prayers rise up from every church, caterers and cloth merchants make a bit on quiet profiteering, and munitions factory owners are coining money. Everyone is in an agony of uncertainty.

And here we are, safe and quiet at sea, tied to world events only by a voice which we can summon from the air or leave silent, as we choose. We have, at the moment, very little money, but we have enough food to eat and a little wine, and there is the sun; we have enough, and no one need have more.

30 AUGUST

Wireless news: everyone preparing for war. Messages have passed between England, France and Germany which, Chamberlain says, it would be unwise at this stage to make public. British ships are warned to keep out of the Mediterranean, so we will try to reach Portugal, by which time either a war will have started or all will be settled peacefully. The line-up is England, France and some Balkan states versus Germany and Italy. No news of Spain. Japan is angry and astonished at the Russian–German pact; the cabinet has resigned and they are 'reconsidering' their European policy.

1 SEPTEMBER

Warsaw and other Polish towns and cities have been bombarded by the Germans. Hitler has declared himself supreme head of the army. Children are being evacuated from London and all other big coastal cities. All officers have been called up. Food buying is restricted ('This does not mean there is a shortage,' says the BBC soothingly). Roosevelt has ordered all American battleships to be ready to sail, saying that war has begun between Germany and Poland.

Last night the Bay of Biscay decided to give us a piece of its mind. The wind, which had been against us all day, dropped completely, and the sea, whipped up by a thunderstorm, rose. *Zareba* lay rolling among the huge billows, each of which struck her a terrific blow on the sides. At every impact she groaned and shook, like a mortally weary trek ox about to founder.

About 2 a.m. the sea subsided, and the creaks and groans and bangs grew fewer and quieter. This morning the sea is quietly heaving – regaining its breath, as it were, after last night's tumult.

3 SEPTEMBER

The Germans invaded Poland, so we have kept our promise and declared war on Germany at eleven o'clock this morning.

5 SEPTEMBER

A perfect day! The sun and sea and sky are like a benediction; so peaceful are all our surroundings that a war seems as fantastic and silly as a bad dream. But a Spanish cruiser is patrolling near us, and though we hoisted the red ensign and saluted, she made no sign of recognition.

The liner *Athenia* was sunk off the north-west of Ireland; she carried fourteen hundred passengers, of whom a thousand were women and children and over three hundred were Americans. There are no mines there, so she must have been torpedoed. All were saved, except those killed in the explosion. Our aeroplanes flew unmolested over north and west Germany one night, and dropped six million pamphlets in German. As if this would stop the Germans! Our planes also bombed Kiel, and there were some casualties.

7 SEPTEMBER

Late last night we came into Vigo. After so many days at sea, and the shrieks and groans of a boat tortured by stormy weather and tumultuous seas, shore sounds and scents seem strange and yet familiar, like an old house revisited after a long absence. A dog barking, a car hooting, a train whistling, become curiously interesting.

This morning the first sound I heard was Don: '*Ooh là là! Ooh là là!*' and when I went on deck, where should we be lying but in the middle of a German merchant fleet! There we were, safe in port, completely surrounded by enemy ships, forty-four of them. The sailors hung over the rails, bored and disconsolate, and presently a ship's boat put out and rowed right round us, with two high-collared, peak-capped, glaring, glowering ship's officers, who looked at us loathingly. We all sat on deck in pyjamas, eating porridge, laughing at them and looking scruffy on purpose.

10 SEPTEMBER

We went to see the British Consul, who seemed very harassed.

'This is not the time to be pleasure cruising,' he said. 'I must advise you to keep near the coast and not to sail at night. There will be vessels without lights and – er – other things.'

Don said, 'Any submarines about?' and at the look of horror he got, he added, 'Or am I asking an indiscreet question?'

'You certainly *are* asking an indiscreet question,' said the Consul, and with that he vanished with no apology or goodbye.

We went to the Spaniard who was acting as French consular agent to talk about Corentin's position since he was on the reserve of the French navy. He said he felt more French than Spanish, through long association with the French, that the Germans were *une race infâme*, and that there would be no peace or safety on earth while any were left alive. We parted bosom friends and promised to write. He was a pleasant contrast to his British counterpart.

Around the hill from the castle is a bar, and there we found Heather and an Englishman who had introduced himself. When he had left us two Germans sat at a nearby table, so by way of committing our first act of war we asked them to come and drink with us. They were pleasant, non-committal, upset about the war, hoped it would be over soon, and wished for trade and peace. One was captain of a ship with twelve passengers and a lot of cargo, while the other had just come back from Madrid, where he said there were very few houses left in the poor quarter [*after the Civil War*] and the people were living like animals.

It is hard to get food here. People are rationed, and hospitals have the best of what's going. The poor people steal bananas and fruit off the quay. It is worse in Madrid and the south, and yet the food is there, for Cordoba alone produces enough oil for all of Spain, and Spain has exported oil this year.

Farewell to Vigo was a battle royal with the ship's chandler, who charged us nearly double for everything. Don stormed at him, laughed at him, twisted him inside out, threatened him, and in the end kept the stores and cut the bill in half. The old man recognized a master bargainer in the end and seemed amused.

Who wants buoys? We saw a dark lump floating, and when we passed it saw it was a branch of bananas – great big, ripe, yellow ones. Corentin started whooping about the deck, and Don unshipped the boat hook and amid the wildest excitement we made the captain turn the ship round and hunt bananas. Corentin yelled and blasphemed, gaffed the bunches and passed them up. More and more appeared in the sea, and after a while we were going through great shoals of them. A torpedoed ship's cargo, we thought – it couldn't be anything else.

12 SEPTEMBER

Yesterday we arrived off Portugal. Fishing boats came out to us, we traded two branches of bananas for seven fish. The fishermen asked for bread; it seems strange there should be none here. Unfortunately we could not spare any.

War news: Canada and South Africa have come in. French troops are in Germany on a twenty-kilometre front. All the Arabs have declared for us. The Poles are nearly beaten but still fighting hard – seven German divisions have not yet succeeded in breaking them down.

Friendly messages come through from the German workers to their British counterparts, saying that though watched and persecuted by the Gestapo they still work for peace and a 'Socialist world'. They need bread, butter, oil, meat and trade, they say. Posters have been pinned on trees reading: 'Rather the heaven-appointed Kaiser than the beast of Berchtesgaden'.

13 SEPTEMBER

Very early in the morning a fishing trawler came up to us; the men asked what nationality we were, and when the captain answered, 'British,' they said we must not stay here; a German submarine was hanging around and had fired on a British ship two days before.

They would not even wait for us to start our motors, but put a man on board us, made fast a line, and started for the shore. We had been lying outside the three-mile limit on account of the fog. They towed us right in before they turned and steamed down towards Leixcos. They would not take any money; all they wanted was to get us safely into harbour. They said a ship had been sunk recently, and another had arrived in Brest with her engines hot from dodging a submarine.

The Portuguese have been wonderful to us, they are kind and courteous, friendly and hospitable. They are Britain's oldest allies, and they never forget it.

15 SEPTEMBER

We found a berth for *Zareba* at Leixcos, and now we can all go ashore. We go to Oporto by tram along the beautiful, balustraded seafront, through the awful slums where the houses are like kennels and the rooms like small boxes, the streets are narrow as footpaths, dark and curving, and into the fine, big square, under the seven-hundred-year-old cathedral, standing splendidly on its hill commanding the town.

The British Consul here was kind and helpful. He said that communications between here and France were very bad indeed, and the railways congested with troops. He knew that U-boats were along this coast, but thought it safe to go to Lisbon, so long as we stayed within the three-mile limit.

18 SEPTEMBER

At sea again. Before we left there was a message to say we must see the British Consul, so into Oporto we trailed once more. The message said there were no laying up facilities in Lisbon, the trip there might be dangerous, and would we not rather return to England with the yacht, hugging the coast all the way. In any case, said the Consul, he thought the two lady passengers should go by train and not risk the submarines. They might not sink us at sight, but they might force us ashore and then destroy *Zareba*.

Very crushed, we went to a café and held a council of war. We decided to stick together and chance it, so we went back to Leixcos where my spirits completely recovered when I bought a lovely Portuguese peasant hat for fivepence. We sailed out on the evening wind, and the northerly breeze carried us along in fine style. It was good to feel the boat moving again, and hear the familiar creak of wood and the hum of the rigging.

1 OCTOBER

Despite – or perhaps because of – all our precautions, for Heather and I packed a box of food and one of clothes in case we were sent ashore in the dinghy, there was never a sign of a submarine until we came into Lisbon harbour, where three Portuguese ones were lying. This was a disappointment to us, but not to the skipper, who was sunk twice in the last war and has not even yet quite got over those awful experiences.

6 DECEMBER

We are returning to England – we can't get any more money sent out, Don wants to get into the air force, and Heather and I want to see Mother.

The lovely *Zareba* lies up here, guarded by an old pilot.

24 DECEMBER

Trains again. We left on 12 December carrying a good hamper of food and wine, since everyone said we could get nothing in Spain, though heaps in France. But we gave it away to the Spanish.

The last time I saw Irun it was burning, and the flames seemed to leap halfway to heaven. The roar they made, and the crash of falling walls and roofs mingled with the sound of rifle fire, the snarl and crackle of machine guns and the booming of Irun's solitary big gun, were all very exciting. Now it is a cold, dreary, tragic place, half in ruins still. Walls pitted by bullets. Windows with no panes. Grey faced, hard-eyed, stricken people.

The Customs and passport people gave us no trouble and we walked over the bridge to Hendaye. Last time I stood there the bullets sang past. This time it poured with rain – no question of a drive into the Pyrenees. Instead, we sat in a sad, dark hotel and finally slept till it was time to catch the train. We had no money left, so did without sleepers. There was no restaurant car, so we did without food too, bitterly regretting our lovely hamper.

26 DECEMBER

At 7 a.m. we arrived in Paris, and stayed, very comfortably, at the Hotel Crystal. Money was sent from England. Heather and I sacked the shops.

The shops are quite brightly lit at night. They are not as they were, but you can see your way about. The restaurants are crammed, but everything shuts at 11 p.m. A barman sadly said that before the war he never got to bed before 8 a.m. but now he had to get up at 8 p.m. It had upset his system. Here and there English women in uniform walked about the streets, regarded by the French with polite and veiled amusement.

On the whole – very few uniforms – great gaiety – and money circulating freely.

After six days we started for England.

The train was normal – warm – good food – scheduled for Calais, but ran on to Boulogne.

The steamer, painted grey, was very full, mostly troops on Christmas leave. All civilians were herded below as we left port, and made to put on their life-preservers.

The biting wind which swept the deck kept us in the saloon, so the sad thrill of seeing again those white cliffs was lost to me.

Again we had to go below as we drew in, and finally emerged to find ourselves in Dover. The customs people were charming to Heather and me, and passed us, and our smart new clothes, through with the slightest of duties. But they pounced on Don. His passport issued in Shanghai, visaed for Russia, was too much for them. There were endless questions – where did he get the camera. Who owned the yacht, who were we. How long had I known him. They went through his diaries, and he started reading out an endless letter to his father. Three hours after the train had gone, they decided he was harmless.

They became angelically kind and solicitous. A taxi was found, then a restaurant, then a train. Tired, fed-up, and cold, we silently sat in a black carriage, gloomily approaching London.

1940

18 MARCH

We've been in England for three months. There is a war, and yet there isn't. At night the streets are pitch-black. First we ran into lamp-posts and fell over sandbags. Twelve hundred people were killed by vehicles in December. Then a glimmer of light was allowed from odd posts, and now you can just see your way. There are many girls in uniform and dozens of women's services. But nothing ever happens. Nurses go to lectures and firefighters have practice fires; they get bored and depressed. The ambulance drivers keep their engines ready and drive their trucks about the East End nightly – collecting drunks.

On our front there is still hardly any war. Fishing boats are machine-gunned from the air. They fight back. Some are mined, some sunk by U-boats. Our planes fly right over Prague and Austria, dropping leaflets.

18 MAY

Here in England local defence forces have been formed to deal with parachutists if they try to land and air raids are expected on London. All the regulations are being tightened.

Yet London is madly gay – everyone works all day, and dances at night. Every night club and hotel is packed – the clothes are lovely, the food luscious. The Battle of Waterloo dance spirit. Why not? We may take our pleasures sadly (as the French love to say we do), but how we revel in our troubles! We are a very quiet race when at peace, thus deluding foreigners. The moment we *have* to, we snap into top gear, producing miracles of courage and fortitude, astonishing our friends and foes – and even ourselves!

JUNE

The French have laid down their arms. Now we are alone, and we know we can trust ourselves! Reynaud's government fell and Pétain became Premier. Weygand is his deputy. There were Armistice talks. The Italians had declared war on the Allies a short time ago, sure they were now on the winning side. The French had to accept their terms, as well as those of the Germans, before fighting ceased altogether. Those terms were hard: release

217

of all German prisoners; handing over of the fleet and air force; part of the north of France to the Germans, and part of the south to the Italians; all colonies, gold, and arms to be given up. This was a shocking blow to the British, and there was only one thing to do: withdraw our men (losing the second lot of equipment we had sent over). All available boats rushed across the Channel, and a marvellous evacuation took place. Quietly, quickly, a large part of the British army was saved and brought back to Britain.

After the first paralysed hours London again went back to normal – on the surface. Women shopped. Men went to their clubs. People dined out. The invasion has not come. Air raids are still very minor and not over London. A few people get killed every night. But that does not seem to affect Londoners, who will not imagine what a raid is really like until they are in one.

When Italy came in, the police swept up all the Italians in London. Ferraro, the Quaglino brothers [*restaurateurs*], Luigi, Sovrani, the waiters and small shopkeepers, they have all been taken away. Quag's was very quiet and rather strained. James, the English hall porter, said it was awful to see them being taken out one by one, with their solitary suitcases, and put into vans and driven away. James has been with them for many years and was terribly upset. The few French and English waiters left are carrying on as best they can. Before they were arrested I went to see these famous and charming brothers – they were distraught and could only keep on saying: '*Quelle salade!*'

The British and French were doing their best to evacuate troops and refugees. Ships came in a steady stream, their decks so crowded that men were sitting in the lifeboats and on the rails. The ships were weighed down till the gunwales were almost in the water. A skipper I knew, Everson, brought the Rothschilds to England. One man held up a small, battered bag, and said: 'This is all that's left of three houses in Italy and two in France!'

8 JULY

Air raids at Falmouth, near where I am staying. Eleven people killed yesterday. A bomb on a camp near here. Air raid warnings here and the sound of enemy planes overhead. The children are packed away in the local shelter, but the grown-ups take hardly any notice. They won't until the first bomb drops among them – then they won't be so *insouciant*. Personally, I just can't imagine a bomb dropping near me. My lack of imagination is to be envied.

Some of the French fleet is in British ports, some in Alexandria and some at Oran [*Algeria*]. To the French admiral in Oran the following terms were offered: to hand over the ships to the British, and the men to be demobilized and repatriated; to take the ships to a French West Indian port for the duration; or to stay where they were, immobilized. It was explained that the British must take *any* steps to prevent the French ships falling into German hands, and that if the admiral refused these alternatives the British fleet would be obliged to open fire. The French admiral, nearly distraught, refused all these offers, so the British opened fire. It was appalling, firing on our own allies, but it was the only thing to do. The British ships all had their boats ready, and sent them out at once to rescue the French sailors. Some of the ships were sunk by gunfire, and some bombed from the air. The death toll was heavy. A few ships ran the gauntlet and managed to escape, but the beautiful *Dunkerque*, the fastest boat of her class in the world, was completely crippled.

The officers and crew were completely shattered by the collapse of France, and the truth is that they did not know what to do, and they had no one to turn to. Perhaps they thought we were bluffing.

What a ghastly war it is. This morning, in retaliation, French aircraft attacked our ships in Gibraltar harbour.

Some Cornish fishermen, now in the navy, were detailed to accompany marines in taking over a French ship in a nearby harbour. In the dark, before dawn, they crept alongside and got quietly on board.

The British were silent. Just as it grew light a French sailor appeared on deck and went to the rails. While he made himself comfortable the British politely waited. The Frenchman turned round and went sleepily towards the companionway. Then the marines moved forward and he found himself surrounded by armed men. He let out a yell which roused the ship. Up from below rushed the French sailors, dishevelled and bewildered, all shouting at once. But in a few minutes they realized what was happening; they listened to the interpreter and went along quietly. They were given the choice of fighting with us, or of repatriation. Most of them elected to stay with us.

Some days ago the Channel Islands were partly evacuated and completely demilitarized, which was announced on the BBC. The next day the German bombers raided the islands, blowing up everything they could and machine-gunning the islanders. I heard they killed about ninety.

9 JULY

General de Gaulle, the [*Free*] French self-appointed leader in London, made a fine broadcast speech about the *Affaire Oran*. He said that, like all true Frenchmen, he had heard with 'rage and pain' of the firing, by their own allies, on the French fleet, that anyone who represented such an action as a British naval victory was lying cruelly and vilely, and that the loss of their splendid ships and valiant *matelots* was the hardest blow they had suffered. But he asked his countrymen to understand that if these ships had fallen into German hands they would have been used to shell English, and probably French, ports; and that the only hope for ultimate liberty for France, and a decent life for Frenchmen, was in the strength of England, and in her victory. He said the blame for this tragedy must be laid at Pétain's door, not that of England. [*Marshal Pétain had signed the Armistice with Germany, and was now head of state in unoccupied Vichy France.*]

Tonight we hear the same thing happened at Dakar [*French West Africa*]. The British officer bearing the message was not allowed to approach the French ships, but the message was somehow conveyed to the French admiral. Though the officer waited until long past the appointed hour there was no answer, and at last he returned to the British flagship.

During the night depth charges were dropped under the French ships' sterns, and the ships were finally crippled by air attacks. Ghastly, fratricidal tragedy – yet it seems strange that the clever and practical French did not realize we could never let their beautiful ships fall into German hands.

Things look grimmer and grimmer. Taxes are going up again. We are now spending *£9 million* a day on this awful war.

The *Arandora Star*, carrying German and Italian civilian prisoners to Canada, was torpedoed by a U-boat. About 160 Germans and 430 Italians were drowned. The Germans fought with the Italians for places in the boats, and of course the Germans won. Many 'famous chefs and restaurateurs' were said to be on board – my poor Quaglinos, perhaps? [*Many years later I found the Quags in a London restaurant – we had a happy champagne reunion.*]

Two bombs were dropped by a fleeing plane near Dartmouth. Robin says: 'Two new bunkers in the golf course!'

18 JULY

Utterly bored and fed up with being alone and having nothing to do, I went to Falmouth for the day. During luncheon we heard the roar of a Spitfire overhead. Then the proprietress came bustling in and said would we please come down to the shelter. Such a nuisance, she said, that one didn't get longer warning. Cups of coffee and hot dishes were left cooling on the tables as we trooped downstairs. I had longed to stay up and see the sights, but the first great Boom! from a ship just beneath the window made the panes jump, and me too. A sailor said it really would be wiser to go below. So I went.

In the cellar were about thirty people, all utterly calm and blasé, just annoyed that their shopping and meals should be constantly interrupted. A Grimsby woman with a little girl of two has not had a single full night's rest since the raids started. First they darted between their bedrooms and the shelter. Now they stay in the shelter, and sleep in the pauses between the firing and the bombing. The child didn't mind in the least – she thought the raids were a game, and the noise didn't bother her at all. Everyone was extremely brave. On all sides you heard these women saying to each other, with a sort of wonder, 'I ain't scared – is ee?'

'No – an' I never wus.'

'I do'n mind they bombs, s'long's they do'n fall in the middle o' we!'

Terrific shooting went on. There is a Dutch ship here with a fiery skipper who fancies himself with an anti-aircraft gun. Never waiting for orders, he bangs away the minute he sees an enemy plane, praying to bring it down before our fighters spoil his fun. He truly is a marvellous shot, and has bagged several.

29 JULY

A good story, perfectly true. Paul Maze, a French-born, naturalized British artist, Jessie, his wife, and Pauline, his step-daughter, were staying with Jacques and Consuelo Balzan [*formerly the American Duchess of Marlborough and a cousin by marriage of Winston Churchill*] at Les Moulins near Dreux. As the Germans came nearer and nearer, Paul kept saying hadn't they better go, or anyway evacuate the two hundred babies and twenty-five nurses from Consuelo's clinic. But the Balzans said the Germans would never reach Dreux.

One fine morning Paul woke up to find that during the night the Balzans had evacuated themselves only, without a word to anyone else. Paul was left with all the babies and young women on his hands. [*Later it transpired they had received a signal from Churchill that they must secretly and instantly leave. Hitler wished to capture any English person of importance, with which he hoped to blackmail the British government.*] Paul rushed about, and by some miracle collected trucks, petrol, milk and food, and bundled his 227 protégées on board for Bordeaux. Very soon German planes found them and machine gunned them. Paul and his party got into the stream of refugees and crawled along those dusty roads, under fire all the time, but eventually reached Bordeaux.

Paul dumped his babies and nurses in a hospital, and started to look around for a ship. He found a stranded RAF officer, and three other British people. There was a Dutch ship just ready to sail, so Paul and his companions went aboard. But the Skipper was a Dutch Nazi, and refused to take them. Then they crept away in the darkness in the ship's own dinghy, which they had 'liberated', to a British destroyer. After explaining the situation to her captain, they returned to the Dutch ship with some sailors they had borrowed. In silence they climbed on board – there was no look-out. They pounced on the captain, arresting him and six of his officers, then took them ashore and left them there. Then the British sailors returned to the ship, and Paul persuaded the Dutch crew to take her out to sea with the entire party, while her skipper stood gibbering on the quay.

After a fantastically awful journey they reached England. Paul, with his wild looks, funny accent and British passport, was immediately removed to an internment camp. For two or three days he was too tired to mind where he was. Then he came to, went to the commandant and insisted on being taken somewhere where he could send a wire to Winston Churchill. Still thinking he was a fifth columnist they let him send the wire, and were thunderstruck when orders came back that Paul was to be released at once.

I went to London, and it was very dull. So I went to Pauline's sister, Kirsty Watney at Cornbury, where all was comfort and gorgeous food. One day was spent placing logs in a field to prevent enemy aircraft from landing – soon no British pilot with engine trouble will be able to come down anywhere in England! Togo Watney and Ronnie Quilter were making Molotov cocktails – empty beer bottles filled with pitch and petrol. Great trouble with a fuse which wouldn't burn properly, until a guest made one of loo paper which worked beautifully. At weekends in the stately homes of England, it used to be: 'Won't you come and feed the horses?' Now it's 'Won't you come and see my bombs?'

Later Prince Bernhard of the Netherlands and some friends came over. One man, a Mexican, was an air gunner; he had just shot down his first Heinkel and hadn't got over the thrill. After all, it must beat big-game hunting hollow.

19 SEPTEMBER

A few weeks ago heavy air raids began, first over Kent, then on the suburbs, and now they have been bombing London itself. Buckingham Palace, the East End, Bond Street, Piccadilly, Park Lane and Holborn have all been badly knocked about.

There was an air battle over Anstie, which Mother, all the servants and villagers saw. A bomber was attacked by three Spitfires; they went so fast past it – *swish* – *swish* – that it appeared to be standing still. They simply poured lead into it, and soon a plume of black smoke floated out behind it. Then white puffs appeared, which blossomed into parachutes. Very slowly and gently they floated down, while the bomber put its nose down and plunged earthwards with a scream which rose higher and higher. It burst into flames, the wings fell off, the engine fell out, the rest of the machine crashed into the ground, and the bombs blew up. Two of the crew were still in the machine. Five other Germans came floating down, as did the pilot of the Spitfire, who had rammed the German bomber and then baled out.

26 SEPTEMBER

Robin came to Cornwall and we camped out. He and I tried to pretend to ourselves we were on safari, but oh how different it was! Here – mud, rain, chill winds, a fishless river, washing up, cooking, smoke in your eyes. There – sun, scented air, beautiful wild animals, hurricane lamps swinging from the trees, nice servants, guineafowl and trout.

After Robin had returned to Dartmouth I went to London, arrived in the evening, changed, and went to the Park Lane Hotel with a friend for a drink. There were a score or so of people there in the underground bar. About 8.15 a man stepped inside and called out: 'Air raid!' No one took any notice. Faintly you could hear distant booms, and occasionally the sharper bark of our anti-aircraft guns. Suddenly there was an explosion and the building rocked. Then came a frozen silence. People half rose from their chairs and remained suspended so for a second. The paralysed moment passed. The barman was first to speak: 'Someone's dropped their money. My windfall.' People laughed, sat down again, and had their drinks. A few descended to the shelter, but soon returned, as the atmosphere there was appalling.

Later we went into the street. The bomb had fallen fifty yards away on the roots of a tree in the park. All the lower windows of the Park Lane and the Splendide were in the street, and we trod on a carpet of shimmering glass splinters. The faint *zoom-zoom* of German engines sounded overhead. The Hyde Park guns barked furiously. Tiny sparks flashed and vanished in the sky. Distant sheets of light flared and died like summer lightning as the bombs fell and burst.

We started for Quaglino's, but before we got there shrapnel came spattering down and we dived into an underground garage.

A row of weary people sat round the walls. One old woman made my heart ache – she was so tired, with a white exhausted face; her head fell first to one side and then to the other as she dozed fitfully. One man was swathed in bandages, with blood on his face. He never moved – he must have been under morphia. We stayed there about an hour until the planes had gone and the firing had died away.

When we reached Quaglino's there were about twenty people there. The band played flatly; no one danced; the food was mediocre. One of the waiters whistled as he passed our table; a tart, rather tight, got up and jitterbugged in front of the band; a Canadian soldier swooped on her and danced her around. This, where once the Dukes of England and the Royalties of Europe used to dine!

Next day I walked around. The corner house of Davies Street and Berkeley Square has fallen down and the wrecked staircase of the house behind it hangs over the ruins. Gieves is nothing but a hollow shell; only a few twisted girders remain.

In the City, more devastation. I walked round behind the wrecked houses. Where a street led into the ruins a rope was slung across. A very old slum woman, an Italian, stood by the rope, glancing up and down the street. No one was looking but me. She nipped under the rope and ran to the wreckage.

223

Back she came with a black cat in her arms. Before she reached me the cat had slipped out of her arms and returned to his ruins, walking with great dignity, slowly waving his tail. The old woman ran after him, picked him up again, carried him a few steps, and then the cat left her and walked back once more. At last she persuaded him to go with her, and they slowly walked away together down the street.

One day I went to Poplar to work with the Women's Voluntary Service. Down there, in the depths of the East End, the destruction has been terrible – hundreds of people are killed and more made homeless every night. For the homeless ones there are rest and shelter depots: good food, mattresses and blankets, with a kind and sympathetic man in charge. There are great rooms stacked with clothes, and fleets of cars, mostly with women drivers, to take the evacuees away to their new quarters.

On the day I went there, the superintendent, Miss Gretton, had been working all through the day and night before. She was so exhausted that she fell asleep at the luncheon table. When she revived she went out to look over the arrangements made for the thousand people whose homes had been destroyed by incendiary bombs the night before. Canteen workers had been out since two that morning keeping hot drinks ready for the ARP men and firefighters. Marvellous people.

London has become the most heroic city in the world, with the most heroic people. For centuries it has stood in perfect dignity. Its traditions and its own special privileges have never been encroached upon since Boadicea sacked it. In the heart of it, the oldest part of the City, each church is a gem and the streets have such lovely names – it is the most romantic city I have ever seen. It has kept the atmosphere of the olden times, from the Knights Templar to the lovely old eighteenth-century houses which still stand among the back streets. Now it is being bombed and burnt night after night, and just seems to become more splendid and beloved the more it is hurt.

Firefighters climb about the smouldering wreckage, playing water on burning buildings; demolition squads tunnel endlessly under tottering walls digging out wounded, dying and dead people; and during air raids, wardens patrol the streets with shrapnel spattering onto their helmets. The bomb destroyers, who dig out and remove unexploded time bombs, are called the Suicide Squad. Sometimes they can render them harmless, sometimes not. It is always an even chance whether the bomb will go off before it is safely defused or not.

Here is a true story told me by men of a demolition squad, to whom I had brought my van with tea and cakes, as I lay beside them behind a wall. At the bottom of a crater lay an unexploded bomb. An expert was lowered into the crater, and the men above saw him bend over the bomb and listen carefully to the ticking. Suddenly he let out a yell: 'Pull me up quick! Pull me up!'

They hauled him to the surface and all rushed away from the crater. 'What's happened?' they said, glancing back, expecting the bomb to go off at any second.

'God!' gasped the man. 'There's the biggest black rat in that crater I've ever seen!'

26 SEPTEMBER

I went to Paddington to catch the night train back to Cornwall. At 8.10 the siren screamed – up and down – up and down – like a thousand hyenas howling.

The boom of bombs and bark of guns started at once. I ate something and then retired from under those acres of glass into the deep shelters. As I went down flights of steps and along tunnels I thought I would almost as soon have stayed nearer the open air. I sat among the crowds of brave and weary people, waiting, while the crashes came ever nearer. Sometimes a voice came through a loudspeaker announcing the time of the next train's departure.

The voice was just saying: 'The 9.15 will leave from platform 10 in a –' when a roar shook the air. The ground jumped, the walls moved, and the air had that terrifying compressed feeling. There were a few screams. A short rush towards the entrance. It seemed as if the tunnel would crack open, and all those hundreds of tons of masonry come crashing in on us. The loudspeaker voice had stopped, broken off short.

Then a man came strolling down the tunnel calling out, 'It's all right! Nothing's happened.' Everyone at once reseated themselves, looking pale and grim, but steady. That one man's voice had made us all pull ourselves together.

The voice came over the air once more: 'This is the station announcer. The 9.15 will leave from platform 10 in a few minutes.' Canteen workers in tin hats brought cups of tea. Wardens and nurses walked about, chatting to people and soothing the children, who were scared and shaking, but not making a sound. The train left at last. Two bombs had fallen in the goods yard. We crept out of the station in utter darkness.

A long time later I looked out of the window. Stars – a small moon – silence. The silent serenity of the countryside on an autumn night. The crazy violence in London seemed like a dream.

1941

For Kenya, from England

Far lie the golden plains;
Silent and still in the hush of the noonday heat
Only their silken grasses ripple and sway
Where the small winds stray
On invisible feet.

The plains sweep out to the hills,
Whose virgin forest stretches to meet the snow;
Where giant trees toss their heads to the windy skies
And the buzzard circles, uttering his lonely cries;
Watching the world below.

(Here, in this fortress isle,
Nerves taut with mastered fear, we await the nights.
The noisy nights! When bombs come screaming down,
And buildings shudder and crash, and the whole sky lights
With the glare from a burning town.)

But in my memories
Once more upon your rolling plains I stand.
I hear the wind go singing through the trees,
I feel the sun again. And, more than these
I feel your perfect peace –
Oh lost and lovely land!

APRIL

The War gets worse.

One night in London I heard that Joss Erroll had been found dead in his car – I was miserable. So few friends, and so precious they are. And Joss, such fun, so loved life, so quick and bright, with a wit like sparkles on water.

Later, the story got dark and horrible. A very rich, elderly friend of mine, Sir Jock Broughton, was arrested for his murder. Joss, and Jock's new young wife Diana had fallen in love. Jock tried not to mind, but he got more and more hurt and angry. Then he started practising revolver shooting on Jack

226

Soames's farm. Jock and Diana stayed together in June Carberry's house near Nairobi. One night there was a party somewhere, to which they all went. Jock and June, Joss and Diana returned late to Jock's house. Joss left, and was found next day, shot, in his car. Now an ammunition expert has said that the bullets found in his body, and those fired by Jock on Jack's farm, came from the same gun, so it looks black for poor Jock. [*Jock's South African lawyer brought a ballistics expert to examine the cartridges. He said it was impossible to say for* certain *that these bullets had come from Jock's gun. Jock was acquitted, but no-one would speak to him. They went to Ceylon – not a success. They parted and went their ways. Jock committed suicide in England. My theory is different. There was a German gunsmith's shop in Nairobi. Joss spoke good German. He never joined up, I think he was asked to watch these Germans. I think they got him murdered.*]

The raids almost ceased, and no one quite knew why. London became much safer. All the night places were packed with gay, smart people dancing and drinking, and it was as much fun as it's ever been. Sometimes bombers came over, but no one took much notice.

You walk through the blackness to the Dorchester – you go through the doors and are blinded with light. You go to the basement ballroom. You drink and dance and drink and see your friends. You hear music and chatter. You eat marvellous food. You decide to go on to the Suivi. You go upstairs – through the doors into the inky darkness. Instantly you are in danger – in the war. Flashes light up the sky. Searchlights move across it. Shells burst above your head, making sparks of light. Shrapnel falls with a faint whistle and splatter – *zoom-zoom-zoom-zoom* go the bombers' engines – guns roar, and at intervals there is the thud of an explosion. Sometimes a great glare flares up – a bunch of incendiaries floating slowly on a parachute, or a house blazing.

You go carefully, listening – if the sounds of firing and engines and falling shrapnel come too close, you stand in a doorway. But you reach the Suivi, go inside, and are in the intimate gloom of a night club. Instantly the atmosphere engulfs you, and the war shrinks away.

25 SEPTEMBER

For weeks there had not been even an alert. Then one night we got it. Guns cracking, bombs whistling down – far away! – coming nearer – one that made the walls jump – a short pause – the drumming of Jerries overhead – more bombs. Each one made me tingle all over till I could hardly bear it – that and my heart jumping about. Then I read the Bible, and got quite calm again.

Some of my friends were in Blenheim bombers which fly at low level. Ten feet above the water they go for a ship and swoop up over the mast, dropping their bombs with all their guns firing. On land it's the same thing – ten to fifteen feet above the ground, too low for ack-ack guns and too heavily armed for fighters to attack them. But one mistake on the pilot's part and they crash into chimneys or high-tension wires, and that's the end. Losses have been very heavy.

26 SEPTEMBER

Northampton. First night I got here, there was an air battle just overhead. A Jerry fighter kept roaring past the house, shooting streams of lead and tracer at one of our bombers. You could see pencils of light flashing across the sky, hear the machine guns and the lead falling, as the Jerry hunted our plane. Our bomber pilot made a mistake, switched on his navigation lights and called the aerodrome that the port engine was hit. Then silence, and they found what was left next day.

15 NOVEMBER

Skoropalsky, the Ukrainian leader, is in Berlin, awaiting events. His son, and his greatest friend, are near Anstie; Mother dotes on them since they are foreigners. The authorities regard them with the utmost caution. Anstie is now strictly out of bounds to everyone, since Heather took them there. Mother has acquired a Ukrainian chauffeur, so perhaps she, also, is now under the watchful eye. These people, being of the aristocracy, are refugees from the Bolsheviks – I feel sorry for them, but don't like them. Sometimes I can hardly believe that such curious things happen in my life.

1942

18 JANUARY

Kenya returns to me ceaselessly. Scented wind, whisper of grass, the dappled light and stir of life in the forests. Wide, golden plains, a buzzard swinging round and round in the sky. Sunshine like a benediction, and at night such great, soft stars, such a velvet sky. And the animals moving as softly as dreams.

27 OCTOBER

I went to the investiture at Buckingham Palace, where a friend of mine received his Distinguished Flying Cross from the King. First came the navy, then the army and finally the air force. All the airmen had the same alert, taut look on their faces. After the air force came the commandos, then policemen, wardens, three women, a fifteen-year-old boy from Norwich, and last of all a wounded airman, who went slowly limping up to the King. The King talked to each man, asked him where he came from and how long he had been in this country.

That night we all had a party which went on till the place closed. Everyone was worn out, and one of the pilots lay down in Bond Street and went to sleep on the pavement. He woke to find a thrilled little newsboy shaking him by the shoulder. The boy asked him where he was staying, and proudly escorted him home.

1943

JANUARY

I am installed in Norwich in a very nice flat with a charming, cheerful servant and a tortoiseshell kitten.

I also have the sort of job I have longed for for two years – driving mobile canteens for the Church Army and the YMCA. We mostly go to aerodromes. On my first visit to a bomber station I met a large truck on a narrow path, and humbly crept out of the way. The truck stopped and the men tumbled out, with designs on the tea van. And out stepped George Ross, the Rhodesian who was at Paignton when I was there. George is now a pilot officer, more grown up and tidy to look at, but just as wild when he gets going.

From here the bombers take off on their long flights over the Alps to Turin and Milan. You see them in the morning, their ground crews climbing all over them like flies, testing and repairing and retesting. The bombs and mines emerge from the bomb dumps on long trains of carriers, drawn by a truck or tractor. I'll never forget the tableau of a train of mines halted beside my van, their fabric caps being fastened into place while men came up and bought a cake or a bun. Someone dropped his Swiss roll on the ground, picked it up, dusted it and put it on the top of a landmine, where ninepenny-worth of chocolate cake and cream sat on top of a thousand pounds of death and destruction, blindness, madness, agony and desolation.

The carriers trail across the aerodrome to their various planes and the bombs disappear into their bellies. All is tested and ready. The planes taxi out to the centre of the ground and wait in a long line. Lorries appear, and out come the aircrew, five men to each plane, bent a little with the weight of their Mae West, parachute and harness. They look very small and lonely, standing beside their large, silent machines. They climb in, the machine turns, taxis out, roars down the runway, leaves the earth and disappears into the night sky.

Then there are hours of waiting until they begin to come home. And sometimes there is an awful, deadly pause while one special ground crew, and the special friends of the aircrew, and the adjutant and officers, and the mess waiters, wait – and wait – and wait, for one machine which is late. They ring up various aerodromes, but are told that the machine has not landed, there is no news of her. They wait on, watching the clock and calculating the amount of petrol left in the tanks. The hours pass, morning comes, and everyone knows that that machine will never return.

The families are visited by senior officers – a tragic duty. Nothing more is said in the mess about the machine or the men on board. The places at table are cleared away until a new plane and a new crew arrive to replace the lost one. Sometimes the crew get home, and what happened to them from the time they landed on the Continent, until the time they suddenly reappear in the mess is a secret.

But I heard one good story. A crew baled out over Holland. As the pilot floated down he saw a lorry full of German troops watching him – waiting for him to land. He managed to land some way off, then buried his parachute after tearing a patch off it. He ripped off his battledress and put it on again inside out, threw away his helmet, then made a bundle of the parachute strip and tied it onto a stick. When he heard the German lorry coming down the road he turned his back and was privately occupied. All they saw was a loutish peasant with no manners. On they drove, and never found any British pilot.

We work hard six days a week, eight or ten hours a day in all weathers – we always get through. With snow up to the axles, and buses held up, or rivers in flood and even trees across the road, we always get to our men and give them their tea and cakes and chat. We go round the airfield perimeter, to every plane and gun pit, dodging the incoming aircraft, followed by flocks of lads on bicycles, hearing the gossip, knowing the jokes, being part of the airfield.

1944

MARCH

My life has changed very much. I had to have a rest from work. With the dogs and a small car I moved across Surrey and Sussex looking for rooms or a flat, but it was a hopeless quest.

Kenyan interlude:
Right: Genesta learns to fly

Below: Offshore at Mombasa

On safari in the African landscape

Above: The Spanish Civil War:
Irun in flames,
3 September 1936

Right: Families flee from Irun
with their treasures
loaded on cattle

Above: A family, including a dazed old
lady, reaches safety at Hendaye

Right: A deserting red soldier shields
his face from the camera

The German Czech border:
refugees seek to cross

Below: Life on a Soviet collective farm

Genesta in 1943. During the Second World War she
served as canteen driver for the YMCA

At last I found myself in Brighton, where I took a flat in a house which once belonged to Kitty O'Shea [*mistress of the nineteenth-century Irish statesman Charles Stewart Parnell*]. It is a charming flat, with high, spacious rooms and good furniture. The sea is so close that the sound of it is always with me, lapping against the wall just below the windows. From the bedroom I see nothing but water. I look across the horizon and think of those foul Germans being so close, almost within eyesight! It fascinates me. There are ack-ack guns all along the front, a big naval station outside the flat, and Canadians stationed in the streets all round. I couldn't be in better company.

Every Wednesday the Canadian Black Watch come and drink beer with my friend Vera and me. They talk of their homes, the friendship and equality and freedom of mind they enjoy in Canada, and of books and politics and history, and how they want to see the world a better place after the war. One was an American from Georgia. Four years ago he gave up a good job and left his home and his own people to enlist as a trooper in the Canadian Army. It wasn't his war, but he felt it his duty to fight for the people of England.

One day Deneys Reitz, [*the author of* Commando *and the High Commissioner for South Africa*] came here, and I gave him and his staff luncheon at Southwick. We went over the shipyard where we saw barges, motor torpedo boats and air sea rescue craft in all stages of production. There were also boats which had staggered into port with their engine rooms torn out and their hulls riddled; here they were repaired, refitted, recommissioned and sent out to sea again nearly as good as new. All round the coast of Britain little yards are working day and night, turning out masses of little ships. Hundreds of thousands of people, men with weatherbeaten faces, women in dungarees with tar on their cheeks and hands, are hammering and welding and planing and painting, turning out our invincible armadas.

6 JUNE

D-Day. All night the planes have roared overhead, each one towing a glider. The entire sky was full of planes and the noise never stopped.

This morning I walked down the line of the Irish Guards tanks, who have taken the place of the Canadians, and found Arthur Cole from Kenya and some of his friends, including one called Lord Claud Hamilton. As usual, Arthur was smothered in grease and oil. He came close to me and said in a low voice, 'It's begun.'

'What has?'

'The invasion.'

'Good God! How do you know?'

'It's on the radio.'

'Those gliders – were they full of troops?'

'Yes, of course.'

We were so security-minded that we talked in whispers, and I walked on. I saw various friends, customers of my van, sergeants in the Irish Guards, the searchlight crews, and finally my boss, Lady Eva de Paravicini – no-one mentioned the invasion, until it suddenly dawned on me that our security-mindedness was getting a little out of hand – since the great news we were all being so discreet about had already been blazoned to the entire world on the radio.

Every moment and movement were covered by the BBC, all day and all night reports from their teams of eye witnesses came pouring over the radio.

Claud Hamilton came to supper some nights. He is the brother of my friend, Mary Gilmour, and a charming person.

The Irish Guards officers work in the oily tanks along with the men, and buy each other cups of tea, and have a lovely camaraderie which seems to me missing among some of the English regiments.

Not long before D-Day I got ill, and then, being really very tired, I got worse and worse, so that I had to give up work altogether. Some friends came down to Brighton from London, and somehow my friend Vera and I squeezed them into our two-roomed flat. It was all good fun.

Then we saw our first doodlebug. Fred Drolet, French-Canadian public relations officer, and Hal Griggs, on headquarters staff, and several others were in my flat when the guns began, and among the sounds of engines we heard several great crashes. To keep away from the window we all sat on my bed while the walls jumped and the doors shook in usual air raid fashion. Then we saw IT – the flying bomb.

It came humming along Brighton front out to sea with a little white light in its tail, looking like some Walt Disney animal busy upon its own affairs. All the guns opened up, but it flew unconcernedly on, with its little light shining, through clouds of white and crimson stars; as it went exasperated gunners ceased firing as it passed out of range, while other hopeful ones took up the battle when the flying bomb came abreast of their guns. Yet, though they must have hit it, it still kept going.

Just as it was nearing the danger spot of Southwick a Spitfire leaped out of the dusk at it and gave it a short burst. The doodlebug's tail light instantly spread all over it, it became a flying torch, and in a great arc it dived over into the sea and exploded. You should have heard the gunners cheer!

We learned later that these unmanned flying bombs were Hitler's secret weapon. He has been bragging about it in an effort to boost German morale, which gets lower and lower – and no wonder!

Doodlebugs came over day and night in a steady stream. I must say I was scared stiff, but at the same time wildly excited and elated, and unwilling to leave this thrilling spot. I used to sit on the Leas at night and watch the flying bombs coming at us. Tiny points of light, and a faint humming, which quickly grew to the vicious thing glowing and roaring across the sea, greeted with frenzied outbursts from the guns like frantically barking watchdogs.

But one had to go to bed some time, and then the fear began. You hear that hum, that roar, the guns – then the guns cease and the roar increases, which means the flying bomb is over the town. You listen with every nerve; the roar seems now as though it would lift the roof. Then there is sudden, complete silence. The engine has cut and the bomb is diving down to earth. Your heart freezes while you wait, barely breathing. There is a new, shattering roar, the doors leap and the windows hurl themselves violently in their frames, the bed trembles, but all you know is you are still alive, though your heart bounds and shakes you. And you pray that it fell in an open space, and that no one has been killed. But every morning you hear that people *have* been killed – sometimes many, sometimes one or two – for there are so very many doodlebugs, coming over all the time.

[*I moved to Folkestone.*] The Folkestone and Dover people never looked up at an air raid warning, they barely condescend to glance around if they actually heard a doodlebug, and they took no notice at all of a shell warning. Flashy young girls eyeing the soldiers, burdened housewives standing in queues, and quiet, well-bred ladies in cafés took not the slightest notice of the enemy's efforts to harass and destroy them.

The sea is always a thrilling spectacle. Some days long convoys stream down the Channel – all sorts of odd-shaped craft escorted by destroyers and corvettes. The convoys are always shelled, but almost never hit. I once saw a tanker in flames, and a grim sight it was, enveloped first in fire and then in a pall of black smoke. Two men were killed. It was a wonderful and touching sight to see the little corvettes scurrying up to the tanker, trying to help her, trying to put the fire out and take the men off.

I had to leave Folkestone at times – to go and see Mother, or to go back to Brighton. Each time I returned I was so afraid the Canadians would be gone. The town was an amazing sight at night. The streets teemed with some of the finest men in the world, better trained in courage and skill than any soldiers have ever been before. They would stop you and speak to you and ask you to have a drink with them because they were so keyed up, and so anxious for women's company and friendliness before they went over to fight. They were courteous and charming, and never importunate or annoying – though I must admit the Americans were sometimes. But the Canadians' manners were too deep-seated to allow them ever to annoy or insult a woman. Each individual man thought he was going to be killed; they were quite calm and perfectly brave about it, but that was their belief. So I went around with my 'Red Hackles', the perfect escort, very proud to be with them.

Then one day I came back and the streets were empty! All the Canadians had gone, and Folkestone was a very silent place. The Irish Guards had gone from Brighton, too, so now all my friends were overseas. I tried hard to get a driving job, but the drivers clung to their vans and neither shells nor winter would move them. So I went back to London, to my old canteen at Charing Cross Station.

But the Folkestone days had led me to one marvellous thing – to a lovely ship, my future home. Through a shipbuilder at Hastings I heard of a Brixham trawler at Lowestoft, and went up there post-haste to see what I could find. And there she lay, the *Torbay Lass*, the perfect craft for me – oak-built, converted to a yacht, ketch-rigged. She has a big saloon aft with a stove in it, four big double berth cabins, two lavatories, a big roomy foc'sle, and a deck house. She is quite spacious – seventy feet long, eighteen wide, and with an eight-foot-six draft. It was a case of love at first sight, and after a little manoeuvring with my dear bank manager I was able to buy her for £2000. This is less than her value, and when she is fitted out for sea she will be worth at least double that. Now I have something definite and stable to look forward to after the war.

NOVEMBER

[*I moved back to London.*] I had one bad moment with a doodlebug, my nearest escape. One night I got to London late – too late to get to the flat – so took a room on the top floor of a shaky old hotel in Victoria. Victoria was Target for Tonight for the doodlebugs, and they fairly rained down while I lay quivering in bed. I nearly broke my record and went down to the shelter, but then remembered I'd paid for the bed so stayed in it. Every few minutes there was another roar – that dreadful silence, then a crash, and all the jangling accompaniment of shaking doors, rattling windows and trembling furniture.

Then one came – so low, so loud, I lay there frozen. The engine cut and the bomb came down with a loud swishing sound which grew and grew as it rushed towards the hotel. I believed this was the end. I prayed for courage and instantly all fear left me – I thought I was going to die, and I didn't mind. When the explosion came the hotel rocked and seemed about to collapse, but everything subsided and steadied, and though the bombs came over until morning I fell asleep at once from pure exhaustion, having passed the peak of fear.

The greatest sadness. My mother died.

I inherited Moorhurst, a sixteenth-century farmhouse, which had been in my family for over 150 years. Life became very different. I had a home, servants, a garden – plenty of space for me and my friends and my dogs. Susie and Sally, the Scottish terriers, were delighted to be in the country. They are such good friends to me, so patient and uncomplaining. All those months in London, while I was away at the canteen all day long, they sat alone in the flat with no one to speak to, and when evening came they sat alone in the dark with no fire and waited until I came home. There was never a whimper out of them. A kind woman fed them and took them out three times a day, and that was all the fun they had. Now life is very different for them, and for me too.

Two of my Canadian Black Watch family came back, wounded. Gordon McLaren was very ill indeed. His leg was shot through and through, and he nearly died on the road in France before he was found beside his bike. Then he was very ill again in England, but eventually was sent to Canada. Jimmy Barclay's carrier drove onto a mine and the whole thing blew up. Jimmy's ears were badly hurt, so he had a spell in England. I was happy to see these two fine men again.

The Black Watch have taken terrible punishment – the battalion has been wiped out and reformed no less than four times. One time when they were surrounded the colonel called up the cooks, batmen and etceteras to drive away the enemy. Pop, the old cobbler, who must be at least fifty but insists he's thirty-eight (white hair and all), was in it, to his joy. He wrote to me: 'Well Jinny, I got three of the German SS b——s, not bad for one afternoon. When a Canadian gets mad he's a bad bad boy and the German SS b——s know it. The Dutch girls are OK. All we have to say is, 'You sleepie with me, yes – no?' And they say OK to the Black Watch boys.' Pop and the rest fought their way through the German SS b——s and the battalion fought its way out – but at what a cost! Almost all the officers and men I used to see swinging about Hove and looking so magnificent and carefree are dead. My own five special friends survived, thank heaven.

In November I had another hard blow to take – Denys Reitz died. [*Then South African High Commissioner, he had guarded Churchill during the Boer War when he was a prisoner. Churchill escaped, and they had been friends ever since.*] Angry and excited, he came to my flat in London for tea. He had just come from a pompous and futile City lunch where he had to make an impromptu speech to men he despised and disapproved of. After a time he calmed down and we talked of ships; he asked me to find him one like mine. Then he left, smiling that sweet, boyish smile – and that was the last time I saw him. A few days later he had a stroke, and was taken to Charing Cross Hospital where he died. Brave, conscientious and uncomplaining, he died of overwork.

To me he was a most beloved friend, adventurous, debonair and warm-hearted.

1945

MARCH

The war is nearly over! It is fantastic. From hour to hour we turn on the radio, expecting that one magic word 'Peace'. This is much more than the defeat of an army – it seems like the death of a country. And yet, true to type, the Germans hold grimly onto the V2 sites, from which came those deadly 2000-ton rockets they've been murdering us with for the last few months. These things are as long as a telegraph pole and as thick as a letterbox. They shoot straight into the sky to a very great height, then curve over and rush down with the utmost speed on London. Where they hit they are quite deadly, but as they are faster than sound there is no nervous tension waiting for them to fall, for by the time you hear the bang it's all over. Once I heard the swish before the roar, and that was pretty close, but again I escaped.

Robin came home. He just walked up the garden path at Moorhurst – what a wild surprise! He looks so brown, so well, and has grown taller – a handsome young naval officer, and very sweet. We have a lot of fun at Moorhurst: Doffy lives there with me, Nannie cooks, and there is an old Austrian exile, Baron Fuchs, who usually stokes the fires. The house if always full of Canadians; hardly a day goes by but there is a staff car at the door, with men from thc hospital nearby. I love to entertain – it is such fun. After many dreary years Moorhurst is at last a gay and happy house.

Then came the liberation of the civilian concentration camps, when such ghastly sights came to light as one would not have thought possible in this age, in Europe. Hundreds of thousands of political prisoners were held in these camps – Belsen, Auschwitz, Buchenwald and others. They were starved, beaten, and tortured with fire and water. The dead and the nearly dead were burnt in huge ovens, and their ashes used to fertilize the fields. A camp commandant's wife picked out men whose tattoo marks pleased her; they were killed, and their skins made into lampshades. When our men found these hell camps thousands of survivors were mad, and thousands more died while the liberators watched helplessly. There were mountains of corpses, the bodies so thin that their insides had wasted quite away, leaving only skeletons with skin stretched tightly over them.

What punishment can ever fit these crimes? More important still – how can we prevent such things happening in the future? When I re-read at the beginning of this diary my smug and complacent remarks I feel *ashamed.*

MAY

The Russians were pouring over East Prussia, the Americans rolling forward from the south, the British and Canadians advancing from the west. The Germans were completely encircled and finished. Strange how repetition makes a statement into a fact. Back in 1939 Hitler was always screaming that he was surrounded, and now indeed he is. The last battles took place in Berlin, with Germans fighting in the subways and the Allies marching overhead. At last the enemy leaders were trapped in the Reichstag, and there Hitler and his girlfriend Eva Braun, whom he married in those last few hours, were killed, and their bodies burnt.

8 MAY

VE-Day. I was in London. Huge crowds waited about all day in an atmosphere of tense excitement. I joined up with two South African former prisoners of war and another woman. About 8 p.m. the announcement was made in a laconic fashion over the radio, without the sirens and carillons of church bells I'd been so hoping for. It was the ultimate in understatement. Then people poured into Piccadilly, waving flags, singing, kissing, dancing, making bonfires and climbing lamp-posts. A little tart seized a big policeman and kissed him – he kissed her back. A Scotsman danced a reel in which we joined. A Norwegian sailor shed his shoes and jacket to climb a high, swaying lamp-post and flew the Norwegian flag from the top. Searchlights trellised the sky, and the most lovely, heart-stirring sight of all was to see the multitudes of Union Jacks, each one with a light on it, floating proudly and freely out in the wind. I joined with friends and strangers, snowballing along the streets among all these happy, cheering people who looked so released and fear-free. At 4 a.m. I crept into the Overseas League and slept on a sofa.

9 MAY

Today every church had a service and every church was full. I thought of all we'd been through, how nearly we were invaded and beaten, and what would have happened to us then; of all the young boys who flew or marched or drove or sailed against hopeless odds and lost their lives; of Robin's safety, and of the work I've done, driving vans and working in canteens; of how our royal children stayed here in England with us when others went away – and I was thankful and proud. Later I went to the Palace and stood among three hundred thousand others cheering and blessing the King and Queen, who came out on the balcony. These two days have been the greatest and most stirring in my life.

1946

21 FEBRUARY

Today Claud Hamilton and I were married, first at Caxton Hall and then at St Dunstan's in the West, Fleet Street. I knew this little church well. If I had a Sunday in London during the war I always went there.

MARCH

Claud and I are having a quiet and peaceful time. He is not well, and very tired now the strain of war is over. The wedding was a quiet, family affair, the church service touching and inspiring. Dr McDonald's sermons were always grand; when the war was at its very worst he always found the brave and stirring thing to say. Now he has married me to Claud, and this is the happiest moment of my life.

I remember the first day I met Claud. Lady Eva dé Paravicini, our YMCA boss at Brighton, had promised to put me on a country run, but instead I was put on the gun sites along the front, and try as I would I could not get onto a country run. They flattered me by saying I was the only one who could drive that van and manage that route – what rubbish! – but there I remained. And then one day the Irish Guards and the Grenadiers appeared in my streets, and one of the very first to come to the van was a tall officer with a kind face and inquiring eyes.

A few weeks later they had all gone, then I began to get letters from Claud, and as a week-by-week record of the war they are the most interesting I have ever had. He wrote of the landings, the pause in Normandy, then the attacks and the gallop across Europe, and what horrors they found in the concentration camps in Belgium, Holland and Germany. Finally he reappeared in England, and we saw each other every day as the time came nearer and nearer to my departure for Kenya. He asked me to marry him, but immediately became terribly ill and spent over three weeks in the London Clinic. His mother and I went there every day – though I was in some pain from my side. At last he recovered and we got married. The party afterwards at the Mirabelle was great fun – everyone drank happily and got very chatty, and finally we drove down to Brighton for a week where we relaxed and rested. Soon we are going to Ireland, and then to Kenya.

Claud's cousin is Lady Alexander, wife of the Field Marshal, the new Governor-General of Canada. Her parents had a party for them, to which we went. It was thrilling to see these famous and splendid men, who were too damn clever for the Germans. Alex carries six or seven rows of ribbons; he has a strong quiet face and a very bright smile. Lord Alanbrooke, Air Marshal Portal, the Archbishop of Canterbury, lots of lovely ladies – *tout le beau monde* was there. We arrived early, and soon afterwards the Queen appeared. She has a very pretty, lilting voice. She shook hands with Claud and said 'Congratulations.' I was presented and made a curtsey; then she kissed my mother-in-law and stood about talking to people who were brought to her. There is always a little empty space around royalty when they go to a party; the rest of the people don't look at them and pretend they're not there – except, of course, that nobody sits while royalty stands, or leaves while royalty stays. If you meet your friends while they are with royalty you cut them as if they were with some undesirable person!

We went to Ireland, to stay with Claud's brother, Jim. Claud went by sea and train, I by air, for my side has hurt so much lately that I cannot face a bumpy train journey.

We landed at Belfast, and there was Claud to meet me. The train crawled along to Newtonstewart, the station for Claud's home, Baron's Court. A chain of lakes lies along a deep valley, and overlooking one of these is the immense, grey house. It was burnt down once, and rebuilt very magnificently by the 1st Marquess in Georgian times.

It is vast, cold and beautiful. They do their best to keep it warm, but the coal shortage makes it very difficult. Jim, his wife Kath and their children were lovely to me.

One day there was a presentation cheque to Claud and me from the 'elders' among the estate people; in their best black suits they stood in a solemn semi-circle with red, embarrassed faces, and one of them read a speech wishing us luck and happiness. Claud replied; he speaks excellently in a strong, steady voice. Then I was introduced to everyone, the whisky and cakes appeared and the tension relaxed. They adore the family and are extremely clannish, calling themselves 'Duke's men'.

We stayed two weeks in this heavenly place, but my side hurt so much, day and night, that it was spoilt for me. We fished and shot rabbits and rowed on the lake.

We finally returned to England, Claud again with the luggage and me by air. My side got worse and worse until I could hardly endure the pain. That and the mountains of aspirin I have swallowed in the last seven months made me very tired and depressed.

MAY

After endless telephoning, interviewing and magnificent efforts by Cook's, we got our seats to Kenya by air. Having adored Kenya ever since I first went there at the age of twenty-two, I have missed it terribly. I have dreamed I was back so very often, and was so happy – until I woke up again and found myself still in cold, uncomfortable, overcrowded England. And now we are on the way, in the air south of Khartoum.

The plane from Hurn to Cairo was a Dakota. Rather small, immovable seats, with sandwich-and-Thermos meals. First England, then France, unrolled beneath us until we landed at Marseilles for lunch. And what a lunch! The first taste of French food for seven years is something to remember; greedy as we all suddenly became, there was far more than we could eat. Then on again until it was night, and we flew over the sea to Malta. Poor Claud with his great height was terribly cramped and had no sleep – I was wiser and took a sleeping pill, so that I was quite dopey at Malta and fast asleep from then on. It did strike me that in this land plane we flew over a vast amount of sea, just as now, in this flying boat we changed to in Cairo, we are always over land. After Malta, Benghazi. Now it grew light, and we saw tank tracks and abandoned and destroyed vehicles in the sand beneath us. At Cairo we went to the Metropole Hotel and slept – and slept.

It is so warm and comfortable in Egypt. We spent some hours in the bazaar, and from the scent shop called the Garden of Allah ordered scent for Claud's family in England. We managed to get in the order and fix the price before giving our names, but when he saw the addresses the man said, 'If I knew your mother is a duchess, Lord, I not show you cheap, small bottles!' When we explained that in England we were all paying fifteen shillings in the pound tax he was quite shaken.

The current political crisis is about the English leaving Egypt. Naturally the masses of people who live on the British army and their wives, and on English commerce, are going to be deprived of their incomes when the English have gone. The politicians must know this, but they are the richest five per cent of the population and it will not affect them – yet.

At last we left, this time in an old-fashioned flying boat with tip-up seats, big windows and every modern convenience. Two false starts, then miles and miles of sand, and in the evening Khartoum – hot, quiet, smelling of Africa. Next day we flew over sand, swamp and bush, till in the evening we reached Kisumu. This was a poignant moment for me, hearing and speaking Swahili again, seeing the opal-coloured lake and the shrub-covered hills.

To get to Nairobi was the next problem – no train or plane was going. So BOAC hired for us an old, old Indian taxi, which has presumably never been serviced in its life. Into this we crammed ourselves – two Czechs, Claud and me, and the Jaluo driver. After a time fearful clankings came from the protesting car, and at Londiani we crawled into the garage with broken brake rods. I felt really at home again!

The Czech girl was one of the few survivors from the German massacre at Lidice, though most of the shocking stories they had to tell were about the barbarous Russians. Their government is callous and indifferent.

At dusk we reached the Muthaiga Club, and there I saw Ali, the head boy. He held my hand and said, 'Memsahib – Allah! I am so very, very glad to see you have returned. That is a very good thing. We are all so glad you are back.' Lilian Graham had told them we were coming, but this heart-warming welcome was lovely. We got to Lilian's house and found the true, unchanged Kenyan hospitality. I do feel I am home again.

JUNE

We have been round the countryside staying with friends. I find Kenya much changed and improved. People are very prosperous – some farmers made fortunes during the war, while we others fought, worked, and paid more and more taxes. The Kenyans would willingly have given up much of their food to help the English, but the shipping shortage prevented its being exported. Quite lately a vast amount of bacon and other food was offered to England, but the Minister of Food refused it. Stranger still, they sent a ton of biscuits over here, meanwhile cutting down the loaf in England.

Income tax for settlers here seems to be around five shillings in the pound, and the cost of living, with fuel, water, heat and most of the light kindly laid on free by the Almighty, is exceedingly low. Also one does not need woolly undies, thick boots, fur coats, umbrellas and mackintoshes.

Natives pay about sixteen shillings (half a goat) a year in taxes. As farm labourers earn from twelve shillings a month and food, and personal servants from thirty to a hundred shillings a month and food, they do not suffer great hardship. In the Kikuyu reserve, from Thika to Nyeri, the grass is green and long and the rivers full of water and fish; there are bananas, maize, potatoes, vegetables, goats and mission schools in plenty.

One weekend we went to Nyeri, and later to Nanyuki to stay with Jack and Glory Soames. Their big, comfortable house looks at Mount Kenya on one side, and the Aberdare Mountains on the other. The air is warm but bracing. He told us how the British old-timers were mobilized during the war to bring intelligence from the northern frontier when the Italian army was gathering there. They went off in their rattly old cars with a gun, some whisky and a native boy, and disappeared.

In due course they returned, casual, undisciplined, slightly alcoholic, sometimes truculent, but always full of perfectly accurate information, which they handed in with a 'take it or leave it' air before going back to the local for refreshment. Why the Italians didn't just walk in and take the whole country is an abiding mystery, but apparently they thought there might be some unpleasantness or even danger if they tried. So, arguing, they stayed on their side of the border until the South African troops arrived. Then the South Africans and the King's African Rifles started their all-time record race through Somalia and Abyssinia, hunting Italians until they had killed or captured the whole of their army. The enemy were so flustered that they forgot to destroy their petrol and water dumps, which of course proved invaluable to our troops. In the end there were more than fifty thousand Italian soldiers in Kenya – they got here after all, but as prisoners.

From Jack's we went across the vast, dry Laikipia plains to the Aberdares, where we stayed with Pat Fisher and later with Sharpie. Pat has been running her little farm all on her own. She has got ninety-one acres of pyrethrum planted, and the natives work for her happily and docilely. The English women have been wonderful during the war years. Mary Boyd managed their farm while Roddie was away, recording all the milk cows every day, inoculating, mending broken machines, and at the same time entertaining sixteen hundred troops when they had leave. Brian Curry's manager's wife was left quite alone in a windswept cottage with few modern conveniences, to manage thirty-six thousand acres, two thousand cattle and a nine-month-old baby. The natives did all they could to take care of her and the cows; and the baby went round the farm with her. She did the job for eighteen months, the only real trouble being the drought. Brian now has fifty-seven thousand acres, four thousand beautiful native cattle of mythological appearance, and a happy and contented life.

Sharpie [*a former District Commissioner*] has made a lovely garden. Small lakes are covered in water lilies, and every sort of flower, shrub, fruit and vegetable grows there. Wild duck, geese, guinea fowls, peacocks and storks have attached themselves to him. They parade for their breakfast early, and stalk hopefully around the house all day. Just before dawn they begin calling to each other, squawking, yelling and screaming – one makes a noise like a French taxi. They wake up the hyraxes, who gargle and groan; then the frogs and crickets try to out-whistle and out-scream them. Everyone is obviously yelling to everyone else: 'For God's sake will you shut up!' Finally they subside, but by then the forest birds have begun their morning Te Deum. All this African symphony disturbed Claud's slumbers, but it is a taste which I acquired years ago and adore hearing again.

Besides the wildfowl there are two small children, sons of the head houseboy, who run about the place, adoring Sharpie and enchanting his guests. They have perfect manners and do a little mild valeting. In fact this is a happy, peaceful, beautiful and entertaining ménage, and Sharpie is having a very nice retirement after years of government service.

He used to have a young elephant, and they loved each other. She learned to climb the stairs to his room, and would stand there at the window, with her trunk hanging out, surveying the world below. When she finally became too big she was sent to London Zoo.

From here we went over the hills and along the valley to Francis Scott's. The country is more densely populated than when I went away, from Thomson's Falls to Gilgil I saw farmhouses about every five miles.

Francis has been trying to disentangle the local Indians from each other; he wrote a letter to the press praising the loyalty and moderation of the Moslem party, and politely regretting the ways of the Congress Party. This had a great effect, and the Moslems send him their weekly paper, written in very good English, abusing Congress and insisting on their sovereignty over Pakistan. Francis has been here since 1919; he was one of 'Delamere's Young Men' and all the VIPs stay with him.

AUGUST

Claud and I are still in Nairobi, having constant meetings with the lawyer, Ennion, who is first-rate.

My side hurts a lot. The X-rays show a curved spine, and the heavy lifting work I did with the YMCA, moving tea urns in and out of the vans, pulled a nerve which has since got inflamed. Two ribs were also overlapping. The pain was not as bad as it used to be, but always there, waiting to gnaw at me. Massage, osteopathy and exercise all help, but it is never completely cured. It makes me tired and depressed, but I mean to beat it.

We stayed a weekend at Naivasha, at Carnelly's lovely place, right on the lake. Sapphire-blue water, distant green hills with purple shadows, groves of yellow thorn trees standing by the shore. Hippos grunting in their grumbling and protesting way, fish eagles screaming, geese honking, and forest birds all whistling and singing at dawn.

21 AUGUST

Claud and I have been married six months today.

27 SEPTEMBER

Today Claud and I came home. As we drove through Kekopey and Soysambu it seemed so strange, forgotten yet familiar. The huge plain, the big, blue hills and the lakes were wonderfully welcoming.

When we reached the stables behind our house all the grooms, their wives and children were waiting. They seized our hands, and gave us such a welcome as I never dreamt of. Down at the house stood the houseboys. My dear Ahamed kissed my hand, and Claud's; he was almost in tears, and so was I. He bowed, and said, 'Salaam, salaam, aleikum, Karibu, Karibu.' and then led me into the house, still holding my hand. As we walked through it Claud whispered, 'It's a lovely house, darling.'

Everything looks just as I left it. Ahamed has done all in his power to preserve my things, but he has had a wretched time. All the pigeons are dead – killed by bees which a former manager kept in the house. My dogs have gone; my poor Lakri had had to be put away just before we came home – she had, I was told, incurable mange. All was ready for us that they could think of here: a lovely meal, and a bottle of champagne on ice. We are waited on hand and foot, with an etiquette and ceremony which I had quite forgotten. We really are home.

1 OCTOBER

The head Masai and other herders came to the house to welcome us. I introduced them to Claud, and everyone shook hands. They seem so happy to see me again! Kofia, the head Kavirondo, said, 'We wept for you. We said, "Why has our Memsahib thrown us away?" ' My old driver said, 'Why did you go away and take all the medicine with you? We've had no medicine since you left.'

We sleep on the verandah, are called at sunrise, get up at once, eat, and go out. There is much to see to and to restore. Despite all Ahamed's efforts, the furniture is damaged, rats ate the foundations of the house, borers ate the roof, and the place is full of swarms of savage bees. The fences are down, the huts ruined. There was a submarine forest of weed in the water tank, and small frogs came swishing down the pipes into the baths.

The cattle have been counted – all 3554 of them! They look fat and well, but all the best milk cows have been sold and the herds must be rebuilt. The grass is in good shape, but there is a lot of weed.

1947

16 JANUARY

The farm progresses; we are very busy and very happy. We have a charming manager called Mr Nicoll, an honest, steady, quiet Scotsman. He has an equally charming wife and three grand little boys. We have sold some cattle, weeded out the stumour cows, and tried to segregate the bulls so that each type gets his own type of cow. I am sorting out the horses.

Polisi, the head Masai, told me once of all he'd been doing in my absence. Bumping and shaking about on these awful tracks on an old bicycle till his arms and legs swelled and he had pains all over; keeping order, giving injections, watching the herders and their herds, with no help. He was now thin as a rail and worn to death. I asked him why he had stayed, and he said, 'I don't know. Perhaps I like the place and the cows.' Then this very reserved and undemonstrative Masai added, 'We are very happy you are back – very, very.'

25 JANUARY

Claud and I have reached Baringo, on the first lap of our first safari. The hot, dusty road got more and more stony, and at last the little tin car Kebe was driving completely failed on a hill. Whereupon Claud, with perfect aplomb, simply turned the car round and roared up the hill tail first! Our camp is on the edge of the lake; it is hot and stony, and only three thousand feet above sea level. What a fearful journey Speke must have made, stumbling over these miles of scorching slabs of volcanic rock, through scrub and bush and 'wait-a-bit' thorn, when he first found the lake.

26 JANUARY

The natives are Njemps, a sort of Masai, very thin and black and lethargic. The women wear shell-covered belts and beaded cloaks, the men mostly just large tin ear-rings and a loincloth (often in rags). They stand in the water and fish, throwing in stones to frighten the crocodile away.

The crocs are pale green, and apparently not very dangerous. Two are basking in the shallows thirty yards away as I write, and this morning, when Kebe brought the tea, there were two, asleep, just on the edge of the water. We have seen them sleeping on a rock in the sun, with their mouths wide open and their pink tongues showing. Beyond the lake, mountains are piled up against the hot blue sky, and at night the myriads of stars shine down and everything is silent except for the lapping of the little waves. We sleep under the stars – no tent between us and the sky. This is the Africa I love, remote and wild.

30 JANUARY

At Maragat, the police post, we were told that the road to Maralal was impassable, so we headed for Nakuru. Both cars gave endless trouble, and I thanked God that we had not attempted that steep, waterless, uninhabited piece of country from Baringo to the north, for a breakdown there might mean disaster. After a night camping outside Nakuru, and another night in the Conduits' lovely house, outside which we conveniently stuck, we finally reached Thomson's Falls, where McDonogh and his wife have a comfortable pub; and here we rested and repaired the cars.

2 FEBRUARY

Mac arranged for us to hire a lorry, so we left the little tin car here in disgrace, and finally set off with Filipo in the Mercury with us, and everything else, including Kebe, in the three-ton truck, with a nice Indian driver and various boys. We reached Timau with the Mercury failing all the way due to dirty petrol. Claud, in despair, kept saying, 'It's hopeless, we'll never get there.' I, *au contraire*, believe in never giving in, and at Timau we drained the tank, cleaned the pump and cured the car.

3 FEBRUARY

With the Mercury cleaned and chastened, we moved on to Isiolo. This tin township is the meeting place of the Turkana and the Somali. The Turkana are a wild Nilotic tribe, the men very tall and thin, with steel tubes thrust through their lower lips, and at the back of their heads a mound of mud-plastered string, which holds their father's hair, surmounted by two or three little feathers. The women wear ten or more iron necklaces, and bead-embroidered cloaks. The Somalis are tall, elegant, handsome and fiery-tempered, with large turbans and long skirts called kikoys.

In camp here we spent a most miserable night, for the mosquito nets had holes, and the mosquitoes were queuing up about a mile long to feast on us.

4 FEBRUARY

Claud saw a big bull elephant last night, only about fifty yards away. The askari he was with very wisely removed him from the danger zone, for the elephant was downwind.

Spent all day in Isiolo, mending the Mercury's radiator. In order to deprive the mosquitoes further on of a taste of our blood we motored halfway to Garba Tula, through the most hot and desolate country – all dead scrub and lava rock. Nothing can ever have happened here; there are no water, no natives and no animals. To be lost on foot here would be the end. We carry our water with us.

5 FEBRUARY

Arose at 4.30 a.m., thankfully left the lava rock and ran into an all-grey country of grey, dusty sand and grey, dead bushes. At Garba Tula there is a police post and a well. We camped at Benare, ten miles beyond. Here there are palm trees and sand, rhino dung and tracks everywhere.

6 FEBRUARY

Two rhino came to the camp last night, standing two hundred yards away and staring. Then they lost their nerve and bolted. On to Garissa, where the nice District Commissioner, Webster, entertained us, and we met the stock controller, Mr Low. We sat under the moon having drinks, looking like an East African scene by Hollywood, while Low told us where to look for elephant and other game. Garissa is a lost, lonely place on the Tana river, singing with mosquitoes and crawling with snakes and scorpions. It is one of the hottest places on the northern frontier, and has only two or three inches of rain in a year.

7 FEBRUARY

On to Bura, where we camped under some fine thick trees on the river. We walked a long way looking for elephant, but saw nothing. Took some photos of Somalis, each more beautiful than the last – tall and slender as spears, with fine, chiselled features, deep-set eyes and mops of wild hair. They are by far the most beautiful people I have ever seen anywhere; they move with stateliness and grace and they have exquisite manners. We walked such a long way – all in vain, and I got very tired.

8 FEBRUARY

Away again at dawn looking for elephant, but they were always just ahead, and though their tracks were fresh and the dung still hot we never saw them, nor the rhino and buff, of which there were traces everywhere.

So we packed up and started for the coast, coming into fine grassy country with thick trees. We drove through a lot of bush fires but suffered no damage, and the trees gradually changed from tall bush to palms, till we arrived at the sea – and so, on in a dhow with a lorry engine, we came at last to Lamu.

11 FEBRUARY

We stay in a primitive but quite comfortable pub owned by 'Pioneer Percy' Petley, who has been crushed by an elephant, almost swallowed by a hippo, and has endured the usual run of near misses incurred by the very early settlers. He has studied the coast natives and knows them well.

There are riverine tribes living just on the banks of the Tana, and Somali and Galla living in the bush. During the war the Somalis, far from aping, and being ruined by, white troops, avoided them whenever possible, and drove their cattle through the bush some way from the road. They had not the faintest interest in the war, and merely wished to be left in peace, but they did watch out for stranded airmen, and brought them into camp where they were well rewarded. The riverines are small, primitive, very shy, great hunters, say they have always been here, and may be the aboriginals.

On the coast, and in Lamu, there are many different races, from coal-black Swahili and slaves' descendants to the golden-skinned Arabs. There are several dhows in the harbour – one came from Bombay, and some from Muscat. They are quite small, high-sterned, with one forward sloping mast and one vast sail; and to tack, everyone rushes forward and turns the sail *inside-out* – and round she goes! The dhows never carry emergency supplies and often run out of water. They have large crews for their rather clumsy craft, but are brilliant sailors and don't often come to grief. Lamu has been lived in since Phoenician times, and one of the mosques is built on the site of a Phoenician temple. Under a hill nearby is an old, buried town, and in the sand dunes a battle was fought between the Lamu and other Arabs – there lie the skeletons, and the wind blows the sand over them and away again. Down the channel an Arab fort commands the entrance. This little paradise is cool and healthy, and everyone looks fit and well set-up.

I went to an Arab ladies' bridal party. About a hundred women and some children squeezed themselves into a small room open to the sky. Five men appeared in the women's rooms (I was rather shocked), but they were the band; they played three drums, something that sounded like a *debi* [*petrol tin*], and a pipe which screamed in my ear. The women sang, the chorus girls danced. The dancing girls were all dressed in red, black and white *shukas [coloured cotton cloths]*, rather short in the skirt; in their hair they wore flowers, tinsel and paper, and they had applied powder, lipstick and dark red circles of rouge. They danced by waving their hands and moving their fingers, bowing and bending forwards and sideways. It was not very exciting. Sometimes onlookers put money into the dancers' mouths as a tribute.

Out of this pandemonium I was taken to see the bride. She sat in a chair, propped up with cushions, dressed in yellow, a gold coin stuck on her forehead, two yellow beaded plaques stuck on her cheeks, a cap of paper flowers on her head, flowers and tinsel ornaments in her dress, and a ring on every finger. Two women fanned her. Her hands spread out on the cushion before her and her eyes were cast down, she sat like a statue. I gave her mother a pound and had hung round my neck a lovely garland of bougainvillaea and jasmine. This was the second night of the party. On the third night the husband comes for her, 'looks at her,' my friend said, 'and sleeps with her.'

There is a strong class-consciousness in Lamu; the descendants of the free-born do not mix socially with the descendants of slaves. Well-bred Lamu women never go out until evening, and then closely veiled. Some of the older ones carry a little tent made of a *shuka* on two sticks, a relic of the days when slave girls carried these over their ladies' heads out walking.

Admiral Fremantle and my grandfather, Admiral Sir Leopold Heath were hunting slave dhows on this coast, with their gunboats. At a conference in London in 1861 they said the only way to stop the slave trade was to 'acquire' Zanzibar, probably buy it. MPs and churchmen said they could never contemplate 'dispossessing the native owners', and were deeply shocked. So the Royal Navy continued to patrol the seas, and thousands of miserable slaves died of suffocation, thirst and drowning, or were killed by sharks, during their ghastly voyages to Muscat and Persia. When Arabs saw British ships approaching they often threw the slaves overboard. Many British sailors also died. Several years later the British government did just what the admirals had suggested and bought Zanzibar and all the coastline from the then Sultan, whose descendant still reigns there.

12 FEBRUARY

The oldest type of dhow was sewn together with coconut fibre, and the huge sail was made of palm leaf matting. In these frail and clumsy boats the natives traded up and down the coast, going south on one monsoon and coming north on the next. Only fairly recently have they built their ships with the planks fastened together with iron rivets, though the pattern of sail (now made of canvas) has never changed, nor have the devil-scaring eyes and charms painted on the bows.

I was told the Phoenicians first came here in the sixth century BC.

Ptolemy, whose first map was made in AD 930, shows Lamu bearing the lovely name of Seraption. The Portuguese touched here, but did not settle, and there is only one grave in the town with a Portuguese coat of arms on it. A branch of the Arab royal family from Muscat settled and ruled here. Their relations and friends came with them, and for their harems they brought beautiful women from Arabia, Circassia and Persia.

Not long ago Lamu was famous for the beauty of its women, and I well remember an early settler telling me with gusto of the lovely, pale-skinned Arab mistresses he and his friends had here, of the scented oils they rubbed on their bodies and the jasmine they wore in their hair. In those days Lamu was more prosperous than it is now, more dhows came in, and the slave compensation money was still fairly new. These lovely creatures have vanished, for at the party I went to there was not one of even passing good looks, except the Barjun chorus girls, and I have seen many Masai and Somali women of far greater charm.

This was a great export town for slaves. Besides the traders there were hosts of pirates in the creeks and among the islands, who would kidnap natives on their own account, and seize and wreck ill-armed vessels. The story goes that they buried their treasure in the vicinity of Lamu. Many people have searched, some with the help of the usual tattered map, all crosses and secret signs – but in vain.

Ambergris is sometimes washed up on the shore. This and powdered rhino horn are said to make splendid aphrodisiacs, and fetched high prices among the ageing, failing gentlemen of Persia and India. Bêche-de-mer [*sea slugs*] was also exported to China, where it is made into a very popular soup, and some of the local cowrie shells were exported for currency and to make a fine lime used in enamels.

Lamu was technically part of the Sultan of Zanzibar's dominions, but these islanders were always very independent, though they allowed the Sultan's crimson flag to fly and let the Arab Governor and his small guard live in peace. In 1875 Ismail, the Khedive of Egypt, sent an expedition under an ex-Royal Navy officer named McKillop to take Lamu, or some other coast town, and establish a line of garrisons inland up to Lake Victoria Nyanza. This was General Gordon's idea [*Gordon was then in the employ of the Khedive*]. Apparently he did not know where the Sultan's lands began and ended, and he thought an Egyptian empire stretching to the coast of East Africa might help to crush the slave trade.

Poor McKillop, equipped with a few hundred ill-trained troops and with practically no stores, arrived at Barawa, north of here, where he tried to establish himself. He sent feelers along the coast, only to discover that Lamu and the other little towns were quite ready and willing to fight, that the Indian traders were moving out in alarm, that not one respectable Arab or Swahili was on the side of the Egyptians, that even the aloof and independent Somali were hurrying to proclaim their allegiance to the Sultan of Muscat, and that his only supporters were the bandits and scallywags who welcomed any form of disturbance because of the chance of loot.

Then a British warship came along the coast and threatened a naval bombardment. So McKillop, the former naval captain, found his force under the guns of the Royal Navy. The Egyptian invasion completely collapsed. Lamu relaxed.

A few years later some Germans arrived and travelled to Witu, saying they were going to set up a sawmill. They went about the country taking measurements and making surveys, watched anxiously and suspiciously by the people and their Sultan. After they had gone the people came to the conclusion that it was not just timber the Germans were after, but the whole country. They decided not to let them return. But the Germans did return, and one bad day the party reappeared in Lamu. The British Consul advised them not to go on, and twice the Sultan of Witu sent messages warning them to stop. But they would not stop.

At the town's narrow gate they demanded to see the Sultan. They were told to disarm, which they did – all but one. There seems to have been an argument with the gatekeeper who was shot. The Sultan's guard fell on the intruders and killed all but the one who still had his gun. He escaped to the forest chased by a crowd of maddened natives, but he fought them off, killing or wounding a man with every shot. At last his ammunition ran out, the natives closed in on him and cut him down.

Witu and Lamu were by this time in the British sphere of influence, and the German government insisted that the British government should punish the people of Witu. A small Royal Navy force landed and after due warning shelled the town. Witu was burnt and the people fled. Some time later the Sultan died; his brother succeeded him, only to be deposed in favour of the commander of his army, Sultan Omari bin Mohammed, the last Sultan of Witu.

Omari was once the great friend of Sultan Jatina of Paté, but jealous people lied to the Sultan that Omari was the lover of the Sultan's favourite young wife. In a mad rage Jatina seized Omari and had him hung up by the heels, head downwards, in the marketplace. All day long he hung like this, and when night came he was barely conscious. He was to be left there all night, and killed next day. But hiding in the shadows was a woman who loved Omari. She faced a dreadful death if she was caught, but she reached him safely, unseen by the guards. She cut him down, chafed his deadened limbs and feet, and helped him to a creek where a canoe was waiting. Together they stole away to the mainland, a long and dangerous trip through the shark-infested sea, and there Omari took service with Sultan Ahamed bin Fumo of Witu, known as Simba [*the lion*].

After the English had punished the people of Witu they sent messages telling the people to return and live in peace under British protection. Sultan Simba refused to come in, but at last Omari, tired of living in the jungle and unable to persuade the old man to change his mind, came with a large following to the British, made his submission, and remained their faithful friend until his death.

13 FEBRUARY

Claud's birthday. 'The fortieth!' he says gloomily. He looks so much better than when we first met – he is quite sunburnt and ruddy now.

We walk about this strange old place in the evenings. Some streets are so tall and narrow there is barely room for us two thin ones, abreast. The women emerge in the evenings swathed in black, their large, dark eyes just showing through the slits in their yashmaks. The men wear small, embroidered white caps, and white jackets over long white *kanzus*. They stroll down the single shopping street buying spices and cloths. Nearly every house has a heavily carved door, studded with nails and sometimes with spikes. The spikes were to repel fighting elephants if they ever came here.

We had tea with the Liwali in his large, cool house. A very charming, well-educated Arab, he used to be port interpreter at Mombasa, then was promoted here. He tries petty cases, and gives them quite stiff sentences. He arranged for us to visit a big dhow from Muscat. Her boat, which was sent for us, was manned by sixteen oarsmen, a wild-looking lot with thin, hard faces and staring eyes. They pulled on their oars while the drums banged and cymbals clashed; between each stroke they paused and sang, then pulled again. At the end of the trip the oarsmen stood up, clapped their hands, stamped their feet and danced. They do not seem sleek and happy like the Lamu – they really look like a gang of cut-throats, but the sort I would like to have in my ship.

When we came up the ladder and over the side, a row of pale, turbaned Arabs was waiting for us, very courtly, bowing and welcoming. The ship was spotless. We sat on cushions and carpets in the poop, surrounded by the ship's officers, the owners and the captain. The black sailors were on the deck below. This lovely ship carries two hundred tons of cargo; she has two masts – the mainmast, raked forward, and a mizzen. Her stern is decorated with black and white patterns, and she has a lot of fine carving on the companionways and poop. They had taken so much trouble for us – at least twenty-four dishes of food lay at our feet, as well as scented tea and very good, slightly scented coffee. There were forty men in the crew, and several ship's boys – very attractive children, all smiles and big turbans. How I would love a trip in this great dhow. We were brought back to shore with singing, drumming, blasts on the conch-shell horn and one last dance.

19 FEBRUARY

Lamu is filling up for the festival of Maulidi tomorrow, Mohammed's birthday. All day little boats sail up to the steps and jetties, drumming, singing and blowing their horns. The boats are packed, and the colourful people from the Barjun islands cling to the rigging with a toe and a finger like flies, waving their spare arms and legs and singing, while others stamp and dance in the crowded boats. People come from Mombasa, Dar-es-Salaam and even Zanzibar. They expect ten thousand people in this tiny town, and I only hope the food holds out.

The Arabian dhow's crew have been doing sword dances in the evenings. They jump high in the air, flicking their swords round in their hands and hitting their own tiny shields. There are two groups with drums, one on each side of the circle, who sing and sway. Then two men dance towards each other, jumping, feinting, striking and catching the swords on their shields. One falls on his knees, trying to disembowel the other. They separate, and dance slowly apart and round the circle, eyeing each other all the time. Sometimes they jump at each other with their big, curved daggers. All the time their eyes are glaring and their teeth are bared – they look brutally savage.

One little black man jumped and fought at a tall, pale Arab, then lost his nerve, flung his sword, shield and turban in the sand and dived through the legs of the crowd. The other danced away, at which the small one, his face a mixture of fear and fury, dashed out, grabbed the sword and went for him again. The crowd howled with laughter, and I realized this was the ship's funny man making a clown of himself. When the dance came to an end he tied his turban on tidily and brushed the sand out of his robes, wreathed in smiles.

We went to the dhow again, and though we were quite unexpected they were most hospitable, and the ship was spotlessly clean as before. They produced carpets and cushions and cigarettes, and talked about the ship, *Abdulraman*. She is fifteen years old, cost £5000, and took one year to build. The timber came from Calicut, as did the very thick mainmast, the sails came from Bombay. She is expected to last only ten more years. She has a very roomy cabin for women passengers, with two little carved rosettes for windows, and a lavatory and washing room. The dynamo for the ship's electric light lives here, and it is obviously the soul of the ship, the beloved of every man's heart. They started it up and it shook and roared so that no one could speak. Back on deck I told them how we would love to sail to Muscat with them. Truly there's nothing I should like better; these charming, wild, gentlemanly people are men after my own heart.

20 FEBRUARY

After dinner we walked through the streets to the square outside the mosque to watch the festival. It was quite dark, a lamp shone here and there. The Liwali met us and took us to the chairs. There were ten thousand people sitting on the ground round the mosque – the women, with only their eyes showing, in one spot apart from the men. Everyone was quiet.

From inside the mosque came the sound of chanting, to which the men in that huge crowd sang the responses. The Liwali led us round the mosque through the crowd. A lane had been kept open between the people, and an askari walked in front. Thousands and thousands of white-clad figures with dark faces sat there, all reverent and silent except when they sang the responses. When we returned to our chairs we all remained standing during more singing, and then the priest came into the minaret and preached, beginning and ending with the traditional call to prayers. It was all so impressive and moving in the light of just a few lamps and the stars, and in the scent of incense and jasmine with which they sprinkled the crowd and us.

21 FEBRUARY

Sadly we said goodbye to Lamu, picked up the car on the mainland and set off for Malindi. All the way to Witu we passed deserted shambas and mango trees, where for centuries the Arabs' slaves worked the ground and made farms and gardens. Now it is all abandoned to the bush. Witu is just a village. The Sultan's Palace is a long mud building with the usual huge uprights, beautiful carved door, and an Arabian version of an English coat of arms carved over it. Now the place is used as a native hotel.

After a long, terribly hot drive of 150 miles we reached Malindi. Lawford's is a nice hotel with the long sea breakers rolling almost to our feet. They make a steady roar day and night, which I love to hear.

22 FEBRUARY

To Gedi. This mysterious place is an old city in the heart of the forest; no one knows who built it or why it was abandoned. The legend is that it was built about AD 1000 by Shirazi Persians, and later lived in by Arabs. There are wells, baths, mosques, splendid houses and tombs everywhere. The wall only surrounds thirty-three acres, but there are ruins all the way to the sea, six miles away, and right on the ocean are a mosque, a fine tomb and a gaol. The Giriama guardian saw a ghost there once, an old turbaned man who grew taller and taller till he was like a tree. Ptolemy's papers and maps do not mention it, nor do the Portuguese, who took infinite pains with their cartography and marked every little village and creek on the coast. The guide who said he got his knowledge of Gedi from his father, who in turn had it from his, told us that the old people always knew of it, but it was full of devils and they did not think the white people would want to go there. So it lay hidden and unknown until 1920, when some surveyors stumbled upon the ruins by accident.

25 FEBRUARY

On the road again – the long, hot road to Nairobi. Through dry, volcanic country, small, steep hills and scrubby bush. We broke down five times, with the same old petrol pump trouble, before reaching Mtiti Andei. But the hotel was very nice and comfortable, and two tame cheetahs were most attractive.

26 FEBRUARY

To Clare Dorman's nice house at Machakos. Tony, a brother officer of Claud's, is now the vet here. They are two darlings – Clare especially witty, civilized and amusing, and the sort of true friend I do appreciate. Machakos is the usual government village – a group of government villas, called the *boma*, inhabited by a District Commissioner, a policeman or two, a vet and so on. The other day someone was transferred and the newcomer was a bachelor, so the departing wife went to the home of the next government official, who happened to be Tony, and said to Clare importantly, 'Now don't forget, dear, when we've gone you will be the First Lady of Machakos.' Clare was overwhelmed.

MARCH

We sent the Nicolls away for a holiday, and Claud and I *chunga [take care of]* the farm.

When we first came the then manager gave us several bits of advice, one being to plough in the lucerne, another *never* to try to raise two calves on one cow. When I found his advice was entirely wrong, I did the reverse: the lucerne still flourishes, and we have a special foster-mother herd. This man assured me the Ulu people had given this up after fearful losses; however, this was quite untrue, and we soon found they all do it. Our herd is a great success, and now each calf has a mother instead of growing up all alone in a little hut and drinking gallons of milk which should go to the creamery. The stumour cows go to the butchery, and are not sold as heifers, as we hear was done in the old days. The milk records are honestly kept – not as before, when each cow's best day was multiplied by seven and that written down as her average weekly record.

I have the herds all sorted out in their colours and types – the Friesians on one side of the river, Guernseys on the other, with their respective bulls. We only use pure-bred bulls now, imported from Europe or bred here. The Boran cattle and half-breds have their bulls with them, in the charge of Ndarara, one of Polisi's fine brothers. And I have one white, pure-bred Boran herd, the apple of my eye, with three splendid Boran bulls, in the charge of still another of Polisi's brothers.

One of the nicest things that ever happened to me was when the Masai

254

gave me a name of my own – hardly ever done for a woman. They call me Keramadisho [*She Who Takes Care of Everyone*], and the farm is now called Keramadisho's Farm. And I used to worry so, fearing I couldn't handle the Masai!

APRIL

Here is a story of the old days – too good to lose. The hostess was having one of Her Parties, everyone was plastered. Derek Fisher was put in a big chest and locked in, like the girl in The Mistletoe Bough. After a time he wanted to come out. He hollered and yelled but no one took any notice. Finally one of the women, very drunk, went and sat on the lid, and kicked at the sides with her heels. Derek in despair drew his bushman's friend (a short knife) and stuck it through the chest's thin lid, straight into the girl's behind. With a wild scream she fled, pursued by the hostess. Back in her room she lay on the bed howling, and bleeding. The hostess brought her some lint and plaster, telling her to put them on the cut, looking in a looking-glass, and then to take a sleeping pill. Then she tripped back to the party. Hours later she looked in, found the girl in a perfect stupor of alcohol and sedatives, a pool of blood on the floor, and the lint and plaster carefully stuck onto the looking glass.

22 MAY

We drove to Nderit. I am not very well. Some days I lie out in the garden, where herds of cattle come to visit me while the head boys bring me all the news. It's the loveliest way to be ill – Claud being perfectly divine, the boys waiting on me hand and foot, the softly coloured gold and blue view to look at, two dogs and a prancing kitten keeping me company.

But I do wish I could get out and ride.

NOVEMBER

We flew back to England in June, and I was very depressed at leaving the farm. All the head boys came up in twos and threes to say goodbye. They made little speeches and said how happy we'd all been together, and how they would do their very best and obey Mr Nicoll 'just as if you were here, Keramadisho.' They have all been so kind and made me so happy, I do love this beautiful place; we are making a real success of it, and Mr Nicoll and his wife and sons all help the farm's progress.

One of the head Masai, Ndarara, came and asked if his wife might massage me. With nothing to lose, I said 'Yes', and Dobari certainly smoothed a lot of pain away and got me so well that I could go out in the car again. She was delighted, taking endless trouble, and was so kind and gentle.

We went by train to Kisumu and caught the plane on 12 June, arriving in London next day at lunchtime. As I saw those drab streets and dreary faces closing round me once more, something that makes life gay folded up inside me and went to sleep, like a bear hibernating for the winter.

Dukie and Dolly gave us a lovely welcome. I am most devoted to my parents-in-law. Dukie is wonderful to talk to, and Dolly grand to go out with; I love being with them. We saw lots of people and stayed away for weekends – the nicest being at Welbeck Abbey with Aunt Winnie Portland, she and Morven were kindness itself. He told us of the good old days when they kept seventy servants, seventy gardeners and a fire brigade; and with the farmers, foresters, roadmenders etc. there were several hundred people living in and around Welbeck. When his parents went riding their route was examined the day before, and all the rabbit holes filled up. He took us through the subterranean passages and into the vast ballroom, where the family pictures were slashed by soldiers billeted in the house during the war. Aunt Winnie had had some encounters with Ribbentrop [*Hitler's ambassador in London, 1936–38*], whom she snubbed on every occasion. He said no lady in Germany would be as friendly with miners and labourers as she was, and she replied that perhaps they were afraid of them. When local miners crowded round her car, stretching their arms through the windows to shake hands and calling out, 'God bless you', she turned on the shrinking Ribbentrop and said, 'Now you see why we'll never have Communism in England! These people are just as good as you or me – probably better.' She heard later that when the German leaders were choosing the houses each would live in after they had invaded and conquered England, Ribbentrop had picked Welbeck. After that Aunt Winnie loathed him more fiercely than ever.

In August we went to Ireland, first to Barons Court, then to the Lough Erne Hotel, and finally to Dublin. I saw some of the 'stately homes'.

Castle Coole, belonging to the Belmores, is disintegrating; these people, with all the charm in the world, seem impervious to comforts. But their houses are full of museum pieces. Went to the Maze races when Princess Margaret was there, and had a long talk to her in the Governor's box. She is a tiny little creature, with lovely dark blue eyes and a very easy way with her. She went straight to my heart by saying how her parents had adored Kenya, and how she and her sister were longing to go there.

We tried hard to find a house for the winter, and finally were lent Crom Castle, Co. Fermanagh, by the Woodhouses, who were going to England. So we moved into this modest little spot of Victorian Gothic, 106 rooms, no light or heat, and draughts which screamed like air raid sirens all day and night. The servants worked like beavers carrying mountains of firewood to warm my trembling limbs. Crom is at the very end of Lough Erne, a lost and lonely spot. Claud was ill most of the time, and I was cold, devitalized and sick with boredom. Sometimes people came to shoot and it was delightful to see them, for everyone in this country seems to be charming, but that was practically our only contact with the outside world.

Then came an invitation to a party at Buckingham Palace before the royal wedding [*of Princess Elizabeth and Lieutenant Philip Mountbatten*]. Claud was ill and couldn't go, but I dashed over, dug the jewels out of their safe places and went with the family, all dressed up.

DECEMBER

The Queen wore a vast cream and gold crinoline, with great diamonds round her neck, orders across her breast and round the elbow, and on her head a perfect sheet of diamonds – a crown of square-cut, modern, blue-white stones. The Queen talked to Dolly, and gave me a small smile for myself; Princess Elizabeth stopped and talked for quite a time, looking radiant in the diamonds given to her for a wedding present by South Africa. She said, 'The whole place is packed with kings and queens – isn't it exciting!', as thrilled as any small girl. Dolly presented me. We told her it was a lovely party and that everyone was all dressed up in her honour, and she replied, 'I'm very honoured, I assure you.'

I returned to Crom by air, and the weeks dragged by. I am so happy with Claud but life is so short, and if I have to spend part of it in the wilderness I would rather be warm, interested and surrounded by beauty – as at home in Kenya – and not cold, bored and drowned in blue-grey damp.

1948

JANUARY

We returned to London. There was a record gale in the Irish Sea and no one had any sleep. In England the train wandered all over the Midlands and arrived three hours late, and I am quite, quite worn out.

21 FEBRUARY

One evening Queen Mary came to tea with the family, but I was ill and missed the party. She very kindly arranged for us all to go privately to see the royal wedding presents: a gold toilet set in a vast case from the Corps Diplomatique; some raffia shopping baskets from old ladies in villages; exquisite dinner plates from 'some ladies of Georgia'; hats made by pupil milliners; breathtaking jewels from the royal family and Indian princes; gloves; furniture; lampshades; a very beautiful tall lampstand from Dukie and Dolly; hand-worked boxes from Ukrainian prisoners of war; priceless glass from President Truman; little glass brooches and ornaments from schoolchildren in Prague; linen; feathers; treasures and junk – all signs of love and admiration from various parts of the world. The newly-weds are very short of carpets – they have been given several objets d'art only fit to hang on walls, but hardly anything to walk on.

Everyone who knows Prince Philip likes him immensely. Only poor little Princess Margaret is very lonely without her sister, as they are such great friends and did everything together.

MARCH

Had lunch with Vi Hamilton, who has just come back from a cruise to South America in the very smart ship *Andes*. She saw Eva Peron, wife of the Argentine President, and said she is very beautiful, very clever and very ill, having to keep going with the help of too many tonics and restoratives, which have turned her skin yellow and sunk her beautiful eyes into her head. Wearing long diamond necklaces and lovely clothes she talked to the workers, whom she calls 'my shirtless ones'. They adore her, attracted by her air of richness and condescension, but they are beginning to take her attitude seriously and strike for higher wages. Eva's sisterliness towards the workers is turning rather into a boomerang. I hear Lord Winterton and others prophesy an economic crash in Argentina for March or April.

Colonial and Dominion land is booming; there is so much food, clothing and money in some parts of the world, and so much want in others – why can't they get together?

The discomfort in England penetrates everywhere. Last year Queen Mary was in bed with a chill, and Dolly was asked to go and talk to her. She found her up, and shivering, wrapped in a rug by a tiny fire in a vast room. She said her bedroom was so cold she could not bear it, and was forced to get up. Sometimes, it seems to me that the grander the people, the more uncomfortable their houses, and the ones who stay warm and cosy are the ones in little houses easily heated.

27 DECEMBER

We're back in Kenya. Have sorted out a herd of half-bred Jersey-type heifers and Jersey-type Borans, who will have only Jersey bulls. Having swept the board at the show and won the supreme championship with our imported Jersey bull, I feel it's good policy to emphasize this attractive breed.

Some weeks ago two fat cows vanished, then Nur Mohammed's house was broken into at night. The other day N.M. asked leave to bring a *mganga [witchdoctor]* here, to locate the thieves. A Kikuyu appeared – young, overdressed and conceited. Then the only bottle of whisky I had had in six months vanished. I told the witchdoctor he'd better begin by finding it. After 'rolling the dice' for hours he accused everyone in the house except Claud and me and the cook. But the cook was plastered last night and not for the first time, either.

The *mganga* then demanded ten shillings, but I would only give him five. He went raging round the Kikuyus, saying he should have had a hundred shillings, not five, and that he would burn them with fire. They just laughed, which made him madder than ever. That night Kisu's store was broken into, some mule harness mutilated and a horse book and files stolen. Everyone assured me this was the work of the witchdoctor, who hoped to be sent for to discover the missing things and to get a hundred shillings. But we got the police instead, and they arrested the witchdoctor. I don't know what happened to him, but being a witchdoctor is illegal in Kenya.

29 DECEMBER

I am in bed with flu. Have decided to switch the farm's main industry from milk, which costs a lot and does not even pay the wages, to beef. This is a momentous decision, but I hope and believe I'm right. It is rather a complicated thing to do, but *can* be done quite successfully.

Some weeks ago, as the dog and I were walking round a calf *boma* among some rather agitated cows, something struck me a sudden blow in the back which made me scream with pain and surprise. A cow, trying to horn the dog, got me instead right at the base of the spine, missing the rectum (which would probably have killed me) by less than half an inch. Dripping blood, I struggled to get home but could go no more than a few yards.

Then Gatama on his bike saw me and flew off for Claud with the car. He was going to Nakuru, but thank heaven hadn't yet gone. He came and took me back to the Naishi cottage, where we were staying for a month during the Turners' holiday. Then came Mrs Nicoll and later on the doctor, who gave me a very mild local anaesthetic and put in five stitches which hurt far more than the cow had. At last they got me back to Nderit House, trembling with cold (from shock) and in some pain.

Two days later the darling Masai women appeared with eggs and tears saying, 'My Keramadisho, what would have happened to us if that cow had killed you?' All this was very soothing and pleasant and made me feel much better. But now, more than four weeks later, I am still feeling knocked about and shall be thankful to start on our holiday.

31 DECEMBER

Am in bed with a sore throat, but hoping to struggle down to the races today. Water on Collier has stopped flowing. It comes from Soysambu, and this time of year they need more themselves, so we suffer.

Claud and I, out walking one evening, saw two figures fleeing through the forest; behind a bush was one of our wheelbarrows carrying one of our drums, half full of drink – fermenting and bubbling beautifully. After fearful scenes on my part and stopping the Christmas bullock and the children's Christmas sweets, Kisu [*the head stable boy*] self-righteously produced the culprit – the tractor driver. Everyone of course, was completely ignorant, though naturally they all knew the brewing was going on. My rage knew no bounds and we sent him off to jail.

1949

DECEMBER

We went to Zanzibar for our holiday, where I basked in the sun and the warm, silky sea and wandered about the narrow streets of this strange, white-walled, black-shadowed old town, and bought carpets in an Arabian dhow and wrote a good deal. Claudie was ill, which spoilt things a lot, but we had a happy time just the same. We stayed in a small, quite primitive hotel owned by an Englishman and his wife. He said he had been at Oxford when he and that group of left-wing undergraduates vowed 'never to fight for King and Country'. Very soon came the war; all of them rushed to join up, and many were killed. No wonder foreigners can't understand us English!

Flew back to England in May, leaving Nderit in the capable hands of Nicoll, Turner, Taju, Ndarara, Waweru and Omolo. Very sad, as always, to leave my lovely home, natives, cattle and the dogs. Found Dukie and Dolly not very well, but thankful to have Claud with them again.

At Goodwood we were in the Richmonds' box when Princess Margaret appeared and refused to sit down, though people kept offering her chairs. So we all stood wearily, wishing she would sit or go! She went.

There is to be a general election. We went canvassing every week in the very poor streets of North Kensington. The people living there are invariably kind and polite; many agreed they had voted Labour before, hoping all those wild promises would be fulfilled, but they are now disappointed and disillusioned and swinging slowly to the right. I made several friends. One was a very nice Roman Catholic Communist sailor! He said I would find this a very odd combination, and promised to vote Conservative.

Labour won the election with a small majority.

I find England terribly cold, dark and dreary during the winter. The streets are still only half-lit; every capital in Europe has more lights and more fun that we do. But no one seems to mind much. I believe there is a type of English person who thoroughly enjoys cold, dirt and discomfort. It seems to please some puritanical smugness buried not very far down in their chill bosoms. But we do produce the hardiest and finest soldiers. Mother used to say, 'Anyone who can stand the English climate can stand anything!' She loathed it, and so do I.

1950

JANUARY

I long for sun, sea and sand. I think I am a rootless person, never *really* homesick for anywhere, not *really* loving any place or country. I like Kenya far better than anywhere else, but never hanker for it as I used to – only for the sun.

17 MARCH

St Patrick's Day. Alex and Maggie have flown from Canada for the Irish Guards' fiftieth anniversary. At Chelsea Barracks the regiment stood at ease behind their officers while their band played. When the royal party arrived the King took baskets of shamrock from an officer and they were distributed to the men. When the King and Queen left the stand the crowd ran towards them, and the Queen, sweet, smiling and lovely, went and spoke to people. How they are loved!

Some days ago we were asked to Buckingham Palace to watch from Delia Peel's window [*a lady-in-waiting*] the arrival of French President Auriol and his wife. We were joined by Prince Charles and his nannie. He is a stout, strong baby; he seized Claud's umbrella, and I thought he would break it. He adores horses and got excited when he saw the mounted policemen. He looks rather pathetic, with a puzzled expression – which I think is only caused by the set of his eyebrows.

On the evening of St Patrick's Day we went to the Irish Guards' party for all ranks. It was wonderful; Claud met so many old friends and they were overjoyed to see him again. He was a very good officer and beloved by the men, as he was always trying to help them; and as legal adviser to the battalion he was a great comfort and help to those in trouble. There were over eleven hundred men there and scores of officers and wives. I don't believe any other regiment except the RAF has this feeling of comradeship. It was a wonderful, heart-warming experience, and I only wish I could do something really useful for the men of the Irish Guards.

3 DECEMBER

The summer passed in a ceaseless hunt for a small farm in England; in frights about Dukie and Dolly, who were quite ill alternately; and in various parties which were never really very much fun. Now it has been quite dark since 3.30 p.m., snowing and blowing, cold and sad. Claud is not well, and I sit here by an electric fire and pine for hot sun, blue seas, the outdoor life, rich, opulent flowers and strong southern scents. The weather forecast tonight says: very cold, snow showers. I am reading Lord Frederick Hamilton's account of Jamaica: 'Wonderfully beautiful under the blazing sunlight, in the crystal clear atmosphere ...! Entrancing beauty. Just a fortnight before we had left England under snow, in the grip of a black frost ... had fallen straight into the most exquisitely beautiful island ... bathed in perpetual summer.' Oh, lucky Great-Uncle Freddy! He did not believe in enduring the British winter, or living like a true Englishman in 'our rough island story' – the operative word being 'rough'!

31 DECEMBER

The war in Korea drags on, backwards and forwards, everyone on tenter-hooks, while the diplomats do their best and the Communists laugh at us. All the same, we've given them fearful losses with high-powered bombing.

We have bought our little farm with 103 acres; Stockenden Farm. A very olde-worlde oaky-beamed house, but genuine and full of possibilities. And Warm. It has a priest hole in a chimney, which is said to have a tunnel leading to the nearest convent, but no one has ever found it. Off a bedroom is a small alcove, built onto the outside of the room at first-floor level. A famous architect came to see the house, but when he saw the alcove he dodged away. I was intrigued at this, and kept asking what it was? At last he said, with some embarrassment, 'That was a Tudor convenience. They hung their clothes there, to discourage the moths.'

1951

DECEMBER

We went for a week's holiday to Pemba in the Gilfillans' truly luxury yacht *Umbrina*, sailing by day and anchoring at night. Bob is a wonderful seaman,

Genesta in the 1940s – a formal portrait

Above: Nderit House
Below: Flamingo and Cattle at Nderit

Above: The drawing room at Nderit

Right: Mutual admiration: Genesta with Lakri

Below: On the farm in the floods

Above: Befriending a Thompson's Gazelle

Left: Perched at Assouan

Below: The bullfight on Pemba

Right: Fishing boats sail home to the East African coast

but poor Mildred got malaria. The first night stop was in a creek called Shimoni, where once the Masai used to raid right down to the shore.

Next dawn we crept out of the creek, very early and quietly, under a pale gold sky and sailed south for Pemba. In the evening we entered a fairyland bay. There we lay for the night, on a star-shimmering sea under a star-flecked sky, dreaming of darkest, loneliest Africa – until we heard, far away, the sound of the Pemba motorbuses!

Next day to Wété: a steamy, hot, heavily overgrown village, the capital of Pemba. A bullfight was arranged for us and here is the account I wrote for the *Mombasa Times*:

> The bull fights of Pemba are a relic of the Portuguese settlers. Though they may lack something of the sartorial splendour and the flashing movements of those to be seen in Europe, Lourenço Marques [*Mozambique*] and Mexico, they are still a unique form of entertainment.
>
> The crowds, the noise, the excitement, the barking men, the chanting women, the setting in a forest glade, all add to the interest of this extraordinary spectacle. Bullfighting here is regarded in much the same way as cricket in England. Just as there are matches on nearly every village green, besides the grand inter-county affairs, so in Pemba every sizeable village has its fighting bull and its forest clearing; besides which there are twenty or thirty bullrings scattered about the island, with grandstands built all round. They all have their matadors, beauty choruses, flute players and drummers.
>
> Led by the Mudir, we reached our stand. There were two other Europeans perched on the edge, and when we had climbed the rickety, home-made ladder our party brought the white visitors up to nine. The stand quivered as the Africans with which it was already crowded milled around, seeking room to sit down. The noise never ceased for a second. The Mudir and I, seated side by side, yelled at each other.
>
> 'The last stand broke,' shouted the Mudir. 'Many people broke their arms. These are new stands; very strong!'
>
> They needed to be, for more and more people were squeezing themselves onto them.
>
> From the forest, with fresh clamour, there now came the procession of matadors. They carried branches of trees, their arms were round each other's shoulders, their heads were down, their legs jerked and kicked as they moved along and they were barking at the top of their lungs.
>
> A dozen girls followed, dressed in bright *kanzus* with flowers and tin combs stuck in their hair and daubs of red paint on their cheeks. Their shoes were on strings around their necks; they clapped their hands and raised their voices in a chant which easily penetrated the other sounds.
>
> Out from the crowd there dashed from time to time, the clowns, the *makungu*, rushing with bent knees about the arena, tumbling in the dust, lying as though in a fit, their limbs doubled up and jerking, their lips drawn back from their teeth, their eyes rolling. Many Africans were drunk, for although drunkenness in Pemba is usually extremely rare, this was a special occasion when everyone was going to enjoy themselves, and coconut wine is easy to get.

263

The matadors gathered against one end of the stand, jerking and barking – the high-pitched sound with which the men of Pemba incite themselves to action. One of them clutched his head with both hands, another moved about crouching with his behind stuck out, jerking in time to the beat of the drum. Led by the drummers, the barking started and stopped at a signal; and in the pause barkers, released from their strained attitudes, relaxed and stood getting their breath for a minute.

Then the drummer, with a yelp, attacked his drum again and the barking was resumed. Behind the legs of the stand stood the chorus, clapping and singing traditional songs, while the flautist with lungs of iron, blew three unvarying squeals from his pipe, almost without a pause.

A group of men came into the ring, pulling a long rope. They heaved and tugged and at last there appeared, with his front legs stuck out protestingly and his hind feet dug into the sand, a very 'reluctant dragon' of a bull. He was small, black and white, with short horns and a big hump. They towed him over the sand by sheer force, tied him to the stand, threw him, held his legs and rolled him onto his back. While the matadors crouched over him barking more shrilly than ever; women sang, flutes played, drums beat – suddenly the bull was released and everyone sprang back.

He was on his feet in a second and rushed at the nearest fighter, who shook a cloth at him. The bull charged the cloth, the fighter dropped it and rolled away in the dust. The bull passed on, having successfully disposed of his enemy.

His only idea was to get out of the ring and go home, but men were everywhere flapping cloths or bits of coconut matting, making noises like dogs, running towards him and dropping on one knee or stamping on the ground, shouting at him.

The bull charged and charged again, hitting nothing but the cloth, ignoring the men who rolled away from just in front of his feet and whom he could easily have gored. Sometimes there was a rush under our stand, and then the row of white, brown and black legs dangling over the edge were rapidly drawn up, out of harm's way.

At the end of every charge the bull trotted docilely out of the ring, on his way home, only to be hauled back again at the end of the long rope. It was a free-for-all, anyone could fight; while the grown-ups were baiting the bull in the ring, small boys darted in from among the trees, stamped, yelled at the bull (who took no notice) and rushed away again.

It was interesting to see that, even after three hundred years had passed, some of the gestures of the Portuguese bullring had been preserved. The dropping on one knee, the stamping and challenging and the attitudes with the cloths, were all reminiscent of the real thing.

Never for a moment was the tempo allowed to fall. When the bull stood immobile, impervious to noise or flapping cloths, just gazing quietly at his opponents, the clowns rushed about, women clapped, the drummer drummed, men and boys practised that quick run and turn on one heel – almost, but never quite falling over – which is one of the features of African dancing.

The drunks weaved around. One could hardly speak or stand, but tottered about, alternately grinning and snarling. Finally, he lay down in the middle of the ring, completely unconscious, and was removed.

By now the bull was getting tired, bored and more than ever determined to stop charging. He dropped his head, trying to find something to eat in the sand. Once more he was dragged to the stand, and once more the fighters clustered all round him, barking no longer, but patting his back and neck, praising and thanking him for the fun he had given them. His owner took off the heavy rope, tied him to a piece of string and led him away, while the crowd of fighters, barkers, singers and clowns again began their antics.

The second bull, with a reputation for extreme fierceness, came into the ring as quietly but less reluctantly than the first. He got his rope entangled with a palm tree, then wrapped round his own legs. Freed, he looked pensively at the crowd and suddenly whipped round and charged a drunk, who was leaning against the stand, half conscious.

The bull knocked him down, gored him once – then lost all interest and stood quietly by while his head was being tied, preparatory to being thrown. The bleeding victim, hardly awake and barely conscious of what had happened to him, was led passively away.

Three bulls were fought that afternoon, but the third, said to be the fiercest of all, was not in a fighting mood. A disappointed man behind us said to the Mudir, 'Tell the Europeans that only the other day he hit my own son, very hard; he is really a very good bull, very fierce.' But he was led away, quiet and covered in shame.

The scenery was lovely in a lush, hot, heavy way, and it must have looked like a little paradise to the buffeted Portuguese sailors when they first saw it. But it is the sort of place which palls.

1952

FEBRUARY

In February the Duke and Duchess of Edinburgh arrived in Kenya for a few days, *en route* to Australia; there were processions and a garden party at Government House to which we were 'bidden'. The Mitchells' [*Governor*] regime surpassed itself; one card sent to Lady 'Mac' [*a widow*] said 'You and your wife will be presented.' Another was sent to 'The Duke of Manchester and Lady Manchester', and any amount of really important people – like Florrie Wilson, who started the airlines here – weren't asked at all. I took our three heads of tribes and they had a wonderful time, tearing around Nairobi, heading off the royal visitors and seeing them several times.

After Nairobi, the Duke and Duchess went to Nyeri and then to Treetops, where they were when the beloved King [*George VI*] died.

The news of his death was the most dreadful shock to everyone, and all our thoughts were for the poor Queen Mother, for they were the world's happiest married couple; they worshipped each other.

MARCH

Jim and Kath Hamilton have been with us; Kenya made a great impression on them. Nderit looked even more beautiful than usual. A friend of mine, riding with me, looked at the view and said, 'It's so lovely I want to either eat it or roll in it.'

We went to the game camp at Amboseli. The dawns were more lovely than words can say; the crimson glow catching the snows on Kilimanjaro, turning the mountain-top blood-red until the colours paled to gold. Even our natives were struck with the beauty of it. The animals began to wake up and graze. We saw elephant, rhino, buffalo, giraffe and small buck, but no lion. Later we all went to Nyeri, to Treetops. At first there was only one old elephant, but at 5.30 in the evening a herd appeared through the forest trees, slowly and massively progressing down to the water and the salt. We counted sixty-five, all ages and sizes, from tiny calves to ponderous old bulls. They stayed there until far into the night; when they had gone forty-five buffalo and three rhino appeared.

AUGUST

Returned to England in April; found the parents frailer but enduring. The poor royal family are still shocked, and missing the King; the Queen Mother looks quite ravaged, but they all do their work as usual and the people love them even more. Katie, Cynthia and the various Hamiltons in the Household have had a hard, sad time.

This month I came to Venice for two weeks, while Claud is in Ireland. Such beauty and fantasy – the black gondolas, the gondoliers with their big straw hats, graceful gestures and musical voices, the exquisite churches, campanile, architecture and pictures, the water shimmering everywhere, the constant *va et vient* on the Grand Canal and the dark, quiet, secret life in the side canals. I met several charming people, including ex-King Peter and ex-Queen Alexandra of Yugoslavia, a very good-looking young pair.

On 13 August I sadly floated away in a gondola to the Danieli landing stage, where the Italian airline launch took me to the Lido aerodrome and off we flew to Milan. From here by BEA to England, where Claudie was awaiting me with a heavenly supper of the salmon he had just killed and some strawberries.

Addio, lovely Venice.

SEPTEMBER

Terrible account of the Mau Mau [*a secret society set up among the Kikuyus to drive European settlers off their farms*] in Kenya – torturing Africans, killing and mutilating cattle, murdering white people and fellow Kikuyus. They are cowards, cruel and treacherous.

27 OCTOBER

We left Heathrow for Kenya in a Hermes. It was cold, dreary and dingy. We crossed England in the murk and rain, reached Nice, turned round and came back to Heathrow with oil trouble in one engine. Sitting around in drab surroundings for three hours made me more attached to Heathrow than ever. At last we took off again, got as far as halfway over the Channel, steep bank – back to Heathrow; same trouble, same engine. Feeling pretty sour by now. Heathrow three times in one day would really be too much, and I refused to go on unless they gave us another machine, especially as one had been waiting ready and empty all day. Another Hermes had also had to return with oil trouble, just behind us.

When we were told to re-embark I went to the aircraft's nose to make sure we did have a new plane – and indeed, so we had. Off we went, and spent the night in Rome; I revelled in the soft, scented air of a civilized climate.

We enplaned for Kenya. Landed at midnight at Khartoum. Heavy heat, tea and lemonade in the waiting room, everyone sleepy and inelegant. Re-embarked, revved up the engine – *pop-po-pop; spit-spit-spit*; and the poor stewards had to tell the passengers yet again that the Hermes, true to form, had a failing engine. Back we trooped to more tea and lemonade. Half an hour later all was well, the broken plug replaced, and off we went.

Arrived at Nairobi to see Kebe and Mbuthia's smiling black faces, waiting by the Chevrolet. They had been there all day long yesterday and since six o'clock that morning. We were twenty-four hours late.

A rapturous Masai welcome awaited us at home, where one soaking old woman had been put out in the rain, to act as sentry, while the men sheltered in a bull house. With warm hearts and hands plastered with red mud we reached the stables, where we were greeted by a crowd of shy, gauche Kikuyu grooms and their families – doubtless meaning well, but without the élan or the manners of the princely Masai. It was heaven to be back. The garden full of flowers, the blue lake festooned with flamingos, the opal-coloured hills and the dark green of the Mau range – all is beautiful and dear to me as ever.

Various old Kikuyu men appeared and squeezed our hands and said, 'Don't worry. Our farm is clean.' It was not true. [*Later, I asked Kebe in private about the Mau Mau and how we were on the farm. 'Who knows the heart of another?' said he, that cryptic African phrase which means 'I suspect.' He told us never to move unarmed, and not to sleep on the verandah any more, nor to go into our lovely forest.*]

A few days later, as we were walking among the cows one evening, Michael Robinson and another man appeared in uniform. The police in Nairobi had made a sudden round-up, arresting Jomo Kenyatta with various other 'leaders' and flying them off to the northern frontier, where they started work on building their own prisons. State of emergency, everyone alerted, build bonfires, put out a cross of white sheets for the spotter planes to see (if in very bad trouble), join the Kenya Police Reserve, watch your Kikuyu, guard your cattle, protect the good (you hope) Kikuyu from the murdering Mau Mau, who prefer to attack their own tribesmen (probably because they are unlikely to fight back).

Claud and I went to Taju's [*the head Masai's*] village, where we found some Masai, including women, armed with very sharp pangas [*small swords*] and panting to be 'at 'em'. We put them all on guard – children to herd cattle by day, Masai to guard by night. Personally, I am so glad everything is now in the open at last.

1 NOVEMBER

We are all on guard all the time, and so far have had no trouble. We know there is a Mau Mau cell here and that almost every Kikuyu has taken the oath. Now they are worried, and we think would like to be 'cleansed' of it by 'good' witchdoctors; but it's so very difficult for them to do this without us knowing! We all pretend that everyone is utterly pure, as I still hope for a big sweep to catch the ringleaders. We have many more Masai now, thank God – three on the stables and three on the house at night and many on villages and herds.

Several more Kikuyu have been most brutally and savagely murdered at Nyeri – including Chief Nderi, who bravely and rashly tried, with only four others, to break up a Mau Mau crowd of five hundred men and women. He was hacked to death with his escort just before police reinforcements arrived. They also attacked a man called Bowyer in his bath, slashing his stomach until he died, and killing the two Kikuyu children who were cowering in the kitchen. Kingori's old uncle, living in his village near Nyeri, heard a knock on his door one night and a voice saying, 'Police – open!' He came out and a noose was thrown over his head. Then he was dragged away, and the Mau Mau cut off his legs, his arms and finally his head. His old wife they smothered.

The educated Kikuyu are everywhere; we cannot trust the telephone, telegrams or the post, and have been warned against everyone by our grapevine. *All* the educated Kikuyu are in it, say the nicest, oldest Kikuyu! Including of course —, that excitable, drunken politician. Their plan, obviously, was to use him as the 'respectable' party and Kenyatta as the leader of the 'active' one – naturally many people in England believe that the 'political' Kikuyu are what they call 'moderate and decent', which, of course, they are not. Now we, on the farms, are in the ridiculous situation of not being able to get rid of the dangerous Kikuyu when we want to, but having to spend a lot of precious time comforting and protecting them!

The Kenyan settlers are splendid. All the men are in the police or the Kenya Regiment. Claud, Gethin and Nicoll do their turns of all-night duty with the police at Elmenteita. Farmers and tradesmen do the best they can to keep business going and do their emergency jobs too. Spotter planes, lent to the police by private owners and flown by ex-RAF pilots, go over the farms all day, seeing that all is well; and fly over the Mau Mau reserve in the Aberdares, the thick forests to which hundreds of Mau Mau have fled, observing their movements. Farms are patrolled at night by the army, and the owners aroused to see if they are still alive. The army and Kenya Regiment patrols drive through the farms by day, showing the flag.

If only the authorities had picked up all the Kikuyu women and children and old people from the villages at the very beginning, 'for their own protection', and had taken them away to camps and removed the food they were taking to the gangs at night, and burnt the huts, the whole thing would have collapsed by now. But they delay and go slow and try to be firm and gentle – the *last* thing the Kikuyus understand. Naturally they think we are weak, so the murders and maiming and tortures go on.

DECEMBER

We went to Lady Mac's heavenly home near Mombasa for Christmas. The flowers were exquisite – purple, mauve, crimson, flame and white bougainvillea growing against a background of cerulean sea, cut by the snow-white line of reef where the rollers roar all the time. We goggled and swam and lazed, and I sailed in the fishermen's canoes and was blissfully happy. We were tired, and Lady Mac's people, coast boys and Mau Mau-haters, were wonderful to us.

1953

FEBRUARY

There have been endless Mau Mau murders. So far they have only killed about fifteen Europeans, but have slaughtered hundreds of Kikuyu women and children.

One of the worst European murders was that of the Ruck family. As they sat in their sitting room one evening, with six-year-old Michael upstairs in bed, their head groom came to the door saying they had caught a Mau Mau about to maim one of the horses. Roger Ruck looked out and saw a bound man struggling on the grass, while his boys stood round him. When he went out they jumped on him, slashed him, dragged him to a log and there killed him. Hearing his screams and the Kikuyus' maniacal yells, his pregnant wife rushed out. They chased and killed her too, slashing her stomach open, dragging out her embryo baby and stuffing it into her mouth to suffocate her. This is their favourite way of killing a pregnant woman. The newspapers just call it 'slashing to death'. Strands of her long golden hair were found on the grass later, where she had fled from her murderers. Then the groom who had taught Michael to ride and had always been with him ran into the house and up the stairs, followed by the others. Guarding Michael's door they found a solitary Kikuyu who begged them not to hurt the child, so they killed him and the groom kicked the door in. Michael was cowering against the wall, screaming for his parents; they first cut out his eyes, then hacked him to death.

This awful tragedy shocked everyone. I showed the photos of Mrs Ruck – such a pretty young woman, a doctor who had spent most of her adult life ministering to the Kikuyus – and the blond little boy to the Masai, who were horror-stricken. I also showed them to our Kikuyu butler, Filipo, who had nothing to say but went rather grey, as black people do when agitated; I think even he was shocked. A short time after this I went and found Taju, the head Masai, and asked if he thought the Masai would come out as guards on the lonely farms on the Kinankop. He said that of course they would. I went to Nairobi and saw His Excellency, the Chief of Police and various others, all of whom told me to go ahead.

Later I did just that, and went to Narok, the largest of the Masai villages. There were three of us – a driver, Taju and me. In the middle of that vast, waterless wilderness, through which the road runs, the car broke down, but mercifully started again. Later we met an American in a lorry who gave us two bottles of Coke. Next day Taju and I began to collect Masai guards, and so enthusiastic were they that I could have filled a lorry. On the way back the appalling road, an endless succession of bumps and dust-filled holes, seemed longer than ever, but at last we reached Naivasha, then went up to the Kents' farm in the Aberdare forest.

There was a certain element of drama in the house. Every night at sundown revolvers were cocked and laid beside us and the two outer doors were locked; the Kents, who had Sten guns, carried them everywhere. The passage from the kitchen to the dining room was entangled with barbed wire; at dinner everyone else laid their guns beside their plates, but I kept mine in my lap. Every day and most nights patrols went into the forest, but the month I was there they saw nothing.

We had one exciting moment when we heard yelling; we saw the Kikuyu gardener running at top speed along a path, pursued by an askari with his rifle, and a house boy. Not a shot was fired, but soon the three men came panting back – they had been chasing a buck, which had escaped.

I took my Masai all over the forest, putting them in twos and threes on lonely and vulnerable farms. Most had brought their own spears, but some had none so I bought spears for them. I gave them each a coat, two blankets and shoes, and also paid their wages for the first month. I asked the farmers to give them milk and food. The people living in these remote farms were scared, but they couldn't leave, for all their money was in them, and anyway they refused to run away. The women wouldn't leave their men, and the older children wouldn't leave their parents. When the kind people of Mombasa offered Christmas hospitality to the schoolchildren living in the danger zone, they replied that they were very grateful, but did not want to leave their parents and their homes.

Some places I stayed in were too dangerous for my taste. 'Faithful old Kikuyu' – just the sort the Mau Mau have got at and who are under oath to let the murderers in – were waiting at table and sleeping in the house, while their Nandi guards slept outside – locked out! My Jaluo driver said, 'Do not let us ever sleep here again. I was very frightened.' At other more careful farms the food was brought in, cooked and cold, at six o'clock, then heated on the sitting room fire for dinner while the servants were locked out. It is very cold up here at nine and ten thousand feet. The temperature frequently goes down to freezing point.

I drove for a month in wonderful Mercedes-Benz diesel-engined cars over ghastly roads, covering three thousand miles and not having one single breakdown. Some people were charming and others the reverse; in some places the Masai stayed, and others they left. I had Kebe and Gunbearer, both armed with rifles, as guards. They were both brave men and excellent shots. Some of the forests we drove through were dense, but we never saw a soul. I loved every minute of it.

JUNE

In April we flew back to England – Claud had been made a gold staff officer for the coronation of Queen Elizabeth II, and I was given a seat in the nave in Westminster Abbey.

Claud wore full-dress Irish Guards uniform and looked quite magnificent; I had a mushroom pink satin frock with a bodice embroidered in sequins and bugles, and wore all my few jewels and the diamond tiara. Julia, my loving and elderly maid, gave me a silver bag, the top set with real amethysts. We got up at 3 a.m., and left the flat at 6 a.m.

In the Abbey there was a long, long wait, and it was very cold. Then a trickle of diplomats and peers and peeresses appeared, walking up the nave to the chancel, beyond the screen, where the ceremony would take place. Some shambled along as though their feet were still encased in their ancestral mud, while others walked with grace and dignity. Certain couples were (one knew) reunited for the day only.

There was a pause while six white-coated charwomen came and swept the royal blue carpet; everyone relaxed and talked. This moment of domesticity was a relief to us all, for the tension and emotion were mounting.

The Queen appeared, glittering, delicate, young and poised, coming very slowly and deliberately up the aisle with her maids of honour (one of whom was Moyra Hamilton) behind her. As they slowly passed there was a wave of curtseys and bent heads; tiaras sparkled, jewels, medals and orders flashed.

After the ceremony was over we waited until our stand, the last to be called, emptied itself and we trooped out. Claud, being one of the staff for the day, was eating cold chicken and drinking champagne while I got a cup of tepid tea and a sandwich apparently made of wood. Out in the street I found a large, tired black man sitting on a shooting stick, while his wife stood by. He had lost his taxi card and had little English; a kind, worried policeman was trying in vain to help. I spoke to him in Swahili and he cheered up a lot. Claud appeared and we took them in our car on a fruitless search for his hotel. When she saw the splendour, his wife told me later, she said to her husband, 'Never give up the British. They are strong.' He was Chief Paul Mboya, of the Jaluo tribe. It was nice to be talking Swahili again and the crowds were enchanted with us, Claud in uniform and medals, me in pink silk and diamonds, wedged between huge Bibi Mboya and still larger Chief Paul Mboya. We all had tea in our flat and the Mboyas went on in a taxi.

That night we went to Uncle Claud and Vi Hamilton for sandwiches and a view of the crowds and the fireworks from Marlborough House. But I was exhausted, having had only three hours' sleep, for some people outside our window had kept up a rowdy party until after midnight the night before. Everything had been exquisite, magnificent and moving; the most glorious sight I shall ever see.

We returned to Kenya – to the Mau Mau, the strain of heat and work, and the loving, loyal and endlessly helpful Masai. The dogs, sleeping on the verandah with me, were extremely vigilant and alert. They knew there was danger. I had a rifle in my bed and a revolver under my knee.

NOVEMBER

We returned to England for a very short spell. My beloved father-in-law died last September and was buried at Baron's Court. I did not go over to Ireland for the funeral, but stayed in Mount Street to keep Dolly company. She was simply heroic, without a tear. She was, in fact, in a state of shock, and told me long afterwards that she didn't remember me staying with her, nor much about what happened. She was greatly helped and comforted by all the letters which poured in, including those from our three queens [*Queen Mary, Queen Elizabeth the Queen Mother, and Queen Elizabeth II*], and one from the Duke of Alba, who himself died a few days later.

I returned to Nderit the same month, finding things pretty chaotic with one manager having done the stupidest and most expensive things and the other having wrecked the cars, ruined the natives and allowed his side of the farm to become rotten with drunkenness. The head manager, thank heaven, soon flounced out, but the other was there until the following August, getting bossier and bossier. It was a relief when he left.

Claud stayed on in England with his mother for a while. He has taken on the job of part-time magistrate in Nakuru, and I am a district councillor. I find the work interesting and I like it. We now have our own Masai army in this valley; fifty Masai Moran [*young warriors*], paid, fed and armed by the farmers. They are on call at a moment's notice if the police want them; they are very keen but don't get enough to do.

1954

The Mau Mau are slowly going under – they are short of food – but still sometimes pull off some ghastly piece of cruelty. They attacked the house of [*the anthropologist*] Louis Leakey's cousin, strangled his wife and carried the old man off. Then they buried him alive – with a living goat – as a sacrifice. The fact he was a blood brother of the Kikuyu did not save him. These are the creatures whose friends in Britain say they are 'fighting nobly for their freedom'. Meanwhile the poor deluded British government continues to 'educate' the Kikuyu. They sent a party to England early this year to learn trade unionism; and when they returned some were found to be practically foundation members of the Mau Mau. The British, of course, are pained and surprised – but we are not; it is just what one would expect.

We had to get rid of all the servants and most of the farm Kikuyu. We were told that the butler, Filippo, was the local Mau Mau manager, another the chairman, etc., and I did notice F. got gloomier and gloomier every time I told him of government successes. When Kenyatta was arrested he was speechless. The Masai finally persuaded me to get rid of him, so one day I had to tell him that I had been told he would be murdered if he stayed on. He didn't want to go, and it was one of the hardest things I've ever done, but it had to be.

Later on I found ourselves stuck with a lot of other known Mau Mau, so I sent for the government photographer. There was a law that every Kikuyu must be photographed, and the Mau Mau threatened to kill anyone who agreed. I was left with about twenty-five out of a hundred, and was most thankful to see them go. I gave them all presents of money and did the best I could for them, sending milk every day to the camp. All were sent home after a token few days in jail for refusing to be photographed.

1955

FEBRUARY

Started on tour of 'troubled areas' in my capacity as district councillor for the Elmenteita area. At Fort Hall we turned up into the hills. The steep, narrow tracks were all made since the emergency; they are often slippery and Land Rovers are by far the best vehicles. Here we saw Kikuyu guard posts – moats filled with bamboo stakes, together with walls and a draw-bridge. Twenty or thirty 'loyal' Kikuyu, i.e. captured, turned around Mau Mau, all ages and sizes, all with weapons; fairly brave, all now vociferously anti-Mau Mau. 'Loyal' chiefs and head-men seem good people. They are well treated by charming Kenyan boys of the Kenya Regiment, all apparently concerned for each other and interdependent. We saw Chief Sospice's tragically over-run and massacred village. Peter Upson, a farmer from Kitale, met us; he is very nice to his men who seem to like him. The various Kikuyu holdings are consolidated – no longer here and there but all in one piece, planted under white supervision with maize, coffee, cassava beans, potatoes etc., ten acres bringing in three hundred pounds a year. Compounds are very clean, with neat, small houses, pigs, hens and a few goats.

We visited a prison camp; the men are fed on maize, meat, vegetables, fruit, beans and potatoes – much better than their guards, who are annoyed about this. Just like German prisoners and us during and at the end of the war. Windy hilltops hold lonely police posts guarding nearby villages. In Nyeri these have small plots for each house, a village hall, a church and a playground; the authorities are hoping everything will stay like this [*it did not*].

Mau Mau Kikuyu, who once opposed all forms of progress, now beg for them. Kikuyu women, who once flayed a young English policeman alive, and tried to lynch vets when dips were established, now can't have enough of them. The Roman Catholic Chief Ignacio's English-speaking daughter is a school teacher, teaching English, mathematics and science in Kikuyu schools.

25 FEBRUARY

We continued our tour from Nyeri and penetrated the forest, but were not allowed to go far. Tidying up bits of paper polluting the lovely forest trail, I found they were pamphlets urging the Mau Mau to surrender. Many rivers were full of trout. Captured Mau Mau told the District Officer one day that for several hours thirty of them had watched him and his friends unsuccessfully fishing. When asked why they did not attack the Mau Mau replied that they didn't know, so inconsistent are they. All they said was, 'You didn't catch much, did you, bwana?'

MARCH

We were invited 'up the mountain' by Brigadier Lord Thurlow, who gave us transport and a British military policeman for an escort. A wonderful motor road has been built from Nanyuki to the highest post, twelve thousand feet up, and here, in the fine, thin air, above the forest line and on the edge of the moorland, we had a picnic lunch with Roger St John and some of his soldiers. Then we drove on up until we had to walk. Here I could only manage a few yards at a time for pounding heart and panting breath. The soldier escort stayed with me, while Claud and a young Roman Catholic priest attached to the army strode off until they were half a mile ahead. We saw no Mau Mau and I'm afraid Operation First Flute (a great sweep through the forest to catch the Mau Mau) has been a failure because of leaky intelligence (what else can you expect when officers have mission-trained 'former' Mau Mau Kikuyu, able to speak, write, and read English letters and dispatches, for servants?). But the silence, the loneliness, and the sweep of the wind from the snowy summit just above us, were wonderful and strange. We reached thirteen thousand feet.

Over the brow of a hill came a line of soldiers (Lancashire Fusiliers), who for four or five days have been sleeping out in this arctic air at the tarn, just below the snowline and too high for their vehicles. They and their Samburu soldiers often went right up to the snow, where they had snowball fights – something which has never happened to a Samburu before! [*A few years later some loyal Kikuyu chiefs spent a day with us in England and I asked one why he sided with us and not the Mau Mau. 'There was more food on your side,' said this very sensible man.*]

17 APRIL

We are in Egypt now and the Egyptians are having a new honeymoon with England; everyone is all smiles and affability. Personally, I am always taken in by this attitude, but I was delighted to be told by people who *know* that the Egyptians truly *are* kind and affectionate people, and only turn nasty when the rabble-rousers go to work. They certainly went out of their way

275

to help us find the right buses and trams in our voyages of exploration in Cairo.

18 APRIL

Our Ambassador, Sir Ralph Stevenson, and his wife Marjorie gave a splendid dinner party for twenty-two people. During the riots [*against the continued British occupation of the Canal Zone after the Second World War*] they had a dreadful time of anxiety and sorrow at the Embassy. Marjorie spent nearly twenty-four hours on the telephone trying to locate various English people, and Ralph had the heavy responsibility of deciding whether or not to summon British troops from the Canal Zone. Wisely, he did not, as they could never have arrived in time to save lives, and it would have meant a new period of occupation, trouble, bitterness and expense.

Farouk had done the right thing; he had the Egyptian army waiting in the desert, all ready to march through the streets. They were loyal, and saved a bad situation from becoming worse. He had wanted the riots to take place, to prove to his ministers that they could not manage without the British; however, it all went too fast and too far for him and ended in his abdication [*in 1952*]. Some wise Europeans left their flats and houses, with everything in them, and went to their Egyptian friends, who gave them tarbooshes [*traditional Egyptian fezzes*] and passed them from house to house through back doors, thus saving their lives.

About ten white men insisted on going to the Turf Club and playing billiards as usual; when the mob burst in they rushed to an upstairs bedroom and prepared to fight it out – all were slaughtered. Someone saw the Canadian Attaché, Boyer, at a window for a moment, his face streaming with blood. Then he disappeared. His wife waited for news all night long, then the British Secretary had to go and tell her he was dead.

The mob burned down Shepheard's Hotel and most of the shopping. quarter, which they looted. In the British Embassy all the Secretaries and Attachés were ex-commandos, so they had a good chance, and though the mob came to the gates yelling for blood they did not dare to attack. Majorie told us all this quite calmly.

Now all is love and friendship; everyone says that is the Egyptians' true nature. I hope it lasts.

SEPTEMBER

Back in England. The Duke and Duchess of Gloucester came for a drink and I had some Kenyans to meet them; Dolly and Jim [my beloved mother- and brother-in-law] supported us. It really was a success, and I think Princess Alice enjoyed seeing old friends. She has let me have a landscape painting of hers photographed for a new book (which has not yet been accepted anyway).

At the end of August we went to Baron's Court for James Hamilton's coming-of-age celebrations. We met the Duke of Kent and Princess Alexandra. He is a good-looking boy, with charming manners; but she is breathtaking, with large glowing, dark blue eyes, a heavenly figure and a very attractive expression.

On 8 August there was a dinner for 162 estate workers and their wives. Old Joe Duncan gave James a cheque and tried to make a speech, but halfway through he forgot his words; he and James stood side by side in an awful silence, while prompters all round the room hoarsely whispered the missing words. Joe, however, is rather deaf and did not hear them. Finally, he seemed to get into another gear, so to speak, and, skipping the main body of the speech, he reeled off the end and sat down to thunderous applause.

The last evening there was a smaller dance for family and friends in the Round Room at Baron's Court. Everyone looked happy and handsome; Princess Alexandra was easily the best and fastest girl-dancer there, as Simon Hornby was the best man dancer.

Flew back to Kenya on 21 September, and the contrast was *too* painful, though Nderit was heaven.

DECEMBER

Christmas at Wamba. This is a lost and lonely spot in the Samburu country, not very far from the Abyssinian border. We came here to avoid crackers and paper hats. The road from the Maralal turn-off is very rough indeed, but the gallant little Standard diesel made it safely. We left the smart and rather vulgar new Chev. under a tree at Maralal, seventy miles away. At our camp there are two huts and a kitchen place. We slept inside the huts because of the elephants, which are said to prowl around at night. Went for a stroll outside Wamba and met four elephants, as calm as cows, watching us to see we didn't come too near, but quite peaceful and happy. Two young Samburu boys were watching them too, and the Somali camel-herder explained, 'They have known each other since the boys were born.'

The Samburu still wear a long red cloth wrapped tightly round their slim, elegant bodies; they plaster their hair scarlet with mud, and wear it in a heavy fringe in front. Young men have long manes down their backs, and they carry spears and swords. They are smaller than the Masai, not so handsome, but more picturesque. The Masai call them Butterflies (probably because there are large numbers of butterflies in Samburu country) and despise them.

24 DECEMBER

Christmas Eve. We went for a long drive with a native game ranger and saw some distant elephants which, thank God, we stopped to look at – for the ranger wanted us to take a track which he said led back to Wamba. But the District Officer, Mr Hill, arrived while we were watching the elephants and the chiefs in his car said, 'Don't go down that road, it goes nowhere, you will be lost, and there is no water.' I asked the ranger why he wanted to kill us. He just gazed at his feet. Personally I'm sure there *had* been a road, but long ago, and he had simply forgotten.

25 DECEMBER

We went to church in the mission schoolroom; there was wire netting for windows. The service was taken in fluent Masai by two charming Ulster missionary ladies, one with a concertina. The congregation consisted of us, a dog and many Samburu and Turkana in plaits, skins, beads, red mud, ostrich feathers and carrying spears. There was a handful of Kikuyu in shirts and shorts, *à la* British bwana. Outside the wire netting was a crowd of tribesmen and a smartly decorated and well-groomed sheep wearing a collar. They would all have been in the church, but there simply was no room. We all sang, 'Hark the Herald Angels Sing' in Masai with gusto; the dog let out one shy bark.

We asked the Irish ladies about the elephants. They said, 'They are usually quite calm, but the wee boys will throw stones at them. Last week one elephant lost his temper and killed a village woman.'

We gave John and Auma a sheep and some shirts for Christmas; they gave us some very well cooked bits of meat. Sadly we left this enchanting place two days later. This is the best and happiest Christmas I have ever had.

1956

28 AUGUST

England again, and then the Channel Islands. The trip to Jersey is tiring, though I enjoyed seeing the little islands as we passed. They are so pretty, especially Herm – just a series of rocky outcrops.

29 AUGUST

In the morning the sun was shining, the air warm and soft, and I could hear the sounds of birds and the sea. I rang up Jo Leinster [*the Duchess of Leinster*], who asked me to lunch. Since Fitz left her she shares the Bedfords' home. This is a long, low, lovely old house, most beautifully done up with some good furniture from Woburn. The garden was full of handsome children – his, hers and theirs – all very good-looking, with beautiful manners. Jo, as beautiful as ever, presided like a goddess over her huge family. She has twenty-two grandchildren and one great-grandchild.

Jo is a dramatically beautiful person to whom dramatic things keep on happening. She is about seventy-five; tall and straight, a cloud of snow-white hair, vast blue eyes with long, dark, sham lashes, a flawless face, low voice, wonderful clothes and endless charm. Her daughters are Princess Joan Aly Khan, Lady Cadogan, Lady Ebury and the Duchess of Bedford. The Bedfords have handsome young Italian footmen who skip over the chairs in the garden and sing a little while they work. I've never seen such a handsome, elegant, decorative and devoted family, all based on Jo, like satellites moving round a planet. She took me to a small cocktail party and to dinner, so I had people to talk to at once.

I walked for hours up a steep sheep track and out onto wild rocky cliffs, with not a human being to be seen, only 'the sweep of the shining sea', gulls and skylarks. It was perfect. This Jersey sea is soft, streaky blue, and not a cold austerity grey like the Brighton variety.

1 SEPTEMBER

The Iberians, small, dark men from Africa retreating from the encroaching Sahara, came here, and there were Bronze Age people and Neanderthals before them. The Gauls drove them away – perhaps to Cornwall and southern Ireland – and settled in this fertile, delectable, soft-aired island.

The Romans came for a short time, and after they left Norman pirates raided for slaves. The Normans settled and farmed. When William conquered England the Channel Islands were perpetually fought over by England and France. Jerseymen were tough sailors, brave and loyal soldiers, and their hearts were English.

Charles II, while a fugitive, was loyally received here, and there was a long period of peace and prosperity for the island when the King had returned to England. French attacks took place now and then, but a really serious, planned invasion of twenty thousand men during the French Revolutionary Wars was frustrated by the wit of a Jersey man, Philippe Dauvergne, who kept sending help to the Royalist Chouans in Brittany, thus keeping the Republican forces too busy to invade the island.

2 SEPTEMBER

I moved from the hotel to the gardener's brand-new bungalow, very comfortable and all to myself – such a relief. Mr and Mrs Quemard could not take more trouble for me, and drove me all round the island. The north-east is empty and wild, and inland is a maze of tiny twisting lanes – built, they say, to bewilder Napoleon's invading army (which never came!). [*This is just the charming local legend, but not true. The good roads, however twisting, were made by Claud's uncle, Bingham, when he was Governor.*] During the war two young men escaped from France in a boat, carrying a pig's head on which they had written the word 'Hitler'. Reaching Jersey [*German-occupied*], they thought they were in England, and happily went ashore, one of them carrying the pig's head. In the dark they saw a soldier and hailed him, only to be arrested. The one with the pig's head was shot immediately; the other was sent to Germany as a slave prisoner.

3 SEPTEMBER

The Vice-President of the Royal Agricultural Society took me to visit two farms to see some very special Jersey cows. Tethered in lines and moved every two hours, they wear little coats and are pampered, cherished and spoilt. Lovely creatures, elegant aristocrats with fine bone, soft coats and thin skins. The farmers are almost all Norman, dating from the days of the Conquest. They speak English, French and Jersey French, and have kind hearts.

4 SEPTEMBER

I boarded the boat for St Malo, and then the train for Paris, where I am staying in Thérèse de Caraman-Chimay's tiny house at Chantilly.

9 SEPTEMBER

To Naples. The scenery on the journey was of such breathtaking beauty that I just lay on my bunk and gazed. Wooded mountains rising from the sea, ancient villages, craggy, Carrara-marble hills, flat, fertile plains with women in long dark skirts, bright red blouses and big straw hats working with the men, oxen in the carts, the aquamarine sea and misty islands.

At last, Naples; and there kind Paolo Langheim took me off to a drinks party at the house of Princess Carracioli Carrafa, and to see the illuminations and procession in honour of the Virgin. The wagons were decorated with sea horses, dolphins, huge shells in which reclined beautiful maidens in chiffon, also bands, pirates and fishermen. Each was pulled by a tractor which frequently broke down while the delighted crowds milled around and yelled – all quite orderly and very gay, though the romantic vision of the beautiful wagons was ruined.

After dinner for twenty at the Excelsior, we came to the island by boat over the starlit sea. The house is lovely – full of treasures and terraces, marble statues, china and old furniture. This is the complete idler's life; one does nothing but eat huge meals, swim and laze all day. There are vast lunch parties for the local gents – all dukes and princes, of course.

13 SEPTEMBER

Claudie arrived. We left kind Paolo and went to a hotel in Naples.

15 SEPTEMBER

For six hours we travelled by train through breathtaking scenery to the tiny station of Sastri, halfway to Sicily. At this primitive spot a taxi awaited us, and in half an hour we came to the Santavenere Hotel, Maratea. We were sad indeed to find no golden beaches, as we expected, but rocks jutting out of the sea. The hotel belongs to an enterprising northern Italian called Count Rivetti, who has an elegant wife and five small children. They have silky, pale yellow hair, fair skins and blue eyes and look like young canaries. Rivetti owns several woollen mills and employs six hundred people; he is certainly one of Italy's benefactors.

20 SEPTEMBER

Maratea has grown on us; we swim, eat lovely food and walk in the evenings. We climbed a thousand feet up the old walled, paved way called La Via Vecchia to the village of Maratea, where one or two grand houses with stone coats of arms crouch among the huddle of later ones, and the roofs are a medley of colours – red, brown, bronze, gold and burnt sienna. Pythagoras settled a little way south of here, among a colony of Greeks who came to live in southern Italy. Some probably lived in Maratea, for several place names are of Green origin.

22 SEPTEMBER

On our way back to Rome, we stopped at Paestum, once a fine, strong town behind a great wall. Excavations have revealed many temples; one lovely golden one dedicated to the goddess Hera lights up in the setting sun. But Paestum was inhabited long before she was a subject city of Rome. There is a Neolithic necropolis, and some of their primitive tools have survived. Greek settlers called Sybarites came in the seventh and sixth centuries BC, drove away the primitive inhabitants, then raised a walled city called Poseidonia. The river Sele and fertile soil helped to make the city strong and prosperous, and the people traded with local Italians and with the Etruscans.

Paestum remained Rome's faithful friend through good times and bad;

once she offered the mother city all the gold libation vessels (an offer declined with great gratitude), and another time she sent wheat-laden ships which tried to reach the hungry Romans beseiged in Taranto by Hannibal. Rome did not forget this; Paestum alone of all her subject cities was allowed to mint her own coins. The city flourished and her population grew.

But the mountains, de-forested for farming, became eroded; rain and earth rushed down to the plains, the rivers silted up, and in the swamps Anopheles mosquitoes bred. Malaria killed many of the people who, no more than the Victorians, knew that the disease was carried by mosquitoes. By the eight century AD only a handful of inhabitants were left, and a hundred years later their descendants, probably harried by Saracen slavers, abandoned Paestum and took to the hills. Forest trees and swamp rushes grew over the temples and houses and Paestum vanished. For centuries no one knew it had ever existed.

Then in the eighteenth century someone decided to clear away the jungle, and then began the slow discovering and reconstructing of this once strong and lovely city. Inside the walls, well protected by towers, there is a lot of unexplored land. On part of it grow descendants of those roses of which Virgil sang, celebrating their habit of flowering twice a year. In one of the temples were found several jars of honey, still soft and yellow after its centuries-long wait.

The museum contains a collection of exquisite statuettes in terracotta, stone and marble. The statuettes are mostly of the same period – beautiful ladies with their hair elaborately done as in the eighteenth century in France, some wearing veils, their features noble and delicate. Oddly enough, nearly all the statues were found in heaps in pits, all the various periods thrown in together; and no one can think why – except me. *I* think that, when the Saracens over-ran the place, they got tired of smashing the human likenesses as ordered by the Koran, so they shovelled all that were left into pits and covered them up. I told this to the guide. He was pleased and said I had given him something to tell the next tourists.

Paestum is a lost and lovely place, and not too full of tourists. We had a good lunch in the tiny station waiting room and returned, drooping, for a coffee and vermouth before catching the train to Salerno.

24 SEPTEMBER

We continued by train to Rome where dear Vera Mamélie took us out to dine in the Sacristy under the Pantheon – a strange place for a restaurant. The violinist is also a fortune-teller, and the musicians wander round the tables playing for you specifically; the clientele are all Roman, mostly artists. It is very small, very cheap and perfectly fascinating.

We left by South African Airways for Nairobi, arriving today, to receive a touching welcome from Ndarara, Auma, Kipoloi and John Shand, who had brought them down to meet us.

1957

12 MAY

We have decided to visit Istanbul.

During a gale the Turkish ship *Ankara* got into a Military Protected Zone harbour where the land was densely covered with coal heaps, and though we were all told to be there at 1 p.m. sharp it was impossible to get on board. We sat in the taxi eating bread and cheese with the driver for an hour or so, and then struggled across the dockside in the teeth of a strong, coal-dust-bearing storm, carrying our own luggage, and clambered on board.

Customs were very thorough searching all Greek and Turkish luggage (for drugs, obviously) but passed us through with smiles. The Istanbul Hilton fairly took our breath away with its vastness, modernity, fountains, bars, restaurants, sham graveyard in the patio, lifts (with music), servants, Turkish coffee girl in fancy dress – and prices. But everyone was very kind, and the two 'welcome cocktails' (on the house), the basket of flowers and basket of fruit which graced our rooms were all very pleasant.

There was a message from El Sayed Abu Bakir Ratib, a friend of our Ambassadress, Lady Bowker, and on the morning of the 9th he arrived in a grey Rolls Royce to fetch us. He is a tall, grey man with light blue eyes and an eyeglass; Egyptian, but luckily came to his house here a year ago and stayed. He takes the same view of Nasser [*the Suez Crisis had broken in 1956*] as we do, but does not think he will last much longer.

He took us to the Treasury in one of the Royal Palaces. Here are the pearl-studded, gold-embroidered thrones, the ropes of pearls, the diamond head ornaments, the carved jade, the jewel-covered robes, the crystal wands, the gold and precious stone jars and bottles and scent sprays, the exquisite china, the suits of gold chain mail and gold armour dotted with rubies and diamonds, the vast emeralds and jewels of the Sultans and Sultanas. It is an incredible collection, though all the Turkish work is slightly crude; but the French influence under the Empress Josephine's cousin, Sultana Aimée, brought finer things, including the pattern of the clasp on my necklace, bought by my grandfather, Sir Leopold Heath, when on leave in Constantinople during the Crimean War.

We stepped into the dark tunnel of the Spice Bazaar before having lunch at Pandili's, where *le patron* goes from table to table getting tiddlier and tiddlier. The food is Turkish, lavish and delicious; little Turkish strawberries are especially good.

In the evening, still with Abu Bakr, we crossed to Asia and went to the house of my dear old friend Jan Ostrorog, whom I have not seen since 1922. He was thunderstruck to see me again, but charming as ever, courteous, and delighted with Claud. The house is 150 years old, with a strong Venetian influence. It is right on the water, with curved verandahs and wrought-iron grilles leaning over the Bosphorus, Turkish divans, old French furniture and some lovely rugs. I was enraptured with it all, and so very happy to see dear Jan again.

Old as this nation is, the new Kemal Atatürk regime [*since 1923*] upset everything. Now the poorer people have got the worst of two worlds – modern vulgar architecture; Sunday (not Friday) picnics with radio, litter and footballs; dirty, shabby European clothes; no veils, but the mess and inefficiency of any Oriental town.

Abu Bakr, a word from whom opens all doors, arranged for us to see the gallery of the Aya Sophia Mosque, where the ninth- and tenth-century mosaics glow fresh and golden. The huge, dark, quiet mosque was rebuilt sometime after the Crusaders had looted and sacked the town (most of *them* were Germans!). It is now a museum. The frescoes and mosaics are magnificent, and it is interesting to see the rich, jewel-studded robes worn by the early Byzantines, and the way they made the angels and the grandest people in their mosaics fair-haired and blue-eyed.

The Mosque of Sultan Ahmet – the Blue Mosque – stole my heart. Lined from floor to dome with blue tiles in flower patterns, carpeted with fine red rugs, quiet and dark; the light coming through the blue glass windows makes a tender soft blue glow fall on the blue walls. No guide threatened our peace; we wandered round together.

Sultan Ahmet meant to surpass St Sophia in Bulgaria, and was so eager to finish his work that he used to go and help the labourers with his own hands. It has six minarets, which offended the dignitaries of Mecca, which has the only mosque in the world allowed this number, so to pacify them Ahmet built an extra one at Mecca, giving them seven.

Aya Sophia is vast and grand. When Justinian had completed it and entered in procession from the huge doors into the body of the mosque, he cried out in triumph: 'Oh Solomon, I have surpassed thee!' The Blue Mosque is half the size, but delicate and exquisite – easily my favourite.

We lunched excellently at a cheap little workmen's café and tried to get back in a bus, but it was jammed with people, so we finally forced our way into a *dolmus [shared]* taxi.

That evening Monsieur and Madame Nemli came to meet us. He very dark and oldish, she fair, tiny, lovely – a White Russian. Apparently she has grandchildren, though she looks thirty-five. Heavenly clothes and jewels.

We then walked out to the only street where the smart shops are. It looked like Bazaar Road in Nairobi but scruffier. I was exhausted, cross and miserable; we searched in vain for a café from which to watch the crowds. At last we forced our way into a hovel with filthy tables, where a Turkish brandy revived me. Unable to afford Hilton meal prices (accompanied by 'music' from a brass-lunged local Teddy Boy), we tramped the streets to an eating den where the meat was inedible. So we went to bed.

15 MAY

On Sunday Abu Bakr appeared in the grey Rolls and drove us along the Bosphorus shores to a hotel hanging over the water where we had a grand meal – though I, alas, had to stick to only meat and rice. Then we drove along the lovely road, past little old wooden Turkish houses with overhanging storeys and shuttered windows, past burdened donkeys and ponies and gay little red and blue carts, 'Surreys with fringes on top'; then empty, lovely country of low hills and shallow, grassy valleys, badly neglected and carrying very poor cattle and sheep, till we reached Kylios, on the shores of the Black Sea.

Back through beech forest to the *barrages*, the water supply for Istanbul, till we reached A.B.'s home. This is another lovely old house right on the water, looking at Asia, full of exquisite things exquisitely kept. Madame, Russian, is charm itself. She and her sister are both very fair and blue-eyed; their brother, a walking *Almanach de Gotha*, darker – all their friends mostly German, very correct and heel-clicking. In the garden is an early Christian well dedicated to St George, where good Christians in need of help say their prayers. A.B. found a box of candles there once, and his Greek gardener confessed that having received assistance from the saint in return for the promise of one candle, he felt he must not be mean, so bought him a box-full.

In the rooms are photos of the present claimant to the Egyptian throne – the eldest son of an older branch of the family than fat Farouk [*deposed in 1952 after General Neguib's* coup d'etat] – and his beautiful, dark-haired, turquoise-eyed Turkish princess wife. With a pair like that in power we would have no more trouble, and the poor fellaheen [*peasants*] would regain their lost livings.

Monday the 13th was again filled with beauty. Tamara Nemli took us out in her car, and we passed through streets lined by remarkably unshaven soldiery, who were waiting to see the President off. They may be brave, but discipline and drill they have none. We also saw the band, dressed in janissaries' uniform, with gay red and green coats, tall folded felt hats and long yellow boots.

The tiny and exquisite Mosque of Karié is now being repaired and will then be a museum. The gold frescoes, all in miniature, depict the Virgin's life; the colours are as fresh and glowing as if done last week, and not in

AD 500. All were covered in plaster but not destroyed by the Turks, and are now being carefully restored by an English expert.

We saw the vast underground cistern of Constantine's time, half full of water, where the huge pillars, a forest of tall shapes, have withstood earthquakes and fires for nearly two thousand years. In the silence we could only whisper to each other, but fled before a horde of vocal tourists and their uninhibited children.

The Mosque of Suleyman is a vast, silent dome. Here are buried the beautiful, cruel Russian Sultana Roxelana and, I think, Doge Dandolo. Though blind, he stayed here as an envoy from Venice determined to get good terms from the Turks for his countrymen, and here he died, much honoured by the Moslems for his courage and devotion.

On Tuesday A.B. surfaced again, since every 13th of the month he hibernates like a superstitious Christian, despite the fact that he is a devout Moslem. In his usual Open Sesame manner he took us to the Seraglio, which is closed to the public. The curator took us round, speaking good French. We saw the Golden Path, down which the odalisques were led to the Sultan's bed, and the Palace of the Sultana Valideha, the Veiled Crown, the Mother of the Sultan, the Palace of the Crowns of the Veiled Heads (all the lesser sultanas). After the Sultan the Sultan's mother was the most powerful person in the whole Ottoman Empire.

Every room is lined with tiles in blue, green or turquoise – each tile decorated with flowers or some delicate pattern. The doors are panelled flower paintings done by imported Italian artists. The Sultan's bed is in one room, behind gold-embroidered silk curtains; next is the servants' room, then the bathroom, a place of the greatest importance. The Sultan's beds are vast, about fifteen feet long and nine or ten feet wide. I suppose lovely young things lay across the Sultan's toes to keep them warm in winter, when this marble rabbit warren must have been like a deep-freeze.

In the entertainment room the male musicians were hidden in a balcony, and the hundreds of royal relations sat on cushions and divans while singers and dancers performed. The court provided every sort of person and attendant one could need, including a chief abortionist – a comforting presence. The women sometimes went out into the town, driving in heavily screened carriages, and they walked in the gardens, which were famous for their tulips (the national flower) and lilacs.

Some Sultanas became extremely powerful, like the Russian Roxelana and Aimée Dubucq de Riviery, a Martinique (Créole) beauty, cousin of Napoleon's wife Josephine. When the ship carrying her to her nobly born French fiancé was captured by pirates she was sold to the Bey of Algiers, and then sent by him as a present to the Sultan of Turkey. Here she was carefully trained in the Ecole d'Amour des Odalisques, displaced the favourite, had a son, and became one of the most influential people in the Empire. When Napoleon divorced Josephine, Aimée worked on her son's feelings (he was known as Mahmoud the Reformer) so that he made peace with Russia, thus releasing the Russian southern army, which was then able to march against La Grande Armée and help to break up the lines of troops during their retreat from Moscow. She never forgave Napoleon for divorcing Josephine and swore to do him all the harm she could. [*I wonder if Aimée ever knew that the last word Napoleon breathed as he was dying at St Helena was 'Josephine'!*]

A shopping trip in the bazaar (once the stables for the Sultan's two thousand horses) proved a failure, for the prices in these dens far surpasses London, Paris and Rome all put together.

19 MAY

On Wednesday we lunched in Jan Ostrorog's house and met a charming Turk, Emin Bey, who had been *en poste* in England. Left in wagon-lits for Ankara, where we have been asked to stay by the Bowkers at our Embassy. Jim and Elsa were kinder than words can say; and we had a good rest in our wonderfully comfortable rooms before meeting our host.

Mrs Pigott, on their staff, took us to the museum, which is full of Hittite statues of men and beasts – massive, inelegant but strong, and some showing very Egyptian influence. Ankara, once Angora, was captured and lived in by many peoples – Hittites, Phrygians, Greeks, Romans, Byzantines, Persians, Arabs, Seljuk Turks, the crusaders, Timur [*Tamerlaine*] and finally the Ottoman Turks. The last one to take refuge there was Atatürk, before the last Sultan left Turkey.

The walls round the old city are built of all the bits and pieces people could find. Statues lying on their sides, inscriptions upside down, bits of Roman brick, pedestals, pillars and plain rough stone. The streets are narrow and curving. The people I saw were dressed in the usual drab European clothes, except for four splendid Kurdish women wearing their proper dress in the gayest colours: turbans over tall red caps, blouses, long skirts and baggy trousers, all in the most brilliant colours.

We were taken round a milk pasteurizing plant and a stud farm. All the machinery was English, Swedish or Danish, beautifully kept, spotlessly clean, roaring away, making ice cream, powdered milk and pasteurized milk. Everything was explained in a mixture of English and German, and we understood most of it. At the farm are about fifty bull and heifer calves – Friesian, Jersey, Swiss and Hereford; very good ones, and all a present from America, under the 'Aid' programme. One heifer was dribbling. No one took any notice but me. I pointed it out, but probably nothing was done. [*I was sure this was foot and mouth. The Turks said several of these calves were ill – because of the altitude! Some had already died – what an appalling waste!*]

Jim says we have been obliged to agree to Nasser's terms because everyone else has, and if we went through the Canal by force, and on *our* terms, he might block it again. I can't see why we should not divert the Nile water. He also says the [*Anglo–French*] march on Suez was halted under threats from America and Russia – why did we not go straight on and be damned to them? Twenty-four hours more and we would have been in control and Nasser done for. A lost opportunity.

Meanwhile, by an act of God, a plot in the Egyptian Embassy at Jeddah to murder King Saud of Saudi Arabia was discovered. King Saud, Jordan, Iraq and Lebanon are now violently anti-Nasser and anti-Communism. This was a marvellous stroke of luck, and just what we needed.

21 MAY

We came in a good train to Kayseri, once Caesarea, where St Paul preached. This town is shoddy, dirty and smelly. The hotel is exceedingly primitive, and as no one speaks anything but Turkish we feel its name, Tourist Hotel, must be in honour of the solitary European-type WC beside the local, squatting one. The food is deplorable – in fact there is almost nothing to eat. Still, how good for the female form divine!

22 MAY

Inside the old walls there is a market where I found a pair of nice brass stirrups, worked all over. Terrible trouble over changing cheques; the tourist rate is L14.70 to the pound, but here one is only allowed 7. The curator of the museum, who speaks a little French, asked me the name of our Ambassador, and then rang up the bank manager and told us to return there. We did so and were sent on to a garage, where we got 10. Better than nothing – but what a joke to have cheques cashed by an unknown museum curator through a bank manager and a garage owner!

A taxi took us through wild, barren country to Urkub and then to Gorémé. We passed a troup of dark-faced gypsies with their ponies, all in turbans and long skirts, long black hair and slanting eyes.

Some workmen were playing pipes, and one was drumming, spinning round and round as in a trance, lifting his arms high above his head with every stroke of the drum. English Morris Dancing is said to have been brought to England by the crusaders, and the name to have been derived from 'Moorish dancing'.

At Gorémé we found ourselves in a strange, lunar landscape, where wind and rain, through aeons of years, have eroded the cliffs until they stand separate, each one like a craggy castle, spire or turret. One of the very earliest Christian refugee settlements lived here, in this safe, lost valley, growing grain in the pockets of soil, tunnelling and carving caves in the soft rock, touchingly decorating their little churches with crooked pillars and paintings of Christ, the Holy Family and the saints. These have nearly all been defaced and ruined by fanatical Moslem vandals, until there was hardly anything left of all the loving and careful work put into their paintings by those very early Christians. This strange valley is two or three miles long and all of a pale beige colour; everywhere there are caves and steps cut in the rock. Some of the caves are so high up that the inhabitants could only have reached their homes by climbing up ladders, or swarming down ropes from above.

In the valleys a few peasant families live happily and peacefully, growing corn and onions. They smiled and waved to me, and I wished we could camp here for a week. A man appeared on a donkey which he tied to a stone, and we understood each other perfectly, though each speaking our own language.

I said in English, 'What a nice donkey.'

He said in Turkish, 'Would you like a ride?'

'No, not in these clothes. What are you going to do?'

'I am going into my cave to eat my onions.' And then, with bows, we parted.

We wandered about this strange, lost valley, and finally had to return to filthy Kayseri, where we continue to starve.

26 MAY

The train journey back to Ankara took ten hours. We had a flask of whisky, and offered some to a Turk in our carriage. He accepted, to our surprise, then from under his shirt pulled a crucifix on a chain to show that he was a Christian and therefore could drink alcohol.

At last we had two square meals at the Cihan Palace Hotel in Ankara. It was not too bad, but still pretty primitive. It is some days since we had baths.

Arose about six and left at nine by air for Izmir. A Dakota with a very rough port engine, all-Turkish crew, and simply dreadful weather. Belts fastened all the time, clouds, turbulence, mountains over and round which we scraped, just finding a hole in the clouds through which to nip down to earth at Korya. This is practically the bumpiest flight I have ever had, and even the brave Claud pronounced it 'extremely unpleasant'.

Izmir airport was a very welcome sight, and the pilot gave us a beautifully smooth landing. All here is green, fertile, wooded, gentle and quite lovely. They grow vines, barley, wheat, olives and rear nice fat cattle, sheep and even rather woolly-coated camels, to my great joy. It is so lovely here: the air so soft, the sea so blue, the mountains standing guardian round the bay. I would like to stay for a while and explore the countryside.

The Izmir Palace Hotel was full, but we got a room at the Kordon (not yet glorified with the name of Palace). Alas for my dreams of a private bath! Turks who design large and pretentious hotels have no idea of hygiene or comfort. In the whole of this large place there is one solitary bathroom, and on our floor one European and one Turkish WC. The former had the men's arrangements in front of it, so even if you got in the chances are you would never get out without passing several busy Americans. I therefore went native and stuck to the Turkish one. Of course the paper ran out, and when I asked the maid for more all she said was: *'Yok' [No]*. We had a shower in our room, but never got at the bath at all. It is now a week and a day since our last bath.

A spitting, hesitating *dolmus* taxi finally got us to Bergama sixty miles away. We went through some heavenly country, green, wild and empty, lying along the coast between the sea and the hills. A place to dream of. A caravan of gypsies passed us, with people riding ponies and leading a string of camels, haughty and hairy, but pathetically scared of the cars which swooped past their flanks, as near as possible without actually hitting them, just in order to frighten them – and did so.

In the Bergama Museum is a collection of very beautiful and ornate native dresses, long robes covered in gold and silver embroidery, and hats with rows of gold coins (the side ones meaning love of all mankind, the large centre one meaning God, the master of all). The mountain tribes still wear these lovely garments for weddings and special events.

A beautiful child of twelve took us in a taxi to the ruins of Aesculapius, a doctor-god of early Greek times, and father of Hygeia (hence hygiene). The healing here was done with sun baths, contemplation and trances (hypnotism?), and the water of certain springs, which patients drank and bathed in. The boy, quite unselfconscious and full of charm, showed us round and explained everything in a certain sort of English.

'Here is sunny place. Here is dream house. Here is good water – you drink.' In the museum he proudly showed us a tiny jar with a minute spout. 'You see, mister? Here is baby's urinal.' There was utter peace and silence here among the ancient pillars and carvings, the long tunnel to the dream house, the marble paving and the old walls. A donkey browsed contentedly, the mountains stood around, and the air was soft. No wonder people got healed.

The return journey was expensive and hair-raising. Our driver went straight at two small boys on bicycles and missed them by a whisker. The car spat and staggered along but actually got us to the hotel, very tired and pretty hungry.

We took the train to Ephesus, as the buses are so complicated. The station is called Seljuk, and was once an important halting place for Seljuk Turks during their invasions of this country. How appalling they must have appeared to the gentle and civilized Greeks; swarthy men with pointed steel helmets, glaring black Mongolian eyes and shaggy ponies; wild, dark women wearing trousers; and the long-necked, long-haired, shaggy camels carrying food and tents and baggage.

At Ephesus the oldest part of all was the temple to Artemis, whose statue, with twenty-two breasts, stands in the museum. Her temple was magnificent – one of the seven wonders of the world; vast and ornate, a forest of pillars and statues, huge flights of steps all round. It was destroyed and rebuilt seven times and finally fell into ruins, when the stones were taken away to build other things and the earth silted over it.

Here St Paul preached, infuriating the priests and the artisans who made and sold little silver images of Diana of the Ephesians. St Paul must have seemed a pestilential little man, cantankerous, self-righteous and dictatorial; ruining everyone's trade and *joie de vivre*. They finally put him in prison, and then he left the country; but his words were wise, they spread, and Christianity took root.

The town grew as the sea receded; finally the whole lovely bay was surrounded by marble houses, temples, avenues, shops and theatres – all decorated with statues, carved garlands of flowers and engraved tablets (one very touching one was erected to a man and his wife by their two freed slaves). It must have been one of the most beautiful cities in the world, far surpassing anything produced in this stark modern age. How wonderful it would be if just one of these exquisite cities could be rebuilt, complete, and kept intact for people to look at.

The Virgin Mary is said to have been brought here by St John, Christ's favourite disciple, who was told to look after her by Him while He was dying on the cross. Christians were being persecuted by the Jews, some were murdered and some fled, and the Virgin (who was also said to have visited the Camargue, landing at Sainte Maries de la Mer) came here and lived here until she died.

The Seven Sleepers (young Christians) entered their cave here, refusing to take part in some pagan ceremonies, and slept for 309 years, according to Moslem legend. When they emerged a Christian king reigned, and their story was proof of the resurrection after death.

As time went on the river Meander, bringing earth with it, silted up the bay so that big ships could no longer anchor at the port. The sea drew back, and left a marshy, muddy plain where anopheles mosquitoes bred. People began to die of malaria, for which they knew no cure, and trade had almost ceased since the harbour was lost.

As at Paestum the survivors left the dying city and the earth took over, covering everything with mounds, grass and weeds. Centuries later the Seljuk Turks robbed the remaining ruins of the building stone they wanted for their barns and cottages. And that was the end of Ephesus.

31 MAY

Back in Istanbul. Everyone has been so kind, warm-hearted and hospitable. Abu Bakr took us to the ceremony of the taking of the wall. The story is that during the siege of Constantinople in 1453 a solitary Turkish soldier, using his dagger and sword as aids, climbed up the outside of the encircling wall and raised the Turkish flag. The Byzantine guardians of the gate saw the flag, thought a breech had been made and rushed to the spot. They killed the soldier instantly, but meanwhile the Turkish army stormed through the undefended gate and thus was Constaninople lost for ever to the Byzantine Christians.

The ceremony today presented its usual mélange of the rather touchingly naïve and the picturesque. On top of the wall, guarding a flag, stood two Turkish warriors with raised scimitars. They wore brass helmets and fifteenth-century uniforms. Beside them, ruining the picture, stood a scruffy old man in a cloth cap. No one told him to 'move on'.

The janissaries' band and soldiers were dressed as in the sixteenth century with red turbans and tall folded white cloth caps, rather Tibetan-looking. They wore baggy trousers, long crimson or green coats, and cummerbunds with daggers thrust through them. As the band played, some lifted their brass staves crowned with crescents in time with the music while some sang; the soldiers stood unmoving. At the end their leader stepped forward and sang a prayer for victory or death in a quavering voice like a muezzin's call. Then all the soldiers called together: 'Allah! Allah! Allah! Allah!' while the drums sounded a strong, long roll. This was their prayer and chant before a charge. It must have been quite impressive and alarming to the opposing or besieged armies.

We were collected early by Emin Bey and taken for a boat trip round the islands. He told us that all the conquerors have left their traces (*he* looks like a Hittite sculpture), that the Seljuk Turks came from Turkestan in a great wave, seeking more grass and water than their barren land provided, and that some centuries after them came the Ottoman Turks. The story is that an Ottoman Sultan had four sons, who had to travel to earn their fortunes, and land, for themselves. One, with his men, was riding across a fertile plain when he saw two armies fighting; the smaller one was being beaten and driven back, though still fighting bravely. He chivalrously rode to the help of the smaller force and turned the tide of battle. When the fight was over he found he had been helping a small party of Seljuk Turks, whose grateful Sultan gave him the land on which they stood, with its town of Konya. Thus were the Seljuk Turks established in Anatolia.

The islands lie like emeralds on a sapphire bed, some quite bare, some forested, with houses clustering near the sea and thick pine forests above. On Prinkipo, the Princes Island, it used to be the custom to incarcerate for life all the Byzantine princes except the direct heir, to prevent them claiming the throne.

1 JUNE

Arose at 6 a.m., took one last look at the gleaming Bosphorus and the spires and domes rising from the mists, and began the dreary, exhausting flight to

England. Athens–Rome–London; travelling for eleven hours, cramped in third-class seats, with a terrible cold.

1 SEPTEMBER

Claudie and I had the usual heavenly time in England. Dolly is failing; her speech is blurred and her mind slips, but she adores having us so close. We went to a lovely evening party at the Astors'; an Irish Guards cocktail party, graced by the Queen; the Royal Show at Norwich; and my dance, which I gave at the Savoy and which was great fun.

We left on 27 August and came to Jersey. I have spent every spare minute with Dolly, who *never* asks for help, but I know what her inner loneliness must be like. C. is returning to her for a week, but meanwhile I am seeing if he likes Jersey. He went to meet his Bedford cousins. C. likes it very much, but it is no place to live except for the very young, to play on the sands, or for the very old, to die in peace. It is a sweet and happy island, and I especially like the stone seats on the old chimneypots, on which travelling witches can sit and rest so that they do not have to come into the house.

3 SEPTEMBER

I left Claudie and flew by Jersey Airlines to Paris, changing to Pan-American for Rome. We were all strapped in, while the radio played soothing music, when the steward said a brake had gone wrong and would we all get out again and wait for two hours. Finally we took to the air, leaving behind the dense cloud, which had followed us from Jersey, and flew into the sun, to Rome, whence by train to Civitavecchia. Two hours' wait before embarking – tired, hungry, homesick and cold. But once on board a drink and a tiny meal and the sight of the moon's great silver watery path cheered me up. Next day at Olbia in Sardinia I had been promised Vera Mameli's car to meet me, but found nothing, so, helped by the kind station master I caught a train for Macomer.

In this nice country your boat ticket covers porters' tips, so they vanished when they saw me escorted by the station master, who installed me first-class on a second-class ticket – obviously a man with the right ideas. Three and a half hours later I disembarked at Macomer, was met by a kind vet. of Vera's and drove the twelve miles to her house.

Vera is a remarkable person, full of drive, kindness, conceit, honour, charity, beauty and wit – such a strange mixture. A terrific talker and mimic, waving her arms, her fork, seizing the chicken in her fingers and tearing it apart, swotting flies onto the bread, dominating the conversation and the countryside. The local people either adore or fear her – or both.

7 SEPTEMBER

I had a long ride with Giorgio, the Ambassador, who led me through tearing bushes to a mountaintop. On the way we met a party of men riding – some on good horses and some on strong bullocks; most picturesque and handsome they looked. The people up here, living between three thousand and four thousand feet, are blonder and more vigorous than the dark-faced, seashore ones who probably have some Arab blood. The view from the top was terrific – a vast plain ending in steep mountains. Up here was buried Vera's beloved younger brother Gerald, who was found dead beside his motorbike on the road to Sassari. He had a splendid funeral – his coffin drawn by six strong bullocks – but a pagan ceremony, with no priest to bless his grave. Everyone turned out to mourn him – he was so young, handsome and well loved. And a few days later they dug open the grave searching for gold in his teeth and a gold signet ring. The plundering continued for some years, until one dark night Vera removed the body and put it under the altar in her tiny church.

9 SEPTEMBER

Giorgio and I had another long ride, meeting three men whom he thought at first might be *banditti*; they did not run away, but stood up to greet us. He always goes armed; it's quite like old times in Kenya. He showed me a place on the road where they had put a road block to ambush him, but he saw it from some way off, stopped and drew his .45 revolver. They ran away behind the wall, led by a famous bandit who was shot and killed by the carabinieri two days later.

14 SEPTEMBER

After two happy days in Rome we reached Nairobi. Ndarara, Korau and Shand met us; the two Masai showing their lovely manners and Ndarara kissing my hand.

1958

19 JANUARY

Claud's mother was dying and he flew home. Katie Gethin and I did the fences, troughs, pipes, the steers, weaners and milk cows, nearly always riding. We sold very little, but kept expenses down and at last got the farm tidy again. Katie was wonderful and a tremendous help.

Left: Ruy Blas, the Nderit stallion,
sired by the Derby winner, El Cid

Below: Kibiri, the Nderit bull

Left: A beast from the
White Herd at Nderit

A Masai Moran surveys the plain

Above: Masai boy, with vulture-feather pigtail

Right: Another Masai boy in an ostrich-feather headdress

Below: A Masai family at Nderit. Mungani, in the centre, was Genesta's maid

Brave old
elephant at
Treetops

The hippo pool at Nderit

Right: Lord and Lady Claud Hamilton at
the Coronation

Lord Claud Hamilton

Right: Lord and Lady Claud Hamilton at
the Coronation

Genesta meets H.M. the Queen at a charity premiere

Dolly died very peacefully last night, with her children round her. Her last fling was to see Ulster beat Italy at football, on TV. This made her very happy.

25 FEBRUARY

Claud came home safely, worn out; and so was I with the strain.

MARCH

Loderisms [*the elderly English housekeeper at Muthaiga Club*] overheard there. 'In my young days titled ladies didn't 'ave bugs. That there lady says she's got bugs in 'er bedroom. She must 'ave brought them with 'er.

'That there Mrs —— making all that fuss over 'er bits and pieces being stolen. Now if they'd been *my* bits what I 'as from the Royals there would've been something in it.'

'Where's that there Mwangi? 'E wasn't 'ere *jana [yesterday]* and 'e isn't 'ere *leo [today]* ; oh there you are Mwangi, get on with your *kasi [work]*.'

'If any of you boys wants to play about with them there Mau Mau you comes and asks me *rusa [permission]* first.'

'Look at that there floor all bloody dirty. 'Ow many times 'ave I told you to *piga [hit]* the bloody thing?'

8 MAY

Left for Beirut; a faultless flight over a glassy sea.

13 MAY

We went to the fantastic house of Madame Linda Sursock, the Grande Dame of Beirut, a most decorative lady beautifully dressed in wide skirts and heavy jewels. The priceless carpets, the fountains in the main rooms full of flower heads, the place where the slaves danced and sang, below the step, above which 'the family' sat in splendour, the hubble-bubble smoking room into which no one might enter unless in Arab dress, the magnificent purple and red, gold-encrusted robes of the Arab queens, and the lovely collection of coloured glass – all make this house a perfect museum and a thing of beauty.

Madame Farjeallah drove us to ancient Sidon [*Saida*] (great disappointment, no old buildings left and only tatty new ones standing) and then up the mountains to the village of Djoun, where half an hour's walk brought us to the crumbling home of Lady Hester Stanhope. Here, in the eighteenth century, she lived – feared, loved, hated and admired – for twenty years; here too she died, and her lonely little grave stands under the olive trees.

She had great influence, helped refugees from the Egyptian invasion, defied the Egyptian conquerors, fought her Emir neighbour, led a punitive expedition against bandits, and made her mark in Arab history as other brave, eccentric English women have done. She thought she was engaged to Sir John Moore of Corunna, whose first cousin, Anne Dunbar of Durn, was my great-grandmother. Lady Hester never married. She chose this place with its staggering view of mountains and sea, and lived here with her English maid and two devoted Arab servants, the great-grandson of one of whom lives in the village now. She died very poor and lonely, and now her home is in ruins. When I was very young I knew a beautiful old lady living near Anstie. She was Lady Hester Carew, and had been named after her godmother, Lady Hester Stanhope . . .

There are anti-President Chamoun riots going on – bombs, shooting, town full of soldiers, doctors and nurses waiting hopefully for custom, pipeline at Tripoli cut, lots of corpses there and some at Sidon. Americans all staying indoors on orders from their Embassy (but ours doesn't bother about *us*!) and not the faintest chance of getting to the country. So I suppose we must leave Lebanon, as there's no point wasting time and money here and not seeing anything. I don't mind being hotel-bound, though Claud does. People tell us to keep off the streets, as no one loves us English just now, and an angry crowd might wreck our taxi or be careless with bombs (they tend to do this).

14 MAY

We went to tea with Madame Chamoun at the Presidency yesterday, and found her very anxious for her husband and worried, but laughing. I met her during the war, in London; then she had flowing brown hair and large violet eyes and looked about sixteen. Now her hair is going grey and she looks years older, but she is still very beautiful. The Chamouns are heavily guarded, with soldiers at both ends of their barricaded street, the house full of soldiers, plain-clothes men, and one devoted, anxious, suspicious dog. In that uncanny sense that dogs have, he knew there was danger. The President came in for a moment, looking extremely well and determined, and we also met his very pro-Western Foreign Minister, Dr Charles Malik.

The opposition is Arab – pro, and probably paid by, Nasser and Russia. They want at all costs to get rid of Chamoun, who has done *everything* for this country and is completely pro-West.

The respectable shopkeepers, bank officials, taxi drivers and hotel people are all behind him, but there is a curious division in the upper classes, some of whom seem to have turned against him, just as many of ours turned against Eden over Suez. They say his term of office has expired and he means to stay on at all costs. But what Chamoun says is that he wants to see his successor chosen by the people, before he decides whether to stand again or not. The law is that he cannot, but laws can be altered.

The situation gets worse – ten killed here yesterday, and more in Tripoli. All the country roads are shut except the one by Byblos, and at Beit-ed-Deen two vendetta families have seized the opportunity to renew their private war. Many Syrians and Egyptians have been caught here with bombs and guns. Yesterday the Belgian Consul-General at Damascus was caught at the frontier post with his car full of arms and one big bomb, Madame Chamoun told us; he was arrested. Soon after that men came down from the mountains, murdered five Customs people, abducted one and burnt the place down before the army arrived to rescue them. Poor people! One was a typist, another the office boy.

Gangs of teenage thugs roam the Beirut streets, throwing bombs when they can. They burnt the American Library and attacked the University, but were driven off by troops who are extremely loyal to Chamoun.

The Chamouns are two very brave people. They have been living in this tension ever since the Suez Crisis, when the President kept the country on our side. What started this present trouble was the murder of a Communist newspaper owner, who was then given a gangster's funeral, and whose death was used as an excuse for riots. The opposition, mainly Arab, say that they are not Communists but only want to 'save their countrymen from the wholesale massacres being inflicted on them by government troops', etc. etc. etc. – an obvious lie. The troops seem very well disciplined and very patient and calm.

We walk about, quite unmolested, but have to be in by 8 p.m. because of the curfew. The nights are quiet, except for the odd shots and bombs; it is nice to be without the eternal noises of car horns.

15 MAY

One of the President's secretaries, having investigated, told us that the road to Byblos is quite safe, so off we went in a taxi along the coast. All the villages are modernistic, dirty, flimsy and unattractive, but the lovely sea is beside you all the way.

Byblos is said to be seven thousand years old, dating from pre-Phoenician times. It has seven walls and seven churches. There is a crusader castle, from whose tower you look down on the town spread out before you, the temples, shops and fortifications, and the semi-circle of elegant pillars brought all the way from Aswan, backed by oleanders in full bloom framing the sea.

Byblos was a rich, strong city, decorated by the Egyptians, Greeks and Romans. After Osiris was murdered by Seth, his brother, so the story goes, his coffin was set afloat. It grounded at Byblos and was buried under a bush. Later, grown into a tree, it was cut down and made into a column to support the roof of the King's palace. Isis, Osiris's lover-sister, became a swallow, and flew about desperately seeking him. Her love finally brought him back to earth, and this celebrated the cycle of the seasons. Osiris and Adonis were the same person, and Byblos claimed the tomb.

The town became a Roman centre, then a Christian bishopric. It was taken by the Moslems, retaken by the crusaders and held for eighty-three years until ceded to the Saracens as part of a ransom for a prisoner. The crusaders had built quite a big church, whose baptistry, of finely decorated pillars under a dome, stands outside the present church. It is moving to look at the strong walls and think of all they have seen. Despite Moslem conquests the Christian element has remained: Byblos people are mostly Christians who dislike the Arabs and like the Jews. They are gentle, law-abiding, and keep themselves apart from political troubles.

Madame Linda Sursock asked us to lunch; there were about twenty people, all anxious, but brave and cheerful. I sat next to the Italian Ambassador and there was a good deal of political chatter. More bombs had been thrown, and people killed, in the Place des Canous just before we got there; it was cordoned off. The private servants and chauffeurs are loyal and brave; though in some danger all the time, they never let their people down. The Chamoun servants seemed touchingly devoted and disciplined, dressed in smart white uniforms and behaving just as if they'd no idea the whole place might be blown up any minute.

Strangers are infiltrating from Syria all the time, coming down the coast by boat and over the mountain passes. They are stopped and frisked and have their papers checked; most of them have bombs and arms, and the prisons and hospitals are full. We now know that the poor Customs house men who were attacked and over-run by the five hundred men from the hills were not shot, as one had hoped, but hacked limb from limb and finally disembowelled.

A certain European consul was arrested and gave up after two slaps from his captors, saying he had made sixty-three trips bringing arms in, at the rate of five thousand pounds a time. He tried to pretend this last lot belonged to his chauffeur, who had told him it was a box of antiquities to sell in Beirut and who had gone to see friends overnight. I've never heard of a more monstrous betrayal of diplomatic privilege; apparently he did the same thing in Nicaragua.

Madame Sursock gave me a lovely pair of Lebanese ear-rings; I was thrilled and very touched. Everyone now says Chamoun must hold out, or it is the end for all of them.

20 MAY

We came to Rome – an excellent flight with Alitalia – and everyone was intensely kind and hospitable.

22 MAY

By train and boat to Palermo in Sicily, where we stayed at first in a frightful place, the Villa Lincoln – no lift, no telephone, no hot bath, almost no furniture but plenty of smells. Moved next day and then went up the mountains in a bus to a village called Monreale. This is utterly ancient, and the cathedral is vast, magnificent, full of gold frescoes, with a white and pink marble floor. It was built during the prosperous Norman occupation of the island.

Even more lovely than the cathedral is the cloister garden, full of roses, aloes, palm trees and tropical plants, surrounded by rows of delicate pillars, some ornamented with carved stonework and some with inlaid gold mosaics. The peace and beauty of this enchanted place was all the more striking in contrast with the dirt and noise of the streets outside.

There was a simply splendid family row going on in a slum outside our hotel windows – two women screeching at each other and flinging their arms about, while from a building there slowly emerged first a sad and sheepish-looking young woman with a small case and a small boy, and then a young man with a motorbike, carrying a sack and with tears on his cheeks. Someone said it was the wives of two brothers at each other's throats – something about clothes! Finally two policemen appeared and everyone calmed down.

We saw the cathedral of Palermo, a splendid building full of tall grey marble pillars with ornate capitals. It would have been lovely, but was ruined by the little guides darting about saying, ' 'Allo – 'Allo,' and trying to show one round.

In a cramped and dreadful train to Agrigento, once a great and beautiful city, now a heap of semi-skyscrapers, dirt and refuse, pretentious and unbearably noisy. But the Valley of Temples is truly beautiful, with four great temples in a stately row along a ridge, their tall columns stripped of their marble and now a soft gold colour. In its richest period, with the valley full of Greco-Roman houses with their pediments and pillars, it must have been a wonderful place. The valley is planted with almond and orange trees, carefully looked after by the industrious peasants. We had a blissful half hour by the sea, then returned to Palermo.

1 JUNE

A fifty-four-hour journey by train brought us to London.

16 AUGUST

Fearful tragedy has struck Iraq, where the Nasser-bribed mob broke into the Palace and murdered everyone they found, while treacherous army officers shot to death the King, the Crown Prince and every member of the royal family they saw – old and young, women, children and babies. I did not like or trust the Iraqis when I was riding through their country. All the world governments have of course been obliged to acknowledge the new regime – but that does not mean that one will ever forget. The Russians and Nasser, who engineered the murders, were openly delighted.

King Hussein of Jordan, a very brave young man, has frustrated several attempted *coups*; he is greatly encouraged by his mother. His father is mad, and often tried to kill the Queen, so she is used to danger. Hussein has his faults; he sent away his pretty, if bossy, young wife Dina, refused her a royal title and kept her baby away from her. Some years ago he curtly dismissed General Glubb, after twenty years' faithful service, and we withdrew our troops. [*In 1939 Glubb Pasha formed the Arab Legion, a force aimed at policing Transjordan, which had become a buffer state in the Middle East.*] He has had nothing but worry and danger ever since, and recently had to ask us for help, so we sent in our paratroops while the Americans poured thousands of soldiers into Lebanon to protect Chamoun and prevent another Iraqi episode. Massed battleships, troops ashore in Dux, heavy armour, tanks and guns; they certainly saved the situation, but very expensively.

18 AUGUST

We left our charming little London flat and went by train to Venice. Such a lovely journey, through the beautiful Alps and beside Lake Garda.

24 AUGUST

Had several happy days here in the most beautiful city in the world. We met a strange, colossal woman, who in Venice goes by her name from her first marriage, and is a Princess. She has a young man (secretary?) with her, passing as American, who says he was at Harvard. [*Some years later they married – it was not a success.*] She lent us her gondola, one of the most beautiful in Venice, and we visited again the church of S. Giorgio degli Schiavoni with its charming Carpaccio pictures of St George and his tame lion, who adored him. After St George died the lion sat howling and finally died of grief. We also saw S. Maria Giusitu, with its lace-like marble and frescoes inside. They once owned the lovely little palace opposite the Grand Hotel, but she swears the ghosts made them leave.

31 AUGUST

Flew to Istanbul, where we stay with Abu Bakr. Poor Turkey is running down financially, but the government, instead of saving what money they have, flings it away. They are making a vast, wide highway, and from the aerodrome a blaze of street lamps leads across the empty desert but fizzles out before reaching the town. Imported goods are very hard to find and madly expensive.

3 SEPTEMBER

Left by ship for Yalova on the Asian side – a very smooth and pleasant crossing of two and a half hours. At Yalova I scouted round and found a café for lunch, and then we got into a packed bus for Bursa. Lovely scenery with rolling hills and distant mountains, wild and lonely. The man next to Claud waited to see us safely into a cab for the Cilic Palace Hotel – typical Turkish good manners. The hotel is large and well planned; we have a bathroom and a balcony, but have to force the staff to clean the loo properly. They were utterly willing, but just hadn't thought. What dreary evenings the Turks have, with no bar and no drinks; they sit at small tables drinking water and talking endlessly, all looking the picture of gloom.

Today we saw the town. Lovely Green Mosque, lined with turquoise-coloured tiles, dating from 1421. It was damaged in an earthquake but restored by a French-trained architect in the nineteenth century. In the Sultans' tombs their turbans rest on their headstones; three or four are buried in one mausoleum. The Sultan Mohammed II had the charming wish that the rain should fall on his grave, so there is an opening in the top of the cupola.

The bazaar here was nearly all burnt last Sunday, but no one was in it. We watched a frightened and bewildered cat trying to go back into its charred home; it gave up at last and wandered away.

Bursa is in a most lovely situation, beneath Mount Olympus – Ulu Dag – named by homesick Byzantines after their Greek mountain. It is at the head of a fertile, wooded valley. They make a lot of rather bad silk; it is real silkworm silk, but rough and coarse.

The town is any age. One legend says that Hannibal, beaten in battle, was befriended by King Prusa; he built and named the town in his honour, and later committed suicide and was buried here. It had the usual influx from Byzantium, Greece and Turkestan, but all their traces have gone except for one or two capitals, upside down and used to build walls. Mountains stand round three sides of the valley, and Ulu Dag itself was once infested by bandits. We wanted to go up there, but the weather is so beastly, with rain and fog, that it is not worth it.

When we returned to Istanbul the clouds were low and thick, and it rained and rained. So we cancelled our trip to Antalya, and instantly the weather changed. Now we have probably missed the only chance of going to that lovely place, and I'll never forgive myself.

301

9 SEPTEMBER

One day the dining room at the Parc Hotel was overflowing with people on a cruise in an Italian ship. We noticed near us a lovely woman with a 'china' complexion, very gay and chatty, about forty years old; a horsey-type man in a high scarf; and an incredible English lady with a leathery skin and a strange hat. Suddenly one woman stared at us, and then came over – it was Dodie Smith! The others turned out to be Lady Diana Cooper (we had thought this person looked like her, but decided she was much too young), Stuart Perowne, who had given my book *In the Wake of Da Gama* such a good review, and Rose Macaulay, the famous author. They had been right round the Black Sea, and had had a great welcome in Odessa.

1959

19 FEBRUARY

We left by air for Aden.

24 FEBRUARY

Flew to Mukieras in Arabia, starting with some difficulty owing to a sick aeroplane, a passenger trying to enter Aden with no permit, and two unaccounted for people in our plane, who hadn't paid but had got on board. The Arab passengers were very wild, handsome and strange to look at, with aquiline features, fierce eyes and large turbans. They carried loaded rifles – against the rules, but the pilot said it was safer to leave them so than try to unload them; beautifully jewelled, curved daggers; bundles and boxes and carpets.

We started an hour late and reached Loda, at the foot of a three-thousand-foot escarpment. Here more entertainment, for three waiting British Political Officers intended embarking, but we were found to be overweight anyhow, so after a heated argument between the intending passengers and the pilot one was left behind. Now we flew over some rather frightening pointed hills, which seemed to be clawing up at us, black and menacing. On our right rose the jagged escarpment. The first attempt to gain enough altitude failed and we made a second circuit, which brought us triumphantly soaring over the top of the mountain to land at Mukieras.

Here we were met by Colonel de Butz and an officer, the Sultan and the Naib. There were fierce-looking tribesmen on all sides, wearing short *shukas* like kilts to their knees, with long curly hair, bandoliers, guns and daggers. The Sultan and his brother the Naib are both tough fire-eaters; the Naib rather overdoes things, trailing his coat at the Yemeni and provoking battles at the drop of a hat. He is a small, handsome man, full of humour, personality and charm, with a very pretty wife whom I visited and who gave me a head shawl, a tray and a jar of woven straw. The Sultan had been in London, staying at the Regent Palace Hotel. Trying to make conversation, we said, 'Were you all right there? Did they look after you well? It is a fine big hotel.'

'Not bad,' said the Sultan, 'but too near the *suk' [bazaar, i.e. Soho]*.

After a battle the Yemeni send their wounded over to us to go to hospital, and we fly them down to Aden in the most gentlemanly way. When restored to health, they return to the Yemen to fight us. I'm sure they think we are mad. They come to Mukieras market weekly, bringing produce for sale.

After tea with the Sultan, Colonel de Butz took us to the lookout post within a few yards of the border. The Yemen is a wild, desolate land which no sensible person would dream of fighting for, but the Yemeni Sultan has an obsession to own Aden – no less – and all these people adore fighting anyway. [*Some years later we gave him Aden and all that piece of land.*] We could see their town of Beidan not far away, where six Russian 'advisers' live, and where they keep some of their army. An emerald jeep painted with scarlet flowers passed us in the dusk *en route* to Beidan, full of potential enemies; we all waved to each other. Supper party with the Sultan. There are fifty British troops here and a hundred or so levies; all the British are volunteers, very much on their toes and loving it. They are National Service boys, very keen and well trained.

We stayed in the house of Jewah Hassan Ali, very, very cold; bathroom full of gadgets, none of which work. On the airport stood the emerald jeep, having brought passengers from Yemen for Aden – never was there such a war! It is very cold up here (7500 feet) at dawn, but we took off and shot 'downhill' to Aden, arriving in about half an hour with no delays *en route*. Here we stayed with my cousins Maurice and Mary Heath; everything is so clean and civilized in Aden.

Maurice has a vast command – air forces from Aden to southern Tanganyika to Muscat to Yemen to Sudan; and land-sea-air forces for the whole Arabian peninsula. He is quite young for this huge post. Every now and then the Heaths throw up one spectacular person – Father was one, Maurice another.

An amusing man turned up for dinner – Bernard Ferguson, ex-soldier, now journalist, knows everyone. I did not tell him what the Naib said at Mukieras, that there were ninety-seven extra men and four 'cannon' in Beidan, but he was coming to Mukalla with us, and then didn't, so he may have heard something. Later the Sultan of Muscat refused him permission to visit Muscat. He was rather put out when he heard we had got ours.

25 FEBRUARY

Over the sea to Mukalla – a three-hour flight in a plane full of smoking, retching Arabs. The town of tall white houses curves round a dark blue, satin-watered bay with stark, jagged mountains behind. At Riyadh we were met by the British Resident, Mr McIntosh – a very strong character, though he is all velvet without. His team came to dinner – Commander and Mrs Wise, Colonel Snell, Arab Legionaries; Johnny Johnstone, George and Bridget Coles, and Major Gammon from the Northern Province.

The local Hadramaut Arabs go to Java, Sumatra and Singapore and make large fortunes. They spend nothing on their poor – no schools, hospitals or charities – though they sometimes *leave* money (so that their descendants suffer) for water points, wells and cisterns here and there, so that the poor may drink. But one great Arab, Sir Seyyid Abu Bekr Al-Karf, has poured his money out for the country, bribing the tribes to peace, starting to build the one good road, opening up and pacifying the country.

The Residency is large, cool and attractive, and on the sea stands the Palace of Sultan Awadh bin Ghaleb, who is the son of a fine father and is perpetually pestering his councillors for more palaces. The country is ruled by the Sultan and his Council, advised by the British Resident, whose political officers keep the peace (more or less) in the faraway places. They are an *extremely* fine lot of men, who love their job and the tribesmen.

26 FEBRUARY

Walked through the town with a guide. Very narrow twisting streets; men in bright turbans with magnificent curved, jewelled daggers, kilts, scarves and shawls. Wild, shaggy Bedouin come in with their camels, their long hair hanging over their eyes and down their backs, their skins dark blue with indigo.

The children were poisonous, following us in a screeching mob and hitting me often. They have been notorious for their vile manners ever since Doughty first wrote of their revolting ways. Outside the town's gate is a camel park (as it might be a car park), where hundreds of them lie and rest after their long treks of two and three weeks, fed by their Bedouin. The Bedouin are charm itself compared to the townsmen, though they are little devils when it comes to administering them – always shooting at trucks, cars and each other. There is a ceaseless feud between camel-men and truck-drivers, who try to pinch all the up-country transport trade, but are allowed only one trip to thirty camel trains. But they cheat, of course, and the camel-men shoot at them and at government trucks in rage. They are very poor, very tough, can go four or five days without food, are careless of heat or cold and only happy in their howling wilderness of a stony desert, six to seven thousand feet up, called Jol. Bedouin have a short, hard life;

their expectation is only forty-two years, which is sad when one thinks how independent, brave and attractive they are.

We lunched at home and left at once, in a jeep and a lorry full of soldiers and safari kit, for the mountains. Our driver was a genius, but it was a hair-raising drive – up and up and up, curving round mountains past mist-filled precipices a thousand or two thousand feet deep, praying one would not meet a lorry on the bends, bouncing over rocks and ridges and hugging the side of the narrow road. After four hours of tension, fatigue and bruises we came out on top of the Jol, and what a relief it was to have flat ground on either side.

We reached the rest house in the dark, and it was terribly cold and very rough – nowhere to powder one's nose except the stony plateau outside, where one hoped one wouldn't be run into by (a) the Resident or (b) the soldiers. Thick mist everywhere, and all the mountains hidden, but in the night I went out and looked at the landscape. I found a brilliant full moon, clear sky and the wild, empty, desolate country spread around – a great and silent solitude.

27 FEBRUARY

The morning toilette was colder than words can say; but dressing was simplified because we had both slept in everything except our shoes. Freezing and rather dirty, we again took to the road, and continued over this flat plateau for hour after hour. A very few, very poor Bedouin live here at the water points – many are charcoal burners, though where they get the wood from is a mystery. Perhaps they dry camel dung for fuel. They are small, tough, wiry people with fierce eyes, and their faces light up with brilliant smiles, showing teeth that are white and shining. Their thin bodies are half naked, and they wear short *shukas* like kilts with sometimes another round their shoulders. However poor, they all have guns. Every man wears a beautiful curved dagger and every male child has a smaller replica.

In Mr McIntosh's jeep we drove to the side of the Wad Du'an, which is just a huge crack in the earth. I imagined this would be just a cliff with a view, like so many others I have gone to look at. We were astonished to look down into the valley a thousand feet below and see towns and villages of tall brown houses, palm trees, cultivation, water: a different world. Some miles further on we snaked down another frighteningly narrow road, round hairpin bends, until we were on the floor of the valley, where we had a splendid lunch under a tree, with carpet, chairs, table and all sorts of grandeur.

On we went, over stones and boulders, past towns, villages, farms, solitary castles, mansions and palaces. The rich Arabs often build themselves vast palaces away from the town, near their fields and date palms. Then they get bored, abandon them, and erect another monstrous big dwelling. Some years ago they were fortified, as no one could stir without a rifle and an armed escort until we brought them Pax Britannica. Each town and village was guarded by thick walls, with castles on spurs of rock behind them. Some of these had round turret towers, a pattern brought from Hyderabad. The later houses look like cakes, hugely over-ornamented and painted pink, blue and green. Inside all is dilapidated and nothing works, as none of these people care about maintenance.

The valley people are a different race from the Bedouin; they are fatter, paler, softer and infinitely less attractive. They came a thousand years ago from Iraq, and I imagine drove the indigenous Bedouin away from the oasis and waterways, up to the Jol.

This night was spent in the rest house at In'atin. The loo showed Turkish influence with its 'long drop', a concrete shaft leading to a platform below, from where eventually everything is collected by the people and spread on the fields. Above is a hole flanked by two raised places for your feet; everything is infested with flies, who then settle on your food and you. No one seems to have heard of DDT in these parts. I would like to write a book called *Loos I Have Known* – but alas! who would publish it? The neatest were in Kurdistan, over a running stream – *mais ne buvez jamais de l'eau*. We were all exhausted after seven hours' very hard going, and the moment we had eaten fell into bed.

3 MARCH

We have been here and there – first to Shibam, once the capital of Kathiri state. It is over a thousand years old, but of course the mud houses don't last for long – 150 to 200 years is very ancient. And if floods come roaring through the valley many houses just melt away. Shibam houses are six and seven storeys high – fantastic architecture just from mud. The windows have pretty fretwork openings, with an arch you put your head through to talk to people outside. The narrow, twisting streets are fairly dirty with open drains running down the middle.

We have lunch with Sheikh Amin, thirty of us, sitting barefoot and cross-legged on the floor, eating rice, sauce and meat with our fingers – very messy and difficult. We both came away hungry, even though Claud did cheat and use a spoon. Before and after each meal two servants come round with a basin, jug and towel to wash our hands. All the six Englishmen except C. wore long native skirts called *fota*; they looked very fine.

In Shibam we visited the house of a merchant family. The ground floor is kept empty. The first floor is the goatery, the second has the men, the third kitchen and fodder, and the fourth the women. This house is extremely well kept – the beautifully carved wooden pillars and doors shining with simsim oil, everything clean and charming. We had tea with the father and three sons, whose family came from Basra with the Iraqis a thousand years

306

ago. The father worked for his family all his days; now the sons keep him. The women were very pretty, gaily dressed in many colours, with gold clasps and combs in their hair. When I asked the English-speaking son to come in and interpret, the girls (sisters-in-law) rushed into a corner and stood behind a sheet held up by his wife.

9 MARCH

A nice young Captain Johnson got me a camel to ride, and it made me very happy to feel that swaying action again, and to hear the soft shush-shush of the large feet in the sand. Claud and Johnson walked behind me, and we visited an Al-Karf house where the owner keeps tame ibex and goats, quite attractive animals. I would love to do a camel safari here, camping out and really getting under the skin of the country. There is such a silence in the empty places away from the towns; we would be very happy alone with the Bedouin for a time.

At last we had to leave, and after a picnic lunch beside a pool under some date palms Ralph drove us to Ghuraf, where we enplaned – much surprised to find we had the whole Dakota to ourselves! Forty minutes later we landed at Riyadh, where Mr McIntosh met us.

We went for a picnic to a Bedouin school for boys and girls. Here they learn to be clean and obedient, and are well fed and happy. The boys may become clerks or soldiers or policemen; in any case they keep their long hair (but combed, clean, oiled and sometimes curled) and look extremely smart, with bright fillets bound round their heads, vivid short *fuquas*, belts and bandoliers full of cartridges, and their beautiful engraved daggers. Arab lunch at the school – but spoons for Claud and me – and then a bathe in the surf, hoping for no sharks. The schoolboys rushed into the sea and splashed about with Mr McIntosh and Colonel Snell, in mutual delight and affection.

We went to the house of the Fish Officer, a bearded man with a nice, smart American wife. Here they catch, salt, dry, embarrel and sell thousands of tons of fish yearly. The smell was ghastly, and I got fed up with hanging about while the men 'went round'. At last we were all asked upstairs, picking our way round a mountain of zebra and waterbuck skins, buffalo and gazelle heads; this man often goes to Kenya and shoots game.

Before we came here and brought our peace, there was much fighting. I now know the true story of the taking of Shibam. It belonged to the Kathiri, but the Qu'aiti desired it. They attacked, and the war lasted a long time. At last a wise Seyyid was brought from afar to mediate, and he decreed that part of the town should go to the Qu'aiti, and part remain with the Kathiri. To this Solomon's judgement everyone agreed, but the Kathiri Sultan only agreed with his mouth, not with his heart. He arranged a great wedding feast, to which the Qu'aiti Sultan and his family were invited; the food on their side of the table was poisoned. A slave, however, told the Qu'aiti what was arranged, so the Sultan's family sent only a very few members, who mingled with their Kathiri hosts so closely that the guests could not be poisoned without killing the hosts as well. The feast passed off peacefully and nobody died.

The Qu'aiti waited a while for their revenge. Then they invited the Kathiri royal house and their followers to a dinner party, and politely stood back while their guests filed in and took their seats on the floor. The hosts left the room, the doors were shut, and someone put a match to the gunpowder piled under the floor. The whole room and everyone in it vanished in a roar of smoke and flame. The Qu'aiti were now masters of the whole of Shibam. A few small pockets of Kathiri held out here and there, but no one took much notice of them. A year later the Qu'aiti decided to take Mukalla, and, descending from the hills one night, they occupied one house. From here they attacked the town, conquering it house by house until they were in complete control.

Their dynasty was established, and here their descendant still lives, useless and complaining. Last year he married forty-six times, but luckily for the girls he soon tires of them and sends them home to their families, for in these expensive days no one can be expected to keep, clothe, decorate and feed several hundred wives.

Despite the Qu'aiti victories, they had no control of the country districts; a few thousand yards on each side of Mukalla there are white stones which marked the end of the Sultan's jurisdiction. No one could move beyond these stones without the danger of being killed, but now, under the peace of God and Britain, men walk where they will. But these people have forgotten what they owe us, of course, and most houses have pictures of Nasser on the walls.

On this, our last day, we motored about three hours to a royal summer house – quite small, entrancingly pretty, in a bower of trees and shrubs with a coconut wood behind, and a long, straight drive to the gateway, past which goes a procession of camels, people on donkeys, children driving goats, women with loads on their heads – it is like a stage set. In front of the house is a large swimming pool where the men and the soldiers bathed; the water was quite hot. A former Sultan made his weekend amusement by sliding his wives down a chute into the water, trying to catch them as they shot past, giggling and squealing. The village head man had arranged another Arab lunch for us; it was delicious as usual.

12 MARCH

Back in Aden we stayed with Maurice and Mary Heath. Bathed on the beach at Government House, rather alarmed to find the anti-shark net full of large holes. We have had a wonderful holiday; Claud has loved it, and so have I.

9 JULY

Entesirika-Masai land, near the Tanganyika border. We are here to see the E-Unoto, the Masai head-shaving ceremony. Coming over Mau Narok, once clear of the European farms we met the vanguard of a Masai migrating village. Women drove the donkeys, loaded with all their worldly goods; wicker flaps like snow-shoes, fastened to either side of the load, cleverly held in place all the pots and pans, the drugs and barks and blankets. The donkeys were scarred with their owners' brands, and some had slit ears, giving them a surprised, four-eared look. Later an old man passed with some Moran decorated in red mud, driving the most dreadful calves. Seronga said they milk their cows twice daily, so no wonder the calves are starved.

Spent a very cold night in a hut at Narok. I wore Claud's thickest wool vest and some pants, my pyjamas, a woolly jacket, a shawl round my feet, a hot bottle, three double blankets, another huge shawl and a mackintosh, and was still cold. Next day we started early and still cold. We have the two Morris Minors, a minute tent, a car tarpaulin, a loo (much too small), lots of food, two Masai and a Samburu. We couldn't be more comfortable, except for the cold.

After Narok we turned south towards the Loita Hills, thankfully leaving behind us the schools and hospital, the Wazungu's [*European*] Club, the welfare and uplift, and the turning of young Masai into European-clothed spivs. All round us were the silent plains, decorated with a few elegant giraffe, ugly, selfconscious-looking wildebeest and well-nourished zebra – the whole lovely place backed by the silent hills.

A very good earth road took us to the hills and then twisted up between them, frequently bursting out in rocky outcrops where stones and boulders tried to disembowel our two poor little cars, which are gallant and strong, but too low-slung for these jeep roads.

We were delighted to see a procession of Morans. We heard their knee bells coming through the forest, and then a group of elders appeared, in gay *shukas [long red cloths wrapped round them]* and hyrax cloaks, carrying staffs. Behind them loped four young warriors, their bodies copper-red and shining, some with their heads crowned with lionskin hats. These are won by the brave man who first spears the lion; the second most honourable man is the one who first catches the tail of the wounded lion. Then came a youth in a leopardskin hat; these were all sons of the Laibon, the hereditary ruler, witchdoctor, king and priest of this large section of Masai. One, in the warriors' usual head-dress of ostrich feathers on a high frame, tied round the face, followed; then came about twenty copper-coloured young gods, loping along in single file with the strange, long-stepping Masai gait, carrying their spears low and looking neither to right nor left. Last came a cluster of girls, all covered with bright red mud and tinkling with bead necklaces; the *ndito*, the *demi-vierge* lovers of the warriors. Except for the chink of knee bells and necklaces, they passed our camp without a sound.

We drove to the festival ground, a ring of huts for the warriors, with one big hut for the head Laibon, and one holy one for the Olotonu, the sacrificial boy. On the ground hundreds of youths and girls were dancing. The boys leaped up and down, their glistening red hair flying above their heads, looking like fire gods. The girls also jumped up and down, but not very high; at each jump their stiff head halters flew up, showing their small, strong breasts. These girls, from the age of about ten to fifteen, live with the warriors, sleeping with them and even sharing their meat (which grown women cannot do), but they are not supposed to make love to them. Some can't control themselves, of course, and when this happens and there is a baby the girl has to marry some outcast, a person of no account and of poor family. The baby is treated like all the others. There is no penalty for being born out of wedlock. The father is fined two cows, nine blankets and a lot of beer.

After the girls are circumcised they stay apart from the young men, having had their fun and learnt a thing or two. Their parents arrange their marriages (at the very reasonable price of four cows, two blankets and some beer) to a good young man of suitable family. The couple never meet in public before the wedding, though they do sometimes sneak away and have a look at each other.

The *ndito* live in the Morans' *manyatta [village]*, cook for them, dance and sing with them and share their beds. If two or more girls want the same man they share him. No one gets jealous. There is a ceremony when the young men stand in a row, and the girls bring their brothers' spears and give them to the man they fancy. One particularly fine young man may have an armful of spears at the end of the ceremony. They don't seem to fall in love with each other – they just have a lot of fun and they rarely marry the man.

From the oldest times the Masai have had their Laibons. There are two Masai legends about them. One is that they descended from heaven on a ladder, and some enemy cut the ladder so that they could not return. The other is that they came from a hole in the ground in the north; streaming out of this chasm came the Masai race, following their Laibons. This might have been some deep valley, and I have always thought they came from Egypt, for their red fringes, long, loose hair and pigtails, their high cheekbones, long slit eyes and fine, firm jaws and chins have a very Egyptian air. The beautiful carriage of the Masai is achieved not by drilling but just by dancing. They think people should be straight and erect, and the neck exercises of some of the dances produce this effect.

The Laibon has magic stones which he throws and then examines. He can thus watch the thoughts and plots of the other Laibons, and is in turn watched by them. If some rival Laibon wishes another's tribe harm and sends evil men to put a spell on them, their Laibon, being forewarned, can prevent the men coming into his territory and thus protect his own people. The Laibon is a very good witchdoctor, and will help or hinder people at a certain high price – a large number of cows and blankets, and quantities of beer. But, as the charming Masai Assistant District Officer, Philip Eleven ole Massindet, explained, 'He is not interested in Mr X, who might give him one heifer.' Poor Mr X! (Mr Philip got his middle name because his father worked for someone called Mr Leven, and the schoolboys then called him Eleven, thinking the name meant that.) The first-known Laibon was called Kidongoi. The eldest son usually inherits, but the Laibon can appoint another son if he likes. Then there is usually a quarrel, and a split in the tribe. The Laibons are quite uninterested in the welfare of the individual.

We found a boy who was extremely ill – the black dresser said he had malaria and a temperature of 104°. As he had had no blood test it was impossible to say if he had malaria, and when I took his temperature it was 96·6°. He was almost unconscious, but no one thought of asking the Laibon to cure him with his magic powers. Poor Mr Philip was entirely nonplussed, for however delightful the Masai are, they can be helpless in an emergency. Luckily we three were there and the angelic Mr Lloyd-Worth took him and his friend into his tent, put him on his own bed with his blanket and hot water bottle and certainly saved his life. The dresser had given him a huge dose of Epsom salts, so Mr L.W. spent the night helping him in and out of the tent. The sick boy had two older men to look after him, but he was not allowed into a hut in case he died there and spoilt the party. No one bothered to tell his parents, who arrived in our camp much later; the mother, angry and frightened, said, 'Where is the sick boy?' No one had said he was in the white man's tent.

There was a great commotion outside one hut. An elderly woman, held from behind by an old man, screamed and writhed, lost her voice, choked, spat and screamed again, her arms going like flails and her body contorted. I thought she had either been caught *in flagrante delicto* (but I couldn't imagine any Masai husband minding) or her son was to be the scapegoat, the *olotonu*. Not at all. Her father had spoken harshly to her, I was told, and she lost her temper.

We spent nearly all day at the *manyatta*. The youths danced and sang and loped round, or stood in statuesque groups, their arms round each other, their beautiful, thin bodies shining red, their cherished hair reaching their shoulders in glistening manes. Their *shukas*, worn over one shoulder, or round their chests, or only from the waist, were copper-red, and all their belts and jewellery were also covered in red mud. They gave up their spears and clubs in order not to fight, but carried long thin staffs instead. They were not disarmed by the tribal police, but it was most tactfully arranged that the elders should take their arms. There was no trouble whatever for, brave as they are, the Masai do not fight barehanded. The dance today was called Engipata Nanyuki – the Red Dance – because they were all covered in red mud stuck on with cow or sheep fat.

The Tanganyika Loita were expected all afternoon. Their last camp was twenty-five miles from here, and of course they were on foot. At seven o'clock the Tanganyikans arrived. The Kenyan Loita met them outside the *manyatta* and escorted them in, and despite their long march they all began to dance and shout. We heard them from our camp. Later the noise died down, but every now and then a wild shriek rang out. This came from the boys in the forest, who had eaten their fill of meat and were calling their friends to come and eat. The *ndito* ate with them, and when everybody was quite full they all returned to the *manyatta* to sleep.

11 JULY

We were woken just before sunrise by loud singing voices – first one, then a chorus, then one, then a chorus. This is the morning psalm of the Morani, *Olkirembe.* I hope to find out the words later. The chanting lasts about five minutes, then there is perfect quiet again until the colobus monkeys awake and call to each other through the forest, with long, soft roars. Soon the birds begin their morning song, a burst of sound and music which I have always thought of as giving thanks for the night safely passed – rather like me during the war! (In fact it is a warning to other birds, to keep off their territory.) They seem to sing their hearts out, and in half an hour it is all over.

When we reached the *manyatta* all was quiet, for the young men were hidden in the forest, painting themselves white. This was the day of the Engipata Naibor, the White Dance. At last we heard the chink of knee bells. A long line of warriors appeared loping across the plain. The leaders, about twenty of them, all wore lion head-dresses, and they jerked their heads to and fro as they walked. Following them came the ones with ostrich feathers framing their faces, and last of all the unadorned men. There were about three hundred youths. They marched and counter-marched, circling each other, tossing their furred and plumed heads. They wore their skimpy *shukas* down their backs, and were stark naked in front. Where they had been circumcised each one had a little tag of skin hanging down, which is the Masai custom. They had white patterns all over their bodies and legs – crooked stripes and wavy lines, quite symmetrical and beautifully put on.

They marched into the *boma [enclosed space where cattle spend the nights, safe from lions]*, circled round, broke up and began to dance. This completely upset other Morans inside the *boma*, who went into shakes and fits. They begin to tremble all over, then foam at the mouth and hurl themselves down,

312

limbs jerking at first, and then rigid. Friends hold them until the fit is over, but one man's fit lasted quite half an hour, and at one time four people were holding him. They 'see stars' and don't know what is happening except that they start by feeling excited or angry. Soon they begin to grunt, always the same tone; their breath comes fast and is expelled with this rhythmic grunt. At the end they open their eyes, staring wildly, and in a moment the fit has passed. Without a word or glance of thanks to their helpers, they get up and walk off. These fits are caused partly by the bark of a tree, which they eat before a fight or a party, and partly by hysteria. Before a battle they eat the stuff, begin to tremble and then dance into the fight. They never have a fit while fighting, but the medicine increases their courage. Once one has eaten this bark, the effects last for ever.

Mr Philip himself says he sometimes wants to tremble. It is very catching; within a radius of about ten yards, eight fits were going on. A District Commissioner in the old days tried the medicine and wrote afterwards, 'The effect is to produce an unbalanced state of mind.' This is a really splendid example of British understatement. Perhaps this was the man of whom Elspeth Huxley wrote that he so loved the Masai that once, thinking they were being 'put upon', he covered himself in red mud, put on a *shuka*, took a spear, entered the Provincial Commissioner's office and went into a fit.

Meanwhile the young men in the lion head-dresses, the feather frames and white stripes danced round and round carrying small, bright flags, then broke into parties and danced their leaping, grunting, chanting dances.

In the evening, when we returned to the *manyatta*, some boys were having their heads shaved by their mothers, or any mother of a Moran. This was enough to produce a fit, for the boys love their long, red, glistening manes and now they had to lose them. It is a very sad moment for all; in fact the whole E-Unoto is based on a great sacrifice, and is an unhappy festival.

We saw one boy, grunting gently and foaming a little, being shaved all over his head (and cut a little); then his eyebrows came off, and finally his bald head was covered again with red mud. When it was all finished, and the old woman left him, he threw a really good fit – arms and legs flailing and then quite rigid – and was carried into a hut to recover. The hair is usually kept for life between the hides they sleep on; they sit on the hides on which they were circumcised.

Forty-nine Morans were shaved today, and the Olotonu chosen. The forty-nine are the best boys that this division of Kenyan Loita Masai can produce. They have no physical fault or blemish. A tooth missing does not matter, but a blue eye (the result of VD) puts them out. They must not have killed a human being, or stolen, or made a girl pregnant. They must always have been obedient children, and polite to the elders. They must have been honest and just and brave. The Olotonu himself must be faultless and flawless, pure-bred Masai on both sides, and of good descent for seven generations (or age groups).

The chosen one is the most unhappy boy in the whole gathering, for all the sins of his age group are put on his shoulders – he is the scapegoat. He expects to die within the year, or very soon after, and he usually does. The shock of responsibility and the fear of early death are very hard to bear for a boy of only about seventeen or eighteen. He must marry before any other of his age group – being so soon to die, he must father children quickly. The tall, handsome boy chosen this evening was put into his parents' hut and has not come out. He is afraid and miserable, and so are his parents.

12 JULY

The colobus woke us up, but the Masai, tired after all the marching, dancing, fits and excitement, overslept their dawn hymn and we heard nothing. The morning was quiet; we sat in the sun and I wrote. Mr Lloyd-Worth's patient was taken to hospital yesterday by the doctor, and he had a busy time disinfecting his camp.

When we got back to lunch we found the Morans had left a present of meat here, very touching of them. While still in the *manyatta* I stood with the elders, and the lion-maned and ostrich-feathered warriors danced round and past us in single file, sweeping their head-dresses at us. At last I got hit on the mouth by the iron-hard top of a lion head-dress, and then the elders pulled me back and moved the Morans off; Claud was hit on the chest.

This is the last and greatest day, the wildest and the saddest. All the morning the young men and the girls eat meat, unseen by anyone else, in the forest. A troop of lion head-dresses moved up the hill, and suddenly the *manyatta* was full of running boys, rushing from the forest to find their families, already wildly excited. They came slowly back towards the sacred hut, the Osingera, where the Laibon has sat. Behind each boy came his mother, holding onto the flag floating down his back, then all his female relations, holding onto each other, and his girlfriends, and his friends.

By now most of them were having fits, foaming and grunting, and sometimes an older man held and helped them. They staggered to the sacred hut and round it. A woman would put some cow dung into the boy's hand, and with this he smeared the side of the hut. These boys have led good lives; and this is, for them, the greatest moment of all. Their train of followers is there to pay them honour, to show the world they are fine and honourable people. Round and round the hut they went, shaking and panting, exhausted with their violent emotions – their heads hanging down, their hands trailing along the hut's wall. At last they were led away, and the ground was covered with other young Morans having fits, their arms held out vertically and their legs pinned down by their friends. Now was the time when the fights might begin, for some kept going round and round the sacred hut and others had not had a chance to begin.

Then the forty-nine pure ones appeared. They stood in a group by themselves, quite calm and still, their shaven heads gleaming, their faces quiet and controlled. When it was their turn to circle the hut each one had a huge following, paying him the greatest honour and sharing in it.

At last the Olotonu came. He wore a necklace of leaves, had white paint on his face and carried a black staff. He was composed, deeply unhappy, very quiet and unselfconsciously dignified. He went round the hut with his father, mother and a vast train of followers. There was nearly a fight when the lion-heads, very excited and hardly knowing what they were doing, tried to push him away. After circling the hut the Olotonu sat outside his mother's hut for a time, with his parents close by him, and then his mother, almost fainting, was helped round the hut. The Olotonu and his 'second' sit on stools onto which a mixture of beer and milk have been poured. Both were very quiet and still, and after a while disappeared into their huts.

The dance grew wilder and more barbaric. Two Morans had a quarrel and broke their staves in half in order to fight. The elders and police moved in, very quietly; they struggled with them and took their sticks away. Others led them off to dance, and the moment passed.

The DC, Mr Denton, had gone back to Narok, and only Mr Philip was left in charge. He and his police and the Laibons managed beautifully, and there was no trouble. Troops of boys in the last stages of exhaustion continued to stagger through their dances. They could not bear to stop, for this is their last day of youth; tomorrow they all – though only seventeen to twenty years old – become old men, marry and have families. No more fun, raiding or dancing.

One elder said to me, 'Why does government cut their hair when they are so young – only children, and tomorrow they become old men?'

I replied, 'You know quite well it is because they are always stealing cattle and fighting, and you, the elders, cannot stop them, and you yourselves asked for their hair to be cut.'

With perfect Masai manners he at once agreed. 'Yes – yes, of course. They should not have stolen.'

The truth is the elders don't care how much the Morans steal and fight, but they do mind the fines they have to pay in compensation.

13 JULY

We left, packed up our little camp and said goodbye to the Endasirika. We drove for eight hours, refuelled at Narok, got news of the sick boy (still alive) and went on and on, changing drivers each hour, until at last we reached home, very tired and filthy. This has been a marvellous and very moving experience which I shall never forget.

1960

29 FEBRUARY

To Muscat. It is a 'closed city', almost impossible to visit, and we only got
here because my cousin, Air-Marshal Sir Maurice Heath, C-in-C Aden,
persuaded the Sultan that we should be allowed to come. The jagged brown
and black mountains crowd down to the sea. On a flat space a tiny town
was built many centuries ago, guarded by Arab forts perched on pointed
hilltops, and, each side of the harbour entrance, two massive Portuguese
castles. The European garrisons two and three hundred years ago must
have been extremely brave to endure the heat and dust and glare, the
perpetual danger, and loneliness lasting for months on end, with no help or
comfort such as this century provides. Now there are a handful of European
men and a few European women; they have air-conditioning, Flit, gauze
windows, jeeps, provisions, radios, endless parties, planes, doctors, books –
everything to make life pleasant. The Sultan of Oman lives at Salalah, takes
almost no interest in the people, never answers letters and makes a lot of
rules, some good, some bad. Women may not drive cars. An English couple
were arrested last week because the car stuck. She drove and he pushed;
they had broken the law. *She* should have *pushed*. No short sleeves, no shorts
for men or trousers for women. No cinemas, lanterns carried at night (to
prevent murders), and no drinking except in private houses. He wants the
people to stay as they are, and I think he is right. We came in the very good
Dutch ship *Waingapoe*, with cattle and small stock, food and eggs from
Kenya. First stop Mogadishu, where the Somalis, now 'free' [*Italian and
British Somaliland had just become independent Somalia*], were eight hours late
loading the goats; not malice but pure incompetence.

Then blue, empty days at sea with dolphins playing and diving around
us, till we turned in between the two forts and were at Muscat.

Colonel Hugh Boustead came to fetch us. We stayed with kind and
hospitable oil company people called Nairn.

1 MARCH

Over to see Colonel David Smiley and Moy, Claud's cousin, at the camp
at Beit-el-Fallaj, where the Persians dug wells and made aqueducts many
centuries ago. In the middle of the camp stands a big Portuguese castle,
guarding the wells and the pass; fierce mountains crowd around.

Before we left Kenya I fell very hard onto the sharp edge of a concrete step in Nairobi – a few moments of blinding pain, then I hobbled about a bit till a friend drove me back to Muthaiga. An X-ray showed a star-shaped crack on the left knee, such as the doctor had never seen before, but it was not broken. So, lame as a cow with three-day sickness, I got home; I was in Nakuru all next day, then gave a large lunch party, followed by a dinner and dance in Nakuru for British soldiers, which was my brain-child and a huge success (except I couldn't dance); then another large lunch party. So by the time we left for Mombasa I was really tired. Several days' idleness by the sea with Claud's care helped a lot, but I still feel pain, even though it is now five weeks old.

The Muscat Arabs are attractively wild to look at, with huge, Semitic noses, splendid eyes and well-shaped faces. The men wear *dish-daks [long robes down to the ground, wrapped round their waists]*, enormous turbans and wonderful gold- and silver-encrusted curved scabbards holding family daggers. Their belts are plugged with bullets, and many carry silver-decorated rifles. They are very good shots. The women are pretty, with pale, thin faces, huge, kohl-rimmed eyes and the brightest clothes. Vivid, flowered trousers, a tunic frock of a different colour, a large headcloth, still another colour, anklets, bracelets, noserings, ear-rings – and the Baluchi women's faces are unveiled. For centuries the Seyyids had Baluchi soldiers, who are more loyal, brave and disciplined than the Arabs. They have stayed here ever since, and though they dress and speak like the Arabs they also have their own language and customs, strictly kept to.

8 MARCH

Left Muscat with Hugh Boustead in a Land Rover and a lorry. We bounced over a very rough stone road, with the jagged hills close beside us and the wild mountains just behind. Miles of stony desert are intersected with oases of date palms, all well guarded by their little forts, and with villages of low mud-brick houses. There have been endless battles and bloodbaths for these date forests, the country's only wealth and priceless to the poverty-stricken people. Just now the Sultan's rival, the Imam of Oman, who is his cousin, is in Saudi Arabia 'training an army'. They have already had one war here; we helped, under our treaty with the Sultan, and lost some British soldiers. Now they are getting ready for the next one, and meanwhile spend a lot of time mining the roads.

As you leave the coast and move into the country you enter rebel territory. For no special reason all these villages are for the Imam, and do what they can to harm and destroy the Sultan's vehicles, forces and allies. But as the Imam is a complete reactionary, we were told, they would not be very well off under him – the roads would break up, hospitals shut, trade collapse, agriculture cease and the country become bankrupt. We camped one night outside a particularly bad village, where the roads had been strewn with

317

wrecked vehicles, but a heavy fine had been imposed on the village, and just now they were behaving. It was lovely to be under canvas and sleep in the open again, beside a murmuring river edged with pink oleander, while soft moonlight lit the mountains and the valley.

9 MARCH

The men met a British officer, Colonel Harrington, who arrived yesterday, had a forced landing, was taken on by lorry and then hit a mine – only a small one, which blew a back wheel off. His third adventure was to be shot up by one of *our* planes, by a dashing young pilot who dived too near – poor man, three shocks in one day.

The huge fort here was built by the Arabs, hundreds of years ago. At the top is a hole twenty feet deep, down which they lower their prisoners, who die fairly soon of hunger and thirst. This is a remote, wild place, rimmed by jagged mountains which light like flames in the sunrise. Strings of camels pass on their way to the coast with cargoes of dates; women in bright clothes with jars on their heads walk in single file to the fields and the furrows; herds of donkeys and flocks of sheep and goats patter past our tents. The animals are all fat and well cared for. The children stand in rows peering at me in bed; I rigged the mosquito net across the opening to frustrate them.

11 MARCH

A beautiful drive through splendid mountains to the enchanted oasis of Samail, where a river flows through the narrow valley with its forest of date palms and its patches of wheat, all guarded by the forts standing vigilantly on the hilltops. Lunch on safari with Hugh is very grand – a tent, carpets, chairs and a table every time, out there in the desert!

Staying now at the British Consulate in Muscat with Bill Monteith; very comfortable and much appreciated.

14 MARCH

No one here has an easy time for the Sultan, who never helps, won't spend money, tries to keep everyone out of the country and does not take care of his people. All the Europeans here are full of plans for defence, security, development, health and agriculture, but HH usually refuses permission so there is almost no progress. The oil companies are leaving, and then I suppose their roads will collapse.

The two Portuguese castles guarding the sea approach are both in use, one as the police headquarters and one as a prison. Jalali, the prison, is terrible. There is almost no crime here, because of the fear of Jalali. All the seventy or eighty prisoners are political. The worst offenders stay in cells deep in the rock. They wear iron bars between their legs, jointed in the middle, with a chain which they must carry in their hands before they can move. They are kept short of food and water, so they suffer greatly from thirst. They have no visitors, never see their families, never see the sky. They stay in their cells, in the near-dark, month after month, year after year, until they die. Any one of them, offered Jalali or death, would take death. For me, this dreadful prison casts its shadow over all Muscat; it haunts me. But the fear of it does keep men honest.

One prisoner who *is* well treated and fed, with a suite of rooms and his own slaves, is the Sultan's uncle. He was offered his freedom, but said he would rather stay in Jalali, as if he got out he might murder the Sultan, having a 'very bad temper'. Politically the situation is quite tricky. One official, Seyyid Abbas, another royal uncle, was so tired and worried that he decided on a sea trip for a safe rest. He and his slave went to their cabin and the Seyyid lay on his bunk. Then, for some reason he could not explain, he got up and reversed his position, putting his feet where his head had been. A bomb under the pillow exploded. He was badly hurt about the feet and legs, his slave was wounded and the cabin wrecked. The Seyyid was taken off the ship and put in hospital; here another bomb was thrown at him as he lay in bed, but failed to kill him. He is now at work again, but never moves without six armed guards, and travels in an armoured Land Rover instead of a vulnerable car.

Everyone has armed guards; a lot of them are slaves. All the blacks here are of African origin, and most of them are slaves. They are extremely fit and look well fed and perfectly happy. If their owner tries to sell them against their wish they can come to the British Consul and be freed, but only about one a month does this.

18 MARCH

We explored the suks, the dark, tiny alleys where the markets are, and found many fascinating things. Arab turbans, with paisley patterns or all in white; gold-banded, silver dagger sheaths, lengths of bright cloth, sandals and a whole street of jewellers. The suks are covered over, so all is dark and cool; there is a maze of tiny, twisting streets, thronged with people. Donkeys stand drooping in the wider streets, carrying loads of lucerne for their lunch, or sacks of onions or dates.

One day, after lunch, while David Smiley was at last having a short rest, the telephone rang. The Wali of Mattrah said would he come and remove a bomb someone had left outside his house? They got there to find a fascinated crowd sitting in a semi-circle regarding the object, which was a small grenade in a tin. They took it away safely, rewarding the little girl who had found it with a thirty silver Maria Theresa dollars. Sacks of these dollars are kept for rewarding mine-detectors, and this system has been a great success.

20 MARCH

We had meant to go to Buraini from Nizwa, but because I was ill, and it rained, and time was getting short, we did not go. Two days ago an army jeep sprang a large mine on the road to Buraini; the jeep turned over and the officer passenger broke his leg. How lucky we were not to go! Hand of God.

The army gave a firepower display to which came practically the whole of Muscat and Matra, including the Sultan's representatives and relations, resplendent in their marvellous turbans, gold-embroidered burnouses and huge, magnificent daggers. They each had a large armed guard who stayed close to them, particularly the guard of Seyyid Achmet, the poor old man who was blown up. The display was very good, especially the Sultan's air force (all British) bombing, and the Ferret armoured cars demolishing distant targets. The crowd was pleased and impressed.

21 MARCH

We left for the north, camping again. The first night was spent at Mussma, a few hours from Muscat. The mountains are hidden in sandstorms, but we sometimes see the lovely sea. Camping is terribly uncomfortable on the stony desert, though better on the sand. The Arabs, as a whole, have regrettable habits, but so have many Englishmen, who let themselves slip when living rough and also leave every sort of tin, paper, dirt and junk around the camps. In Kenya one would not know there had been a camp, except for traces of fire.

24 MARCH

The second night was spent near a garden. We visited the Wali of the district, who lives in a village called Korabur. Shoeless, we entered his reception room and sat on the floor round the walls, leaning against pillows. Hugh talked of this and that with the Wali, getting all the news and gossip. All these villages are fortified with strong castles, for there was endless fighting up and down the coast in the old days as one ambitious sheikh after another tried to take Muscat and murder the Sultan-Imam. The castles, though only made of mud bricks, are impressive, and were quite strong enough for those times to withstand a siege of men armed only with poor rifles, swords and daggers. Sometimes, though, the garrisons were starved out (despite the huge supply of dates stored under the floors) and then slaughtered. Some of the castles are in ruins, but others are still lived in.

They are built to a very simple plan – a tower with living rooms, sleeping rooms and a roof also to sleep on; the Sheikh and his family lived upstairs, the soldiers, slaves and livestock below. The stairs are narrow and steep, easily defended, and of course the villagers and tribesmen would rush to help, or face massacre by their enemies. At night, lit only by flickering candles, the whole effect is grim and medieval.

The Sheikh and his brother, two sons and some guards, were invited to dinner for 8.30. They arrived at 9.30, by which time we were starving and Claud was cross. A feast was brought to the tent, where we sat on the floor, faced by two mountains of rice and goat's meat, bowls of sauce, onions, tomatoes and peppers; and plates of fruit and custard. A cluster of old men sat silently at the end of the tent. The vast remains of the huge meal were for them.

En route again, with Hugh's Indian clerk called Mani driving – rather cramped with three of us in front, very jolting and rough. We camped at a quite dreadful place called Aswad, beside a village, all stones, and no bush or cover at all. I was tired and rather fed up. All night it rained, and at dawn a gale nearly blew the tents down. Hideously uncomfortable and cold, I was glad to start off again, though sad to say goodbye to dear Hugh and the boys – Jahn Mohammed the cook, Bakri from the Hadramaut, a Sheikh's son with a great sense of humour and always pulling people's legs, and Ibrahim, a born clown. They have been very nice to us and we tipped them well.

It poured along the road, but Hadji (Inspector of Public Works) drove fast and well. We left the stony country and came to lovely, softly rounded sand dunes, a red-gold colour. This is the eastern edge of the Empty Quarter; how I would have loved to camp among them. After four hours and eighty-six miles we came to Dubai, known as the Venice of the East. I never saw anything less like Venice, except that there is a creek. The old town looks quite picturesque; otherwise the usual frightful modern houses have sprung up, surrounded with litter, tin cans, bits of paper and smashed-up cars.

We are staying in the very nice and comfortable house of Major Lorimer, the Police Chief. It seems to me extremely luxurious, with everything that opens and shuts, pulls and lets go.

We went to visit the ruler, who received us in a reception room lined with chairs and floored with the most exquisite carpets. I could hardly resist admiring them out loud, when he would have had to give me one. Claud sustained the conversation, with Major Lorimer interpreting. This ruler has about forty thousand subjects, including a lot of Bedouin – a very floating population, as one never knows where these nomads are. There is no oil here and the people are not very rich, but they are happy and content.

321

28 MARCH

Ramadan is over and this is the festival of Id. These ceremonies, the fasting and then the festivities, correspond to the Christian Lent and Easter. Now all the women and children are glittering with sequins, gorgeous new clothes, emerald trousers, purple dresses, scarlet headcloths and gold masks, instead of the black bird-of-prey horrors they normally wear. Drums beat, people chant, sheikhs and elders are in clean white robes with gold-edged burnouses, large, new turbans and their best daggers. All this colour and glitter made the streets of Dubai look very happy. But it was not such a happy Id for one double murderer in jail in Sharjah, whose public execution had been saved up for this auspicious day. Most of the population of Dubai flocked to see him killed; the usual methods here are shooting, beheading, hanging rather slowly, or stabbing to death. We did not find out in what way he died. We were told that murderers die in the way their victims did, killed by the victim's family.

1 APRIL

We drove to Sharjah on the 28th and flew to Bahrein. We thought this the dullest, dreariest, deadliest place we have ever seen. On the 29th the day began for us at 3 a.m. We took off at 5.30 a.m. and finally arrived at Istanbul about 3 p.m. where we stayed the night, too tired to go on today.

1962

20 MAY

It is lovely being in England again. I have almost sold Nderit to Robin, who insists on having it. I shall be thankful to be free of the worry and responsibility, the work and the bills. I love the Masai, but the political problems are enormous.

1963

10 DECEMBER

Two days to Uhuru ('freedom' in Swahili). All the *canaille* boiling up, our Luo kitchen boy sulky and swollen-headed; drumming in the Olkalau forests all night; newspapers squirming before the former murderers, like dogs on their backs. Long-haired Mau Mau with filthy beards emerging from the forests to greet their former bosses.

If it wasn't for Claud and the Masai I wouldn't stay one more day. I am bored, slightly scared, and utterly fed up when I think of my forty-one completely wasted years here, when I might have been building up a lovely, safe and permanent home in some civilized country.

13 DECEMBER

We were asked to the Government House garden party. Black Kenyans in cheap and badly fitting European suits, with tight shoes, monkey-skin capes and rugs and even hats! Dark glasses and selfconscious faces. Their women wore long ball dresses, short ball dresses, or very tight skirts over ballooning behinds above thick, stumpy legs. One had even powdered her beige face orange to match her headscarf. Some, in long brocade native dresses, looked grand, but most made utter jokes of themselves.

It was all quite comic until the Union Jack came slowly down, for the last time in this – as I used to think – my beloved country, which once I loved and now I loathe. That was a heart-sore moment.

1964

27 JANUARY

We have had a series of mutinies in the African army and a very bloody and cruel revolution in Zanzibar. About ten days ago there was an outburst of killing and maiming of Arab men, women and children by the negro population. The royal family were away in Mombasa, and the Sultan, the Prime Minister, the British head of the police force and over three hundred Arabs managed to reach the *Seyyid Khalifa*, the boat which goes to Pemba. They waited offshore for a time, while the fearful din of shooting, slashing and burning went on. At last they left for Mombasa. [*The army and police in Nairobi stood by their planes, awaiting orders to fly to Zanzibar, but these orders could only come from the Sultan now that the island is independent. He refused to give them, not wishing his people hurt. The result was seventeen thousand Arabs slaughtered in one night.*]

A man called Okello, who promoted himself to field-marshal, seems to have been the leader. His men broke into the police armoury and then ran wild. Okello ordered the Sultan's ministers to go to the police, when, he said, they would be shot, hanged or burned alive. The Sultan was refused

323

permission to land at Mombasa and join his family, just when they most needed each other, but it is true that his presence might have sparked off an Arab–Negro fight. He sailed away, and my heart ached for him. He was given temporary asylum in Dar-es-Salaam (the Harbour of Peace, built by his ancestor Seyyed Majid), and the chivalrous inhabitants booed and cursed him as he came ashore.

The next night Zanzibar asked Tanganyika for three hundred policemen 'to help to restore order'. Nyerere [*President of Tanganyika*] ordered the manager of East African Airways to have them flown over; he refused, for in the air rules it says you may not carry arms or ammunition. Nyerere, in the usual manner of these new rulers, had the wretched man deported! Clearance was finally given, and 130 police askaris crossed to Zanzibar. Okello then came to Dar 'for a rest'. Meanwhile the Sultan and his sixty-strong suite had been flown to England.

No sooner were the police out of Dar than the 1st Tanganyika Rifles [*formerly the King's African Rifles*] mutinied. They wanted all the usual things – more pay, better living conditions, quicker promotion (regardless of merit and ability) and no British officers. These officers removed the nameboards from their houses, hoping to confuse the mutineers and protect their families. But of course the men knew where they were, burst in and marched them to trucks which took them off to the barracks. Here they were paraded before a 'minister' called Kambona, who, after hours of arguing, persuaded the mutineers not to kill their officers. Next morning the negroes in Dar ran wild, attacking the Arab and Indian shops, burning, smashing, looting and killing. At last the officers and their families were flown to Nairobi and then to England, some still in shorts and vests and the women and children half dressed. Nairobi women whipped round and got them warm clothes and shoes.

Nyerere had vanished. The remains of his cabinet begged for help from Britain, having in vain asked their friends, Uganda and Kenya, to send troops. Next day the 2nd battalion the King's African Rifles mutinied at Tabora – same complaints. Their British officers and families were flown to London. Tanganyika was really in a mess, their splendid independence and self-rule quite useless. We sent ships, commandos and troops to restore order, but the 'mopping up' is not over yet.

The day after the Tabora mutiny, the battalion in Kampala mutinied, and more of our men were sent there. They stopped the mutiny and disarmed the men. Then, as we were all catching our breath and wondering what next, the 11th battalion, here at Lanet, mutinied on 24 January.

Our troops, forewarned, had come from Gilgil in the dark and were encamped on the rifle range on my land; but the mutineers had already broken into the armoury at Lanet and were roaming around the camp. Surrounded by our men and black police (who stayed wonderfully loyal) they could not break out, but it must have been frightening for the white families. These were sent to Nakuru at 4 a.m. and were so unprepared that the children were still in nighties. They might have had their bags ready packed (as we did during air raids on England) – but no!

Aumu, my driver, and I set off early to see what we could. Claud wouldn't come. At the Lanet turning were some very tired police. We went to Nakuru to see if any wives wanted asylum, but all were well looked after. We went back; about fifty more troop carriers had arrived and black police were lining the ditches, while white troops were advancing in extended order. We were waved on and couldn't stop. On the bridge we halted and watched, but then there was a sudden burst of fire and I took off for the hilltop – *how* stupid it would have been to be hit by a mutineer's bullet after coming untouched through the Kaiser's war, the Spanish war, Hitler's war, the Lebanon revolt and Mau Mau!

By evening it was all over. Our troops had calmly disarmed the mutineers, five hundred of whom were now sitting in barbed-wire cages run up by the sappers. One mutineer was shot – a sort of hard core individual who kept on firing at our men. The mutineers hit nothing but one car and one poor old black man walking to his job in Nakuru. They had fired thousands of rounds. Aumn and I had enjoyed ourselves. He said, 'that was better than a cinema!'

16 FEBRUARY

Called on Sheikh Salim Mohammed, who was charming and interesting. Three thousand people have been slaughtered in Zanzibar, all Arabs and Asians, mostly the very old, very young, and women. [*Later we heard that the actual death toll was seventeen thousand.*] The blacks ran mad for blood, as they so easily do. Many sad, penniless, homeless, bereaved Arab refugees have come to Mombasa, where their friends are taking them in and helping them. So is the Red Cross. The Sheikh drove me to the train, where I spent a sleepless night, bumping and shaking behind a black driver.

30 SEPTEMBER

Had a wonderful time in England, as usual, with some interesting moments. We went to a Lord Mayor's party, asked by the Edgars, High Sheriff of London; everyone in full evening dress and looking like a Noël Coward *mise-en-scène*. Also to a soirée for the visiting Prime Ministers, invited by the Douglas-Homes. Kenyatta's ADC found Claud and asked us to 'meet' K., so we spent an amusing evening taking evasive action, and saw many friends and had a lot of fun. We had tea with Elizabeth Douglas-Home at 10 Downing Street; it is a beautiful, quiet house, with lovely rooms and pictures. Alec looks tired, but he is so witty and honest, and she is so natural; everyone loves them both.

I spent much time at Coldharbour. Claud got some fishing. It is so wild and beautiful in those hills and I long to live there and be near the villagers again. I hope God will help me find a home in my own country – the older I get, the more I long for my own tribal background! Claud, who once hated it, alas loves Kenya more and more, as I detest it more and more.

Finally came to the new little house in Jersey, larger and quieter than Bretonnerie. We sailed once, then the weather broke, and when it got fine again there was no more time. Claud finally left me to go to Kenya, and I came to Paris, *en route* Corsica.

4 OCTOBER

Left at 1.20, stopped at Marseilles – oh, the sun and the sea and the smell of salt water, and shrubs at the airport! Reached Ajaccio about 4.15 p.m. and once more saw those wonderful mountains.

12 OCTOBER

Have motored about this wonderfully beautiful country; I found a nice old house agent who motored me in a tiny, stout-hearted Dutch Daf over wild mountains to Propriano, where the hotel is much smaller, nicer and cheaper than at Ajaccio. I found an excellent taxi driver, Monsieur Luciano, who drove me to the lovely little creek of Tizzano.

Luciano took to the *maquis* when he was twelve and the island was over-run with Italian troops; he did liaison work, and killed his first man when he was thirteen. An Italian soldier was bullying his grandfather for eggs, shaking him by his white beard. The boy stood by, then admired the soldier's rifle and asked how it worked. It was handed to him ('Take care – it's loaded!'), and saying 'This is for pulling my grandfather's beard' he shot the soldier dead – then off to the *maquis*, with the gun. I don't know what happened to his grandfather! The Italians never followed into the *maquis* because they were too scared, and the resistance groups lived there for four years – very well, on fruit and game and village food. But some were caught. Luciano's leader was taken and tortured, but never said a word; then he was shot. After the liberation Luciano 'fixed' his age and joined the French navy.

I came up the Ospedali valley and over the Col de Bavella, four thousand feet high, between jagged mountains called the Needles, and a pointed range like dragons' teeth, to Solanzara. I went to Pinarelli, lovely and lonely and almost untouched. Today, because I was going to fish, it pours; and last week, because I was going to sail, a gale rose in the night, tearing down branches, small trees and the telephone wires.

16 OCTOBER

Solanzara is a dead place at night – all these places are.

I drove up a narrow, tortuous valley with jagged rocks leaning towards the road and a foaming river below, to a café at Ghisone, where a fourteenth-century fanatic religious sect was caught, massacred and burnt by government troops. A hermit came from his cave to read the mass, and as he said Kyrie Eleison (Lord have mercy upon us) the assembled villagers repeated this so loudly that the rocks echoed the cry, and the highest mountain has been called Kyrie Eleison ever since.

Again to Pinarello, where I found a perfect paradise bay, with blue and emerald water curving round, and a small island with an old Genoese tower rising from the water on the left. There are pines on the ridge and a little lake behind. Alas, the whole place has been bespoke by an Italian company, who will shortly ruin it with villas and bungalows. There is a nudist camp in the *maquis*; two of them walked past me on the sand. They were fat and pink and ungainly, and were anyhow cheating, because they had bathing caps on.

12 OCTOBER

In England we have lost the election! Only by about twenty seats, so the Socialists can't last long, but poor Alec [*Douglas-Home*], who is so brave, clever and honourable!

The Chinese have let off their nuclear bomb.

What can happen next?

20 OCTOBER

Labour finished the election with a majority of only four. James Hamilton got in, thank heaven, for Fermanagh and South Tyrone.

Came to Calvi via Agriates – a truly magnificent, wild, uninhabited place, all tumbled rock and hills, ending in mountains by the sea. Here our submarines landed arms for the *maquis* resistance during the war.

Bandits lived on in the mountains till quite lately; the French swept them out in the 1930s, but one man would still easily murder another to avenge an insult, or his 'honour', or that of his family. Vendettas are over, and that is good; though I think the great spirit of protective chivalry which Corsicans have for their families and their women is attractive.

1 NOVEMBER

Monsieur Baretti, owner of the Hotel des Etrangers where I have been staying, was friends with some of the bandits and liked by them. He went into the mountains and persuaded one to give himself up, on condition his life was spared. The man said he would surrender to Baretti but to no one else, for his honour's and pride's sake. He had a few years in jail, but now lives in Bastia. When Baretti was on a mountain road one day he saw about eight cars lined up. This could only mean a bandit hold-up. He refused to stop, drove straight on, and was shot at – the bullet just missed his head. Next time he went shooting in the mountains he found that bandit chief and reproved him, receiving many apologies. Most Corsican bandits were *bandits d'honneur*, killing for family honour's sake, but some were just plain highwaymen.

I decided to try to buy one hectare at Algajola near Calvi, as a speculation, since the places I really wanted were either too dear, sold, or not for sale.

Quelle drame! Monsieur Filipini, the estate agent, sent for a *notaire* from Niole in the mountains, as mountain people are more honest than the Ajaccians. He arrived, we discussed all, and arranged to meet at ten next morning. My friend Frederica Rose and I got there at ten, and waited – and waited – for one and a half hours. At last the man arrived – not sorry at all. We then tried to retype the form necessary for the Bank of England to release the money. Bumble Bee's [*Filipini*] typewriter wouldn't work, and he had no ribbon. (He had given his good typewriter to an old mountain woman whom he thought needed some money.) I finally had to write it myself, to a background of babel. The whole thing was too disorganized and Corsican for words, but we got it all written out, and Frederica seized it to post herself.

I left Ajaccio on Friday the 30th by train, and had four bumpy hours of breathtaking scenery – brown bracken, gold trees, snow mountains, tiny grey villages which seem to have grown out of the rocks, rushing, foaming rivers, and the emptiness, the loneliness of this silent country. Country Corsicans – especially the mountain people – seem to me a race apart, with their fair skins and their princely manners, their honesty and uprightness. When taking and leaving a taxi you always shake hands, and I'm sure the drivers feel this is more important than a tip.

Santoni, my Ajaccio taxi driver, took me to see a cheap and wonderful place to buy – of course it was all *maquis* and rocks, quite hopeless – but *en route* we stopped at Auntie's cottage. She was a beautiful old Carg, with deep blue, very Corsican eyes and fine features, speaking only Corse. I was cold, so they put me near the fire and added to it scented spruce wood. They gave me a glass of their own year-old prune brandy – prunes soaked in eau-de-vie. I wanted my handkerchief and opened my bag. I could feel the tension rising – they feared I was going to try to pay for their hospitality! So I had fun, fumbled and took everything out slowly, including the purse. They watched in growing horror till I produced my handkerchief with a sigh of relief, and everyone relaxed almost audibly.

I am now in Rome, and leaving at the grisly hour of midnight for Nairobi.

Overjoyed at the thought of seeing Claud again; loathing and dreading the thought of Kenya.

8 NOVEMBER

Now at Naishi, where all the people gave me the sweetest welcome. Under the present government things are more uncomfortable than ever. Roads very bumpy. Radio not worth hearing – nearly all the 'international' news is about Africa: more farms confiscated in Tanganyika, more riots in Sudan, etc.

5 DECEMBER

Such appalling things have happened in the Congo that one can hardly believe it possible.

I can now get Voice of America on the radio daily, and their estimated deathroll of blacks murdered by other blacks there is thirty thousand since October, a million in the last four years. Nearly all European families have been wiped out; a few escaped to Kenya.

1965

JULY

We left Kenya on 20 April for Rome. On 8 February I motored to Nanyuki to stay with the Boyds and see the film *Born Free* being made. The dust was so awful that soon I felt as if a burning razor had been stuck in my throat. Virginia McKenna and her husband Bill Travers are acting; I lunched with them. They are brave people! The lioness acting with them wouldn't act; she prowled among the cars and I had to keep putting the window up and down. She jumped on Travers's back and onto the white hunter; both had small sticks and hit her on the nose, whereupon she snarled and jumped off. If she had knocked them down she would have killed them. Mrs T. was rehearsing in the bush with 'Little Elsa', a half-grown cub, guarded by a boy with a rifle – the son of Robin's manager Mr Remnant . . .

I was sad to leave the servants – they do touch one's heart. The reserved and dignified Naigisi saying with difficulty, 'We pray God to bring you safely back to us'; and Morda, 'When you are not here, I am not happy.' But I, who once loved it so, now loathe Kenya – the politics, the boredom, the inefficiency and the dust.

8 DECEMBER

A nice – and true – story. Donald Graham was trying to sell his farm to a black syndicate who *wouldn't* pay and *wouldn't* pay. At last his lawyer told him to speak to them himself, as they never answered letters. Donald sent for them and they said: 'The lawyer told us we must bring the seal for the form. We didn't know what a seal was, so looked it up in the dictionary. It said "a fish-eating marine animal". We tried to find one, and could not, so we did no more about it.'

1966

25 MARCH

I left Claud again and flew to Rome, where Vera had installed me in a rather dull pensione not far from her.

30 MARCH

Vera had arranged for me a semi-private audience with the Pope [*Paul VI*]. There has been much to-ing and fro-ing and excitement over my dress – long black wool skirt; high-necked, long-sleeved blouse; huge black lace veil to my knees, arranged over very high coiffure; lots of jewels; and black gloves and bag, last two and veil lent by Vera. The hotel maids, who were very excited and pleased, came to dress me. Vera lent me their diplomatic car and driver.

The Swiss Guards in their bright sixteenth-century uniforms, carrying their long halberds, were most impressive – tall, blond, handsome men; and the Vatican chamberlains in crimson brocade coats, knee breeches and buckled shoes were splendid. There were fifty people for this semi-private audience, and in due course we processed to the main room. As I was alone I walked down the middle, being unwilling to cringe along on one side.

The Pope came in with just a few attendants; he wore a white robe and small skullcap. I curtsied deeply and we shook hands. He said he would pray for me – I nearly said I would pray for him but thought that rather cheeky, as from an amateur to a professional. But I did say, '*Nous autres, nous Protestants, nous avons la plus grande admiration pour vous, Saint Père.*'

He looked surprised, and rather pleased. He has a very sincere expression and splendid, large, grey-blue eyes; a northern Italian, I should think, and a great aristocrat. I then made another curtsey and backed away. It was a marvellous experience, very magnificent and very simple.

5 MAY

James Hamilton is engaged to a most attractive girl called Sacha Phillips, and Moyra also engaged to sailor Peter Campbell. Everyone delighted.

25 OCTOBER

My brother died. He had been so ill so long – his voice had gone, and the use of his hands. The cremation service was very small and quiet; the memorial service later, in Coldharbour church, very touching, the little church full. Many Heath relations, and Margit, as always, elegant and dignified, shattered with grief, but restrained.

12 NOVEMBER

James Hamilton and Sacha Phillips were married in the [*Westminster*] Abbey, watched by the Queen and Prince Philip, Prince Charles, Princess Anne, Princess Marina, the Duchess of Gloucester, Claud, me and twelve hundred guests. A large party of tenants came from Barons Court, and some more from Phillips territory. Sacha looked heavenly; lots of little bridesmaids and three pages, including Prince Andrew. The singing was exquisite, as were the flowers, and the clergy in their magnificent cloaks and robes, bowing gently to the Queen, looked quite medieval.

So many friends – such fun! And my white and gold, rather medieval-looking dress and long coat, with the large amethyst tam-o'-shanter to match the amethysts I wore, were really quite a hit at the St James's Palace party.

1967

We have bought a house in Sussex called Rudgwick Grange, very old, done up in Georgian times, now very elegant, and it does look lovely with all the pictures, the collection of fans in their green alcoves and our nice furniture and ornaments. This old house was said to have been used by smugglers, who brought their booty up the river Adur and lived in what is now the cellars. They probably quarrelled and fought among themselves. Nothing would make our lion-dog, Mango, go down those quite easy cellar stairs. She pulled backwards, very scared, and the ridge on her neck stood up. I think she saw ghosts.

[Worn out by the war, with all the strain and work and danger, Claud died, very suddenly and with no pain. I was quite unable to write for over three years. Then I began to travel and to write a little.]

1971

14 OCTOBER

There is so much violence in the world – Ulster is being persecuted by the IRA (Irish Republican Army, as they call themselves) who blow places up and murder our soldiers, police and civilians.

Amin has thrown Obote out of Uganda, and killed a very great number of people. He likes throwing them to the crocodiles in Lake Victoria. The Sudanese murder the Christian Nilotic tribes in the south. Yahya Khan of Pakistan has killed and tortured the people of East Pakistan so cruelly that nine million refugees have fled to India.

1 NOVEMBER

I left London by Air India *en route* Nepal, in a thick fog. Landed Paris. Fog. Landed Geneva. Fog. Then down the coast of Turkey during a black night and over Persia to Teheran. By now I was all in and had taken a sleeping pill and slept. But not for long, since the Indian captain's voice came booming into the cabin: 'This is your captain speaking. We are now over Arabia, etc.' – as if one cared! At last reached Delhi, where pandemonium in the airport was indescribable. Hundreds of people in a small space, and very few staff. Dozens of forms, permits, Customs, and passport things to be seen to. We reached the splendid Maidan Hotel about 10 a.m., having been up since 7 a.m. the day before. The air-conditioning in my vast room was full on. I froze, and six appeals and promises of an electrician brought no help, so I finally had a tepid bath and slept through the rest of the day. I thought Delhi frightful. Myriads of begging children; dirt, dust, starving ponies and (holy) cows, miserable cannas and bougainvillea, groves of stunted thorn trees, crumbling buildings and gloomy people – like Nairobi when we left, but more so – set in a vast, flat, monotonous plain.

Arose at 3.15 a.m. for take-off at 4.45 for the two-hour flight to Kathmandu. In Delhi we were put in the wrong plane, and after the usual frisking (anti-hijack, very superficial – no one found the notes in my brassiere) we wandered all over north India. But the small, two-engined plane was far nicer than the big one we had left London in. This one flew

332

low and slow and was not crowded and one could see the country, which got hillier and prettier the further north-east we went. At Patna more delay, more frisking; finally we were told our plane to Kathmandu was cancelled because of 'bad weather', though several planes continued to fly placidly in and out. At last we boarded one and reached Kathmandu.

2 NOVEMBER

Contacted Colonel Malla's charming brother and sister-in-law, who gave me a huge, delicious Nepalese lunch and took me to the temple of Sway-ambhu on a hill beyond the town – said to be two thousand years old. There is a tall tower covered in gilded copper, very ornate and striking, and dozens of shrines to the Lord Buddha, in one of which knelt two priests, dressed in robes and hats of scarlet and yellow, chanting and waving their hands very fast in a sort of holy dance. There were processions of 'businessmen' chanting and praying, wreathed in garlands – *how* nice if our City gents did this! Countless women and children, with flowers in their hair, throwing rice and flowers into the shrines.

I went with Professor Malla to a folk dance and song display at the university, mostly done by students, quite brilliant, clever and graceful. The singing was charming – no harsh nasal twang, nor operatic braying, but musical, harmonious voices with a big range. The funny men made me laugh just with their expressive faces and voices – though of course I could not understand a word – while the audience rocked. The dances were all glitter and sparkling, whirling bodies and arms.

3 NOVEMBER

Left by air over dramatic mountains covered in cloud for Pokhara, where we arrived with hardly a bump, forty-five minutes later. It is a grey rainy day. My pony, cook, cook's wife, and groom were awaiting me, other porters having gone on. Pony and I made dubious friends, porters all smiles and greeting *wais [the greeting gesture of hands joined before you and a bow]*, while I did my best.

Then away to the hills! Lovely feeling, riding and walking with these charming people into the wildest country – sadly, for me, meeting many other British tourists – all on foot, brave people. It rained and blew, and there was one awful crazy fragile bridge which pedestrians had to cross. Thank heaven I was obliged to ride the pony through the river, saving face *and* nerves. Camped now on a bluff above the main trail, up which tramp brave, wet British tourists with their dripping porters. Hope to get away from them tomorrow. I am camped by a Gurkha village, and Sona, head boy, says they think only 'money-money-money'. They come to my tent constantly, trying to sell me rings, shawls, scent sprayers and lamps. Poor people, all refugees; they had a dreadful time escaping from their Chinese overlords, through fearsome mountains. They have lost their homes, money, families, land and all they had in the world – no wonder they try to make a little money.

4 NOVEMBER

A shocking night with tummy upset due, I think, to the bad egg the hotel put in my dreadful lunch.

Villages have very pretty houses – ochre-coloured bricks with rich carving on doors, windows and balconies. It was a fine, sunny day and the clouds rolled off the steep, snowy mountains. We reached a large valley full of rice fields; smiling women in huge, flowered skirts and folded turbans were gathering a good harvest. At the end was a tall mountain and a terrible path up it, all steps and stones and boulders and struggle.

The pony stopped trying to carry me up so I walked for at least an hour, climbing, slipping, panting, legs trembling, heart hurting, stopping more and more often, almost unable to breathe, staggering on and on, determined to walk to the very top – but I failed. The track got better and the sherpas *made* me ride. Pony so fed up he pretended to bite me. We must be about four thousand feet up now – perched on a mountaintop, with a three-thousand foot precipice just outside my tent, and these monster mountains standing sentinel all round. It is wonderfully beautiful, savage and silent. And I *am* tired. I have climbed three thousand feet.

I have the most enchanting lot of boys – Sona is sherpa, cook and head boy [*who has climbed to the top of Mount Everest*]; his wife Kanji, sweet and pretty, and as plump as a pumpkin, strides out under a heavy load and is charmingly kind and helpful to me. How I wish I could take them home. A Tibetan groom and five Sherpa porters, who carry their heavy loads up this mountain goat track and never get tired, or stop smiling, complete the party. In the evenings I sit in the door of my little tent with a basin of burning firewood at my feet, the little kitchen camp before me, the great mountains all round, and perfect peace, while the porters sing gently.

7 NOVEMBER

A fearful descent next day, pony slithering, me on foot scrambling and sliding and more exhausted than I have ever been. I lay on the ground while Kanji massaged one leg and a Tibetan groom took over the other. Passed a few lonely hamlets and finished at the bottom of a valley, beside a roaring river.

I was dead beat and beginning to wonder if I can manage any more mountains. I woke up yesterday still tired, with a spinning head, and again had to walk, as Pony can't carry me up *or* down these monstrous trails. Met a wan American woman, obviously with a high temperature. She said the next mountain was truly terrible, and she had been carried up in a basket. 'If you take my advice you won't even try' – but one always does try.

Therefore, as God knew I wouldn't listen to good, first-hand advice, He arranged something else. At last we came to a flat bit above a small precipice, and the groom brought my Pony too near the edge for me to mount. So I pushed his quarters a little, like one does any horse, and he kicked sideways like a cow, caught me on the right hip, and flung me through a small, dry-stone-wall and down the precipice. I rolled over and over, clutching vainly at grass, rocks, everything – barely conscious – till I managed to stop just a few yards from the wild river and its huge boulders. Sona was with me in a flash, crying. He thought I was dead or at least very badly hurt. There was blood everywhere, but I managed to keep saying, 'I'm OK,' then Kanji held me in her arms and put her cheek to mine, crying; the others were all round me, some in tears – they had had a worse shock than I had. I could not stop laughing: shock, I suppose.

They washed the blood off and nothing hurt at all. All my joints moved. I staggered and was pushed and pulled up to the path, where the poor groom looked as if he'd seen a ghost. After a time I could walk – then rode, afraid of 'losing my nerve' if I didn't get on, at once. Head hurt, not much, and right shoulder; then ribs began.

When we got to lunch-place ribs were quite bad. I lay under a tree for an hour, then tried to go on, and did ride about two miles, but the pain got much worse and I knew I'd never get up the next mountain. So God had stopped me after all, as I truly believe I might have had a real heart attack and even died – awful for the Sherpas.

We turned back, ribs hurting badly with every jolt and cough; and at some places I had to walk. Then came a hailstorm, with stones as big as marbles; one hit the cut on my head. I met such a charming Englishman, a Gurkha officer, Colonel Alistair Langlands, who looked at me hard and said, 'Are you all right?' I said, 'Not really,' and he came with us, then went ahead to the village, found the Nepali doctor, and searched for a room for me. The whole village stood and gaped while I chastely held my clothes, above and below my rib cage. The doctor felt all my ribs, said nothing was broken, dressed the rather deep, bad head cut and bound my ribs up. I started shivering with shock while a bed was being made up in the hut and the tiny loo put in the yard beside it. Tibeti and another gently put my red stockings on my legs, brought in a basin with fire, and did all they could think of to help and comfort. They really are darling people, as kind and gentle as the Masai – I have no higher praise.

Ribs now hell when I move. Sona and Kanji sleep in my room with a blanket between us and the other sherpas.

About ten young Gurung rice harvesters came into my room to talk to

Colonel Langlands. The rice harvest has been ruined by the hailstones, which have cut it to bits. All these months of preparing soil, planting, caring for young shoots, guarding, weeding, and finally cutting a small part of a very good harvest – wrecked in fifteen minutes. It is heartbreaking. Many people now will have no food. I asked Langlands if I could help with money; he said yes, through the Embassy in Kathmandu. They are so brave and quiet, no complaints.

Funny: if my bedroom was full of Europeans, I would go mad; full of sherpas, and I like it! I must be very odd.

8 NOVEMBER

At 5 a.m. a cat fight broke out under and all round my bed – two screaming, scratching devils. Sona and Kanji turned a torch on them and they fled, yelling, through the village.

Pain under ribs still fierce, but today I must dress and walk a little, as tomorrow the trek to Pokhara begins. First I must cross that awful swinging bridge with two guard chains, just too far apart for me to hold both sides. The sherpas will help me over. I am very weak – get a spinning head and stagger when I walk.

People come into my room, stand and stare. I look ghastly – one eye half shut, swollen above and below, and badly bruised all round. Patches of white plaster on head and forehead. I was so lucky my eyes weren't touched and no limbs broken, and that Pony kicked my hip and not the cracked knee. Colonel Langlands brought me this poem by Wordsworth he found.

> One adequate support
> For the calamities of mortal life
> Exists – one only; an assured belief
> That the procession of our fate, howe'er
> Sad or disturbed, is ordered by a Being
> Of infinite benevolence and power;
> Whose everlasting purposes embrace
> All accidents, converting them to good.

6 NOVEMBER

I like this peaceful village life and all the village sounds – even the cats! Two water buffalo live in stalls next door to me – they look so calm; and the chickens cheeping, cocks crowing at 4, 5 and 6 a.m., just as in Kenya, and there are even crickets! A nostalgic sound. There are long caravans of donkeys, the biggest and best at the head, adorned with big scarlet plumes – even the smallest and humblest have a little decoration on their harness. They go to Pokhara for food and supplies, reminding me of the camel caravans of Muscat. They all wear bells, all with different voices.

Nepali doctor has been wonderful, clever and kind. Head wounds nearly healed now, dysentery better, ribs a bit better too. He has patients nearly every day – a horse yesterday, who also rolled down a slope (but not very far), and cut his leg; a horse today with terrible saddle sores, as the beastly Filipino on his back couldn't ride, had no mercy and forced the poor horse on and on, in great pain. Two people, Swiss, are trying to reach the glacier at Annapurna, twenty-three thousand feet, on foot – I do hope they make it, but they are being very brave.

The doctor has another medical station three days' walk away up the mountain; he has stayed on here to care for me these two days, and will see me on my way tomorrow – over the dreaded bridge, I hope (I hope the money I can spare will mend the bridge), and into the basket on someone's back. He himself had once carried a hurt Japanese tourist on his back for many miles down a mountain.

11 NOVEMBER

Rather a nightmare journey here (Pokhara) for two days; much pain but not when I walk, only if I stretch or cough. Left this sweet village, regretfully, in a basket on a porter's back. Very uncomfortable – one keeps slipping forward and nearly out. Besides, vertigo assails me at glimpses of vast precipices beside the track. Poor, brave porters sweat and grunt at each step, and change at each stop. I am nearly as tired as they are, but they keep laughing and joking – superb people.

I walked a long way, getting stronger all the time, but my heart spins and bumps and pinches. The endless trail keeps rising and the huge precipices never cease. It took three hours up to the top of Naudana, and we camped on a freezing small plateau; I had to borrow the camp's solitary big lamp to keep warm. This safari, though very expensive, is ill equipped – the bed three feet off the ground; awful sleeping bags to get into, with sheet sewn like an ice-cream cone for your feet, very hard to get in and out of. So much simpler to have one nylon sheet and two normal eiderdowns. They gave me no loo paper, towel or pillow.

The last lap is always the worst. I got into Pokhara very tired and went to the hospital. An English lady doctor, Watson, felt all round and said ribs not broken, but cracked; hence the pain. Head quite cured and clean – clever Nepali doctor. Finally went on to the camp site, of dream-like beauty, on the shore of a lake, hills all round and, towering behind, Annapurna and her attendant peaks. The lake is a pale, soft blue, twisting away in the distance.

12 NOVEMBER

I was told that one man had been brought to the General Hospital (which has a Nepali doctor in charge), badly mauled by a black panther, which he still managed to kill. The doctor just washed his wounds and bound them up – no antibiotics, no healing medicine, nothing. Dr Watson was there, but helpless as this is a government hospital. The Nepali said the man would be quite all right, but he will probably lose the use of his hands, if not his arms. I was so lucky with my Dr Bhattchan, who took endless trouble with my head wounds.

Cows and water buffaloes here are desperately thin; people can't afford grain to feed them properly, and the grass is short turf. Two starving dogs haunt the camp; there are very few in this country, where rabies is rampant.

13 NOVEMBER

Leaving soon for Kathmandu. This has been the roughest, toughest safari I've ever been on; and one of the most beautiful, but I do like a modicum of comfort. As for lots of the tourists I passed – carrying their own supplies, no tents, living off the land, and climbing these appalling mountain trails – their courage seems beyond praise, especially that of the women and girls.

I have ridden since I was two, on various camels, horses, ponies, donkeys, mules and an elephant, and never been kicked down a precipice before! I do think it's funny.

Last night the porters gave me a half bottle of local 'whisky', and then some of their chicken I had bought them, then some raksi to drink, and finally sang me a concert in their charming melodious, harmonious voices. I was so touched, and found today's farewells very difficult, especially from Sona and Kanji, who came to the 'airport' (just a small airstrip) with me and cherished me right to the end. Back at noisy Kathmandu, wishing I was in the hills again.

17 NOVEMBER

Mrs O'Brien, the Ambassadress, sent flowers and asked me to dine and to a piano concert; John Clegg, a travelling pianist, played Chopin, Mozart, etc. most beautifully. The O'Briens are very easy to talk to. I gather the political situation is tricky because of Indian–Pakistani border tension. Poor little Nepal, wedged between India, China and Tibet, is in a dangerous situation. Also very poor, not receiving much aid.

I gave Dudley Spain of our Embassy fifty pounds to mend the bridge at Bori Thanti; he was very pleased. And so will they be, I'm sure. [*A few years later a great storm destroyed much of the village and smashed the resthouse they had built with my money.*]

I took the daily flight along the Himalayas, past Everest and Kanchenjunga. A most wonderful and glorious sight.

To Panta, a strange old place, once the home of the Malla kings of

Cherati Province. Their palace is built of dark rose brick with intricate carving on every bit of wood; there is a vast, ornate pool, the King's bath, in a courtyard, where the King bathed in icy water in full view of all the village inhabitants. There is another pool fed by mountain streams which is washed in and paddled in, by women and ducks; they also drink, from the spouts, water from heaven knows what polluted places. One grows immunity, of course. There are shrines, pagodas, temples, and pretty old houses everywhere.

18 NOVEMBER

To lunch with Clive Giboire, who lives in the heart of the bazaar at the top of a rickety house. You take off your shoes before entering his room with its strange Tibetan rugs, all hand-dyed and sewn, its odd futuristic pictures and local ornaments. He knelt on the floor, native-way, talking to us, and in came a White Russian countess, now a Buddhist nun, very intelligent, amusing and charming; a newspaper man; a Chinese lady; a Dr Whittaker from London; an elderly and very important sherpa; and a Nepali doctor.

The Buddhist nun intrigues me. Does she really think her grandfather was an earwig? They teach that each earthly life depends on your former one – Hitler and Rasputin might well now be scorpions, snakes or native-owned animals, to be killed at sight or ill treated. I much prefer our Christian beliefs – 'In my Father's house are many mansions.' I hope we may keep on working and helping people in real need.

From this hilarious and interesting lunch walked through slum streets, between fascinating old houses milling with people. Women with flowers in their hair, for some festival; a party of tall, handsome Tibetans, stately in rags, with battered, smiling faces; mounted police keeping an eye on the crowds; begging children, persistent and pestering like flies. Took a taxi for tea with Mrs Malla. She is very good-looking, intelligent and aristocratic. Her husband's family were kings of the Western Hills thirteen hundred years ago; she herself has Rana blood. The Rana clan had vast palaces everywhere; this hotel was one. Some of these people are still very rich, some penniless. All were well paid for their homes and land. Her mother still has four houses and twenty-five servants; four are personal maids, and she spends her time travelling between the houses and trying to think of something for the maids to do.

A Malla ancestor was so shocked at a proposed *mésalliance* for his daughter that he left all his vast lands (a hundred thousand acres) and took his family to India, where he got a commission in the Sind Regiment and became their colonel. Now these Mallas live in a little bungalow and he teaches political science (whatever that means, with politics changing every hour) in the university here.

1972

16 JANUARY

I am nearly well now, but get very tired. I think a lot about Nepal. Some small things I remember so clearly. A caravan of about fifty mules and donkeys came down the track; we stood aside to let them pass. The going was awful and one poor little donkey, loaded with paraffin drums, was so frightened he stood with hanging head, his long upper lip quivering with anxiety, as he searched with bent head for a safe way down the boulders. Finally he staggered down, and on they all went, carrying their heavy loads, on their six to eight days' trek, up ever higher and rougher mountains, to Jomson, about nine thousand feet up.

And I remember Sona and Kanji looking up at me where I stood on the aircraft steps, as we bowed to each other with our hands together – *Namasté*, goodbye. And the Sherpas' soft velvet voices singing, that last night, at Pokhara.

25 MARCH

Back in England. I have had two marvellous days with the army. On 17 March Brian Synge took me to the Irish Guards' St Patrick's Day celebration at Pirbright. There were tremendous security precautions, as the Queen Mother was coming. We were stopped five times by military police, questioned, and asked to show our tickets. In the car park soldiers searched every car – the bonnets, boots and cushions – and on the news that night I heard they had found a gas pistol under the seat cushion of a press photographer's car. They took it away and returned it when he left.

At the parade I had been given a seat in the front row – great honour – and then told I was to lunch at the Queen Mother's table – even greater honour. She took the parade with her usual perfection, and gave out the shamrock, including some for Fionn, the wolfhound who, I think thought it was something to eat. I was presented, along with the others; and then we all went to the mess and drank champagne for at least half an hour, which was marvellous. I do adore pomp and ceremony, and am always so surprised and delighted to find myself included among the mighty.

23 SEPTEMBER

Corsica. Came to the house of my Polish friends the Skorjewskis, to dear and charming Mouche and Léontine, who made me welcome. They began telling me the odyssey of their wartime escape from Poland. They had two large, beautiful country houses and one town house. Her jewels were all in a Warsaw bank. One night in 1939 the captain of the Polish patrol told them to go – there was no one but him and his few men between them and the Germans, and he had to withdraw. So with the maid, the cook and his family they left in cars, driving several hundred miles to an uncle's land, where there was no more petrol. So they took horses and troikas and headed for the Romanian frontier. They were frequently under fire from German planes; houses, farms and villages were flaming all round them. They found peasants who helped them – Léontine's beauty and wit, and Mouche's charm, courtesy and personality helped. They had with them their own two children, Léon, five, and Christine, eleven, and the cook's three children. They crossed rivers, lost a lot of horses, nearly starved, and came to a place twelve miles from the frontier where there was a man who helped refugees through to Romania, via a woman whose cottage was on the frontier road. It cost a lot of money, but they had brought some.

By now the Germans had withdrawn, and the Russians had come in. Siberian guards arrived, magnificent men, tall and handsome and very fair, wearing spotless white leather coats with the fur inside, not feeling the cold at all. The time came for the Skorjewski family to move on, but they could not cross the frontier road. They had been joined by other refugees, including a policeman. All their horses were gone or were dead by now. Their guides took the fugitives away from the frontier and up the mountain at midnight. Fifteen miles later they reached a house where they were given some food and rested for an hour. Then down the mountainside, sliding on the ice, they went again. Mouche was sometimes up to his chest in snow, holding Léon's hand, while the lightfooted five-year-old child walked on top of the snow beside him.

At the frontier road the osier hedge had been cut back to give the armed guards a view, to shoot fleeing refugees. The Skorjewskis and their companions crossed two at a time, after the guards had passed – all got over. On the Romanian side the osiers had been left, thick – here they hid. Now that the danger was over, Léontine almost collapsed. They were taken to a house, fed and put to bed on rough straw mattresses, and they slept, worn out, but flooded with the feeling of being free and safe – an impossible, incredible feeling of utter relief.

25 SEPTEMBER

The odyssey continues. They stayed some days where they were, and then went on their way towards Bucharest. Mouche told the colonel in charge of the district that he was a cousin of King Carol's, and he let them sit on an ox-drawn vehicle which was carrying water pipes to Bucharest from the mountains.

In Bucharest they were looked after by their Embassy and given visas for Paris and Madrid. They then went to Paris – France fell, and among all those thousands of frightened refugees the Skorjewskis got through to Spain on their Madrid visas.

Here they were mixed up in politics. Mouche's first job was to persuade the Italians not to fight the Poles, who had never declared war on Italy, and his first success was to ask a British fleet, sailing to fight an Italian fleet, to remove the two Polish ships who were sailing with them.

Later the British asked him to try to arrange a separate peace with Italy. As King Umberto (another cousin) was perfectly approachable, and Mussolini by now (1942) hardly counted, said Mouche, he naturally contacted his royal relation. This was a supremely delicate job, as, although the Italians hated to fight and longed for peace, spaghetti and songs, Mussolini's government still wanted to put on a fiery show from the safety of their own offices.

26 SEPTEMBER

They were in Rome for a time while Mouche proceeded with these difficult negotiations. One day as they came home to their villa they found a large car and two officials in front of their door. They were told they were urgently needed in one of the government offices, and were driven away fast.

It was not an office but a prison they were taken to, where they were separated. No one would answer Léontine's questions. She could not imagine what they were supposed to have done. A nun visited her next day, very silent and withdrawn, who rebuked her for not having cleaned out her cell. She was taken for questioning, and given a 'confession' to sign. The confession of a spy. If she signed, she and Mouche would be set free and lent a villa with servants and food. But Léontine would not sign. She said, 'Be good enough to tell me what I am accused of. Am I supposed to have stolen my own jewels, or is your friend here preparing to sell them?' (They kept asking where her jewels were.)

27 SEPTEMBER

Léontine's interrogations continued, but she never gave way. They questioned her often from 6 a.m. till nightfall without food or drink. The questioners came and went in relays. Once or twice she was called out and told she would not need to take her bag. She thought this meant the end, but it was just one more form of mental torture. Always she asked the jailers and others for news of Mouche, and found he was still alive.

Then Mussolini fell and was imprisoned. All the prisoners were delirious with joy, thinking they would be let out. Some were, but the Skorjewskis were sent to Germany. They saw each other in the distance. In Berlin the questioning was worse, but she never lost her head or her courage. Then the grapevine told her that Count Bernadotte, head of the Red Cross, and the Pope and various others were demanding their release, as Germany was collapsing and there was now no question of exchanging them for prisoners.

During the interrogations Léontine (a Radziwill by birth) was frequently asked if she had Jewish ancestors. She said certainly not. But when they asked Mouche, he said, 'Look; I have twelve quarterings, my father had thirty-two, my grandmother twenty-six – how do you expect me to know if one of my four hundred-year-old family married a Jewess?' This bit of vulgar snobbery impressed the Germans, and he was not asked again.

Then, suddenly, they were released and reunited. They looked for a home – Léontine said all she wanted was a safe place where she could grow potatoes. They found it in Corsica.

28 SEPTEMBER

Rather sad to leave Corsica, as always, and the wild mountains round Cap Corse, with its last little finger of land pointing north, saying goodbye, seemed somehow poignant.

NOVEMBER

My beautiful sister-in-law, Cynthia Spencer, is dying, very slowly, of a tumour on the brain which began a year ago. Most of the time now she is unconscious, but it is a long-drawn out agony for Jack and the family . . .

Cynthia died, quite peacefully, in a coma, and I went to the memorial service in Northampton church. It was a lovely service, uplifting and gentle, and suited her so well. Lunch afterwards at Althorp, nearly all the family. Poor Jack lost his pallor when the rooms were full of people, and was, as always, the perfect host. But it makes one's heart ache to think of him, living on alone in that great house. He will be so terribly lonely.

1973

24 DECEMBER

Coming back from a cinema in London one night I saw something lying in the road in the dark, and discovered a man in leather hippy clothes, unconscious. A black attaché case lay in the gutter. A few men stood on the street, and a car had stopped. I asked the men (Spanish) in French, to put him on the pavement, and at last they did so; then some furtive little

Londoners appeared, saying he had been 'rolled' [*this word is interesting; in French 'roulé' means attacked and robbed*], and I must not get involved, being a 'lady'. I was rather touched at this, and went off to ring up the police, having seen blood on his temple. I went into the nearest pub and the owner came out with me. The man was by now standing up, beating on a door and swearing. The publican told me not to bother the police, as this sort of thing went on all the time. So I came home, rather shaken.

I do miss the Masai, especially my sweet friends Mungani, Morda and Rahel. Robin is being pushed off Nderit by the Kenyan government, and there will be no one to look after them. Though I had many unhappy moments there, I can never forget the sympathy, kindness and lovingness of these Masai women, and the splendid loyalty of the Masai men to us both.

25 DECEMBER

My new little house, made from four old cottages and standing in a silent valley in Leith Hill [*Surrey*] called Broadmoor, is a great comfort to me. I go every weekend, and my labrador Susie takes me for walks. Deer come into my tiny field, and I hear vixens screeching and deer barking at night. It is all wild and remote and beautiful. It is in country I always rode in as a child, and some of the oldest people think it is much more important to be born Miss Heath than to become Lady Claud Hamilton. This is very nice for me.

1974

16 FEBRUARY

Left London for Paris and Lisbon, then over the Atlantic to Caracas. As we were going west all the time the sun took simply hours to rise – I thought we'd lost it for good. Landed at Caracas, changed to local crew, landed at Bogota, very rough, and reached Quito in Equador twenty-four hours after leaving England.

This place is nine thousand feet up, and I feel the height. Today we were bussed off to Indian markets in the country, twelve thousand feet up; thousands of Indians selling fruit, flowers, pots, pans, stews, shoes, ponchos, hats – the fleas were free. The women wear vast long skirts, coloured bodices, several shawls and ponchos all of different colours, vivid and glaring, topped by high felt hats. Their faces are flat, pink or brown, Mongolian, the whole place a mass of moving colour and noise.

We lunched on a lovely lawn belonging to a *rancho* (not a cow to be seen). Two transistors and a uniformed brass band competed in din-making. Two attached llamas stood in dignified aloofness under trees.

17 FEBRUARY

Tour of museums, where our group leader explained everything very well and at length. There was an invasion by Japs in cave-man times, said she; using currents and winds they came across the Pacific on a northerly route and made a tiny settlement in the Andes. In the museums were squat, hideous little figures with squashed Pekingese faces, and some actually made of gold, such as tempted the Spaniards. I wish I knew more about *their* times – I can't get over the courage of these few men, marching in their heavy armour through the hot valleys of the hills and mountains, fighting off native tribes (some of them very brave), with no idea of what awaited them around the next corner.

20 FEBRUARY

In a small ship, *en route* the Galapagos Islands. My cabin mate and I lie like two fishes still barely living, gasping on a hot marble slab. Our porthole is locked and there is no air-conditioning. But today we reached the first Galapagos Island, called San Cristobal. Lord Chatham (my ancestor) came here. Went ashore to the dreary village and a crushingly boring museum – shells, fish, bones, pickled snakes.

That was last night; today we went ashore and walked over miles of broken lava rock. Wonderful birds and animals, all so tame you have to be careful not to tread on them. Blue-footed boobies displaying their beautiful blue feet and huge spread wings to their lady-loves, whom they also try to seduce with presents of twigs and a lot of bill clattering. They were courting, nesting, displaying ceaselessly all round us, totally unafraid. If you get too close there are angry squawks, and you sheer off. The very young are white and fluffy, with Mum forever preening their feathers and making them look even more beautiful.

But my favourites are the splendid sealions, diving and rollicking through the wild coastal water and surfing through the waves to the shore. In splendid isolation on a rock sits a huge male, guarding his females from intruders and seeing to it that humans don't get too close. They are fast, agile and elegant, with melting eyes. There are enormous scarlet and yellow crabs and the famous iguana lizards, with fearsome faces, spines down their backs, and no brains or guts at all. I saw a movie of a snake moving among the iguana and finally catching a young one to eat – no big ones took the slightest notice.

We landed in a mangrove wood – very wet indeed – and walked along flat volcanic rock to a large colony of lizards. Dozing in the mangroves was a sea lioness who regarded us with soft, disinterested eyes and did not move. The lizards exactly match the rocks and are truly unattractive to look at; from one angle they look just like Harold Wilson without his pipe. They slide into the water for no apparent reason, and sometimes a sealion will play with one, holding his tail and dragging him backwards through the huge, breaking waves. The poor little iguana is terrified, of course, but usually gets away to crawl up a rock, palpitating with fright and shock.

23 FEBRUARY

One morning we spent on an island where the dark grey, rather nasty-looking sea iguana give way to very smart land ones, with orange or scarlet heads, the same spines and endlessly jerking heads, but more intelligence. They come up to you and hope for some cactus flowers to eat; though we were told not to feed them, several American women did, while their doting males took their photos. There are thousands of iguanas here, living in small holes in the ground; when Darwin came he could find nowhere to put his tent because of iguana holes, and walking was difficult for fear of treading on them.

And so back to London.

1976

12 AUGUST

At Barons Court, with darling Jim and Kath. He has been desperately ill but is much better, though not very mobile.

The UDR [*Ulster Defence Regiment*] are out in strength: one hundred Belfast women made a demonstation against the IRA yesterday, joined by a thousand today from a Catholic district. This might mean a crack in the violence. I saw a group of deaf and dumb children get off a bus in Enniskillen yesterday and they instantly picked up stones to throw at police and soldiers. Their teachers quickly disarmed them.

15 AUGUST

The Mountbatten party arrived to stay with James; they had a nasty accident on the way. Lady Pamela Hicks was driving her father and a dog in the first car, while David Hicks brought the others. They had a conspicuous motorbike security escort out of Eire. At the border these went back and the party had one small fast red car, with several police in it, to look after them – much less conspicuous and therefore safer. Pam got into a skid, and the car went into the ditch, hit the bank and turned completely upside down, wheels in the air. They hung in their seat belts while the frantic dog was walking on the ceiling. The police, watching in their mirror, saw it all happen, tore back and managed to release them, by which time petrol was pouring through the car. Asked if he was all right Lord M. replied, 'I am indestructible,' and considering what he went through in the war this seems true.

There are two guards patrolling Barons Court, armed with Luger rifles, day and night while Lord M. is here; they come from the local police, and are changed at intervals. It all strikes me as being quite familiar, as when the Governor stayed at Nderit during Mau Mau, with ten Masai guarding him all night and several staying around all day.

22 AUGUST

Douglas and Patience Campbell took me for a lovely drive to the west coast. Through a gorge in the mountains called Barnswell Gap and eventually to Adara, where high mountains go tumbling down to the sea, and in the narrow space between them and the water a little lane winds along between fuschia hedges. The loneliness and remoteness were a blessing after the traffic, houses and people on the main roads. I would like to stay here a few days in one of these solitary cottages so close to the water.

But, of course, the awful drought and beautiful sunny days we are having, and have had for several weeks, are very different from the grey, weeping skies which are normal Irish weather. The drought is especially bad in Surrey and Sussex, where old trees turn brown and die and the fields and gardens look like the Athi plains in Africa. It is still worse in mainland Europe.

A man I know was driving near Londonderry one day when he came to a road block and two thugs in stocking masks pushed guns through the windows at him, got into the car and ordered him to drive to Letterkenny – a good way off. So he did, and took them straight to the police station.

The Bishop of Derry and his wife came to lunch. He told two good, true stories. When he first came to Derry he asked if it was safe to walk about the streets. 'Certainly, sorr,' said the police sergeant. 'They can't risk the bad publicity they'd get for bumping off a bishop.'

Another time he was in the Shanklin Road area where no fewer than five pubs were blazing. He tried to get the women and children away to safety, then a very drunk man reeled up to him and took him by the shoulder. 'Look at that, will you?' said the man. 'You bloody bishops have been trying to get the pubs shut for seven years, and it's only taken us one night!'

1977

17 FEBRUARY

Princess Alice, Duchess of Gloucester, told her lady-in-waiting to ask me to tea, to my very great delight. She and I used to ride a lot in the old days in Kenya and she is still the sweet and gentle person she was then. She has lost her son, Prince William and her husband, who had a stroke some years ago and became paralysed and dumb. Then she looked very ill and drawn, but now she looks much better. She shares her Kensington Palace apartment with Prince Richard, his wife, their son Alexander, two and a half years old, and a loving labrador called Beatnik.

6 AUGUST

To Belfast, where Anthony was nearly an hour late meeting me, having been stopped and searched among a long queue of cars. The Queen, Prince Philip, Prince Andrew and Prince Edward are due here next week for two days.

8 AUGUST

Ulster seems so beautiful and peaceful – here, in Fermanagh, Union Jacks fly, cows, sheep and horses graze, children play in the streets, people shop and chatter; here and there are bombed shops and small, ruined houses; the sun blazes and all is calm. Now the Ulster Defence Regiment is under arms, five hundred special Scots Guards have arrived, frogmen will guard the Royal Yacht *Britannia*, there are checkpoints and armoured cars on every road – and our soldiers and policemen keep getting murdered by snipers, mines and bombs. There are hundreds of desolate, bereaved families whose happiness has gone for ever. I know how lucky I am not to be too involved.

14 AUGUST

Most interesting talk with Kath; we are alone as Jim has had to go into hospital for rest and treatment for his heart. They have both had a gruelling time. Jim is much better but not strong; he had to go to Coleraine College, of which he is Chancellor, and give away prizes in July. Then last week there were the rehearsals for the Queen's visit; they went to the parties and the banquets; and motored one and a half hours each way to Belfast and back nearly every day for rehearsals. Then, when the Queen was here, Jim, in his splendid Chancellor's robes, received her, climbed a long flight of steps with her, made an excellent speech, talked and walked and laughed with her for two days running. When it was all over a small time bomb was found in the hall, set to go off while the Queen was there. By an act of God it was badly set, and was defused after she had left.

1978

JULY

There have been some beautiful and interesting moments this year. To the Garter Ceremony at Windsor: very magnificent. The royal family in Garter robes walking slowly up the aisle, with Yeomen of the Guard lining the sides, armed with halberds; and the Gentlemen at Arms in scarlet uniforms and plumed helmets, standing to attention all through the long and splendid ceremony. They are all quite old, and must have got very tired, but they never flinched or quailed.

There was also the Abercorns' golden wedding party – about two hundred people in the Westminsters' beautiful, huge flat in Eaton Square. Jim and Kath looking splendid; so many people I knew, such fine men and beautiful women, in wonderful clothes and jewels. It was a very happy evening – so English, so grand and magnificent.

I have persuaded the Chairman of the British Legion, Sir Charles Jones, to get a first night for the Legion, as that does make a lot of money. We have to share with the Variety Club of Great Britain, and hope it will be a great success. I am on the committee. There is a lot of work: telephoning for hours every day to city firms to get advertisements for the programmes, and to other people to buy tickets and to arrange my supper party after. I do what I can for the BL and SAAFA and mentally handicapped ex-servicemen and for no one else; I think these surviving ex-servicemen and the forces families have done more for us than we can ever do for them, and we need a lot of money to help them now we are at peace.

10 AUGUST

To a drink with Johnnie Bevan, who is dying of throat cancer. During the Second World War he was sent for by the Defence Cabinet, being on the reserve of officers; they told him he was to organize the Deception of the Enemy Operation. He tried to put himself in Hitler's mind and thought

H.'s priority must be the invasion of England from Calais or via the Channel Islands. How to divert this? False information through British double agents and Ultra, the marvellous encoding machine invented and built by the Germans, parts of which were stolen (by Polish agents I believe) and sent to us.

Every sort of wrong information went to Hitler; the strength of our and our allies' armies, navies and air forces; our home defences, and the deception of the Man Who Never Was (a dead body in RAF uniform with fake instructions in his pockets to our army in Sicily, which was put in the sea off Spain, badly mauled in a supposed air crash, fished out by Spaniards and the information sent to Hitler).

When Johnnie started his job he had two or three radio sets; when he finished he had over three thousand, sending lies to Germany all the time. It was largely because of Johnnie that the Allied invasion of Normandy was such a success.

3 OCTOBER

I flew to Corfu a fortnight ago. Now I was taken for a lovely drive into the hills, winding up through olive groves and tiny old villages. This evening I went to 'The Village', where we saw carpets being made by hand; two girls sit, one at each end of a very large carpet, weaving the different-coloured wools into a most intricate pattern – so fast, so clever and so accurate. I hope they made a few mistakes, as I've been told the only way you can tell a hand-made rug from a machine-made one is by looking carefully at a repeated pattern – the hand-made ones show slight mistakes, the machine ones never.

Then to a large pottery factory where many jars and plates are copies from ancient ones found at Delphi – very rude and pornographic, according to our prim eyes. But how silly we are! These love-making attitudes were greatly admired two thousand years ago and surely brought more fun and gaiety into life.

The island of Corfu is covered with olive trees and cypresses. The story is that when the Venetians occupied the island they had a great feast; and when they came to, next day, they decided to visit some villages. They were appalled at what they saw. Huts of clay, with thatched roofs full of holes. People in rags, walking skeletons, children with the swollen stomachs of starvation. The rains had failed. Their crops had died, they were starving.

The Venetians held a conference and finally decided to give the country people food and money to help them through this bad season – provided every person planted an olive tree. Thirty years later the olives produced fruit, and as olive trees are thought to live for ever the country people had a revenue which never failed them.

Some olive trees have two main trunks, joined at the root. This happened because, it is said, long ago a god came down from Olympus to see conditions on earth for himself, as the gods were tired of the endless complaints and cries for help which ceaselessly assailed them from Corfu. This god went from house to house, asking everywhere, 'Any complaints?'

The complaints were endless, until he found an old couple sitting in the shade of their olive tree. They had no complaints and were full of gratitude for their happy lives together. The god was so impressed and pleased that he promised to grant any wish they might express. They asked that they might die peacefully together, and be buried under their olive tree which had sheltered them all their lives. This wish was granted, and when they had been buried the tree produced two trunks, as many of these trees have ever since.

We went to a village one night and were given plates piled with chicken legs (Corfu chickens apparently are hatched without breasts or wings, and all their eggs are tiny and white) and huge slabs of something called 'lamb'. There were also some beans, which I was able to eat, and endless jugs of wine, most comforting. Six pretty village girls appeared, wearing head-dresses of gay feathers and sparkles, white blouses, velvet waistcoats with gold and silver embroidery, huge, gay skirts and aprons. All the clothes are heirlooms. They moved sedately round in circles, waving red handkerchiefs; they looked nice, but dull.

Then men came on; two or six at a time, leaping, crouching, kicking, all in perfect time with wonderful rhythm. They were led by an oldish man in local dress with a wide red sash and shoes with pompoms. He was a marvellous dancer. The excellent band consisted of only a violin, an accordion and a drum. The diners did conga dances out into the street and back round the rooms. Alas, I could not join in because my knee hurt. But it was a grand evening, and everyone looked happy.

24 DECEMBER

At Bridgers, my Surrey home, taking Susie out, I slipped on ice and fell very hard. I lay there rather stunned; Susie sat with me. No one came. At last I struggled up, hurting everywhere, and crept home. The postman arrived and gave me some water; later Mr White came, lighted the fire and gave me brandy. Mrs Bayles came and tied my wrist up beautifully. Susie and I slept on the drawing room floor.

25 DECEMBER

To London, Mr W. driving – to Dr Eppel. Broken wrist – to Middlesex Hospital; X-ray and plaster for six weeks. Right wrist, very inconvenient and hard to manage. People are being very kind.

351

1979

3 JANUARY

To Heathrow. Plane to Kenya was two and a half hours late taking off. Many broken limbs here today; people falling on ice everywhere. Dreadful, narrow cramped seats in these new planes and chairs don't tip back, so no sleep.

7 JANUARY

A bit of shopping in Nairobi. It was nasty enough before, but ten times more so now. Not much in the shops except some pretty *kikois* (patterned, coloured wraps) and nothing seems very orderly.

Robin and Liza brought me to their pretty prefab house at Naivasha – the lake and hills look lovely and I was glad to be in the Rift Valley again.

18 JANUARY

We have reached the coast. It is wonderful for me to see the Indian Ocean once more: 'So wide, so soft, so bloomin' blue', as Kipling said. And the palms and baobabs. Mombasa has grown terribly, but the countryside looks the same as ever, except that native men now wear shirts and trousers and look like spivs, instead of *kanzus* or *kekoys* which give dignity to every black face. Back to Nairobi and then to Naivasha. Saw dear Auma and Taju [*formerly my head cattleman, with six thousand cattle to watch over*] in Nairobi, a little older but very charming. Taju was wrapped in a pink blanket from chin to toe and looked every inch a chief. He always did look very smart, even at work with the cattle and carrying only a club.

27 JANUARY

On the 23rd, Georgina picked me up to go to Nderit. Twelve miles from Naivasha we got a flat tyre. G. struggled to get the wheel off but it was jammed hard. Hundreds of cars passed but no one stopped to help. At last a Sikh stopped, a very strong man, but he could not move the wheel. He took us to Naivasha where Kamau, a nice Kikuyu mechanic, took us back to the car, got the wheel off, found the ancient tyre had split right through and the spare tyre was bald. That is the normal occurrence nowadays in Kenya. We sat on the road for four and a half hours, inhaling diesel fumes

352

FEBRUARY 1979

from the endless lorries, until at last Kamau reappeared with the mended tyre.

Next day Rahel appeared and we fell on each other's necks. She has been here three days waiting for me; I truly think she is the best and dearest friend I ever had.

28 JANUARY

We drove to Nderit and once more I saw that marvellous view from the top of the hill where the stables once were. The line of scented acacia trees, the plain beyond, the blue, blue lake and the dark forest with the Mau Hills behind it. It was so beautiful, but did not make me sad, for since Claudie died, I have very little emotion left.

But saying goodbye to Rahel I felt very sad. She had tears in her eyes as she said, 'God has brought you back to see us and perhaps He will again. But if not, we will meet up there,' and she gestured to the sky. I could not speak when we kissed each other goodbye. She died soon afterwards.

We drove down to Nderit House and were shown round by a man who runs it for National Parks. It was not so awful as I had been told, except that the fine stone fireplace was painted hideously in black and white stripes, the big drawing room a vulgar green; a large red plastic bar is now in the verandah and my bedroom wing is locked up. The pond is still there; the garden has gone but there is a mass of cannas and my huge bougainvillea, in front of the house.

We drove to the waterfall and picnicked – all the baboons have gone. Then to Naishi – the dear little house looks just the same from the outside – through the forest, where there are a few waterbuck, giraffe and impala, then back up the hill and so to Muthaiga. Dust everywhere. And the famous flamingoes have vanished.

I leave tomorrow at 8 a.m. for Cape Town; not sorry to go.

31 JANUARY

Somerset West. Had some lovely drives up the mountains and down to the sea. I have not been to the Cape since I was two – when Father and Mother, two children, two nannies, a maid and a manservant set forth round the world in the old ship *Corinthia*.

The mountains stand round the plain. It must have been a wonderful sight for Vasco de Gama, when he first sailed past this empty coast.

7 FEBRUARY

Cape Town, at the Tudor House Hotel. A doctor took the plaster off my hand; it was like iron – it took all his strength and a twenty-minute struggle. It still hurts rather.

353

Julian and Joan Bevan are being angelic to me. He took me for a long, lovely drive round the mountains and beside the silky, shimmering, freezing Atlantic. Just beyond the mountains and round to the east coast is the warm and sharky Indian Ocean. It was most beautiful and such a joy to get out of this dull and noisy town.

Up Table Mountain again with a 'tour' – hundreds of yelling tourists, like the Tower of Babel. The hyraxes hid and I sat alone, my own apartheid, and looked at the stunning view.

15 FEBRUARY

I have lots of friends everywhere and just enough money to travel and entertain mildly. Yesterday I went in a boat from Hout Bay to see the seals. There are thousands of them, on two rocky islands – not quite as attractive as the Galapagos ones, who waited for the ships' boats bringing us tourists ashore, then dived into the sea and came up all round the boat, gazing at us with their large, dark eyes. But it was a lovely trip on a lovely day, with enough rollers to make the boat dance a bit.

20 FEBRUARY

Janet, one of Pat's employees, drove me to High Noon – a beautifully run game park. There, on a road, was a tall giraffe being pestered by a cock ostrich who had already driven a perfectly harmless water buffalo off the road into the bush and was now going for the giraffe. With wing feathers extended in what an ostrich thinks is a war dance, its beak wide open in a threatening way, it actually *kicked* the giraffe continually for about fifty yards up the road – the giraffe only gave one half-hearted kick (he could easily have broken the ostrich's leg, but was too much of a gentleman to try).

Further on there was a cage of chimps; one put a stone in his mouth, climbed a tall post, then hurled the stone over the top of the fence and hit the car with it. Then he descended and flung pebbles and sand at us where we sat in the car, and never missed. A very bad-mannered and clever chimp. There were lions and tigers there, lying together, being fed; and hundreds of other animals which I know well, but have never seen so tame.

2 MARCH

Left for England this evening in a 747 jumbo of South African Airlines. A sardine-like crowd at the airport. The seats didn't tip back as in the old planes, so no sleep for fifteen dreary hours.

5 MARCH

Last May, Kath asked me to tea with her and Jim in London. I haven't seen him for a year, since I was last at Barons Court. He has a clot of blood in his foot which gives him endless pain; and his heart bothers him. But no complaints. He was in marvellous form, full of funny stories and so kind and charming. A few days later Sacha rang up to say he was dead – of a heart attack, in Ulster. Kath was away with the Queen Mother on a cruise in the Scottish lochs. This was a fearful shock and blow to everyone, and to me. I love Jim and Kath, and all the family. The Hamiltons feel to me more like relations than in-laws and have always been fun, civilized and warm-hearted. Jim was the head of this splendid family and this branch of the Hamilton clan; adored all through Ulster and much of the South too. He was so like Claudie to look at and talk to, it brought back all my memories. I feel very bereft, though thankful he is now happy and, as Moyra wrote, reunited with Claudie, Cynthia and his parents. 'Think of the jokes!' wrote Moyra – wonderful girl.

17 JULY

Buckingham Palace garden party with Maurice and Mary Heath. Eight thousand – very tiring indeed but most exquisitely done, as always. Maurice, a Gentleman Usher to the Queen, has been lent today to the Queen Mother. He looks splendid and does his job magnificently.

18 JULY

To the Royal Tournament with Eddie Goulbourn; he does not look or feel well, but enjoyed the splendid display. We had seats near the royal box and to my delight the Queen Mother saw me and waved – this made my day!

We now have a Conservative government under Mrs Thatcher. Things are getting tougher, but she inherited a financial mess and it is very difficult to get things right again. She is fearless, honest and patriotic. She has managed to increase the forces and police pay and reduce income tax, but unemployment and inflation continue to go up. This is bound to happen until she gets things straightened out, as I pray she will.

3 AUGUST

Nex Monday I leave for Belfast to stay with the family; always one of the best months in the year.

6 AUGUST

The usual wait at the airport and a crowded, small-seated plane to Belfast, where Anthony awaited me. He brought me to his charming Georgian house which needs almost everything doing to it, but will be lovely when finished. All seems calm just now, even in Enniskillen, but you never can tell.

9 AUGUST

There were riots in Belfast yesterday, the tenth anniversary of the day the British troops – at the urgent request of the *Catholic* priests and leaders – arrived over here. A can of paint was thrown at three British soldiers and the paint got into their eyes, I hope and pray not blinding them permanently. Others were stoned.

12 AUGUST

The Mountbatten party are staying with James. Lord Mountbatten, Pammy Hicks, Edwina (what a beauty) and two retrievers. Sacha has a lot of work to do, besides breast-feeding her enormous baby, Nicholas, ten and a half pounds and growing hourly. It has been so lovely here and so warm; James has a splendid wood-burning stove which heats the whole of his huge house.

This is a curious country. Away from the bad parts it is so peaceful and feels somehow prosaic, though the Irish have been fighting and murdering each other for two thousand years at least; and yet there seems to me to be no drama in the air here. Rather a sort of Presbyterian calm.

28 AUGUST

In Jersey with the Sinkinses. Yesterday we heard on the news that Lord Mountbatten has been murdered by the IRA, who blew up his yacht by remote control just as he, Patricia, her son Nick, Doreen Brabourne, John Brabourne and a local boat boy were going out fishing. This has been a most fearful shock to everyone. Lord Mountbatten was killed instantly, Nick also, and the boat boy. The others were picked up, and today I hear Doreen has died.

29 AUGUST

The Mountbatten deaths have had a terrific impact on the world. Mrs Thatcher paid a flying visit to Ulster, saw some of the bomb victims, did a 'walk-about' among the people and saw, among others, a young policeman with both legs and one arm blown off by an IRA bomb.

6 SEPTEMBER

Back in London. We saw Lord Mountbatten's funeral on TV, magnificently done and very moving. The whole royal family was there and many foreign royals. Prince Philip and Prince Charles very nearly in tears. Sailors carried the coffin into the Abbey, their faces set. The Royal Marine buglers sounded Last Post and Reveille. Our own Archbishop of Canterbury made a splendid sermon and the Catholic Cardinal Hume also spoke. This dreadful crime has shocked the world – except for the IRA representative in the USA who said, 'I applaud his death.'

Lord Mountbatten's body was taken to Romsey Abbey and buried there. I am glad he did not have that terrible, lingering torture of extreme old age and helplessness but went out in a flash, on his beloved sea.

13 SEPTEMBER

Started a frightful journey by getting up at 4 a.m. on 11 September, having slept at Gatwick in a most pretentious and expensive hotel, full of clever gadgets. A TV, of course (unmanageable), a thing to wake you up, a thing to make your tea, a thing to draw the curtains, and double glazing (again unmanageable).

Once in Paris I got into a plane for Corsica and arrived at Calvi, where the Cheybans met me. Too tired to risk driving a strange car on the wrong side of the road, so came to Algajola with the Cheybans, who cherished and fed me and gave me wine and flowers.

Today to Calvi to get the car – man not there. Madame Cheyban rang up, car came, man said I must pay *him* for car as he was responsible, though card said 'Charges to this office'. But the man said it meant him, as *he* was Avis, and sixteen hundred francs please. At last we settled it that I would go to Ile Rousse tomorrow, pay there, return to Calvi, get the car – oh dear, I was so tired and in pain I could have cried. But the man was suddenly angelic and said I could take the car and pay tomorrow.

Just as we were leaving, a handsome young *gendarme* shouted, 'Come back and have a drink with us!' So Madame Cheyban and I, plus *gendarme*, Monsieur Cheybau and police inspector, Avis man and some woman cleaner had a lovely party, with lots of jokes and leg-pulling. It was such fun – it could only have happened in Corsica or Ireland. At last Madame Cheyban and I set off and they all clustered round the door to see me drive off on the *left* – but I didn't!

17 SEPTEMBER

Walked through the lovely old village of Algajola, past the castle built in AD 900 and now belonging to some commercial person who is letting it all fall to pieces inside. It is also, I'm told, very cold. The battlements have been rebuilt by the Foreign Legion, and they have done a splendid job. There are 'half walls' all along the sea, where you can sit and listen to it.

18 SEPTEMBER

Yesterday I woke at 4 a.m. and at 8 a.m. was on the quay awaiting the ship for Girolata. We got away and steamed past the rocky and precipitous Corsican mountains, and I wondered all the time where our wartime subs had managed to land the huge amount of arms we sent them, which were met by the *maquisards*, loaded onto mules and whipped away to mountain caches.

Put in at Galeria, a dull little port, and then sailed through a marine forest of the huge red *calanche* rocks, which turn scarlet in the sunset. They go on endlessly, all the way from Galeria to Girolata. As we snaked in and out of them it was like something by Jules Verne. We steamed through tiny openings between great red monsters, cut by the wind and sea into animal and human shapes – a group of *gendarmes*, a sheep's head, a woman scolding her cowering husband; past arches through which you saw the sky, and past jagged rocks of every description and size, going straight down into the sea. The captain knew his way like his own home and the excellent ship never made a mistake or had an engine miss. But if there had been an accident it would have been the end, as I never saw a Corsican ship with *canots de sauvetage* on board – not even a dinghy tied on behind.

Girolata is very pretty, completely run-down. It has a big board up saying, '*Girolata n'est pas une réserve, il est un village, et il veut vivre.*'

The Corsicans could have very good farms, but they bring every single thing they eat from the mainland! And Girolata should cash in on those marvellous *calanches*, run boats out to them, even import seals which would live happily on the local fish, and use the lovely bay for peacetime tourists. But they do *nothing*, and I think are frightened of the sea.

So much of Corsica is wild and empty and beautiful. I wish I'd chosen a wilder place, but then I would not have had the Cheybans, who do make life so easy for me. My tiny house is all right for a few days, though quite primitive and there are insects everywhere. Algajola, full of tourists, is littered with debris of every sort, unlike Cape Town where you never even see a dead cigarette on the ground because they have bins *everywhere* for the rubbish. Claudie once said, as we sailed past a lonely bay in the Agriates, where one blue plastic bottle rested on the sand, 'How they *urbanize* everything!' The perfect description.

19 SEPTEMBER

Went to tea with Comtesse de Savelli. No tea but floods of excited, very French talk. The old house is handsome with very old black nineteenth-century furniture, some fine Spanish chairs and many family portraits. Her husband (now dead) said he was descended from Romulus and he may well be, as the Romans did come here and some must have stayed. He said he had 'electric powers' – he meant he was a warlock. He said he took electricity from his alsatian dog (who did not look well) and recharged his own batteries with it.

20 SEPTEMBER

By train to Léontine Skorjewski through endless, gorgeous scenery and many mountain tunnels. In one was a cow, who was in no hurry, though the train stopped and the driver made the local cow noises designed to move her on. At last she did, but soon after there was another pause while a herd of sheep were persuaded to leave the cool of the tunnel for the heat of the sun.

Léontine's house, once a convent, is about a thousand years old with enormously thick walls.

23 SEPTEMBER

We flew off for France. Just before Nice there was a great blue flash and a loud bang inside the cabin – we had been struck by lightning! No one took the slightest notice, not even the children or the dogs. I was very impressed by them, but I think most of them were Corsicans.

1980

8 JANUARY

On 2 January I spilt boiling water on my leg, put a teabag on it at once and the pain stopped instantly. On 3 January there were two large burns, but not hurting. That evening I got into one of these uncomfortable new 747 planes, where the seats don't tip back, there is no leg room, and one is squashed three a side. There was a gorgeous scarlet sunrise when we landed at Nairobi, but we were not allowed to get out. My burns hurt a lot. At Johannesburg a long queue waited as Passports, where a black lady's papers were investigated, an old Indian had no visa, etc. etc., and I had a heavy bag and a *very* sore leg. Then I saw my suitcase pass on the belt – and vanish. I waited in vain for the suitcase to come round again when a kind man took pity on me and retrieved it from the far end of the hall. No porters anywhere. Pushed the awful trolley a long way, until I saw a crowd of several hundred people awaiting friends. I hopelessly pushed on and suddenly saw my hostess, Mo MacMurray. She made me sit down while she fetched the car.

She took me to their lovely house, with a garden growing all the flowers I love. She put me to bed with a tumbler of milk and another of whisky, and when I came to a doctor came to see my leg. He said it was a bad, deep burn, so I stayed on in this very lovely and happy home with six handsome sons, two beautiful daughters, various grandchildren, and delicious food.

11 JANUARY

The Drakensberg Mountains are terrific, jagged, wild and steep. When the heroic Voortrekkers travelled through them they had a hard time. They often had to take the wagon wheels off and put on skids, while their best and cleverest oxen put all their strength into holding the wagons back as they slid down the precipices; they forded fast rivers, climbed up terrible ravines on the other side, were harassed by Bushmen and other natives, and quarrelled with each other. And *still* they got through, though many died – murdered or fighting or ill. Babies were born, and the people still went on. They travelled two thousand miles, largely on foot, though the women drove in the wagons when they could. They had fearful battles with the Zulus when they laagered their wagons, the men shot, the women loaded, and their black servants fought beside them, utterly faithful to the end.

16 JANUARY

Came to Pietermaritzburg, a rather nice little town, and *en route* saw the Brahmin stud at Bar O farm; eighty head of gloriously beautiful creatures, who are very tame and love being petted and talked to.

While in the mountains, I met various friends of the Harrises – Ross and his half-Norwegian wife; Murless, ex-navy, with a small and famous herd of Red Sussex. And others – all British, no Afrikaans. They don't mix much. They get on all right and the Boer War is much in the past, but their customs, houses, churches and backgrounds are entirely different from ours.

Today has been marvellous. First I was taken to a cattle auction, but the auctioneer talked so fast I couldn't catch a word. The cattle were all high-grade Afrikanders, Guernseys, Simmenthals and Herefords. The farmers were very mixed – English, Afrikaans, Indian and Zulu, all sitting together.

Then I went to the memorial for the Voortrekkers, and was shown some of the terrible country they had trekked over, until they came to the last ridge, overlooking the plains. There are still marks of wagon wheels on some of the stones, and the track these thousands of people used can be clearly seen. The names of the leaders are inscribed on a stone. I found it very moving, and am glad the South Africans have made this gesture to their forbears.

4 MARCH

Very bad, sad news of the election in Rhodesia. It was won by Mugabe. This is a fearful blow to East and South Africa, and perhaps to the world.

22 MARCH

I embarked in a 747 for London. We got to Nairobi in the dark, and then one engine would not start. At last we were airborne, but had to divert to Rome for petrol. There, another very long wait while the captain rang up the chief engineer in London (who of course was asleep at 2 a.m.) asking for permission to start with this sick engine. I don't know who he finally contacted, but we did take off (hearts in mouths) and came safely to London where, of course, it was raining.

21 JUNE

Coldharbour village fête (known as the 'fate worse than death'). The Sixth Gurkha band marched through the village, playing beautifully, marching, counter-marching and wheeling over that rough ground in perfect order. I adore them and still think nostalgically of the eight sherpas I had on that trek in Nepal. The fête was a huge success and made over nine hundred pounds – largely gate money, for which I had pleaded in vain for about three years and which the committee finally agreed to ask for.

27 JUNE

William Hunt gave me a ticket to the presentation of colours by the Queen to the Honourable Artillery Company – only the third time in this century. These are all part-time soldiers and the HAC is the oldest regiment in our army, formed by Henry VIII from the medieval 'trained bands' raised by the nobles and squires of England, for battle. They are all stockbrokers, bankers and so on. There was a parade of about fifty musketeers and pikemen, dressed as in the time of the Civil War. They marched very slowly, to drumbeats – in those days the roads were muddy and rough, the country paths even worse, and foot soldiers *had* to go slowly. They carried very long muskets on the right shoulder and a long staff with an iron V on the top on the left. When required to fire, the staff was stuck in the ground, the clumsy musket loaded and then rested in the V. For the second shot it all had to be done again – they must have been very slow-motion battles in those days.

16 JULY

Father's company sent a car to take me to their cocktail party at their City office to launch a book about my father. I felt very proud, being treated like a queen and photographed. The chairman, Frank Holland, told me it had always been his dream to get a book written about Father, so that the world might know what a wonderful man he was: a saint, a genius and a millionaire – a unique mixture.

31 JULY

Some funny stories. A vet friend of my neighbours the Sprawsons got an SOS from a woman to come at once, urgently. He found a 'stripper' with a boa constrictor; the poor snake had boils and was in the bath. There he lay, yards and yards of him. The vet and the woman began to haul him out, which took some time. The vet knew he could not give a boa an anaesthetic, so he tried to lance the boils. The boa objected and poured himself away into the drawing room where he curled up on the floor. The woman put a blanket over him, then *sat* on him.

Another SOS to the vet. This time it was a brothel, with an indoor pond containing some very sick terrapins. He asked what they were fed on, as the water was so dirty and slimy. 'The girls,' said the woman, 'eat their polony sandwiches sitting on that sofa and throw the bits in the pond.' She was told no more polony sandwiches into the pond and to change the water.

'What do I owe you?' asked the woman.

'Eighteen dollars.'

'How very odd,' she said. 'That's just what *we* charge!'

9 AUGUST

Have been to Ireland, to Viola [*Duchess of*] Westminster. The view from the house, across the garden to Lough Erne is very beautiful. She has a splendid man looking after her and the house; he is very devoted to Viola and the family. He loved Pud [*Viola's husband*] and refers to him as 'His dear late Grace'. When Pud died it was a fearful blow for poor Evans, who was as stricken as the rest of the family. Some time later, when they were all together for Pud's memorial service – Gerald and Tally Westminster, Viola, James and Sacha Abercorn and Kath, Guy and Janey Roxburghe, and Sally Westminster (i.e. three dukes and six duchesses) – Evans flung open the door and intoned, 'O come all ye Graces. Luncheon is served.' I'm sure no other butler would have dared, or had the wit.

1981

2 JANUARY

Left yesterday for Nairobi. At Naivasha with Robin and Liza. Good road until you come to the lake one, then mountains of dust, deep holes, hellish surface. But bliss to be in the country – all quiet, lovely lake view, charming dogs and birds. Nairobi is dreadful. Boys at the Muthaiga Club begging for baksheesh! I was extremely shocked and very firm. American tourists, knowing not the etiquette of English club life, give tips, so of course local club boys are ruined. I think I've had this place – it is no longer worth the awful journey.

Went to Nderit last week in a hired car with an excellent driver. The place is ruined. They have hacked the house about and smashed the lovely big rooms, making several cell-like bedrooms out of each one. Food unspeakable. Very bad drought here; most of the game and flamingo have gone. Went back to Muthaiga utterly disillusioned. The whole trip was very expensive and a total waste of money, except that I've learnt a lesson.

9 JUNE

I've just heard that Prince Charles is going to marry Johnny Spencer's daughter Diana.

29 JULY

The royal wedding day. I was invited, which was a great honour and thrill, and quite unexpected. I was called by telephone at 6 a.m. and was ready at 8 a.m. New frock (pink and yellow flowers on a pale grey background), bright yellow cloak and a small pink feathered hat. Also the lovely emerald and diamond clasp from the bank.

The streets were jammed with people. Thousands of them had slept on the pavements. Union Jacks and decorations were everywhere, waves of cheering rippling along the crowds, all the way from the Palace to St Paul's. They even cheered *me*! All the royal family arrived to frantic cheers which we inside the cathedral could hear through the fanfares. Johnny Spencer held his daughter's arm and managed very well, though he was seen to stagger once. He has been *so* ill, and only survived through Raine's devotion and a new drug, still unobtainable in England.

The service and singing were superb. As the royal family walked slowly up the aisle, my yellow coat caught several royal eyes; Alice, Duchess of Gloucester and Queen Elizabeth the Queen Mother both gave me tiny smiles. One spent a long time curtseying, standing up, and curtseying again. When the Prince and Princess of Wales came down the aisle, at the end of the ceremony, her veil was thrown back and she looked stunningly beautiful, like a fairy queen, both of them so happy. No one can do all this pomp, ceremony and magnificence, with split-second timing and friendliness, as well as we do.

ENVOI

Reading my diaries has brought back memories of matchless scenery, interesting varieties of people, experiments in manners of locomotion, interests, excitements, pleasure, exasperation, discomfort, and amusement.

Most of all, I am so thankful to have seen fascinating places which are now no more, and never will be so again. I am very glad I was in England during the War, for I might have got stuck in Kenya, as many of my friends were – England is still the best country I know.

G.M.H. July 1986

INDEX

Compiled by Gordon Robinson